Medieval Chinese Warfare, 300–900

China's history has been shaped by war. Shortly after 300 AD, barbarian invaders from Inner Asia toppled China's Western Jin dynasty, leaving the country divided and at war for several centuries. Despite this, a unified imperial order gradually took shape again. *Medieval Chinese Warfare, 300–900* explores the military strategies, institutions, and wars that reconstructed the Chinese empire which survived into modern times.

Drawing on classical Chinese sources and the best modern scholarship from China and Japan, David A. Graff connects military affairs with political and social developments to show how China's history unfolded. Between 300 and 900 AD, both Chinese and barbarian regimes experimented with many different forms of military service, including the tribal warrior, the hereditary military retainer, the part-time farmer-soldier, and the full-time mercenary.

Medieval Chinese Warfare, 300–900 is the first survey of medieval Chinese military history to be published in English. This pathbreaking text will be of interest to both students of military history and to anyone with an interest in China's past.

David A. Graff is Assistant Professor of History at Kansas State University. He received his PhD in East Asian Studies from Princeton University in 1995.

WARFARE AND HISTORY
Series Editor: Jeremy Black
Professor of History, University of Exeter

AIR POWER IN THE AGE OF
TOTAL WAR
John Buckley

THE ARMIES OF THE CALIPHS:
MILITARY AND SOCIETY IN THE
EARLY ISLAMIC STATE
Hugh Kennedy

THE BALKAN WARS, 1912–1913:
PRELUDE TO THE FIRST WORLD WAR
Richard C. Hall

ENGLISH WARFARE, 1511–1642
Mark Charles Fissel

EUROPEAN AND NATIVE
AMERICAN WARFARE, 1675–1815
Armstrong Starkey

EUROPEAN WARFARE, 1660–1815
Jeremy Black

THE FIRST PUNIC WAR
J. F. Lazenby

FRONTIERSMEN:
WARFARE IN AFRICA SINCE 1950
Anthony Clayton

GERMAN ARMIES: WAR AND
GERMAN POLITICS, 1648–1806
Peter H. Wilson

THE GREAT WAR 1914–1918
Spencer C. Tucker

ISRAEL'S WARS, 1947–1993
Ahron Bregman

THE KOREAN WAR: NO VICTORS,
NO VANQUISHED
Stanley Sandler

MEDIEVAL CHINESE WARFARE,
300–900
David A. Graff

MODERN CHINESE WARFARE,
1795–1989
Bruce A. Elleman

MODERN INSURGENCIES AND
COUNTER-INSURGENCIES: GUERRILLAS
AND THEIR OPPONENTS SINCE 1750
Ian F. W. Beckett

NAVAL WARFARE, 1815–1914
Lawrence Sondhaus

OTTOMAN WARFARE, 1500–1700
Rhoads Murphey

SEAPOWER AND NAVAL
WARFARE, 1650–1830
Richard Harding

THE SOVIET MILITARY EXPERIENCE
Roger R. Reese

VIETNAM
Spencer C. Tucker

THE WAR FOR INDEPENDENCE
AND THE TRANSFORMATION OF
AMERICAN SOCIETY
Harry M. Ward

WAR AND THE STATE IN EARLY
MODERN EUROPE: SPAIN, THE
DUTCH REPUBLIC AND SWEDEN AS
FISCAL-MILITARY STATES, 1500–1660
Jan Glete

WARFARE AND SOCIETY
IN EUROPE, 1792–1914
Geoffrey Wawro

WARFARE AT SEA, 1500–1650
Jan Glete

WARFARE IN ATLANTIC AFRICA,
1500–1800: MARITIME CONFLICTS
AND THE TRANSFORMATION
OF EUROPE
John K. Thornton

WARFARE, STATE AND SOCIETY IN
THE BYZANTINE WORLD, 565–1204
John Haldon

WAR IN THE EARLY MODERN
WORLD, 1450–1815
Jeremy Black

WARS OF IMPERIAL CONQUEST
IN AFRICA, 1830–1914
Bruce Vandervort

WESTERN WARFARE IN THE
AGE OF THE CRUSADES,
1000–1300
John France

Medieval Chinese Warfare, 300–900

David A. Graff

London and New York

First published 2002
by Routledge
2 Park Square, Milton Park, Abingdon, Oxon, OX14 4RN

Simultaneously published in the USA and Canada
by Routledge
270 Madison Ave, New York NY 10016

Routledge is an imprint of the Taylor & Francis Group

Transferred to Digital Printing 2007

© 2002 David A. Graff

Typeset in Bembo by BOOK NOW Ltd

British Library Cataloguing in Publication Data
A catalogue record for this book is available from the British Library

Library of Congress Cataloging in Publication Data
Graff, David Andrew, 1962–
     Medieval Chinese warfare, 300–900 / David A. Graff.
        p. cm. — (Warfare and history)
     Includes bibliographical references and index.
        1. China—History, Military—221 B.C.–960 A.D. I. Title. II. Series.

DS747.43 .G73 2002
951′.01—dc21   2001052022

ISBN 0–415–23954–0 (hbk)
ISBN 0–415–23955–9 (pbk)

Contents

Maps

Preface and acknowledgments

This book was several years in the making and stands on the shoulders of several earlier projects, including my doctoral dissertation. The list of people and institutions whose contributions should be acknowledged is therefore a rather long one. I will mention only a few of those names here. The list begins with the members of my doctoral committee at Princeton University, Professors Denis Twitchett, Ying-shih Yü, and Martin Collcutt. It also includes Professor Huang Ch'ing-lien of the Institute of History and Philology of Academia Sinica, who provided valuable assistance and advice during a year of research in Taiwan (1992–3) that was supported by a research grant from the Center for Chinese Studies of the National Central Library in Taipei. Additional research for this volume was done during a year as a visiting scholar in the Department of East Asian Languages and Civilizations at Harvard University, made possible by Professor Peter K. Bol. Jeremy Black and Peter Lorge read the manuscript and suggested numerous improvements, while timely intervention by Ken Chase saved me from an embarrassing *faux pas*. Mr. Yang Yu-wei not only helped to clarify some of the more obscure passages in the ancient military texts, but also guided me through a great deal of medieval parallel prose that would otherwise have been utterly impenetrable. Any errors that remain are, of course, entirely my own responsibility.

Though it may not be immediately apparent to the non-specialist reader, I have tried to keep the sinological baggage in this book to a minimum. All official titles are translated, as are most other Chinese terms. Specific dates have in all cases been converted to Western equivalents (for example, April 30, 637, rather than "the first day of the fourth month of the eleventh year of the Zhenguan era of Emperor Taizong of the Tang dynasty"). References to months are trickier, since the months of the Chinese lunar calendar rarely coincide with those of the Julian and Gregorian calendars. In order to avoid repeated use of awkward locutions such as "between the middle of April and the middle of May 758," I have generally chosen to refer to months of the Chinese calender (e.g., "in the third lunar month of 758"). The Chinese lunar months usually begin between eighteen and forty-five days later than their Western equivalents. Thus, the first day of the first lunar month of the sixth year of the Wude era corresponds to February 5, 623. The discrepancy between the Western and Chinese years does not present a serious problem for the purposes of this volume because there is little day-by-day narrative description of military campaigns.

David A. Graff
Manhattan, Kansas
May 2001

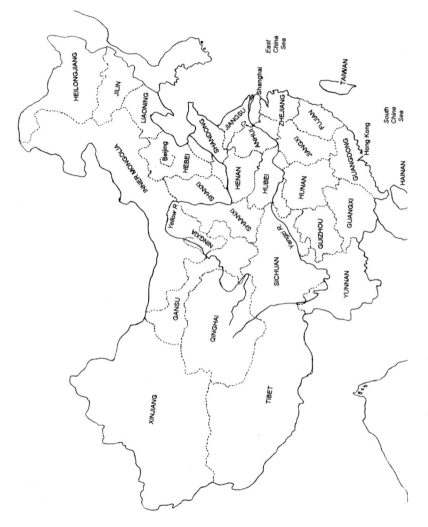

Map 1 Provinces of modern China

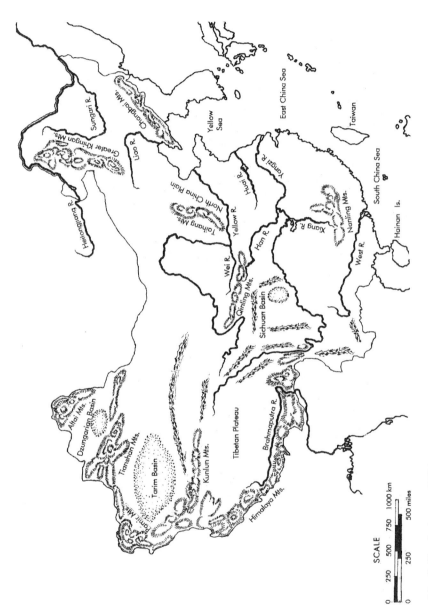

Map 2 Physical map of China

Introduction

The body of writing in Western languages on Chinese military history is not large. Very few students of Chinese history and culture have had much interest in things military, while military historians, for their part, have paid little attention to China. Most general surveys of military history follow in the footsteps of J. F. C. Fuller's fifty-year-old *Military History of the Western World* in that they are limited explicitly to a "Western world" (usually defined as Europe, the Near East, and European colonies of settlement).[1] Even those authors who have attempted to write a more global military history, such as John Keegan with his *History of Warfare* (1993), have tended to give China short shrift even as they perpetuate longstanding stereotypes of an Asian way of war.[2] To be fair, the writers of broad syntheses have inevitably been hemmed in by the lack of a substantial specialist literature in English and other Western languages. And this neglect surely owes something to the fact that from its origin in the middle decades of the nineteenth century, modern Western sinology grew accustomed to scrutinizing a China that was militarily weak and technologically backward, the hapless victim of Western and Japanese imperialists. Stated in the bluntest terms, China appeared to be a perennial loser with little to teach the winners when it came to the military arts.

Such attention as there has been has clustered in two areas. One is contemporary military analysis and the study of recent conflicts, a field that began to thrive after the emergence of Communist China as a significant military competitor in the Korean War of 1950–3. Recent trends in Chinese military expenditures and Sino–US relations suggest that this area of inquiry will continue to flourish in the foreseeable future. The second area of interest has been the study of the ancient military classics dating from the Warring States period (453–221 BC), especially Sunzi's *Art of War*. The thirteen chapters of Sunzi have been translated into many Western languages since the first French translation by Père Amiot was published in 1772.[3] English renditions began with the efforts of Captain Calthrop and Lionel Giles in the early years of the twentieth century, and there are at least half a dozen competing versions currently in print. The market would seem to be insatiable. This popularity owes something to the profundity of the text itself, something to the portability

1

of its teachings to other times, places, and fields of activity, and something (perhaps) to the much wider Western interest in the "wisdom books of the East." From the point of view of the serious student of Chinese military history, this emphasis is by no means misplaced: The "age of the classics" was a formative period for many ideas and institutions, and the influence of Sunzi on later military thought and practice is undeniable.

The emphasis on the early and recent periods has, however, left most of China's military history relatively unexplored. For nearly a generation, the conference volume *Chinese Ways in Warfare*, edited by John K. Fairbank and Frank A. Kierman, Jr. and published by Harvard University Press in 1974, remained the single most important work in English on military operations and practices in "Imperial China" – that is, the entire period from the unification of the empire in 221 BC to the fall of the Qing dynasty in 1912. Those wishing to dig deeper have had to seek out obscure monographs,[4] unpublished doctoral dissertations,[5] scattered articles,[6] individual chapters in books not otherwise devoted to military history,[7] and works in various foreign languages.[8] Within the broad chronological framework of imperial China, coverage of the period from the fall of the Han dynasty in AD 220 to the establishment of the Song dynasty in 960 has been especially sparse, perhaps because the political chaos and disunity that plagued the Chinese world for much of this period could not compete with strong, expansive dynasties for the attention of military historians.

The modern Chinese-language secondary literature is of course much more extensive, but it is of very uneven quality. The most substantial scholarly contributions have been made in the study of military institutions, a subfield of the much broader literature on Chinese institutional history that dates back at least to the *Tong dian* (*Comprehensive Canons*) compiled by the scholar-official Du You in the middle years of the Tang dynasty. Many detailed studies have been produced dealing with military organization, recruitment, and the terms of military service in particular periods of Chinese history; based on the careful study of surviving documents, historical records, and literary texts, these works can be intimidating to the non-specialist. A fine example of this genre is Gu Jiguang's book on the *fubing* or territorial soldiery of the Tang dynasty, originally published in 1962; another, more recent example is Sun Jimin's 1995 book on the expeditionary armies of the Tang dynasty.[9] Military institutions have also drawn a great deal of attention from Japanese sinologists; for the period covered by this book, extremely important contributions have been made by prominent scholars such as Hamaguchi Shigekuni, Kikuchi Hideo, and Tanigawa Michio.

The history of battles and campaigns, as opposed to the history of military institutions, has received relatively little scholarly attention. To be sure, for the premodern period we now have massive multivolume "official" histories such as the ten-volume *Zhongguo lidai zhanzheng shi* (History of Chinese warfare through the ages), published in Taipei in 1967 under the auspices of the Armed Forces Joint Staff College, and the twenty-volume *Zhongguo junshi tongshi*

2

(Comprehensive history of military affairs in China), issued in Beijing in 1998 by the Military Science Publishing House. These works and others like them leave much to be desired, however. Typically written by committees rather than individual authors, they often do little more than paraphrase the narratives of the traditional dynastic histories, with little attention to textual criticism, rigorous analysis, and unconventional lines of questioning. Military history as written by such innovative Western practitioners as Hans Delbrück and John Keegan has scarcely been attempted – in any language – for the more than two thousand years of imperial China.

The aim of the present volume is considerably less ambitious. It is intended not to revolutionize the writing of Chinese military history but to begin to close the vast gap that separates the Chinese and Western-language literature dealing with the interrelationship of warfare, state, and society during the six centuries between the fall of the Western Jin dynasty and the fall of the Tang dynasty. While other volumes in this series have been organized thematically, the unfamiliarity of even the most basic political history of this period for most Western readers necessitates a different approach. This study is built around a fairly straightforward narrative of political and military events, with chronology dictating the sequence of the chapters. Within this basic framework, developments in military institutions, social and political structures, and the techniques of warfare are introduced where appropriate. The goal is to elucidate some of the most important connections between warfare, military institutions, and social change in medieval China.

The term "medieval," when applied to Chinese history, requires some clarification, as does the word "China" itself when we are dealing with the period from AD 300 to 900. Following widespread (but far from universal) usage among historians of China, I have chosen to take the early years of the fourth century and the fall of the Western Jin dynasty as the beginning of China's medieval period. These years saw the final collapse of the unified imperial state initiated more than five centuries earlier by the First Emperor of Qin, and a rapid descent into chaos and disunity that would last for nearly two hundred years; the parallel with roughly contemporaneous developments in Europe and the Mediterranean world is obvious and will receive more detailed attention in the next chapter. The endpoint of the Chinese Middle Ages is much less obvious. For the purposes of this particular study – and to hold this volume to a reasonable length – I have chosen to follow the lead of the pioneering Japanese sinologist Naitō Torajirō and place the end of the medieval world at about the end of the Tang dynasty (618–907). The reader should be aware that other scholars (such as Herbert Franke) have sometimes attached the "medieval" label to the Song (960–1279) and Yuan (1279–1368) dynasties as well.

The meaning of "China" does not at first seem to be problematic. At the beginning of the twenty-first century, the natural tendency is to think of China as the territory of the People's Republic of China (PRC), and the Chinese as the ethnic Han people who make up more than 90 percent of the population of today's PRC. Unfortunately, these assumptions do not mesh very well with the realities of the first millennium. For much of the period covered by this book, the territory of today's China was divided into two, several, or many rival political entities. The vast, peripheral regions of today's PRC, including Tibet, Xinjiang, Qinghai, and Yunnan provinces, and most of Manchuria and Inner Mongolia, were rarely (and in some cases never) subordinated to Han Chinese states or empires, though their inhabitants often posed serious military threats under their own native rulers. On the other hand, at least one area that is not part of today's China – northern Vietnam – was administered as an integral part of Western Jin, the southern dynasties, and the Sui and Tang empires. Another outlying area, the Korean peninsula, had been part of the Han empire; it continued to be included in the sphere of Chinese diplomatic and tributary relations, and faced repeated efforts by the Sui and Tang dynasties to establish direct military and administrative control. The "China" dealt with in this volume is, in other words, not a single imperial state, but a vast subcontinental region of Eastern Asia whose boundaries do not coincide precisely with those of today's PRC.

The population of this region was extremely diverse. An inner zone, "China proper," contained the largest and densest population; this zone included the North China Plain, the Wei River valley, most of the Yangzi valley, the Sichuan basin, and various river valleys south of the Yangzi. The majority of the people here were sedentary farmers who were Han Chinese by language, cultural traditions, and self-identification. Many mountainous regions were, however, inhabited by distinct peoples such as the Man and Liao with their own languages, customs, and ethnic identities. Still other peoples inhabited an outer, peripheral zone including the arid steppes of Mongolia and Dzungaria, the oases of the Tarim basin, the forests of Manchuria, and the alpine deserts of the Tibetan plateau. Most of these people were not agriculturalists but hunters or stockbreeders, and some – especially the steppe dwellers – were full nomads. While the outer zone was generally inhospitable to settlement and exploitation by Han farmers, there was considerable movement in the other direction, especially during the first half of the period covered in this book. Large numbers of "barbarians" from the outer zone settled in North China, and they provided almost all of the rulers of the various northern states until 581. As time passed, these peoples tended to lose their separate ethnic and linguistic identity through intermarriage with the Han majority and the adoption of Han dress and customs. This process was by no means a one-way street, however. There are also examples of Han military families moving to the northern frontier and adopting the language and lifestyle of their "barbarian" comrades. The malleability of ethnic identity in medieval China will be a recurrent theme of this book.

The picture of medieval Chinese warfare presented in this volume is inevitably influenced by the nature of the available sources. There are very few truly "primary" sources bearing on this subject. These include a small number of original government documents (such as duty rosters) from the manuscript caches discovered at Dunhuang and Turfan in China's arid northwest, administrative compendia laying out the organization of the imperial government, several important military manuals dating from the Tang dynasty, and a number of edicts and memorials preserved in encyclopedias and anthologies (most of which were compiled during the Song period). For the most part, however, this book must rely primarily on the "standard" dynastic histories covering the period from 300 to 900, including the *History of the Jin Dynasty* (*Jin shu*), the *History of the Wei Dynasty* (*Wei shu*), the *History of the Sui Dynasty* (*Sui shu*), the *Old Tang History* (*Jiu Tang shu*), and the *New Tang History* (*Xin Tang shu*). Most of these works were written in the early years of the Tang dynasty, though based on earlier records and accounts. The *Old Tang History* was not compiled until the middle of the tenth century, while the *New Tang History* did not appear until the second half of the eleventh century, under the Northern Song dynasty. Another important work of history bearing on this period, Sima Guang's *Comprehensive Mirror for Aid in Government* (*Zizhi tongjian*), also dates from the late eleventh century. With the exception of the *Comprehensive Mirror*, which began as a private historical project and later received imperial sponsorship, all of these histories were produced under the auspices of the state by teams of scholar-officials, men pursuing careers in the government service who had been assigned to the History Office (*shi guan*) or one of a handful of other organs that were charged at one time or another with the compilation of official history. All of these works represent the end result of a very long process of editing, rewriting, and condensation, and none can properly be characterized as a primary source.

Given that we are largely reliant on the official historians for our under-standing of medieval Chinese warfare, it is appropriate to ask what their sources were, how they handled those source materials, and what biases and distortions they may have introduced into their narratives. When it came to describing military operations, the official historians of Tang times should in theory have been able to draw upon a very wide range of source materials including not only primary documents such as proclamations and manifestoes, letters, memorials to the throne, all manner of military records and communications, and imperial edicts conferring appointments, bestowing rewards, and extend-ing amnesties, but also the texts inscribed on the memorial stelae erected at some of the battle sites of the past, the direct testimony of eyewitnesses and participants, court dances commemorating the most glorious victories of the dynastic founders, and even drawings of successful generals and their troops in battle array.[10] Some of this evidence, especially that of a documentary nature, *was* used by the historians, and a great many edicts, memorials, proclamations, and letters were incorporated in the histories in abridged form. When it came to the particulars of what had transpired in a given military engagement, the most important sources were probably the "announcements of victory" (*lubu*) sent to the court by generals in the field, and the "accounts of conduct" (*xingzhuang*), which were biographies of deceased senior officials (including generals) submitted to the government by their relatives and former subordinates.

The "announcement of victory" normally gave the time, date, and location of the battle, along with the estimated size of the enemy force, the names of the enemy leaders, the names of at least some of the subordinate commanders on the government side, the assignments they were given as part of the overall battle plan, and sometimes also the number of troops under their command. The accounts offer few details of the engagement itself, but are careful to record the number of casualties inflicted on the enemy. Judging from the few surviving specimens, the "announcement of victory" was a rather one-sided document. While the losses of the enemy were recorded in minute detail, it seems that government casualties were not mentioned unless they were so few as to border on the miraculous.[11] There must surely have been a system for reporting defeats to the court as well, but the fact that no documents of this type appear to have survived is indicative of the fundamental bias of the reporting system. At a time when successful generals could expect lavish rewards while those who failed faced severe punishments, there was naturally a strong tendency to accentuate the positive. Some generals, such as Yang Su during the Sui period and Gao Xianzhi in the middle of the eighth century, made sure that their secretaries sent in reports that were more flattering than the facts warranted, while others were in the habit of falsifying reports, magnifying small victories into large ones, and passing off defeats as victories – even though the falsifiers could expect to be punished if they were caught.[12] This sort of behavior is supposed to have been especially rife under the Tang emperor Xuanzong (r. 712–56), who took a special interest in military success beyond the frontiers.[13]

The "accounts of conduct" of military commanders would also have been self-serving, insofar as they were usually written by relatives or former subordinates of the deceased rather than officials of the Office of Merit Assessment and were often very similar to the eulogistic funerary writings that served the family's ancestral cult. They were likely to present their subject in the most favorable light, emphasizing his successes and skipping over his failures, and they were sometimes adopted by overworked official historians as the basis for biographies with little checking or serious revision.[14]

In addition to perpetuating many of the lies, half-truths, and distortions that had been introduced into their sources by the generals and their friends and relatives, the official historians also brought their own peculiar set of preconceptions and prejudices to the description of warfare. Western sinologists who have written on Chinese military history have complained that traditional Chinese battle accounts offer very little information about the substance or details of what happened. Herbert Franke, for example, points out that even major military events are often described in the most laconic terms: "'The army of X was defeated near Y', 'the city of Z was taken (or successfully defended)' – such are the usual entries."[15] Not all battle accounts are as spare as this, but there is no denying that medieval Chinese materials tend to be less informative about weapons, tactics, and the details of combat than battle accounts from, say, Greece, Rome, or Byzantium. To some extent this was because Chinese society did not produce people like Caesar or Thucydides – people who were not only chroniclers of warfare but also active participants. In medieval China, there was a fundamental disjunction between the people whose job it was to exercise military command and those who were responsible for writing official reports and historical accounts of military operations.[16] Though not necessarily illiterate, the men who exercised military command in medieval China were normally of limited literary ability and interests, while the writing of official history was the preserve of a "scholarly elite within the civil service," men who moved back and forth between the historiographical and remonstrative offices at court and were seldom assigned to leadership positions in the provinces, let alone to army commands.[17]

With little knowledge of or interest in the practical details of warfare – and with very few details provided by their sources in any case – these scholarly official historians were probably more comfortable borrowing elements of their own descriptions of military operations from models of the genre in earlier histories and recycling conventional literary expressions and allusions bearing on combat than trying to offer a precise and accurate reconstruction of the event. When they did choose to provide details, they usually preferred to focus on a clever stratagem or an unusual or colorful feature of the battle or campaign.

The scholarly elite from which the official historians were drawn was not only unfamiliar with the practical details of military affairs, but was often actively hostile to warfare and the military. Its members esteemed the civil and literary virtues (*wen*) over the martial virtues (*wu*), and regarded the resort to arms as "an undesirable option, almost a confession of failure."[18] They strove to limit or reduce the power and influence of military officials within the imperial polity, and sometimes argued against major military expeditions beyond the empire's borders.[19] The cultural preference for *wen* over *wu* dated back to the early days of Chinese civilization, and had long ago given rise to the time-honored literary convention that C. H. Wang has called "the ellipsis of battle". In Chinese poetry, "the battle, the actual clash of arms, is almost always left unsaid. . . . It is a significant feature in the Chinese literary convention that keeps poetry about the heroic action from developing into a detailed narrative of the battle."[20] It would seem that this same convention applied with equal force both to military reports and to the battle narratives crafted by the official historians. The "announcements of victory" emphasize initial dispositions and the listing of the spoils rather than the combat itself, while the battle accounts in the standard histories tend to focus on pre-battle deliberations and post-battle explanations of strategy.

The literati bias that informs the standard histories is not simply a matter of omission, but may also introduce significant distortions into the sources for medieval Chinese warfare. The histories often have generals quoting from the *Sunzi* and other ancient military classics to justify and explain their decisions. But can we trust this evidence? Highly literate scholar-officials were more likely to be familiar with this body of book-learning than the military men were. Quotes from the military classics are often encountered in the memorials and other documents drafted by scholar-officials.[21] And these men were already accustomed to quoting from the Confucian canon to support their own policy positions and attack their opponents.[22] When the historian chose to exercise his imagination to produce a more detailed picture of military decisionmaking than was strictly warranted by the evidence at his disposal, there is good reason to believe that he was inclined to portray a mode of argumentation firmly grounded in *textual* authority. It is perhaps also worth noting that an emphasis on the mastery of book-learning as the key to success in war is very well suited to the purpose of putting military men in their place, implying as it does that military command at the highest levels can be success-fully exercised by scholars with no skill at arms and no practical experience of warfare.

Another area where the standard histories may present a somewhat mis-leading picture of medieval Chinese warfare is with regard to magic and divination. The most important and extensive of the military manuals surviving from the Tang period, Li Quan's mid-eighth-century *Taibai yinjing*, devotes several chapters to methods of divination and prognostication, but this element is largely absent from the battles and campaigns described in the dynastic histories and the *Comprehensive Mirror*.[23] There are a few tantalizing indications that divination within the framework of established cosmological and cosmographic schemes may have had a significant role in shaping command decisions. We are told, for example, that when the Eastern Wei leader Gao Huan attacked the fortress of Yubi in 546 he selected both the times and locations of his attacks in this fashion, and that in 784 two warlords in Hebei divined to select an auspicious day to unite their forces in order to attack a common foe.[24] Such mentions are, however, extremely rare. It may be that these practices were unusual, but it is also possible that the official historians – who tended to adopt a rather rational, skeptical attitude – looked askance at magic and divination and preferred not to mention it. Magical practices mentioned in the standard histories of the Sui and Tang dynasties usually fall into one of three basic categories: (1) cynical performances put on by generals to raise the morale of their followers; (2) sincerely performed divinations or magic rituals that lead to complete and sometimes laughable failure; or (3) successes gained by men who scoff at superstitious beliefs. An example of the third category is a defeat inflicted on the rebellious province of Huaxi by the Tang general Li Su in 817, as recorded in Ouyang Xiu's *New Tang History*. Despite the objections of his subordinates, Li deliberately launched his attack on a taboo day and thereby succeeded in taking the enemy completely by surprise.[25] This case in particular suggests that cosmological and cosmographic beliefs may have had a widespread and hitherto largely unrecognized influence on military decisionmaking in medieval China.

Another aspect of the traditional Chinese historian's approach to military history that may be viewed with a certain amount of skepticism is the treatment of numbers. Readers familiar with the military history of medieval Europe and Byzantium will very likely find many of the army sizes given in this volume incredible. Modern historians have consistently deflated the army strengths passed down by the medieval chroniclers, in some cases by digging out more reliable documentary evidence and in other cases by pointing to the inescapable limits of time and space.[26] It is now generally agreed that even in the expansive days of Justinian in the first half of the sixth century, Byzantine field armies did not exceed 25,000 and were usually much smaller.[27]

Modern historians of China have similarly questioned the army sizes (and most other numbers) found in traditional Chinese histories. In his essay on "Numbers and Units in Chinese Economic History," Lien-sheng Yang observed that it is "an open secret that generals over-report the number of their soldiers and exaggerate their military achievements," while the Japanese sinologist Miyazaki Ichisada found textual evidence that it was routine procedure for generals of the Three Kingdoms period (AD 220–63) to multiply the enemy's casualties by ten when reporting a victory.[28] The modern Chinese historian Li Tse-fen, a former military officer himself, has asserted that the early historians had a purely literary attitude, lacked common sense, and made no effort to report accurate numbers.[29]

This criticism is not entirely fair. The authors of Chinese dynastic histories and the preliminary historical compilations on which they were based were seldom men with practical military experience, to be sure, but they were also members of a functioning bureaucracy that kept voluminous records and made strenuous (if seldom fully successful) efforts to compile and maintain accurate figures on population, tax revenue, state expenditures, government grain supplies, military manpower, and the number of horses in the imperial herds, to name only a few areas of concern. Sima Guang, the greatest of the medieval Chinese historians, was anything but credulous about numbers and, when confronted with contradictions in his sources regarding the size of an army, almost invariably opted for the smaller figure.[30] Nor should all of the numbers given in the old Chinese histories be tarred with the same brush. There was not the same temptation to exaggerate the size of a government army that applied in the case of, say, the number of casualties inflicted on an enemy force. The great majority of the Chinese army sizes reported in Sima Guang's *Comprehensive Mirror for Aid in Government* and other traditional histories do not seem inherently implausible, given China's large population and administrative resources; most are fewer than 50,000 men.[31] The very large and very vague numbers ("several myriads," "a hundred myriads") are usually attached to armies of rebels or foreigners (often nomads) where the Chinese historian had no reliable documentary sources to draw upon and was therefore able to give his imagination free rein.

Of course, even where the historian had official records and reports at his disposal, there was likely to be a strong upward bias in numbers. This was because it was very difficult to keep track of large numbers of people over time, even for armies as well provided with staff aides, clerks, and bookkeepers as those of medieval China. Soldiers were constantly being lost to wounds, disease, and desertion, while others were sent off in detached columns or left behind to garrison cities and guard supply lines. The size of an army changed from day to day, and if reinforcements were not coming in the change was necessarily in a downward direction. We cannot assume that all of these fluctuations were being accurately recorded and reported to headquarters, or that such records as did exist would have made their way into the hands of the official historians. Owing to these difficulties, it is likely that most recorded army strengths tell us the approximate size of the force that began the campaign, not the reduced force that arrived at the battlefield days, weeks, or months later.

How large were medieval Chinese armies? The best answer from the very limited evidence available to us is that they were usually smaller than the figures reported by the traditional historians, but in most cases probably not very much smaller. Reports of government field armies of 50,000 or less can be accepted almost without reservation, and armies in this range seem to have been by far the most common during the period in question. It is probably no accident that in his treatise on the art of war the early Tang general Li Jing used a force of 20,000 men as his example of a typical expeditionary army.[32] Although some of the larger figures are suspect for various reasons, armies of 100,000 or more are not inherently implausible given China's very considerable demographic, material, and administrative resources. (The empire's population was recorded at more than 57 million near the end of Western Han, at 46 million under the Sui dynasty, and at just under 49 million at the height of Tang power in 742.[33]) It should be borne in mind, however, that size always carried a price. Such massive armies would have been extremely cumbersome to move, supply, and control unless broken down into several smaller armies which would have been difficult to coordinate effectively from a single center. Only the very largest figures for campaign armies should be rejected out of hand: if the numbers reported for these forces are anywhere near accurate, they must represent not a single army marching together, camping together, and fighting together on a single battlefield, but the aggregate of several separate armies operating over a wide expanse of territory.

This volume consists of eleven chapters. The first chapter deals with Chinese history prior to AD 300 in order to identify the military inheritance from the Warring State period (453-221 BC) and the Qin and Han empires (221 BC-

AD 220) that contributed to shaping the warfare of the medieval period. This legacy included not only weapons, tactics, and a body of prescriptive literature on the art of war, but also several key normative concepts. One was the ideal of a mass, conscript army, with all adult males of the farming population trained to arms and capable of serving the state as soldiers whenever necessary. A second was the ideal of imperial unity, with strict central control over all the armed forces of the realm. Another was the ideal of civilian supremacy, with subordination of the military command structure to the civil bureaucracy (headed by a ruler whose duties did not include military leadership in the field). Closely linked to this was the ideal of the scholar-general, capable of exercising military command on the basis of his mastery of texts rather than any practical miltary experience or skill at arms. These ideals and preferences underlay the military institutions of the Western Han dynasty (202 BC–AD 9), but they were the product of an age when wars were fought mainly between Chinese states. The rise of a strong nomadic power, the Xiongnu, on the steppe north of China at the beginning of the second century BC posed a new sort of military challenge and tended to undermine the arrangements that had emerged from the Warring States period.

The second chapter examines the collapse of the Western Jin dynasty (AD 265–317), which ushered in nearly three centuries of disunity. By the beginning of the fourth century, the need for permanent standing forces had resulted in the replacement of the farmer-conscripts of Han times by men of unfree status who resembled a hereditary military caste. Considerable military authority was delegated to princes of the imperial family, while the task of frontier defense was largely entrusted to barbarian groups that had settled within the borders of the empire. Reliance on such forces reflected the need for skilled warriors capable of standing up to the nomads, and also indicated the increasing importance of cavalry in East Asian warfare with the introduction of the stirrup and heavier armor for both horse and rider. These military arrangements contributed to the undoing of the Western Jin empire, which was ravaged by a civil war of the imperial princes and then faced with a rebellion of its barbarian auxiliaries. The capital, Luoyang, was sacked by the rebels in 311, and North China fell under the rule of a congeries of squabbling and unstable tribal statelets.

The third chapter examines war and society in North China from the fall of Western Jin to the reunification of the north by the Tuoba Wei dynasty in the middle of the fifth century. Incessant armed conflict and the absence of a stable ruling authority capable of enforcing a monopoly of violence over a wide territory led to the fragmentation of Chinese society into self-sufficient local units, often dominated by local strongmen who built hilltop fortresses and organized their dependants into private militias for self-defense. Despite this pervasive militarization, ultimate political control remained in the hands of barbarian rulers whose authority derived from control of a core following of tribal cavalry. Even after the reunification of the north by the Wei dynasty of the Tuoba Xianbei people, North Asian cavalry remained the nucleus of the state's military power and society remained deeply divided between Han Chinese and those they regarded as barbarians.

A rump Jin government in the south survived the debacle of the early fourth century and lasted until 420. It was replaced by a succession of short-lived southern regimes, the Liu Song, Qi, Liang, and Chen. All save the last of these were established by families that had emigrated to the Yangzi valley to escape the chaos in the north. This chapter will examine the security problems common to all of the southern dynasties, including the need to defend against attack from the north, the desire to reconquer the lost territory, and the difficulty of controlling both powerful elite families and the court's own military commanders. The need to maintain strong military forces coupled with the inability to maintain effective control over those forces made for extreme political instability and helps to explain the rapid succession of regimes, most of which were established by military coups d'état.

The fifth chapter deals with developments in the north from the middle of the fifth century to the founding of the Sui dynasty in 581. The Wei rulers found it necessary to deploy strong forces to the northern border to guard against nomadic newcomers, and in the 520s their empire was thrown into chaos by a rebellion of the garrison forces, who were in part protesting the increasing sinicization of the Wei court and its lack of solicitude for the frontier warriors. In the wake of the Wei collapse, the north was divided between two rival successor states, Western Wei (later Northern Zhou) and Eastern Wei (later Northern Qi). In order to defend themselves against their more powerful opponent, the rulers of Western Wei–Northern Zhou found it necessary to supplement their small force of North Asian cavalry by drawing the militias of local Chinese magnates into their military establishment. This was the origin of the celebrated system of territorial soldiery (*fubing*), which eventually evolved into a highly cost-effective force of soldier-cultivators. These *fubing* formed the backbone of the armies that unified North China under the Zhou banner in 577 and then conquered the south for Zhou's successor, the Sui dynasty, in 589. Not only did the new military institution play a role in the reunification of China, but it also tied the interests of local magnates to the imperial court and contributed to the formation of the mixed-blood aristocracy that dominated the Sui regime and the early Tang court.

The sixth chapter traces the conflict between the regional regimes in north and south China from the establishment of the Eastern Jin dynasty in the Yangzi valley in 317 to the conquest of its successor, the Chen dynasty, by Sui in 589. The north–south division was prolonged for a number of reasons. The north was usually divided between several states, but even when it was united the structural weaknesses of the northern regimes with their deep ethnic divisions often placed limits on what they could accomplish militarily. Northern invaders were also hindered by the south's climate and geography, especially the mighty Yangzi River barrier guarded by southern naval forces. The southern regimes, for their part, lacked the resources to reconquer the more populous north, and eventually they also lost the will to do so. The division was finally ended in 589, when the Sui dynasty controlled all of the north down to the Yangzi itself and was able to build powerful water forces to challenge Chen's control of the river barrier.

The seventh chapter focuses on the last Sui emperor's disastrous campaigns against the northern Korean kingdom of Koguryŏ in 612–14 and their consequences for China. If the Sui conquest of the south illustrates the constructive or integrative potential of war and military power, the circumstances surrounding the collapse of the Sui dynasty afford an example of war's destructive or disintegrative power. The Sui efforts met with failure due to the difficulty of overcoming Koguryŏ's strong border fortresses (compounded by the difficult geography and climate of southern Manchuria), and also because of the difficulty of supplying the unusually large armies that had been mobilized for these operations. The requisitions of manpower, foodstuffs, and other resources needed to support the gargantuan military effort, coming on top of natural disasters and routine corvée exactions, imposed an impossibly heavy burden on the peasantry of northeastern China and helped to fan the uprisings that brought down the Sui dynasty.

The eighth chapter is devoted to the civil wars that followed the Sui collapse and led to the consolidation of the Tang dynasty (618–907). With a number of regional warlords competing for power and an even larger number of local strongmen – some plebeian bandit leaders, others local elites, and still others former Sui officials – watching anxiously from the sidelines and hoping to end up in the winning camp, Tang military victories played an important role in attracting supporters and pacifying large regions of the empire. The principal Tang field commander, Li Shimin, the second son of the dynastic founder, developed an extremely successful formula for dealing with his various opponents, one that involved occupying a fortified camp, avoiding a general engagement while raiding the enemy's supply lines, and only going over to the attack when it was clear that the enemy had begun to weaken. The new dynasty's last serious domestic opponents were disposed of in 622–3.

Once the Tang court had succeeded in firmly establishing its hegemony within China, the focus of its military concerns shifted to the northern frontier. Developments there from the 620s to the 670s are the subject of the ninth chapter. In a series of offensive campaigns which began in the late 620s and extended over several decades, the Tang won the submission of the Eastern Turks and other nomadic peoples. In many of these campaigns, cavalry forces provided by steppe peoples who had aleady been subjugated played a more important role than the *fubing* farmer-soldiers from the interior of the empire. In the northeast, Li Shimin, now emperor, began a new war against Koguryŏ in the 640s. After temporary success during the 660s, the Tang government was distracted by threats to other sectors of the frontier and its armies were driven from the Korean peninsula by the end of the 670s.

The tenth chapter traces the decline of the *fubing* system and the emergence of permanent frontier armies made up of longserving regular troops. The *fubing* were not especially well suited to long-range expeditions beyond the borders of China proper, and after the late 670s, when the Turks threw off Tang suzerainty, they proved even less well suited to the task of providing strong, permanent border garrisons. By the middle of the eighth century, powerful regional military commands had been set up along the northern and western frontiers. The military governors appointed to these commands led armies composed of full-time, long-service troops. By the middle of the 750s, most of the military governors and a great many of their soldiers were of barbarian origin. These forces proved extemely effective in guarding the empire's borders against the Tibetans and a variety of nomadic peoples, but this security came at a high price. Not only were the armies costly to maintain, but the imperial court relinquished effective control over the military governors, whose troops came to owe primary allegiance to their immediate superiors rather than the distant authorities in the capital. This situation made possible the devastating rebellion of the frontier general An Lushan, which raged from 755 to 763 and came close to bringing down the Tang dynasty.

The book's final chapter explores the impact of the rebellion on politics, society, and the economy during the second half of the Tang period. The failure of the imperial court to crush the last of the rebel generals completely, coupled with the autonomist tendencies of many nominally loyal commanders, meant that the imperial court lost control of a large part of the empire, territory which was divided among a number of unstable warlord regimes. The existence of these autonomous provincial military governments had significant social and economic consequences. They promoted greater social mobility by recruiting officials from a broader range of backgrounds than had been tapped by the imperial court, while the multiplicity of jurisdictions weakened the state's control of the economy and helped make possible the flourishing of commercial activity in the last century of Tang rule. These developments laid the groundwork for the very different social, economic, and political structures of the Song dynasty and "late imperial China."

Notes

1　J. F. C. Fuller, *A Military History of the Western World* (New York: Funk and Wagnalls, 1954–6); an example of a more recent effort is Archer Jones, *The Art of War in the Western World* (London and New York: Oxford University Press, 1989).

2　John Keegan, *A History of Warfare* (New York: Alfred A. Knopf, 1993), pp. 214–21, 380–7, and passim. For a more sustained and systematic analysis of Keegan and others, see Jeremy Black's chapter in Hans van de Ven (ed.), *Warfare in Chinese History* (Leiden: E. J. Brill, 2000), especially, pp. 428–31.

3　Sun Tzu, *The Art of War*, trans. Samuel B. Griffith (New York: Oxford University Press, 1971).

4　For example: Hans Bielenstein, *The Restoration of the Han Dynasty*, vol. 2: *The Civil*

War, in *Bulletin of the Museum of Far Eastern Antiquities* (Stockholm), 31 (1959), pp. 1–287.

5   For example: Terrence Douglas O'Byrne, "Civil–Military Relations During the Middle T'ang: The Career of Kuo Tzu-i" (Ph.D. dissertation, University of Illinois at Urbana-Champaign, 1982).

6   For example: Benjamin E. Wallacker, "Studies in Medieval Chinese Siegecraft: The Siege of Yü-pi, A.D. 546," *Journal of Asian Studies*, 28.4 (August 1969), pp. 789–802.

7   For example: Ray Huang, *1587, A Year of No Significance: The Ming Dynasty in Decline* (New Haven: Yale University Press, 1981), ch. 6, on the Ming general Qi Jiguang.

8   For example: Herbert Franke, *Studien und Texte zur Kriegsgeschichte der südlichen Sungzeit* (Wiesbaden: Otto Harrassowitz, 1987).

9   Gu Jiguang, *Fubing zhidu kaoshi* (Shanghai: Shanghai renmin chubanshe, 1962; rpt. Taipei: Hongwenguan chubanshe, 1985); Sun Jimin, *Tangdai xingjun zhidu yanjiu* (Taipei: Wenjin chubanshe, 1995).

10 For examples of imperial edicts dealing with warfare and the military, see Song Minqiu (comp.), *Tang da zhaoling ji* (Beijing: Commercial Press, 1959), chs. 59 and 60; for mention of stelae, see Stanley Weinstein, *Buddhism Under the T'ang* (Cambridge: Cambridge University Press, 1987), p. 13; for court dances, see Sima Guang, *Zizhi tongjian* (Beijing: Guji chubanshe, 1956), ch. 200, p. 6323; for drawings, see Liu Xu et al., *Jiu Tang shu* (Beijing: Zhonghua shuju, 1975), ch. 187A, p. 4867.

11 See Li Fang et al. (comps.), *Wenyuan yinghua* (Taipei: Huawen shuju, 1965), ch. 647, p. 17a, and other examples of *lubu* in the same chapter.

12 Denis Twitchett (ed.), *Cambridge History of China*, vol. 3: *Sui and T'ang China, 589–906, Pt. 1* (Cambridge: Cambridge University Press, 1979), pp. 68–9, Sima Guang, *Zizhi tongjian*, ch. 216, pp. 6888 and 6906–7; also ch. 217, pp. 6926–7.

13 Du You, *Tong dian* (Beijing: Zhonghua shuju, 1988), ch. 148, p. 3780.

14 For a discussion of the "account of conduct," see Denis Twitchett, *The Writing of Official History Under the T'ang* (Cambridge: Cambridge University Press, 1992), pp. 66–71. The epitaph of the early Tang general Li Shentong skips over the period from 618 to 621 to avoid mentioning his defeat and capture; see Mao Han-kuang (ed.), *Tangdai muzhiming huibian fukao*, vol. 1 (Taipei: Institute of History and Philology of Academia Sinica, 1985), pp. 143–4.

15 Herbert Franke, "Warfare in Medieval China: Some Research Problems," in *Zhongyang yanjiuyuan di er jie guoji hanxue huiyi lunwenji* (Taipei: Academia Sinica, 1989), vol. 5, p. 806.

16 Li Tse-fen, *Sui Tang Wudai lishi lunwenji* (Taipei: Taiwan Commercial Press, 1989), pp. 214, 218.

17 For the scholarly elite, see Twitchett, *The Writing of Official History Under the T'ang*, pp. 11, 15. According to D. L. McMullen, "many scholars prided themselves on avoiding involvement with military office"; see his article, "The Cult of Ch'i T'ai-kung and T'ang Attitudes to the Military," *T'ang Studies* 7 (1989), p. 62.

18 McMullen, "The Cult of Ch'i T'ai-kung," p. 66 and passim.

19 McMullen, "The Cult of Ch'i T'ai-kung," pp. 70–1, 75; Michael C. Rogers, *The Chronicle of Fu Chien: A Case of Exemplar History* (Berkeley and Los Angeles: University of California Press, 1968), p. 46.

20 C. H. Wang, "Towards Defining a Chinese Heroism," *Journal of the American Oriental Society*, 95.1 (1975), p. 29.

21 See, for example, Sima Guang, *Zizhi tongjian*, ch. 205, p. 6481, and ch. 232, p. 7465.

22 D. L. McMullen, *State and Scholars in T'ang China* (Cambridge: Cambridge University Press, 1988), pp. 67, 71, and passim.

23 Li Quan, *Taibai yinjing*, in *Zhongguo bingshu jicheng*, vol. 2 (Beijing and Shenyang: Jiefangjun chubanshe and Liao-Shen shushe, 1988), chs. 8, 9, and 10.

24 Wallacker, "Studies in Medieval Chinese Siegecraft: The Siege of Yü-pi," pp. 794–6; *Jiu Tang shu*, ch. 142, p. 3875.

25 Ouyang Xiu, *Xin Tang shu* (Beijing: Zhonghua shuju, 1975), ch. 145, p. 4875.

26 For an example of the former approach, see J. H. Ramsay, "The Strength of English Armies in the Middle Ages," *English Historical Review*, 29 (1914), pp. 222–3. Ramsay found that surviving muster rolls listed 13,374 effectives (not counting contingents from York and Durham) available for the Scottish expedition of Richard II of England, while the chroniclers gave figures of 100,000 to 300,000. The foremost practitioner of the latter approach was surely Hans Delbrück; see his *Numbers in History* (London: University of London Press, 1913).

27 See John Haldon, *Warfare, State and Society in the Byzantine World, 565–1204* (London: UCL Press, 1999), pp. 99–101, and Warren Treadgold, *Byzantium and its Army, 284–1081* (Stanford, Ca.: Stanford University Press, 1995), pp. 59–64.

28 Lien-sheng Yang, "Numbers and Units in Chinese Economic History," in idem, *Studies in Chinese Institutional History* (Cambridge, Mass.: Harvard University Press, 1961), p. 80; Miyazaki Ichisada, "Tokushi satsuki," *Shirin*, 21.1 (1936), p. 134.

29 Li Tse-fen, *Sui Tang Wudai lishi lunwenji*, pp. 15, 28, 33.

30 For examples, see Sima Guang, *Zizhi tongjian*, ch. 206, p. 6515; ch. 217, pp. 6943–4; and ch. 258, pp. 8404–5.

31 See David A. Graff, "Early T'ang Generalship and the Textual Tradition" (Ph.D. dissertation, Princeton University, 1995), Table 2.2, pp. 49–53.

32 Du You, *Tong dian*, ch. 148, p. 3792.

33 For the Han figure, see Ch. 1, note 4; for Sui, see Wei Zheng et al., *Sui shu* (Beijing: Zhonghua shuju, 1973), ch. 29, p. 808; for 742, see *Jiu Tang shu*, ch. 9, p. 216.

CHAPTER ONE

The legacy of antiquity

There has long existed a rough-and-ready, generally accepted periodization of the military history of the Western world. Though exact chronological boundaries remain subject to debate, changes in technology, tactics, and military institutions have enabled historians to distinguish between an ancient period dominated by the infantry-based armies of Greece and Rome and a medieval period characterized by political fragmentation, the primacy of cavalry on the battlefield, and the great advantage enjoyed by the defenders of castles and fortresses. This medieval pattern in turn gave way to an early modern warfare marked by the resurgence of effective infantry forces, the use of gunpowder weapons, and the centralization of military authority.[1] In contrast to this familiar picture of historical change, the periodization of Chinese military history remains extremely murky. At the ancient and modern extremes, to be sure, certain changes are fairly obvious. The aristocratic chariot warfare of the seventh century BC was profoundly different from the conflicts waged by disciplined mass armies of infantry and cavalry four centuries later, and, at the other extreme, the struggle to assimilate Western military technology, organization, and ideas in the late nineteenth century marks another obvious watershed. In the more than two thousand years separating these points, however, significant developments are not easy to identify. It is not at all clear that medieval Chinese warfare – however we choose to define the term "medieval" in the Chinese context – differed very much from what came before or followed after. The starting point for this survey, AD 300, coincides very loosely with the appearance of the stirrup in China, while the endpoint of AD 900 falls just prior to the introduction of gunpowder into Chinese warfare. Yet, for a variety of reasons both institutional and technological, neither of these innovations seems to have had the same sweeping impact on the conduct of warfare in China as in the West.[2] Nor can this period be sharply distinguished on the basis of military institutions or organization, since there was little that did not have an analogue in earlier or later times. The choice of 300 and 900 as the chronological boundaries of this work has less to do with developments in the art of war than with changes in the broader background of Chinese society and the imperial polity.

At the beginning of the fourth century China was a unified empire ruled by the Jin dynasty (house of Sima) from the ancient capital city of Luoyang just south of the Yellow River. The Jin regime was heir to the administrative and political traditions of China's first unified empire, which had been founded by Qin Shihuangdi of the short-lived Qin dynasty in 221 BC and continued in much the same form under the rulers of the Han dynasty from 202 BC to AD 220. Between the final collapse of Han rule and the advent of the Jin dynasty, China had experienced a half-century-long period of civil war and disunity when the land was divided between the so-called Three Kingdoms – Wei in the north, Wu in the southeast, and Shu in the Sichuan basin of the southwest. Each of these regional regimes claimed imperial legitimacy, but the Wei state, larger and more populous than its rivals, enjoyed a distinct advantage. In 263 Wei armies succeeded in conquering Shu. Two years later the last Wei emperor was deposed by the dominant minister of the Wei court, Sima Yan, who took the throne as the first emperor of the Jin dynasty. The Jin forces completed the conquest of the south by eliminating Wu in 280. The wars of the Three Kingdoms were the longest period of conflict and disorder since the founding of the empire in 221 BC, but their impact was limited by the fact that they were *civil* wars waged by Chinese against other Chinese with the aim of reconstructing the Han empire. There was actually a great deal of continuity in government during this period, especially in the north, and many of the officials who served the Jin court at the end of the third century came from families that had already been prominent under the Han dynasty.

The crisis that overtook the empire in the first decade of the fourth century was of a very different sort. A new round of internecine conflict initiated by feuding members of the Jin imperial house created an opening for revolts by non-Chinese peoples who had settled within the borders of the empire, and for invasions of North China by their pastoral cousins inhabiting the mountains, deserts, and grasslands beyond the frontier. The Jin rulers retreated south of the Yangzi River, leaving the north to be divided among a number of violent and unstable "barbarian" regimes. Some three centuries passed before the empire was reunited by the founders of the Sui and Tang dynasties, who had themselves emerged from the new, mixed-blood Sino-Turkic elite that had taken root in North China during the age of division. While the Tang dynasty was able to impose a high degree of unity and order on the empire for more than a century, the great rebellion of the frontier general An Lushan in 755 badly weakened the power of the court and ushered in a new period of warlordism and regional autonomy that lasted well beyond the fall of the dynasty in 907.

The period from 300 to 900 was a time when disunity and disorder were the dominant themes. China was subjected as never before to invasions by peoples that the Chinese – or more precisely, their literate elites – chose to regard as barbarians. Much of China was conquered and ruled by the invaders, another unprecedented development. And during this period outside influences were felt strongly not only in the political sphere, but also in religion and culture.

The chaos and violence of the age set streams of refugees in motion, especially from north to south, and gave rise – at some times and in some places – to autarkic, manorial systems of production. This period was also an aristocratic age, when hereditary status counted far more than had been the case in Han times. A distinguished pedigree could command popular respect and access to government office, and high birth was among the most important qualifications for leadership. China's "medieval" period was also an age of religious faith, as disorder and insecurity created fertile conditions for the spread of Buddhism with its otherworldly promises to people of all classes and conditions in all parts of the country. Buddhism was first introduced to China from India during the Han, but it was during the age of disunion and under the Sui and Tang dynasties that this foreign faith was fully accepted by the Chinese and enjoyed its greatest influence over thought and behavior, politics and the arts. As others have pointed out, parallels for many of the characterics of China's "medieval" period can be found in the Europe of the Middle Ages. The resemblance should not be pushed too far, however. Buddhist monasteries could be locally powerful, for example, but the Buddhist clergy was never able to claim the same monopolistic position that the Catholic church enjoyed in medieval Europe. Literacy, the written heritage of antiquity, and traditions of public administration were far better preserved in China than in the Latin West.

Just as the period after 300 was in many ways distinct from what came before, Chinese society of the Song dynasty (960–1279) and later was very different from the "medieval" world that preceded it. Sinologists have long regarded the transition from Tang to Song as one of the most important divides in all of Chinese history. It would be absurd to try to date this transition, based as it was on gradual processes of social and cultural change, to a single year such as 900, 907, or 960, but the changes that occurred in China between the middle of the eighth century and the end of the tenth were no less profound for being so difficult to locate precisely in time. These two and a half centuries saw the replacement of the old aristocracy with its hereditary claims to office by a more broadly based elite of landholders and bureaucrats recruited on the basis of merit rather than birth. The rise of the civil service examination system over the course of the Tang period certainly played a major part in this development, as did the rampant provincial warlordism of late Tang which opened many local government positions to men of humble origins, the chaos of the late ninth-century rebellions and civil wars which destroyed many of the aristocratic families, and the emergence of a free market in land which enabled newly risen bureaucratic elites to secure their family fortunes as landed gentry. The same period saw the burgeoning of a market economy and increasing urbanization, the invention of woodblock printing leading to a much wider distribution of reading materials and correspondingly greater literacy, and a decline in the fortunes of Buddhism coupled with a revival of Confucian philosophy. One of the most influential Japanese sinologists of the twentieth century went so far as to label the Song dynasty as the beginning of "modern"

China, primarily on account of the disappearance of aristocratic privilege and the enhanced power of the emperor, no longer first among equals, over all of his subjects.[3]

Of course, any scheme of periodization must inevitably do violence to a complex historical reality. Political and military turning points cannot be assumed to coincide with significant social and economic developments, and none of these are necessarily connected to new intellectual departures or innovations in technology. Some phenomena change quickly and others, the stuff of Braudel's *longue durée*, change slowly or not at all. The basic agrarian pattern of Chinese life and the family-oriented Confucian value system must be counted as part of this relatively static substrate, as must a number of ideas and practices that were already quite well established by the beginning of the medieval period. One of these was the ideal of imperial unity, the belief that China – the lands and peoples that had been ruled by the Qin and Han dynasties – should form a single political entity under a single legitimate ruler who would serve as ritual intermediary between the human world, nature, and the cosmos. Even before Qin's creation of an administratively unified empire, the relatively loose hegemony exercised by the earlier Zhou kings had planted the notion that a single paramount ruler for all the Chinese lands was both desirable and necessary. Under the Qin and Han regimes, this craving for unity attached itself to the structures and pretenses of the centralized, bureaucratic empire. Imperial unity acquired an aura of legitimacy that became a valuable ideological resource for would-be unifiers. After the fall of Han, each of the Three Kingdoms claimed sole legitimacy for itself and dreamed of reuniting the empire under its own mandate, though only Wei–Jin had the strength to realize this ambition.

Another core normative principle was the centrality of China and the superiority of its civilization. Peoples who existed outside of the community of Chinese culture (as defined by customs, rituals, written language, and self-identification) were regarded by the Chinese as "barbarians." The pastoral peoples of the northern steppes were characterized as having the faces of humans but the hearts of wild beasts, creatures for whom armed robbery directed against China was the natural way of life, while the aboriginal peoples of the south were viewed as simple, primitive types who could be brought around to a Chinese way of life through the transforming influence of benevolent local officials.

The ideology and practice of government were also very firmly established during the centuries of Han rule. Alongside the well-publicized official endorsement of the Confucian emphasis on government by ritual and moral suasion, there was also a lasting inheritance from the Legalist statesmen of the Qin dynasty in the form of a penal code providing harsh punishments for lawbreakers and detailed regulations governing the conduct of government business. The administrative structure inherited from Qin and Han reached down to the local level, the county (*xian*) with a population of several thousand or several tens of thousands; it relied heavily on written records and documents, and sought to maintain a very high degree of control over the population. The state counted the population on a regular basis (the census of AD 2 recorded 57,671,400 individuals[4]) and kept detailed household registers recording family members and landholdings to facilitate the extraction of taxes, corvée labor, and military service from the populace. Though many individuals and families were surely able to slip through the cracks, the state's intention was uncompromising.[5]

Just as the underlying framework for medieval statecraft was established in the Han dynasty and earlier, so too were the basic tools and techniques of medieval Chinese warfare. The Warring States period (453–221 BC) in particular saw a number of new developments that would permanently alter the shape of Chinese warfare. These included the rise of large infantry armies, the introduction of cavalry, the adoption of new weapons such as the crossbow, and the development of new techniques of siegecraft. During this period there was a vast increase in the scale of armed conflict, reflecting the greatly enhanced power of the state to mobilize resources for war.

This picture differed greatly from the style of warfare that had been practiced during the Spring and Autumn period (722–481 BC), when North China was divided among a large number of competing city-states ruled by a warrior aristocracy. Although small forces of infantry were present on the battlefield, most of the fighting was done by chariot-borne noblemen. Wars were fought for prestige and honor more often than for territory, and combat was hedged about by ceremonial and ritual restrictions. Divination and sacrifices were performed before battle, and it was customary for the two sides to agree on the time and place before the action began.[6] The *Zuo zhuan*, a narrative history dealing with this period but committed to writing several centuries later, contains many examples of restraint and what might be described as chivalrous behavior on the part of the combatants. Commanders often refused to take unfair advantage of their opponents. In a famous case from 638 BC, the Duke of Song refused to attack an enemy force in the midst of a river crossing but waited until it had completed its deployment on the opposite bank, and in 554 BC an invading army withdrew from the state of Qi when it learned of the death of the Qi ruler.[7] On the battlefield, warriors prized heroic feats and gallant gestures. Winning was by no means irrelevant, but the battle narratives of the *Zuo zhuan* often give the impression that the most important thing was to show off one's bravery and individual style.

However, the increasingly intense interstate conflicts of the late Spring and Autumn period precipitated significant changes in both the state and its approach to waging war. In a process that spread over several centuries, the stronger principalities gradually succeeded in annexing their weaker neighbors and transforming themselves into centralized territorial states, of which only seven remained standing by the middle of the third century BC. As Mark Lewis has pointed out, a key step in this process was the tightening of administrative control over the rural population which was now called upon to perform compulsory military service.[8] This, together with population growth and increases in agricultural output stemming from the introduction of iron tools, permitted states to raise much larger armies than had been the case in earlier days, and the chariot component of armies came to be dwarfed by the growing mass of foot soldiers. By the late Warring States period military obligations were nearly universal for males; the state of Qin, for example, is supposed to have mobilized all of its men over the age of fifteen for a campaign against Zhao in 260 BC.[9] The new mass armies fielded by the warring states were also equipped with new and deadlier tools. Iron weapons and iron armor first came into widespread use during this period, and crossbows were being employed in large numbers on the battlefield by the middle of the fourth century BC. Some two centuries later, the crossbow had become, in the opinion of one authority, "nothing less than the standard weapon of the Han armies."[10]

Another major development of the Warring States period was the introduction of cavalry forces. Horseback riding was probably first adopted by the pastoral peoples living to the north of the Chinese states sometime between 650 and 350 BC. Among the Chinese, however, it does not appear that horses were ridden before the fourth century BC. This lag can perhaps be explained by the fact that the Chinese did not come into contact with the nomads of the steppe until their northward expansion had absorbed "alien communities of mixed shepherds and agriculturalists" that had long served as a sort of buffer.[11] Once the northernmost of the Chinese kingdoms had come face to face with the nomads, however, the advantages of mounted combat must have been obvious. In 307 BC King Wuling of Zhao ordered his troops to adopt the clothing of the barbarians (trousers and tight sleeves in place of flowing robes) and practice mounted archery.[12] In the middle of the third century BC a Zhao army campaigning against the northern nomads reportedly included 13,000 cavalry as well as 1300 chariots and 150,000 infantry.[13] Other states organized cavalry forces of similar size, all of which were used more for scouting and skirmishing than for shock action.[14]

Along with the rise of mass armies composed primarily of infantry and cavalry rather than chariots, the Warring States period also saw the development of new techniques of siegecraft. Ruling groups in North China were building massive ramparts of pounded earth around their cities as early as the first half of the second millennium BC. Archaeological excavations have shown that major cities of the pre-imperial period, such as Linzi, the capital of the state of Qi, might have had walls more than twenty meters thick.[15] During the Spring and Autumn period sieges of such well-fortified centers were unusual; it was more common for an attacking force to raid to the gates of the enemy's capital and set fire to the suburbs before withdrawing. The military attitude toward cities seems to have changed during the Warring States period, however, perhaps because such centers now contained more people and greater wealth and had thus become more attractive targets for attackers. Texts of the period tell of a tremendous range of sophisticated poliorcetic techniques, including the use of engines such as arcuballistae and lever-operated stone-throwing catapults (trebuchets), approaches by means of siege towers and covered vehicles, sapping to bring down the walls and tunnelling to pass beneath them, or even the diversion of a nearby river to inundate the city (as was done to the Wei capital of Daliang in 225 BC). There was to be very little change in the Chinese art of siege warfare from the Warring States until the introduction of gunpowder more than a thousand years later.[16]

The result of all of these developments in the art of war was that conflicts came to be waged with greater intensity and on a much larger scale than ever before. Large, centralized territorial states could mobilize more men and keep them in the field longer. Before the sixth century BC, armies of ten thousand men or less were the norm. Campaigns seldom lasted more than a few weeks, and battles were usually resolved in a single day's action. By the second half of the third century BC, however, the major states were accustomed to fielding forces of several hundred thousand men; wars could drag on for years, and entrenched armies of crossbowmen might confront each other for months along a front extending for many miles. A major defeat could spell the destruction of the state. Under these circumstances, the conduct of warfare lost much of the ritual restraint and air of sportsmanship characteristic of the Spring and Autumn period. Armed conflict was now unequivocally a means to an end rather than an end in itself. Tricks and stratagems were much admired, and generalship became a ruthless and highly rational search for the advantage that would lead to victory.[17]

The increasing scale and complexity of warfare during this period gave rise to a new genre of military treatises which offered instruction in military leadership, tactics, and the conduct of operations. The best known and probably the earliest of the extant military treatises, the "Art of War" (bingfa) attributed to the legendary strategist Sunzi, is thought to date from the second half of the fifth century BC, and many other texts were written during the Warring States and into the Han period.[18] The contents of these works, ranging from general principles of statecraft to specific tactical deployments, are too rich to be summarized in a paragraph or two. Suffice it to say that most of them place considerable emphasis on intelligence, deceit, and the psychological element in war. The target of strategy is not so much the enemy army as the mind of the enemy commander, and the general is advised to manipulate the morale of his own men – whether by ostentatiously sharing their hardships and privations or by throwing them into desperate situations so as to stimulate them to fight for their lives. Above all, this literature emphasized careful, rational calculation as the basis for military decisionmaking. Rulers were urged to weigh the balance of forces before going to war, and field commanders were advised to look for signs of weakness in the enemy camp, wait for just the right opportunity, and join battle only when the conditions made victory a foregone conclusion. This aversion to risk-taking is especially evident in the thirteen chapters of Sunzi: "The one who excels at warfare first establishes himself in a position where he cannot be defeated while not losing [any opportunity] to defeat the enemy. For this reason, the victorious army first realizes the conditions for victory, and then seeks to engage in battle. The vanquished army fights first, and then seeks victory."[19]

While this passage seems to be compatible with a strategy of delay and the temporary avoidance of battle, other parts of the same book show a keen awareness of the economic cost of war and point to the desirability of bringing the fighting to a speedy conclusion. These points are not necessarily contradictory, but they do highlight the fact that the classical military literature of the Warring States period often appears to offer conflicting advice, imposing upon the reader the intellectual burden of reconciling two or more passages, or determining which might be the more applicable to the particular situation at hand.

One theme that runs throughout the military classics is the notion that command of an army is a matter of brains rather than brawn; bravery and prowess at arms are dismissed as unimportant or even harmful qualities, while superior perception and intellectual acumen are extolled as the most important characteristics of the general. One of the strongest statements to this effect can be found in the *Weiliaozi*, a treatise probably dating from the late fourth or early third century BC, in the form of a parable about the famous general Wu Qi. Once, on the eve of battle, the general's subordinates offered him a sword, but Wu Qi refused to accept it on the grounds that banners and drums, the tools of command, were the only weapons a general required. "To command the troops and direct their blades, this is the role of the commander. To wield a single sword is not his role."[20] If the general was to be the brain of the army, the soldiers were to respond as the limbs. Here, too, there was no room for individual heroics; what were expected were obedience and perfect coordination. This point is underlined by another of the *Weiliaozi*'s parables regarding Wu Qi: Before the battle was joined, one of Wu's soldiers was unable to restrain his enthusiasm. He left his place in the ranks, charged the enemy line, and then trotted back to his own position with two heads as trophies. The general ordered that the man be put to death. When his officers protested that he was a fine warrior, Wu Qi replied, "He is indeed a fine warrior, but he disobeyed my orders."[21] As Mark Lewis has observed, these lessons ran directly counter to the heroic ethos of the Spring and Autumn period and served the agenda of the centralizing despots of the Warring States who sought to impose discipline and control on the fractious warrior aristocracy.[22] But that was not the end of their usefulness. The emphasis on discipline served not only the needs of rulers, but also those of generals who were faced with the task of making the huge new armies of infantry conscripts effective on the battlefield. "Gongs, drums, pennants, and flags are the means to unify the men's ears and eyes. When the men have been unified the courageous will not be able to advance alone, the fearful will not be able to retreat alone. This is the method for employing large numbers."[23] Armies had become too large to be led effectively from the front, or for the individual warrior to make much of a difference in battle.

One of the most significant differences between the new style of warfare and the chariot battles of the old nobility was that military leadership now demanded a great deal of specialized knowledge and training. The early military treatises were one response to this need. Another was the appearance of a new class of military specialists who were appointed to command positions on the basis of ability, technical skills, and education rather than noble birth. By the third century BC, it was common to find such people leading the armies of the major contending states, and specialized knowledge of military command was in many cases passed from father to son as a sort of family business.[24] It is important to note, however, that military specialization was never carried to completion in imperial China; military men were never really able to set professional standards, control the admittance of new members to their ranks, or enforce a monopoly over the exercise of military command. Civil officials, especially those with responsibility for territorial administration, were often called upon to take the field with local forces to deal with "barbarian" incursions, banditry, and rebellion, and a man might move back and forth between civil and military positions over the course of his official career. During the Han dynasty in particular, it was not uncommon for male relatives of imperial consorts to be put in command of military expeditions despite a lack of obvious qualifications for the job.[25] The various military treatises facilitated this sort of amateur generalship, inasmuch as they held out the possibility that book-learning could be substituted for real military experience.

This result was not necessarily intended by the authors of the military treatises. Judging from the contents of most of these works, their authors were speaking for the emerging class of military specialists and attempting to claim the largest possible sphere of professional autonomy. Several texts argue that the general should not be subjected to interference from the ruler once he has been placed in command of the army and sent into the field. "There are commands from the ruler which are not accepted," declares the author of the *Sunzi*.[26] When the general is deciding whether to join battle with the enemy, he should resist the instructions of the ruler and follow his own judgment. According to some of the treatises, the ritual by which a general was invested with his command authority included the ruler's formal acknowledgment of the general's autonomy in decisionmaking. During the ceremony, the general was presented with a pair of axes symbolizing his authority to impose capital punishment on the men under his command (normally a prerogative of the sovereign).[27] The general's authority was probably never as unfettered as this prescriptive literature would have it, but there is ample evidence from Warring States and Han that it was still considerable. In 158 BC, for example, the Han general Zhou Yafu refused to allow the emperor to enter his camp until he had presented the proper credentials.[28] The leeway given to the commander of an army on campaign surely had much to do with the difficulty and danger of trying to micromanage the conduct of operations from a distant capital in an age when detailed reports and instructions could travel no faster than a horse and rider. There was a real need for command autonomy in the field. On the other hand, Chinese rulers also took various measures to keep the power of the military within bounds – especially in time of peace when command autonomy could be more easily dispensed with. The Qin and Han dynasties employed a system of tiger tallies. Bronze tiger figurines were divided in half, with one half kept by a troop commander or local official and the other by the government in the capital; troops could only be called up or set in motion when the two halves were matched. The principle of the superiority of civil over military leadership was firmly established at the very beginning of the Chinese empire. The rulers of the Warring States and the emperors of Qin and Han were not war leaders. They seldom took the field in person, much less risked their lives in battle. Their place was in the capital, governing the realm through the civil administration and the powerful symbolic propaganda of imperial ritual. The founder of the Han dynasty, Liu Bang, took the throne by force, but was soon advised by the scholar Lu Jia that he could not expect to rule the empire effectively from horseback.[29] Liu chose to follow this advice, as did almost all of China's other dynastic founders.

That the authority of the military commander was temporary and provisional in nature was underscored by the assumption, prevalent among statesmen and political theorists by late Warring States, Qin, and Han times, that the soldiers who filled the ranks of the army and the peasants who tilled the land (and constituted the vast majority of the state's population) were essentially the same group of people. This assumption, a reflection of the earlier extension of compulsory military service to the rural population, can be found in many writings of both the Legalist and Confucian schools.[30] In this view, there is no permanently existing military sphere that remains separate from the wider civilian society. All adult males are potential soldiers and can be called to arms when the need arises, but when the crisis has passed they are to be returned to the primary occupation of agriculture. The military institutions of the Western Han, ultimately descended from those of the predynastic Qin state, appear to have matched these normative assumptions very closely. This was especially true in the early years of the dynasty, when the Han system of military service was remarkably similar to the "cadre-conscript" pattern favored by European powers in the late nineteenth and early twentieth centuries.

Under the Han system, all males became subject to military service upon reaching the age of twenty-three.[31] They served for one year in their home areas, during which time they received military training and some men were assigned to specialist units (such as cavalry, water forces, and elite crossbowmen). After the completion of the first year of service, some of the conscripts might be sent to perform a year of guard duty in the capital or on the northern frontier. It does not seem that this additional service was required of all of the conscripts, since the number of men entering the system each year would have far exceeded the relatively small number of troops garrisoning the frontier and the capital.[32] After their one or two years of service, men returned to their home communities and their original occupations. They remained liable for call-up in the event of emergency until they reached the age of fifty-six and received some refresher training during that time, with great military reviews being held annually by the local governors. Large armies were assembled on an ad hoc basis by summoning "reservists" from the commanderies (provinces) and appointing a general to lead the army on campaign. When the campaign was finished the soldiers were sent home and the general's appointment came to an end. This sort of military service was not sharply distinguished from the corvée labor that Han subjects were required to perform for one month of each year. Both were considered to be forms of "labor service," and a man called to serve for a year on the frontier could pay to send a substitute in his place – an escape route that was also open to men who had been summoned for corvée.[33] Those who had been awarded high honorific ranks by the state were exempt from corvée and all forms of military service. One way to attain such rank was by purchase, which meant that members of wealthy families would have been able to escape from all military obligations.[34] Although military service was in practice somewhat less than universal, the important point is that the imperial Chinese state claimed a sort of eminent domain over the muscle power of its able-bodied male subjects. This claim would not be forgotten during the medieval period.

The administration of the Han system of military service required a tremendous amount of recordkeeping and paperwork, but in this respect the military was no different from most other areas of the imperial government. Local officials were required to report the number of households and individuals in their jurisdiction on an annual basis and to keep detailed household registers.[35] Records of this sort made it possible for the authorities to keep track of which individuals were eligible for corvée labor and military service at any given time. And a well-developed military bureaucracy kept voluminous records of many other sorts. The most astonishing evidence of Han administrative practice comes from Edsen-gol in Inner Mongolia, where the dry climate preserved a large number of documents, written on strips of wood and bamboo and dated between 102 BC and AD 98, that had been left by the Han garrisons of this northern frontier region. The documents include an account book, a record of pay issued to officers, a list of clothing handed out to servicemen, and a register of cattle, "with details of age, height, colouring, and other distinctive features."[36] There are inventories of equipment, records of work assignments, and reports of military incidents. A great deal of attention was devoted to maintaining records of communications. Beacon stations kept logs of signals received and sent, and headquarters kept detailed registers of outgoing correspondence and documents in transit. One such register indicates the destination of each item of mail, the date it was sealed and the name of the sender, and also provides a summary of the contents. It would appear that there was no aspect of importance to the functioning of these garrisons that was not subjected to painstaking inventory control and recordkeeping.

This sort of administrative routine was part of Han's inheritance from the kingdoms of the Warring States period, but the presence of strong garrisons at remote frontier locations such as Edsen-gol suggests an important difference between the unified empire and its predynastic predecessors. Although states such as Qin and Zhao did take steps to protect their northern frontiers against nomadic incursions, Zhao was much more concerned with the threat from Qin than with that from the nomadic Xiongnu people. The primary concern of all of the warring states was to triumph (or at least survive) in the armed competition with their Chinese rivals, and all of the classical military treatises assume that one's opponent will be a fellow member of the Chinese cultural community. The position of the Chinese vis-à-vis the inhabitants of the steppes took a sharp turn for the worse in 209 BC, when the Xiongnu were brought together in a powerful confederacy under a new leader named Maodun. Within a decade, the reorganized nomads had surrounded a very large army led in person by the first Han emperor, Liu Bang, who was forced to agree to a humiliating peace. There is some disagreement as to the underlying causes of the sudden emergence of the Xiongnu as a major power. One school of thought holds that it was the unification of China in 221 BC that prompted the nomads to coalesce in order to strengthen their own bargaining position in relation to the Chinese empire. The Xiongnu sought grain, silk, and other products of China's sedentary economy, and used the threat of violence (raiding) to persuade the Chinese to make these things available to them. In order to effectively coordinate raids, threats, and negotiations in their dealings with a now-monolithic China, the Xiongnu themselves found it necessary to rally around a political center of their own.[37] Another view holds that this reorganization was the nomads' response to the political crisis that overtook them in 215 BC when Qin armies evicted them from their pastures within the great bend of the Yellow River.[38] Whatever the cause of this development, there is no question that political unity transformed the Xiongnu into a much more formidable foe by enabling them to concentrate larger forces and exercise better strategic coordination. Since the Xiongnu were trained from childhood as mounted archers, they already enjoyed certain tactical advantages over Chinese armies that were composed largely of slow-moving infantry units and cavalrymen less expert than themselves.

The Chinese developed several strategies for dealing with the nomads. During the early years of the Han dynasty, when China was relatively weak and the memory of Liu Bang's humiliation at the hands of the Xiongnu still fresh, the emperors adopted an appeasement policy that came to be called "harmonious kinship" (*heqin*). In concrete terms this meant payments to the Xiongnu, the establishment of frontier markets where they could trade with the Chinese, and high-level marriage alliances, with women of the imperial family being sent to the steppe as brides for the Xiongnu rulers. Given the propensity of the nomads for small-scale raiding even when "harmonious kinship" arrangements were in effect, the Han also took to constructing defensive lines, observation posts, and signal stations along the northern frontier. The practice of wall-building dated back to the Warring States period, when the Chinese kingdoms had built defensive lines first against each other and then against the horseriders of the steppe. After the Qin forces cleared the Xiongnu from the bend of the Yellow River in 215 BC, they set about linking the existing defense systems into the earliest version of the "Great Wall." This early construction should not be confused with the massive brick and stone fortifications near Beijing, which date from the latter half of the Ming dynasty (1368–1644).[39] Qin and Han frontier defenses were built of pounded earth or mud bricks, and were more in the form of a series of forts, lookout towers, and beacons connected by a fairly simple rampart rather than the massive curtain wall-cum-causeway of popular imagination. But they were still a major construction project. The Tsondol lines, built by Han forces in the Edsen-gol area, stretched for forty kilometers and included one major fortress and twenty-six lesser towers situated at 1300-meter intervals, each within easy view of the next.[40] Positions such as these were maintained for most of the Han period. It has been estimated that approximately ten thousand men were needed to staff the beacons and watchtowers, exclusive of logistical support personnel and mobile reserve forces controlled by the frontier commanderies.[41] The Han established military agricultural colonies (*tuntian*) to support these defenses and reduce the cost of transporting provisions from the interior of the empire, and as many as fifty or sixty thousand men may have been assigned to these farms at one time.[42]

During the reign of Emperor Wu, the Chinese shifted from defense to offense. In 129 BC Han forces launched the first of a long series of large-scale campaigns aimed at destroying or subjugating the Xiongnu. This fighting continued with very few respites until the end of Emperor Wu's reign in 87 BC. The Chinese won major victories in the first decade of the war, but the conflict eventually developed into a bloody stalemate. The major Han offensive campaigns were spearheaded by powerful columns of cavalry; though their numbers should not necessarily be accepted at face value, the Han histories routinely mention forces of tens of thousands of horsemen. The first major campaign in 129 BC, for example, involved four separate Han cavalry columns each reported to be ten thousand strong, while the campaign of 119 BC saw two cavalry columns of 50,000 men each. In 97 BC, a total of 70,000 cavalry and 140,000 infantry were sent against the Xiongnu.[43]

The decades-long struggle for mastery between the Han and Xiongnu empires produced significant changes in Chinese military organization. It was during this time that the chariot, which had continued to see some battlefield use during the early years of the Han dynasty, disappeared entirely from the annals of Chinese warfare. In this sort of fighting cavalry forces necessarily came to play the primary role, as they alone were capable of keeping up with the fast-moving Xiongnu horsemen.[44] This presented a challenge for the Han military system because the vast majority of the conscripts were only prepared to serve as infantry. Cavalrymen tended to be drawn from the northern frontier commanderies where the environment was suitable for horsebreeding and the people were most familiar with horses.[45] Such men would have been much more in demand than ordinary conscripts from the interior of the empire during the period of Emperor Wu's campaigns, and they must have been called for service repeatedly – so often that they became full-time, professional soldiers in fact if not in name. Although the basic system of universal conscription and military training was not significantly altered until the first century AD, there is considerable evidence that, in the course of the great campaigns against the Xiongnu, military responsibilities came to be borne by men who were not ordinary conscripts. The wooden strips found at Edsen-gol indicate that at least some of the servicemen stationed there had brought their families with them, and that officers might serve for several years. At least one scholar has suggested that the practice of hiring substitutes could have led to the appearance of professional substitutes who became more or less permanent denizens of the frontier garrisons.[46] The reign of Emperor Wu also saw the use of reprieved convicts in the garrisons and the earliest employment of surrendered tribesmen as a component of Han expeditionary forces.[47] All of this would seem to suggest that the basic military institutions of the Han dynasty were not well suited for prolonged warfare against a powerful nomadic opponent. As one perspicacious statesman of the early Han put it, "If you have soldiers from distant places defend the border and change them annually, then they will not know the skills of the barbarians."[48] There was a real need for experienced, long-service troops with special skills and a good knowledge of frontier conditions.

The trend toward a more permanent soldiery continued after Emperor Wu's time, and became especially pronounced during the Eastern Han period (AD 25–220). There was even more use of convicts on the frontier, and submitted tribesmen came to make up the bulk of the empire's cavalry forces. In AD 31, the Eastern Han founder, Emperor Guangwu, issued an edict abolishing the system of universal military training and one year's service in the commanderies. This did not mean the end of a generalized military obligation; most able-bodied males remained eligible for military service and could be called to arms in the event of an emergency. However, the first-line defense of the empire in ordinary times was now placed on a much more professional basis. A standing army of approximately 40,000 men, drawn originally from the followers of Emperor Guangwu in the civil war that had brought him to power, was stationed at the capital and several other strategic points in North China. Members of this force were long-service recruits rather than short-term peasant conscripts.[49]

At first glance these might seem to be developments of a centralizing character, but the most important long-term military trend of the Eastern Han was the loss of central control over the armed forces. This happened for several reasons. One was the creation of a new and more powerful sort of regional governor (*cishi*) with administrative authority over a number of local commanderies. Another was the gradual abandonment of control measures that had been scrupulously observed in Western Han times, such as the use of tiger tallies and the practice of appointing generals on a temporary, ad hoc basis. The most important factor, however, was surely the pressing need to respond effectively to the wave of Daoist-inspired peasant rebellion that swept over much of North China after the middle of the second century AD. With the standing army now of very limited size, regional and commandery governors found it necessary to mobilize local conscripts to deal with the crisis, and to supplement them with mercenary recruits and even forces of private retainers. Driven by the exigencies of the situation, the imperial court allowed generals and governors considerable leeway in matters of military administration and command. They remained in control of the same forces for very long periods of time, and came to command the personal loyalty of their armed followers.[50] In a word, they became warlords. Once the rebels had been disposed of the victorious generals turned to fighting one another, ushering in several decades of intense, multicornered civil war followed by the three-way partition of the Han empire that lasted well into the second half of the third century.

For the soldiers and statesmen of medieval China, the legacy of antiquity was complex and multifaceted. It included both the ideal of imperial unity and the more recent experience of disunity and civil war; both the military institutions developed during the Warring States period and the very different set of arrangements that had appeared in response to the new challenge posed by the steppe nomads. Venerated classical texts offered more than one model of military leadership, and the ideal of civilian supremacy was balanced by stark lessons in the political usefulness of military power. Antiquity provided the basic parameters of medieval military and administrative practice – cavalry, infantry, and iron weapons on the one hand; strict regulations and extensive written records on the other. But within the framework established by tools and techniques, the legacy of the past offered many alternatives and left room for very different choices. The military pressures of interstate competition had transformed Chinese warfare and society in the middle of the first millennium BC, and the demands of conflict with the steppe peoples had undermined much of the military system inherited from the Warring States. The rulers of medieval China faced military pressures every bit as great as those of earlier times; in some cases, the challenges were of such a nature as to be entirely without precedent in Chinese history. The chapters that follow will explore the choices that the Chinese made when confronted with the harsh demands of armed conflict during the six centuries from the fall of Western Jin to the passing of the Tang dynasty.

Notes

1 Once we begin to look at the details, of course, things are not so clear-cut. Bernard Bachrach and others, for example, have pointed out the importance of infantry in

Carolingian warfare and downplayed the role of cavalry. See Bernard S. Bachrach, "Charlemagne's Cavalry: Myth and Reality," *Military Affairs*, 47.4 (December 1983), pp. 181–7.

2 For an overview emphasizing the essential military unity of the entire imperial period, see Edward L. Dreyer, "Military Continuities: The PLA and Imperial China," in William W. Whitson (ed.), *The Military and Political Power in China in the 1970's* (New York: Praeger, 1972), pp. 3–24.

3 This was Naitō Torajirō (1866–1934); for an introduction to his periodization of Chinese history, see Hisayuki Miyakawa, "An Outline of the Naito Hypothesis and Its Effects on Japanese Studies of China," *Far Eastern Quarterly*, 14.4 (August 1955), pp. 533–52.

4 Hans Bielenstein, "The Census of China during the Period 2–742 AD," *Bulletin of the Museum of Far Eastern Antiquities*, 19 (1947), p. 135.

5 For the origins of the household registration system, see Tu Cheng-sheng, "'Bian hu qi min' de chuxian ji qi lishi yiyi," *Bulletin of the Institute of History and Philology of Academia Sinica*, 54.3 (September 1982), pp. 77–111.

6 Mark Edward Lewis, *Sanctioned Violence in Early China* (Albany: State University of New York Press, 1990), pp. 37–8. This behavior is reminiscent of warfare between the *poleis* of classical Greece; see the articles by Josiah Ober and Michael H. Jameson in Victor Davis Hanson (ed.), *Hoplites: The Classical Greek Battle Experience* (London and New York: Routledge, 1991), pp. 173–227.

7 Cho-yun Hsu, *Ancient China in Transition: An Analysis of Social Mobility, 722–222 BC* (Stanford, Ca.: Stanford University Press, 1965), p. 54.

8 Lewis, *Sanctioned Violence in Early China*, pp. 54–67.

9 Hsu, *Ancient China in Transition*, p. 67.

10 Joseph Needham and Robin D. S. Yates, *Science and Civilisation in China*, vol. 5, pt. 6: *Military Technology: Missiles and Sieges* (Cambridge: Cambridge University Press, 1994), pp. 139–41. For iron weapons and armor, see Yang Hong, *Zhongguo gu bingqi luncong* (rpt. Taipei: Mingwen shuju, 1983), pp. 14–15, 142. Yang's book has been translated into English under the title *Weapons in Ancient China* (New York and Beijing: Science Press, 1992).

11 Nicola Di Cosmo, "The Northern Frontier in Pre-Imperial China," in *The Cambridge History of Ancient China*, ed. by Michael Loewe and Edward L. Shaughnessy (Cambridge: Cambridge University Press, 1999), pp. 890–2, 912.

12 *Chan-Kuo Ts'e*, trans. by J. I. Crump, Jr. (Oxford: Clarendon Press, 1970), pp. 296–307.

13 Sima Qian, *Shi ji* (Beijing: Zhonghua shuju, 1959), ch. 81, p. 2450.

14 Lao Gan, "Zhanguo shidai de zhanzheng fangfa," in *Lao Gan xueshu lunwenji*, pt. 1, vol. 2 (Banqiao, Taiwan: Yiwen yinshuguan, 1976), p. 1172.

15 Yang Hong, *Zhongguo gu bingqi luncong*, pp. 140–1.

16 Needham and Yates, *Science and Civilisation in China*, vol. 5, pt. 6, pp. 254–5.

17 For the changing nature of war and generalship during this period, see Frank A. Kierman, Jr., "Phases and Modes of Combat in Early China," in *Chinese Ways in Warfare*, ed. by Frank A. Kierman, Jr., and John K. Fairbank (Cambridge, Mass.: Harvard University Press, 1974), pp. 27–66.

18 For a survey of this literature, see Robin D. S. Yates, "New Light on Ancient Chinese Military Texts: Notes on their Nature and Evolution, and the Development of Military Specialization in Warring States China," *T'oung Pao*, 74 (1988), pp. 211–48. The most important of the extant military treatises have been translated in *The Seven Military Classics of Ancient China*, trans. by Ralph D. Sawyer (Boulder, Colo.: Westview Press, 1993).

19 *The Seven Military Classics of Ancient China*, p. 164.

20 Liu Chung-p'ing, *Weiliaozi jin zhu jin yi* (Taipei: Taiwan Commercial Press, 1975), p. 109. My translation follows that of Mark Lewis (*Sanctioned Violence in Early China*, p. 114).

21 Liu Chung-p'ing, *Weiliaozi jin zhu jin yi*, p. 110.

22 Lewis, *Sanctioned Violence in Early China*, pp. 103, 107.

23 Sunzi, translated in *The Seven Military Classics of Ancient China*, p. 170.

24 Hsu, *Ancient China in Transition*, pp. 73–6.

25 See, for example, the *Shi ji* biographies of Wei Qing and Huo Qubing, translated by Burton Watson in Sima Qian, *Records of the Grand Historian*, Han Dynasty, vol. 2 (Hong Kong: Columbia University Press, 1993), p. 163 ff.; and Michael Loewe, "The Campaigns of Han Wu-ti," in Kierman and Fairbank, *Chinese Ways in Warfare*, p. 87.

26 *The Seven Military Classics of Ancient China*, p. 171; also see p. 177.

27 Lewis, *Sanctioned Violence in Early China*, pp. 125–6.

28 *Records of the Grand Historian*, Han Dynasty, vol. 1, pp. 375–6.

29 *Records of the Grand Historian*, Han Dynasty, vol. 1, pp. 226–7.

30 Lewis, *Sanctioned Violence in Early China*, pp. 64–5.

31 This sketch of Western Han military institutions is a composite based on several sources, especially Hans Bielenstein, *The Bureaucracy of Han Times* (Cambridge: Cambridge University Press, 1980), pp. 114–16; Sun Yutang, "Xi Han de bingzhi," *Zhongguo shehui jingji shi jikan*, 5.1 (March 1937), pp. 2–13, 23–6; and Lao Gan, "Handai bingzhi ji Hanjian zhong de bingzhi," *Bulletin of the Institute of History and Philology of Academia Sinica*, 10 (1943), pp. 23–55. Due to the difficulty of interpreting the very limited evidence, there is much room for difference of opinion. For one dissenting view of the Han military, see Sun Yancheng, "Qin Han de yaoyi he bingyi," *Zhongguo shi yanjiu*, 1987, No. 3, pp. 77–85.

32 Zang Zhifei, "Qin Han 'zheng zu' bianxi," *Zhongguo shi yanjiu*, 1988, No. 1, p. 95; also see Lao Gan, "Handai bingzhi ji Hanjian zhong de bingzhi," pp. 35–6, and Michael Loewe, "The Campaigns of Han Wu-ti," in Kierman and Fairbank, *Chinese Ways in Warfare*, p. 93. Loewe estimates that the total number of conscripts manning the northern defenses, exclusive of service and support troops, may have been only 9750.

33 Sun Yutang, "Xi Han de bingzhi," pp. 2–7.

34 Sun Yutang, "Xi Han de bingzhi," pp. 12–13.

35 Michael Loewe, "The Heritage Left to the Empires," in *The Cambridge History of Ancient China*, ed. by Michael Loewe and Edward L. Shaughnessy (Cambridge: Cambridge University Press, 1999), p. 1015.

36 See Michael Loewe, *Records of Han Administration* (Cambridge: Cambridge University Press, 1967), especially vol. 1, pp. 19–23.

37 This view is offered by the anthropologist Thomas Barfield in *The Perilous Frontier* (Oxford: Basil Blackwell, 1989).

38 Di Cosmo, "The Northern Frontier in Pre-Imperial China," pp. 964–5.

39 See Arthur Waldron, *The Great Wall of China: From History to Myth* (Cambridge: Cambridge University Press, 1990).

40 Loewe, *Records of Han Administration*, vol. 1, pp. 83–4.

41 Loewe, "The Campaigns of Han Wu-ti," p. 93.

42 Loewe, "The Campaigns of Han Wu-ti," p. 74.

43 These events are summarized in Loewe, "The Campaigns of Han Wu-ti," pp. 111–18.

44 For the importance of cavalry in Emperor Wu's campaigns, see Chang Chun-shu, "Military Aspects of Han Wu-ti's Northern and Northwestern Campaigns," *Harvard Journal of Asiatic Studies*, 26 (1966), pp. 149, 167–9.

45 Sun Yutang, "Xi Han de bingzhi," p. 23.
46 Loewe, *Records of Han Administration*, vol. 1, p. 82.
47 Sun Yutang, "Xi Han de bingzhi," pp. 33–4.
48 Chao Cuo, quoted in Ban Gu, *Han shu* (Beijing: Zhonghua shuju, 1962), ch. 49, pp. 2281–6. Also see Sun Yutang, "Xi Han de bingzhi," pp. 30–1, 46.
49 For the Eastern Han military, see Lao Gan, "Handai bingzhi ji Hanjian zhong de bingzhi," pp. 48–52; Sun Yutang, "Dong Han bingzhi de yanbian," *Zhongguo shehui jingji shi jikan*, 6.1 (June 1939), pp. 1–34; and *Zhongguo junshi shi*, vol. 3: *Bingzhi* (Beijing: Jiefangjun chubanshe, 1987), pp. 109–19.
50 *Zhongguo junshi shi*, vol. 3, pp. 116–17.

CHAPTER TWO

The fall of Western Jin

In the year 280, shortly before a general named Diocletian established his authority over distant Rome, Sima Yan's newly founded Jin dynasty in China attained the apogee of its power. The conquest of the southern state of Wu restored the imperial unity that had fractured with the collapse of the Eastern Han government at the end of the second century. Sima Yan's grandfather Sima Yi, the scion of a prominent and wealthy landowning family in the flatland region of Henan on the south side of the Yellow River, had risen in the service of the Wei state in North China and, under a succession of weak emperors, emerged as the dominant figure in the northern government. By the time of his death in 251 he was ruler in all but name. His authority was inherited by his sons Sima Shi and Sima Zhao, and then by Zhao's son Sima Yan. In 265 this new leader of the house of Sima deposed the last, feeble Wei emperor and took the throne for himself and his family; his reign lasted until 289, and he would be known posthumously by the title of "Emperor Wu of Jin." The southwestern state of Shu having already fallen to the northern armies in 263, Sima Yan turned to the conquest of Wu. The final campaign began in the eleventh lunar month of 279 with 200,000 Jin troops marching against Wu in six columns, one of which descended the Yangzi River from the former Shu territories in Sichuan.[1] The outnumbered southern defenders were overwhelmed in short order, and Sima Yan was soon in possession of almost all of the territories that had once been ruled by the mighty Han dynasty – from Lelang commandery in northern Korea to Dunhuang on the Silk Road, and south as far as the city that is now known as Hanoi.

Whatever Emperor Wu may have wished, however, the newly reunified empire was very far from being a faithful reconstruction of the glorious Han. Much had changed since the collapse of central power in the 180s, and the civil wars in the north followed by the incessant battling of the Three Kingdoms had not been conducive to the maintenance of the status quo in Chinese society. Perhaps the most significant difference between Han and Jin was a radical decline in the population registered by the state. The Jin census of 280 recorded 2,459,840 households and 16,163,863 individuals. This was an improvement over the lowest figures from the Three Kingdoms period, but it

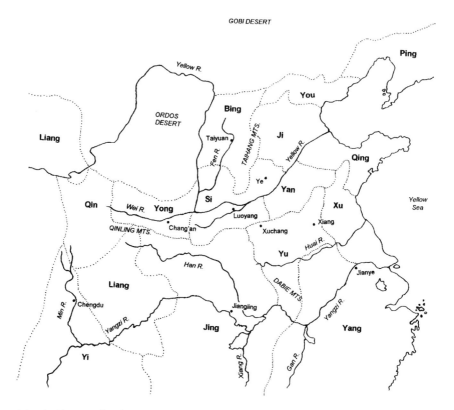

Map 3 China under the Western Jin dynasty, *ca.* AD 300, showing provinces

was still only a fraction of the 10,677,960 households and 56,486,856 individuals reported by the Han census of 157.[2] Where had all the people gone?
Part of the difference can be attributed to deaths on the battlefield and from
other war-related violence, and part to the famines and epidemics that were so
often associated with the movement of armies. Another factor was the
migration of population out of the war-ravaged commanderies of the north
and northwest, a trend that was already underway by the middle of the Eastern
Han period due to steppe nomad raids and the rebellions of other frontier
peoples such as the proto-Tibetan Qiang.[3] The best explanation for most of the
loss, however, is that in the military and political confusion of the time the state
was simply unable to maintain administrative control over the majority of the
population.[4] Large numbers of peasant smallholders absconded to escape the
heavy burden of taxes and corvée labor, increasing the burden on their
neighbors and giving them all the more reason to flee in their turn. Many of the
fugitives sought refuge with powerful landholding families that were able to
shelter them from the demands of the state; they became tenant farmers or
agricultural dependants tied to the land like the serfs of medieval Europe.

Adherence to such powerful families was doubly attractive because they were often able to organize their dependants to provide an effective community defense in unsettled times.[5] These developments meant that the imperial state was seriously weakened as a very large portion of its manpower and tax base was transferred to the control of the great landowning families. The Jin government did make a nominal effort to impose upper limits on the private control of land and population, but the Sima family and its wealthy supporters benefited too much from the existing situation for any reform to be pressed vigorously.

The political chaos of the Han collapse and the Three Kingdoms period influenced the health of the economy as well as that of the state. The treatise on "food and money" in the seventh-century *History of the Jin Dynasty* tells us that China enjoyed peace and prosperity for a generation after the conquest of Wu in 280: "Supplies flowed into granaries and treasuries. Palaces had additional adornments; dresses and playthings sparkled brightly. [The richest people] vied with one another in display. Their carriages, dresses, and food utensils were comparable in elegance to those of the imperial family."[6] This period probably did represent an improvement over what came before (and no doubt looked like a golden age compared to what came after), but for the great majority of the Chinese people it was still a very far cry from the vigorous economy of Han times, which had seen extensive interregional trade and the widespread circulation of metallic currency. Amidst the violence and uncertainty of the late Han civil wars, much cultivated land was abandoned, trade dried up, and copper coins disappeared from circulation. There was a return to barter and a "natural economy"; most of the government's exactions came to be collected in kind as quantities of grain and silk replaced currency as the medium of exchange and store and measure of value. In some areas, the wealthy landowning families with their numerous dependants and tenants had begun to create self-contained manorial economies.[7] It is worth noting, however, that in the Chinese context economic autarky was not associated with any formal division of sovereign powers between central and local leaders. "During the period of division following the Han dynasty China did not move from an imperial system to a feudal one. Government retained its imperial structure."[8]

The internecine conflicts that dominated the Chinese scene during the century after 180 transformed the economy and gave rise to new relationships between elite families and the farming population; they greatly weakened, but did not destroy, the centralized structure of imperial government. At the same time, they also saw the emergence of new forms of military service and military organization. The most important of these changes were the creation of a dependent, hereditary military caste that was clearly distinguished from the general population, an increasing reliance on cavalry forces of non-Chinese, "barbarian" origin, and the development of command structures that left tremendous authority in the hands of local and regional military leaders. All of these developments amounted to the negation of the early Western Han military system that had been based on universal service and temporary, ad hoc command arrangements.

These changes did not occur overnight; as has already been noted, the Han period saw a gradual movement in the direction of long-service, "professional" military forces. The trend culminated during the confused, multi-cornered civil wars at the end of the second century and finally crystallized in the form of new military institutions during the period of the Three Kingdoms. The armies that fought the civil wars were raised largely from voluntary recruits, though there was also some use of press-ganging as well as forcible enlistment of prisoners from defeated armies.[9] Men who turned to military service for their livelihood remained under arms for very long periods of time or even indefinitely. The conditions of prolonged warfare favored the emergence of a soldiery expert in the use of arms and willing to follow their commanders from one region to another over the course of many years as dictated by the fortunes of war, while the stable administrative structures that had made possible the early Han system of military conscription simply ceased to exist. The unsettled conditions of the time also guaranteed that there would be no shortage of willing recruits, who could be drawn from the very large numbers of destitute peasants, fugitives, and refugees.

Many of the larger armies of the period were formed by absorbing lesser leaders and their followings. These leaders included both local magnates who had converted their agricultural dependants into soldiers and military commanders who had recruited their own private retainer corps of armed men serving in the capacity of personal dependants rather than government soldiers. The private fighting men in both of these categories came to be known as *buqu*, an old Han term for regular units of military organization that may be translated simply as "troops."[10] The relationship between commander and *buqu* was in essence hereditary. When the commander died, a son, brother, or nephew would inherit control of his troops, and when a soldier died one of his close male relatives would inherit his position in the ranks.[11] This pattern developed because the *buqu* were not so much individual fighters who had become dependent on individual commanders as they were the heads of families that had become dependent on other families wealthier and more powerful than themselves. The connection was most obvious in the case of armed tenants or agricultural servants for whom survival on the land required acceptance of the same servile, dependent status from generation to generation.

The government armies of the Wei and Jin dynasties adopted a pattern of military service that was to a very large extent modeled after that of the private *buqu* forces.[12] This owed something to the fact that so many *buqu* had been absorbed into the ranks of the government army, and something to the desire to maintain a stable, reliable reservoir of manpower from which losses might be made good. The families of military men were concentrated in the capital and several other major centers, where they might serve as convenient hostages while the soldiers were on campaign. The soldiers and their families were assigned a status as "military households" that was separate and distinct from that of peasants and other commoners. Their names were recorded in special military registers, and they were subject to control by the military authorities rather than the local civilian administration. Once a man became a soldier, he served for life. When he perished or became too old or infirm to carry on, it was expected that a son or another close relative would come forward to replace him. Under the Wei dynasty soldiers and their relatives were only permitted to marry into other families with military status, to ensure that out-marriage would not lead over time to a diminution of the manpower pool. Ordinary commoners – that is, most members of the community – had no regular military service obligation, though in rare cases of urgent need men might still be conscripted for temporary duty. For the most part, however, there was a very clear distinction between soldiers and potential soldiers on the one hand and the general population on the other. The Jin dynasty relaxed some of the harshest restrictions that had been imposed by the Wei rulers, but kept the basic system intact and derived most of its soldiers from this source.

In broad outline, the measures employed by the Jin rulers to meet their manpower needs resemble certain policies adopted by the late Roman emperors to cope with their own shortages of military personnel. During the fourth century, in accordance with laws most likely introduced by Diocletian, Rome attempted to enforce its own version of hereditary military service by requiring the able-bodied sons of soldiers to enlist in the army.[13] After the late fourth century Roman generals and magnates had *buqu* of their own in their private corps of armed retainers, the *bucellarii*. The late empire also recruited troops of foreign or "barbarian" origin, including large numbers of Goths, Franks, and other Germanic peoples. Some were incorporated in regular military units under Roman or Romanized officers while others, especially after AD 382, were settled within the borders of the empire as allied armies under their own chiefs.[14] In this respect, too, the late Roman armies resembled those of Jin dynasty China.

In Wei and Jin times, the non-Chinese peoples who lived not only along and beyond the northern frontier but also in settlements in the interior provinces of North China were an important source of military manpower. The employment of barbarian auxiliaries had begun during the reign of the Han Emperor Wu, when the campaigns against the Xiongnu put a premium on the services of tough, experienced cavalry forces. With the passage of time, the Han empire and its successor states came to place ever greater reliance on ever larger numbers of foreign horsemen. This trend received a major boost in the middle of the first century AD, when a succession struggle among the Xiongnu brought one of the rival claimants and a significant portion of his people to the border to seek Chinese protection. These "Southern Xiongnu" were permitted to make their home within the territory of the Han frontier commanderies, especially in the Ordos region within the great northward loop of the Yellow River and in the northern part of what is now Shanxi province, and they joined Chinese forces in expeditions against their northern cousins. In AD 90 Chinese officials counted 237,300 individuals among the dependent Southern Xiongnu, of whom 50,170 were males capable of military service.[15] Another nomadic people who submitted to Han authority in the first century were the Wuhuan of southwestern Manchuria. Possibly numbering as many as a hundred thousand, they were permitted to settle along the northeastern frontier in the vicinity of today's Beijing, as well as farther west in some of the same commanderies that were also home to the Southern Xiongnu.[16] On the northwestern frontier, surrendered groups of Qiang, a people related to today's Tibetans who supported themselves with a mixed economy of agriculture and stockraising, were moved into the upper reaches of the Wei River valley west of the old capital of Chang'an. Although not always fighting as cavalry, they too were often called upon to perform military service for the Chinese state. Bands of foreign warriors might also be recruited from beyond the borders of the empire. Especially noteworthy in this regard were the nomadic Xianbei people who had once lived to the northeast of the Wuhuan on the slopes of the Greater Xingan range. When the Northern Xiongnu confederacy collapsed near the end of the first century, the Xianbei absorbed many of its people and spread into the territory north of the Gobi Desert to become the dominant power of the steppe for much of the second century. Whether as subjects or as allies, all of these peoples contributed troops to the Eastern Han expeditionary armies. The four columns sent against the Northern Xiongnu in AD 73 included cavalry from the Qiang, Wuhuan, Xianbei, and Southern Xiongnu, and the army of 50,000 men that the Han general Dou Xian led against the same opponent in 89 counted only 8000 Han Chinese soldiers.[17] Some barbarian warriors were also recruited into the regular armies of Eastern Han. One of the five standing regiments of professional soldiers stationed at the capital was made up largely of cavalrymen recruited from among the Wuhuan.[18]

The use of steppe cavalrymen in Chinese armies continued in the Three Kingdoms period and under the Jin dynasty. After defeating the Wuhuan people in 207, Cao Cao, the founder of the Wei state, moved many of them into the interior of China and incorporated the warriors into his army. During the course of Cao's struggles with other regional warlords, his Wuhuan gained a reputation as the best cavalry force in all of China.[19] But they were by no means the only foreigners in the Wei armies. Cao also commanded the services of a considerable number of Xiongnu, and claimed that his army included contingents of Dingling, Di, Qiang, and several other northern peoples.[20] Faced with the need to fill the ranks of their armies with high-quality troops and to replenish the declining population of the northern provinces, Chinese leaders continued to accept the submission of steppe peoples along the frontier. The Jin government, for example, received the surrender of 29,300 Xiongnu in 284, more than a hundred thousand in 286, and another 11,500 in 287.[21] Many of the barbarians who came under the authority of the Wei and Jin governments, both those who had recently submitted and those who had been under Chinese tutelage along the frontiers for several generations, were relocated to the interior of the empire. This was done both to "solidify" the frontier by moving potential troublemakers away from sensitive areas, and in the hope that the newcomers might eventually be assimilated to the way of life of the Han Chinese majority. The result, however, was not exactly what had been intended. In many areas of North China the barbarians came to out-number the Han inhabitants, spreading a pervasive sense of insecurity from the frontier to the interior. The Xiongnu were present in very large numbers in the southern part of Bing province (today's Shanxi), and one anxious Chinese scholar claimed that the Qiang and other alien groups made up half the population of Guanzhong, the land "within the passes" surrounding the city of Chang'an.[22]

The military value of the cavalry forces raised from these peoples and their cousins on the steppe was being enhanced during this same period by several innovations in the tools of East Asian warfare. The mounted fighters of the Western Han period, both Chinese and Xiongnu, were overwhelmingly light cavalrymen whose primary reliance in combat was on the bow and arrow.[23] By the years around AD 300, however, the appearance of heavy armor for both man and horse, the introduction of the stirrup, and the adoption of new patterns of edged weapons greatly added to the advantages that cavalry enjoyed over infantry. To the mobility and firepower of the old type of cavalry there was now added a much greater capability for "shock" combat that would be especially useful in the context of Chinese civil wars, where fighting occurred in constricted spaces and concentrated hitting power might be more valuable than the speed of movement essential to successful warfare on the open steppe. Due to the very limited literary and archaeological evidence it is not possible to determine precisely when each of these innovations appeared on the Chinese scene, nor what influence each of them had on the development of the others, but we can be fairly confident that all elements of the complex were present by the middle of the fourth century at the very latest.

At the time of the founding of the Han dynasty, the form of sword used by Chinese armies was the *jian*, a straight, slender, double-edged blade tapering to a point. It could be used for either slashing or thrusting. Gradually, during the four centuries between 200 BC and AD 200, the *jian* was supplanted in military use by the *dao*. Sometimes translated as "knife," this weapon was really a sturdy, single-edged saber with only very slight curvature. As a chopping weapon that could be used by horsemen against either footsoldiers or other cavalry, it was superior to the relatively fragile *jian* with its redundant edge. By the end of the Eastern Han period, the *dao* had effectively replaced the *jian* as the basic sidearm for cavalrymen.[24] Over the same span of years, the *ji*, a long-handled weapon with several blades that was used as much for hooking as for thrusting, yielded to spears and lances of simpler construction. This switch may have been the result of the adoption of tighter infantry formations, with less room for swinging and hooking, in response to the greater threat posed by cavalry.

During this time the cavalryman was gaining a more secure seat atop his horse. The "rudimentary saddle" seen on the terracotta cavalry mounts from the tomb of the first emperor Qin Shihuangdi (really no more than a small pad, probably made of leather) had also become a thing of the past. "By the end of the Han period (ca. AD 200) we see evidence of a military saddle carefully shaped so as to fit the hips and upper leg, probably to assist the spear-bearing warrior to maintain his seat while using his weapon."[25]

At least some Qin and early Han cavalrymen were provided with simple armor to cover the front and back of the torso; this appears to have been lamellar armor, made from many small squares (lamellae) of iron or leather tied together with cords. About the beginning of the third century AD we find the first mention of horse armor (*makai*) in literary sources. The great warlord Cao Cao boasted that with only ten sets of horse armor he had faced an opponent with three hundred. The very small numbers here are worthy of note, and it is not at all clear whether Cao is speaking of simple chest protectors or complete bardings. By the early years of the fourth century the numbers have increased enormously, with the sources mentioning the capture of thousands of "armored horses" in a single battle. A pictoral representation dated to 357 shows us a fully armored warrior: "The body of the rider is almost completely covered by armor. He wears a plumed helmet that protects the sides and back of the head, a habergeon with high neck and shoulder guards, and chaps. The armor was made of lamellar plate, but one cannnot say whether of iron or of lacquered leather. The bardings almost completely cover the horse and include a chanfron of distinctive shape."[26]

The rapid spread of cavalry armor and heavy cavalry in China and adjacent regions appears to be closely connected with the introduction of the stirrup. The very earliest Chinese representation of a stirrup comes from a tomb figurine from South China dating to AD 302, but this is a single stirrup that must have been used only for mounting the horse. The earliest figurine with two stirrups probably dates from about 322, and the first actual specimens of stirrups that can be dated precisely and with confidence are from a southern Manchurian burial of 415. However, stirrups have also been found in several other tombs in North China and Manchuria that are most likely of fourth-century date. Most of these early Northeast Asian stirrups were oval in shape and made from iron, sometimes solid and sometimes applied over a wooden core, and this form would remain in use for many centuries thereafter.[27] It is interesting that in China, just as in Southwest Asia, heavily armored cavalry appeared before the introduction of the stirrup. Albert Dien has suggested that "it may well have been the increasing use of armored cavalry that provided the incentive and favorable environment for the development and widespread use of the stirrup."[28] This view is supported by the fact that some representations of heavy cavalrymen of the Wei–Jin period appear to show them with their legs encased in heavy wooden sideboards to stabilize them on top of the horse. As several authors have pointed out, the stirrup was never an absolute prerequisite for effective shock action by cavalry.[29] However, there is no denying that it conferred a certain advantage on its users by giving them greater stability and freedom of motion. Once the stirrup came into use, it must certainly have encouraged the employment of heavy cavalry on an even larger scale.

The basic organizational structure of the Jin military was inherited from Wei. There were two major components: an "inner" army of some one hundred thousand based at the capital city of Luoyang, and a much larger "outer" army made up of garrisons stationed in the provinces. The inner army was under the direct control of the imperial court and included both a palace guard and a powerful mobile striking force, while the outer units were subordinated to regional military commanders (*dudu*) appointed by the court. In addition to these forces, there were also local troops raised by the various provincial governors (*cishi*). The Jin army reached its greatest size, perhaps as many as 700,000 men, shortly after the conquest of Wu in 280.[30] Following that event, Sima Yan decreed the abolition of the local forces as a step toward the demilitarization of an empire that was finally at peace after nearly a century of civil war. Civil and military chains of command were separated at the local level, with provincial governors losing the authority to command troops. The local forces were a relatively small part of the total military establishment, however, and the reform was far from complete. Some provincial governors, especially those in strategic frontier areas, continued to command local troops after the reform edict was issued in 282.[31]

Another Jin policy was to place substantial military power in the hands of princes of the imperial house. The Jin founder, Sima Yan, apparently believed that he would be able to guarantee the preeminence of the Sima family and establish a bulwark against the sort of coup by which he himself had over-thrown the ruling family of Wei if he granted territorial fiefs to members of his own large and highly ramified lineage. Twenty-seven princes were enfeoffed soon after the founding of the dynasty in 265, a list which included three brothers of Sima Yan along with six uncles, one great uncle, and seventeen first and second cousins. Many other relatives were made princes later on.[32] Most of the princes received commanderies as their fiefs, with populations initially ranging from five thousand up to twenty thousand households. These allotments were later doubled, and a few princes were given even larger fiefs – up to a maximum of one hundred thousand households.[33] In 277 the princes were allowed to raise their own armies, ranging in size from 1500 men for the smallest princely fief to 5000 for the largest. They were very far from being independent rulers, however. The central government in Luoyang appointed their chief ministers, and the princes had to turn two-thirds of their tax revenues over to the center. The real power of the princes, in the case of those among them who were truly powerful, lay in their appointments as regional military commanders. By 290 six of the princes were serving as *dudu*. They held more than half of the regional commands in the empire, and these included the most important provincial centers: Xuchang on the great plain southeast of the capital, Ye in the rich and densely populated region north of the Yellow River, and Chang'an in the Wei River valley, a former capital and the gateway to Central Asia. All of these places had very large garrisons from the "outer" army and held substantial stockpiles of military supplies.[34] Even the less important of the *dudu* controlled forces of more than twenty thousand men, far more than in their capacity as fiefholders.[35] And the already great power of those princes who served as regional commanders was further augmented after 290 when *dudu* were once again allowed to hold provincial governorships concurrently with their military offices, giving them full control of both civil and military affairs in their assigned regions.[36]

The obvious potential of the princes to become independent warlords was held in check as long as there was a strong leader at the center. After the death of the Jin founding emperor Sima Yan in 290 this condition no longer obtained. The throne went to the founder's feeble-minded second son, Sima Zhong, known posthumously as Emperor Hui, while real power fell into the hands of the new ruler's mother, the empress dowager Yang, and her father Yang Jun. Unfortunately for the future of Jin rule, the Yangs were not the only imperial consort family with political ambitions. Emperor Hui's consort, Empress Jia, immediately began to plot the downfall of the Yang family. Since Yang Jun's followers controlled the imperial guard, the empress turned for support to the princes who were serving as regional military commanders. She found two of the emperor's brothers, the Prince of Chu (Sima Wei) and the Prince of Huainan (Sima Yun), most amenable to her scheme, and both held powerful regional commands. Chu was the military commander at the strategic center of Jing province on the middle Yangzi, while Huainan controlled the headquarters of Yang province in the fertile lower Yangzi region. In the third lunar month of 291, a visit to the capital by the two princes (no doubt accompanied by a numerous armed entourage) provided the opportunity for a bloody coup d'état. Yang Jun perished with several thousand of his supporters, while the empress dowager Yang was deposed, confined, and later starved to death. Sima Liang, the Prince of Ru'nan, an uncle of Emperor Wu and a political opponent of Yang Jun, took over the reins of the government. Within a few months, however, Empress Jia contrived to rid herself of both Chu and Ru'nan by encouraging the impetuous, twenty-one-year-old Prince of Chu to kill his great uncle the Prince of Ru'nan. With Ru'nan out of the way, she arranged to have Chu executed on the grounds that he carried out the murder without imperial sanction. Empress Jia dominated the Jin court for the next decade, but her rule was inherently unstable since it was based on a balancing of the imperial princes against one another rather than a real centralization of military power.[37]

The period of Empress Jia's dominance came to an end in 300 when she was betrayed by Sima Lun, Prince of Zhao and younger brother of the late Prince of Ru'nan. Originally an ally of the empress, Zhao now used his position as commander of the imperial guard to seize power in the capital and kill the empress and a large number of her partisans. He made himself prime minister, placed ten thousand soldiers under the direct control of his headquarters, and appointed his cronies to key positions. Zhao's blatant self-aggrandizement naturally aroused the opposition of other princes who were holding powerful regional commands. The first to act was the Prince of Huainan, who marched on Luoyang in the autumn of 300. Huainan's troops entered the capital and besieged the prime minister's office for several hours before their leader was cut down by hostile cavalrymen who had pretended to be bringing him an imperial edict. Having dealt with this challenge, the Prince of Zhao deposed Emperor Hui, imprisoned him in the citadel of Luoyang with the title of "retired emperor," and assumed the imperial throne himself at the beginning of 301. These moves, however, quickly stimulated the emergence of a much more formidable opposition movement in the provinces. In the third lunar month of 301, Sima Jiong, the Prince of Qi – a nephew of Emperor Wu and commander of the important garrison center of Xuchang, 90 miles southeast of the capital – denounced the Prince of Zhao and moved his forces toward Luoyang. Others raised troops to support him. These included Sima Ying, Prince of Chengdu, the regional military commander at Ye, north of the Yellow River, and Sima Yong, the Prince of Hejian and regional military commander at Chang'an, together with several of the provincial governors.[38] As armies totalling several hundred thousand men closed in on the capital from three directions, the Prince of Zhao's forces were defeated and driven back into the city. Zhao's own followers turned against him as the provincial armies entered Luoyang. Emperor Hui was freed from captivity, and the Prince of Zhao put to death by the victors. The whole affair had lasted only sixty days.[39]

Far from heralding a return to political stability, the victory of the princes of Qi, Chengdu, and Hejian marked the beginning of the Jin dynasty's descent into the abyss. The provincial magnates had openly and successfully challenged the center and imposed their will on the imperial court by force of arms. An era in which power struggles were settled by palace coups and the façade of central authority was preserved more or less intact now gave way to a period of warlordism and civil war in which disagreements were settled on the battle-field. With their conflicting ambitions, their strong regional bases, and their deepening suspicions of one another, the imperial princes were simply incapable of restoring a stable political order. The Prince of Qi assumed the dominant position in the capital, but when he was seen to have designs on the throne the others united against him just as they had against Zhao. The Prince of Hejian once again sent strong forces toward Luoyang, but the decisive blow was struck by the Prince of Changsha, the sixth son of Emperor Wu. Originally a supporter of the Prince of Qi, Changsha commanded a body of troops within the walls of Luoyang, and with this force he was able to make a surprise attack on Qi's headquarters at the end of 302. After a day and night of fighting in the streets of the capital during which "arrow fells like rain and fires lit the sky," the Prince of Qi was seized and put to death – as were some two thousand of his partisans.[40] The new division of power between the Prince of Chengdu at Ye, the Prince of Hejian at Chang'an, and the Prince of Changsha in the capital lasted only a few months. Hejian plotted the assassination of Changsha, who got wind of it and killed a number of Hejian's agents. Hejian then sent an army of two hundred thousand men toward Luoyang, while some seventy thousand of Chengdu's men approached the capital from the northeast. The armies of the two princes menaced the capital from the eighth month of 303 to the first month of 304; within the walls the price of grain skyrocketed and even slaves were mobilized to supplement the badly outnumbered defenders. In the end the Prince of Changsha met with much the same fate that he himself had earlier visited on the Prince of Qi. One of his subordinate commanders in the city, a distant cousin named Sima Yue who held the title of Prince of Donghai, seized Changsha and handed him over to one of Hejian's generals, who had the hapless prince roasted to death over a slow fire.[41]

The court was then dominated, for a season, by the Prince of Chengdu, who had himself made heir apparent and installed a strong garrison in Luoyang while managing affairs at a distance from his base north of the Yellow River. In the seventh month of 304, Emperor Hui and his court rebelled against Chengdu's tutelage. The Prince of Donghai was appointed to lead the imperial guard against Ye, and the emperor himself accompanied the expedition. As the imperial column approached Ye, however, it was surprised and routed by Chengdu's forces near the town of Tangyin on September 9, 304. During the battle, arrows fell thickly around the imperial carriage and one of the attendants died trying to shield his master from the fusillade. In spite of this sacrifice, the emperor was struck by three arrows and wounded on the cheek; his clothing was stained with blood and he lost the imperial seals. Left alone on the field as his bodyguards and attendants scattered, he was brought back to Ye as a captive of the victors. The Prince of Donghai escaped to take refuge in his fief in the remote coastal region south of the Shandong peninsula, while the Prince of Hejian seized the opportunity to occupy Luoyang with his own forces.[42]

The Prince of Chengdu's triumph was short-lived, however. From the eighth lunar month of 304 he came under increasing pressure from the forces of two northern frontier generals, one of whom happened to be a younger brother of the Prince of Donghai. These northern armies were especially formidable because they incorporated substantial cavalry forces recruited from the Wuhuan and Xianbei peoples. After his armies had sustained several defeats in the field and efforts to enlist the Xiongnu of southern Shanxi to counter the enemy's cavalry had failed to bear fruit, Chengdu decided to abandon Ye. With a small escort and the captive emperor in tow, he fled to Luoyang where both he and the emperor became captives of the Prince of Hejian and were soon forwarded to Chang'an.[43] In the summer of 305 the Prince of Donghai reentered the fray, no doubt encouraged by his brother's success against Chengdu and by the fact that two other brothers also occupied strategic positions. Donghai's army advanced on Luoyang from the southeast, while his brothers approached the capital from the north and northeast. During the latter half of 305 the civil war, which had originally been confined to the environs of Luoyang, became general throughout much of North China as local governors raised militia forces and declared for either Hejian or Donghai.[44] The Donghai forces prevailed and took possession of Luoyang early in 306. Rejecting peace overtures from Hejian, Donghai sent his army toward Chang'an and smashed the opposing forces in a battle at Huxian on the south bank of the Yellow River near the mouth of the passes leading into Guanzhong (June 4, 306). Hejian and Chengdu fled into the southern mountains as the Xianbei warriors of Donghai's army entered Chang'an and subjected the city to a frightful pillage that reportedly claimed the lives of 20,000 citizens. Emperor Hui was returned to Luoyang but died before the end of the year, with the throne passing to his youngest brother, Sima Zhi, the twenty-fifth son of Emperor Wu, who would be known posthumously as Emperor Huai. The Prince of Chengdu and his sons were soon captured and put to death. As for the Prince of Hejian, he was offered a post at court by the new emperor, but was treacherously murdered by agents of one of Donghai's brothers while en route to Luoyang. The date of his death, February 6, 307, is often taken to mark the end of what came to be called the "War of the Eight Princes."[45]

This left Sima Yue, Prince of Donghai, as the undisputed master of the Jin imperial court and the only survivor among the major princely contenders. By that time, however, the prize that he had won was but a shadow of what it had been in 301, at the beginning of the civil war. It was not simply that thousands of soldiers had fallen on the fields of battle and thousands more civilians had perished in the sack of several of the empire's most important cities, but that the social and political order had been irreparably damaged during the six years of chaos. Provincial governors ceased to obey orders from the center, internal migration increased from a trickle to a flood as refugees fled the violence in North China, and bandits arose everywhere. Moreover, the agrarian economy was a shambles. The *History of the Jin Dynasty* describes the situation in the following terms:

> By the Yongjia period [307–12] trouble and disturbances were very widespread. From Yongzhou eastward many suffered from hunger and poverty. People were sold [as slaves]. Vagrants became countless. In the six provinces of You, Bing, Si, Ji, Qin, and Yong there was a bad plague of locusts. . . . Virulent disease accompanied the famine. Also the people were murdered by bandits. The rivers were filled with floating corpses; bleached bones covered the fields. . . . There was much cannibalism. Famine and pestilence came hand in hand.[46]

The migration of population southward from Hebei to Shandong, from Shanxi to Henan, from Shandong and Henan to the lower Yangzi, and from Guanzhong to the Han River valley and Sichuan gave birth to local rebellions as the migrants met with resistance and exploitation from the indigenous populations and took up arms to protect themselves.[47] Even more worrisome, however, were the revolts of the non-Chinese peoples in North China. These had begun even before the outbreak of the War of the Eight Princes; some of the Xiongnu in Shanxi had risen in 294 and killed a number of local officials before they were crushed, and a much more serious rebellion of Xiongnu, Qiang, and Di broke out in the Guanzhong region two years later and was not put down until 299. Han and Di refugees escaping from the fighting in Guanzhong launched their own rebellion in Sichuan and occupied Chengdu, the most important city of the region, in 303. By far the most threatening of the risings by non-Chinese peoples, however, was the one begun by the Xiongnu chieftain Liu Yuan in 304, at the height of the Jin civil war.[48]

Early in the third century, the Wei founder Cao Cao had moved the majority of the Southern Xiongnu away from the frontier and into the interior of Bing province (modern Shanxi) where they might be more easily controlled. He split them into five "divisions" (*bu*) that were settled in different locations in the upper reaches of the Fen River valley, centered around the provincial capital of Taiyuan. By the 280s, the total population of the five divisions was reckoned at more than 29,000 encampments (*luo*).[49] Living interspersed among the Chinese population in a mountainous region very different from their original home on the steppe, it seems that these Xiongnu had turned from nomadism to sedentary stockbreeding, with some even taking up agriculture. They began to put down roots, and some became quite sinicized in their lifestyle. The trend toward sinicization was most pronounced among the tribal elite.[50] Liu Yuan, the hereditary chieftain of the Left Division and a descendant of the Xiongnu king (or *shanyu*) who had submitted to Han back in AD 50, was literate and fond of study. He spent part of his youth as a court attendant in Luoyang, and he had received a thorough education in the Confucian classics and also became acquainted with the most important Chinese works of history and strategy.[51] In spite of their participation in Chinese elite culture, however, Liu Yuan and other Xiongnu leaders had a keen sense of separate identity and were far from satisfied with their subordinate position within the Chinese state. As one of them put it, "Since the fall of Han, Wei and Jin have risen one after the other; although our ruler has been given an empty title, he no longer has even a foot of ground as sovereign territory. From being princes and nobles, we have descended to the same level as ordinary registered households of commoners." The Jin government, he complained on another occasion, "uses us as if we were slaves."[52]

In 304 Liu Yuan took advantage of a commission from the increasingly desperate Prince of Chengdu (who was just then being driven from his base at Ye) to gather 50,000 warriors from among the five divisions of the Xiongnu. He then proceeded to proclaim himself "King of Han." The rituals that he performed for this occasion, which included sacrifices to the spirits of all of the emperors of the Han dynasty, left little doubt that he intended to make a bid for the imperial throne as the legitimate heir of the Han rulers in opposition to the usurpers of the house of Sima, his claim in this regard being based primarily on the earlier intermarriage between the Han and Xiongnu royal lines. Liu clearly hoped that his legitimist stance would win him substantial support among Chinese elites, and it may be taken as evidence of the extent to which he had accepted the ideology and political practices of those same elites.[53] However, his main effort involved coercion rather than persuasion. After meeting with frustration in his efforts to capture the provincial capital at Taiyuan, Liu shifted his attention southward and overran the southern part of Shanxi in 307. That same year, he accepted the allegiance of two large bandit forces that had been ravaging the Shandong peninsula and the plains of Hebei and Henan but had come under pressure from Jin armies. The more significant of the two was a mixed band of Chinese and barbarians led by an ex-slave of Xiongnu origin, a man named Shi Le about whom we shall hear a great deal more. Around this same time Liu also attracted the support of certain leaders of the Di and the Xianbei. With these accretions of strength, he sent out columns that defeated Jin armies in the field and plundered all the way to the gates of Luoyang in 308 and 309.[54]

Liu Yuan did not live to see the fall of the Jin capital, however. An astrologer's prediction persuaded the Xiongnu field commanders to postpone their final assault on the city until 311, and in the meantime the "Han" emperor fell ill and died on August 29, 310. Despite its legitimist pretensions, the Han regime proved no better than Jin when it came to managing an orderly succession to the imperial throne. Liu Yuan's eldest son and designated heir was eliminated and replaced by an ambitious younger brother, Liu Cong, before the drive on Luoyang was resumed. The Prince of Donghai attempted to take advantage of this breathing space to buttress the defences of the capital, and sent out a summons to the provincial governors to provide reinforcements. When it became clear that his call was going to be ignored, the prince decided to transfer his base of operations to a safer location southeast of the capital in the Henan plain. He marched out of the city on December 22, 310, with 40,000 troops, heading southeast toward Xuchang. Some four months later, on April 23, 311, the Prince of Donghai died at Xiang County, on the Ying River. His army and entourage took this opportunity to move even farther to the east, in order to return the prince's body to his coastal fief for burial. On the way they were overtaken by Shi Le's cavalry. The barbarian horsemen formed a ring around the Jin footsoldiers, who trampled one another in their haste to escape from the arrows that came raining down upon them. In the end none succeeded in getting away, and the Jin army was reduced to a mountain of corpses. Those killed or captured by Shi Le on this occasion included not only soldiers but also a considerable number of government officials and imperial princes.[55]

Even before this disaster, many in Luoyang had already concluded that the situation of the capital was hopeless. The populace had been short of food for months; robbers went about openly in broad daylight, and corpses were piling up even within the halls of the imperial palace. Moreoever, the departure of the Prince of Donghai had stripped the city of most of its defenders. Given these conditions, reports that eight or nine of every ten officials had deserted their posts may not be very much of an exaggeration.[56] The Han forces began their assault on the capital in the fifth month, and the lead column quickly broke through one of the gates in the southern wall to plunder and burn some of the government offices. It was only two weeks later, however, after substantial reinforcements had arrived, that the Han troops ventured to occupy the rest of the city and force their way into the palace compound to lay hands on the palace women and the imperial treasures. Emperor Huai was taken prisoner as he attempted to flee the palace by a back gate opening onto the imperial park. The tombs of his ancestors were thrown open and plundered, the palaces and government offices set on fire. Later historians would place the civilian death toll in the tens of thousands.[57] The Xiongnu leaders chose not to move their seat of government to Luoyang, since it was surrounded by hostile territory that had yet to be pacified. Instead, they burned what remained of the city to the ground and returned to Shanxi with their loot and captives. At the height of Jin rule before the War of the Eight Princes, Luoyang had had a population of about 600,000 occupying a space of three square miles within the city walls; it was the largest city in eastern Asia and probably second only to Rome as the largest in the world. After the cataclysm of 311, it would be nearly two centuries before the city was restored as an important center of population, commerce, and government.[58]

The fall of Luoyang marked the end of effective Jin rule in North China. After Emperor Huai finally perished at the hands of the Xiongnu in 313, a nephew was enthroned at Chang'an, but his writ did not extend much beyond Guanzhong – and even there he was heavily dependent on the goodwill of the local elites. The nephew, who would be known posthumously as Emperor Min, held out until 316, when Chang'an fell to the Han general Liu Yao. He was then taken to the Han capital and in 317 suffered the same fate as his predecessor. The Jin throne was then claimed by a relatively distant cousin, Sima Rui, who had been serving as military commander of the Lower Yangzi region for more than a decade.[59] Sima Rui and his descendants would keep Jin rule alive in South China for another hundred years, but the north was irrevocably lost; China would not again be united under the rule of a single imperial government until 589. Given the many weaknesses of the Jin regime at Luoyang and the fragility of the newly reunified state after the prolonged disunity of the Three Kingdoms period, it would be rash to view the Jin collapse as simply a consequence of the damage done by the War of the Eight Princes. Had the conflict of 301 to 306 not occurred, it is still possible to imagine another chain of events tipping the empire into chaos and sundering North from South. On the other hand, it is also possible to imagine the survival of the empire under the same set of circumstances. The same cannot be said of the situation that existed in the aftermath of the War of the Princes. Their self-destructive conflict all but guaranteed the success of Liu Yuan and other leaders of rebellious marginal groups, ushering in the longest period of division in all of Chinese history.

Notes

1 Wang Zhongluo, *Wei Jin Nanbeichao shi* (Shanghai: Shanghai renmin chubanshe, 1979), vol. 1, p. 113. The northern regime's ability to conquer the south at *this* time and not earlier has been attributed to the economic recovery of the north after the devastating civil wars of circa 200; see Zou Yuntao, "Shi lun San Guo shiqi nan bei junshi de xingcheng ji qi pohuai," in *Wei Jin Nanbeichao shi yanjiu* (Chengdu: Sichuan sheng shehui kexue yuan chubanshe, 1986), pp. 128–45.

2 Tang Changru, *Wei Jin Nanbeichao Sui Tang shi san lun* (Wuhan: Wuhan daxue chubanshe, 1993), pp. 29–30; also see Lien-sheng Yang, "Notes on the Economic History of the Chin Dynasty," in his *Studies in Chinese Institutional History* (Cambridge, Mass.: Harvard University Press, 1961), pp. 113–14.

3 Rafe de Crespigny, *Northern Frontier: The Policies and Strategy of the Later Han Empire* (Canberra: Faculty of Asian Studies, Australian National University, 1984), pp. 72–3.

4 Tang Changru, *Wei Jin Nanbeichao Sui Tang shi san lun*, pp. 23–4, 30.

5 He Ziquan, *Wei Jin Nanbeichao shilue* (Shanghai: Shanghai renmin chubanshe, 1958), pp. 14–15.

6 Lien-sheng Yang, "Notes on the Economic History of the Chin Dynasty," p. 149, with slight modification of Professor Yang's translation.

7 For the economy of this period, see He Ziquan, *Wei Jin Nanbeichao shilue*, pp. 8–10, Lien-sheng Yang, "Notes on the Economic History of the Chin Dynasty," p. 117, and Tang Changru, *Wei Jin Nanbeichao Sui Tang shi san lun*, pp. 39–41.

8 Charles Holcombe, *In the Shadow of the Han: Literati Thought and Society at the Beginning of the Southern Dynasties* (Honolulu: University of Hawaii Press, 1994), p. 8.

9 He Ziquan, "Wei Jin Nanchao de bingzhi," *Bulletin of the Institute of History and Philology of Academia Sinica*, 16 (1948), pp. 231–5; Gao Min, "Cao Wei shijia zhidu de xingcheng yu yanbian," *Lishi yanjiu*, 1989, No. 5, pp. 62, 64–5.

10 Tang Changru, "Wei Jin Nanbeichao shiqi de ke he buqu," in his *Wei Jin Nanbeichao shilun shiyi* (Beijing: Zhonghua shuju, 1983), pp. 2, 15; Yang Chung-i, "Evolution of the Status of 'Dependants,'" in E-tu Zen Sun and John DeFrancis (eds.), *Chinese Social History* (Washington, D.C.: American Council of Learned Societies, 1956), pp. 142–56; Gao Min, "Cao Wei shijia zhidu de xingcheng yu yanbian," p. 67.

11 Gao Min, "Cao Wei shijia zhidu de xingcheng yu yanbian," p. 66.

12 This sketch of the Wei system of military households is based on Gao Min, "Cao Wei shijia zhidu de xingcheng yu yanbian," pp. 61–75.

13 Pat Southern and Karen Ramsey Dixon, *The Late Roman Army* (New Haven and London: Yale University Press, 1996), pp. 67–8.

14 Southern and Dixon, *The Late Roman Army*, pp. 46–52.

15 Tamura Jitsuzo, *Chūgoku shijō no minzoku idō ki* (Tokyo: Sōbunsha, 1985), p. 11.

16 De Crespigny, *Northern Frontier*, pp. 382–3.

17 De Crespigny, *Northern Frontier*, p. 88; Li Tse-fen, *Liang Jin Nanbeichao lishi lunwenji* (Taipei: Taiwan Commercial Press, 1987), vol. 1, p. 30; Lei Haizong, *Zhongguo wenhua yu Zhongguo de bing* (Changsha: Commercial Press, 1940), pp. 51–3.

18 De Crespigny, *Northern Frontier*, p. 387.

19 De Crespigny, *Northern Frontier*, p. 415.
20 Tang Changru, "Jindai beijing ge zu 'bianluan' de xingzhi ji Wu Hu zhengquan zai Zhongguo de tongzhi," in his *Wei Jin Nanbeichao shi luncong* (Beijing: Sanlian, 1955), pp. 130–1; He Ziquan, "Wei Jin Nanchao de bingzhi," pp. 239–43.
21 Ni Jinsheng, "Wu Hu luan Hua qianye de Zhongguo jingji," *Shi huo banyuekan*, 1.7 (March 1, 1935), p. 39.
22 Tang Changru, "Jindai beijing ge zu 'bianluan' de xingzhi ji Wu Hu zhengquan zai Zhongguo de tongzhi," pp. 127–8.
23 Albert E. Dien, "The Stirrup and its Effect on Chinese Military History," *Ars Orientalis*, 16 (1986), p. 36.
24 Yang Hong, *Zhongguo gu bingqi luncong*, pp. 124, 130–1.
25 Chauncey S. Goodrich, "Riding Astride and the Saddle in Ancient China," *Harvard Journal of Asiatic Studies*, 44.2 (December 1984), pp. 293, 299, 304.
26 Dien, "The Stirrup and its Effect on Chinese Military History," pp. 37, 38.
27 Dien, "The Stirrup and its Effect on Chinese Military History," pp. 33–5.
28 Dien, "The Stirrup and its Effect on Chinese Military History," p. 37.
29 Philippe Contamine, *War in the Middle Ages*, trans. by Michael Jones (Oxford: Basil Blackwell, 1984), pp. 183–4.
30 *Zhongguo junshi shi*, vol. 3: *Bingzhi*, pp. 160, 161–5.
31 Tang Changru, "Wei Jin zhou jun bing de shezhi he feiba," in his *Wei Jin Nanbeichao shilun shiyi* (Beijing: Zhonghua shuju, 1983), pp. 145–50; Chen Yinke, *Wei Jin Nanbeichao shi jiangyanlu*, arr. by Wan Shengnan (Hefei: Huangshan shushe, 1987), p. 37.
32 Fang Xuanling et al., *Jin shu* (Beijing: Zhonghua shuju, 1974), ch. 3, p. 52; Li Tse-fen, *Liang Jin Nanbeichao lishi lunwenji*, vol. 3, p. 460.
33 Wang Zhongluo, *Wei Jin Nanbeichao shi*, vol. 1, p. 211.
34 Tang Changru, "Xi Jin fenfeng yu zongwang chu zhen," in *Wei Jin Sui Tang shi lunji*, vol. 1 (Beijing: Zhongguo shehui kexue chubanshe, 1981), pp. 1–2, 8–10; Tang Changru, *Wei Jin Nanbeichao Sui Tang shi san lun*, pp. 51–2.
35 *Zhongguo junshi shi*, vol. 3, p. 165.
36 Tang Changru, "Wei Jin zhou jun bing de shezhi he feiba," pp. 145–7.
37 This account follows Li Tse-fen, *Liang Jin Nanbeichao lishi lunwenji*, vol. 1, pp. 47–8, Wang Zhongluo, *Wei Jin Nanbeichao shi*, vol. 1, pp. 215–16, and He Ziquan, *Wei Jin Nanbeichao shilue*, p. 49.
38 Chengdu was the sixth son of Emperor Wu. Hejian was a more distant kinsman, the grandson of a younger brother of Sima Yi.
39 Li Tse-fen, *Liang Jin Nanbeichao lishi lunwenji*, vol. 1, pp. 50–2; *Jin shu*, ch. 59, pp. 1597–605.
40 *Jin shu*, ch. 59, p. 1610; Li Tse-fen, *Liang Jin Nanbeichao lishi lunwenji*, vol. 1, pp. 53–4.
41 *Jin shu*, ch. 4, pp. 100–1; He Ziquan, *Wei Jin Nanbeichao shilue*, pp. 217–18; Li Tse-fen, *Liang Jin Nanbeichao lishi lunwenji*, vol. 1, pp. 55–7.
42 *Jin shu*, ch. 4, pp. 102–3; He Ziquan, *Wei Jin Nanbeichao shilue*, p. 218.
43 *Jin shu*, ch. 59, p. 1618; He Ziquan, *Wei Jin Nanbeichao shilue*, p. 219.
44 Li Tse-fen, *Liang Jin Nanbeichao lishi lunwenji*, vol. 1, pp. 61–2.
45 Li Tse-fen, *Liang Jin Nanbeichao lishi lunwenji*, vol. 1, pp. 63–5.
46 Lien-sheng Yang, "Notes on the Economic History of the Chin Dynasty," p. 181. Translation slightly modified.
47 He Ziquan, *Wei Jin Nanbeichao shilue*, p. 57; Wang Zhongluo, *Wei Jin Nanbeichao shi*, vol. 1, pp. 229–30.
48 Tang Changru, "Jindai beijing ge zu 'bianluan' de xingzhi ji Wu Hu zhengquan zai Zhongguo de tongzhi," pp. 144–5.

49 He Ziquan, *Wei Jin Nanbeichao shilue*, pp. 51–3; Tamura, *Chūgoku shijō no minzoku idō ki*, p. 15. An encampment included several "tents" or household groups. The number of individuals in an encampment must have been highly variable. Modern estimates range from a low of ten to upwards of forty-two. See David B. Honey, *The Rise of the Medieval Hsiung-nu: The Biography of Liu Yüan*, Papers on Inner Asia, No. 15 (Bloomington, Ind.: Research Institute for Inner Asian Studies, 1990), p. 5 and p. 31, n. 18.

50 Tamura, *Chūgoku shijō no minzoku idō ki*, p. 14; Li Tse-fen, *Liang Jin Nanbeichao lishi lunwenji*, vol. 1, p. 43; Chen Yinke, *Wei Jin Nanbeichao shi jiangyanlu*, p. 99.

51 *Jin shu*, ch. 101, p. 2645–6.

52 *Jin shu*, ch. 101, pp. 2647, 2648.

53 Tamura, *Chūgoku shijō no minzoku idō ki*, p. 27; *Jin shu*, ch. 101, pp. 2648–9. Liu would declare himself emperor in 308.

54 Li Tse-fen, *Liang Jin Nanbeichao lishi lunwenji*, vol. 1, p. 90; *Jin shu*, ch. 101, pp. 2650–2.

55 Wang Zhongluo, *Wei Jin Nanbeichao shi*, vol. 1, p. 220; Sima Guang, *Zizhi tongjian*, ch. 87, pp. 2746, 2754–5, 2759–61.

56 Sima Guang, *Zizhi tongjian*, ch. 87, pp. 2754–5, 2762.

57 Sima Guang, *Zizhi tongjian*, ch. 87, p. 2763. For a popular account in English, see Arthur Waley, "The Fall of Lo-yang," *History Today*, 1 (1951), pp. 7–10.

58 Waley, "The Fall of Lo-yang," pp. 7, 10.

59 He Ziquan, *Wei Jin Nanbeichao shilue*, pp. 59, 74.

CHAPTER THREE

The north under barbarian rule

The overthrow of the "Western" Jin regime based at Luoyang by Xiongnu under the leadership of the Liu family left China divided into two major segments, north and south, roughly along the line of the Huai River and the Qinling and Dabie mountains. In many ways this split recalled that of the Three Kingdoms period, and reflected the enduring geographical and cultural differences between the dry, temperate north and the warm and watery south, between the land of wheat and millet and the zone of wet-rice cultivation. Over the ensuing four centuries of division, these two vast regions would experience very different histories and develop in different directions. From their new capital at Jiankang (today's Nanjing) on the lower reaches of the Yangzi, the heirs of the Jin ruling class exerted their authority over the south, asserted their legitimacy and cultural superiority in the face of the barbarian usurpers in the north, and dreamed of a return to the ancient homeland of Chinese civilization. In the north, meanwhile, the violent and disorderly rule of the earliest non-Chinese conquerors gave way very gradually to a new Sino-barbarian synthesis, new political and military institutions, and a vigorous new ruling class that would succeed in reuniting the empire near the end of the sixth century. This chapter will deal with developments in North China up until about the middle of the fifth century.

The military successes of Liu Yuan and his heirs did not lead to the establishment of a stable political order in the north. The Han regime of the Xiongnu was not strong enough to extend its authority over all of North China. It faced serious challenges from several other barbarian groups, and was at the same time unable to win the support and cooperation of the Chinese population. The incessant violence and the collapse of the Jin administration produced tremendous social dislocation as many Chinese of the north abandoned their cities and villages to seek refuge from the storm. Migration of population from north to south had been underway as early as the second century AD, but the volume of this flow increased substantially during the late Jin disorders, especially the War of the Eight Princes. With the Xiongnu onslaught and the fall of Luoyang, the flow became a torrent.[1] According to one estimate, the north lost at least 300,000 households in the early years of the fourth century, with the Guanzhong region alone losing 40–50,000 households – approximately one-third of its registered population.[2] On account of the obvious softness of many of the numbers found in the Chinese sources, the exact dimensions of this movement are unknown and unknowable. But all agree that the numbers involved were very large. While the main paths of migration were from north to south, running from Guanzhong to the Sichuan basin and from Henan and Shandong to the middle and lower Yangzi, some people also sought refuge with Xianbei rulers in southern Manchuria or with the Chinese governors of territories along the Silk Road in the far northwest. In some areas the migrations produced a sort of chain reaction; in Sichuan, for example, disorders sparked by refugees from Guanzhong prompted a large portion of the local population to move eastward down the Yangzi River to central China.[3] The upper class of landowners and government officials seems to have accounted for a disproportionate share of this movement; according to one estimate (which is, of course, open to question) more than 60 percent of the northern elite fled to the south between 311 and 325.[4] A common pattern was for a member of the local elite to lead his kinsmen, retainers, and neighbors to make the trek to safety as an organized community of several hundred households.[5]

Those who did not seek safety in flight to distant regions tried to protect themselves by abandoning their existing settlements and moving into nearby mountains or other easily defensible terrain. These people, like the migrants to the south, moved as organized groups. Led by respected members of the wealthier and more powerful local families, they constructed rudimentary fortifications, stored their grain within the walls, and defended themselves against marauding bandits and barbarian horsemen. Such fortresses might offer refuge to self-sufficient communities of several hundreds or even thousands of people. The most famous example of this phenomenon from the Jin period is that of Yu Gun, a minor official of Yingchuan commandery in central Henan. When his home was threatened by troops of one of the princely armies in 301, Yu led his kinsmen and other members of the community into the high country to the northwest. "In this high and dangerous defile, he blocked the footpaths, erected fortifications, planted [defensive] hedges, examined merit, made measurements, equalized labor and rest, shared possessions, repaired implements, measured strength and employed the able, making all things correspond to what they should."[6] On several occasions when bandits threatened his hilltop sanctuary, he was able to deter them simply by deploying his armed followers in orderly ranks.

Defensive communities of this sort had appeared before in Chinese history, as in the civil wars at the end of Eastern Han, and they would be used again and again in imperial China's recurrent times of troubles. As Jin rule dissolved in North China, forts became especially common in Henan and Shandong but could also be found in Guanzhong, Hebei, and Sichuan. One early medieval text tells us that the Luo River valley near the old Jin capital was home to at least eleven of them, while other accounts have the Xiongnu bandit leader Shi Le capturing dozens of forts in the course of a single sweep through Henan.[7] With many cities and towns abandoned by their inhabitants, the forts became the real basis of local government. Fortress chiefs squabbled with one another for power at the grassroots level and were alternately coerced and courted by barbarian rulers and by the Jin émigré regime in the south. Some succeeded in organizing leagues of many forts and even received official appointments as local governors from various ruling authorities. The fortified community of refuge would remain the basic building block of local power in North China for several generations after the Jin collapse, until a stable political order was finally provided by the Northern Wei dynasty in the middle of the fifth century.[8]

Looming over this highly fragmented local scene were several sets of would-be rulers, none of which succeeded in establishing very much control for very long. The most important of these initially, if we exclude the "Eastern" Jin government at Jiankang, was the Han court established by the Xiongnu aristocrat Liu Yuan and his family. This group dominated southern and central Shanxi and, from 316, was also in possession of the Guanzhong region with its ancient capital of Chang'an. From the very beginning the Liu rulers had made a point of adopting the trappings of Chinese imperial government, including rituals, sacrifices, official titles, and a variety of symbolic gestures. This did not compensate for a deep instability at the center, however, and the transfer of power was repeatedly marked by bloodshed. Liu Yuan's designated heir had been murdered and replaced by a younger son, Liu Cong, in 310. Shortly after Liu Cong died in 318, *his* son and heir was murdered, together with many other members of the Liu family, by an ambitious imperial in-law. After more bloodshed, the throne was claimed by Liu Yao, a member of the ruling clan who had been orphaned at an early age and raised by Liu Yuan. Liu Yao moved the capital from Pingyang in the lower valley of the Fen River in Shanxi to his own power base at Chang'an, and changed the name of the regime from Han to Zhao. Preoccupied with its internal struggles, the Liu ruling group made very little progress toward subduing rival barbarian rulers in North China.

By the second decade of the fourth century the northern and northeastern rim of what had been the Jin empire was dominated by the Murong, Tuoba, and Duan clans of the Xianbei and the Yuwen clan of the Xiongnu. The Murong had occupied southern and southwestern Manchuria and set up a government that encouraged agriculture and welcomed Chinese refugees, some of whom received official positions. The Murong leader professed loyalty to the Jin dynasty and accepted official titles from the Jin emperor in the south. The Duan, apparently a somewhat smaller group than the Murong, lived to the south and west, on the northern frontier of Hebei. Though often in conflict with the Murong, the Duan eventually developed a firm marriage alliance with their larger neighbor so that the legitimate heir to the Murong throne was normally the son of a Duan consort.[9] The Tuoba lived farther to the west, at the eastern corner of the Yellow River bend and in the northern part of Shanxi around the modern city of Datong. Between 304 and 314 the Tuoba leader, Tuoba Yilu, sent strong cavalry forces to assist the Jin governor of Bing province against the Xiongnu of Liu Yuan and his heirs. As a reward for his efforts, Yilu was ceded control of five counties by the Jin court and given the title of Prince of Dai (a traditional appellation for the North Shanxi region). Just as the Murong had formed a marriage alliance with the Duan, the Tuoba rulers intermarried with the Yuwen clan of the Xiongnu, who lived to the north of the Murong in the valley of the Sira Muren River. As a result they were sometimes drawn into conflicts between the Yuwen and the Murong, though for most of the period from 308 to 325 the Tuoba and Murong were at peace as the Tuoba focused on their struggle against the Xiongnu in Shanxi.[10]

The northwestern perimeter of the old empire was also beyond the control of the Han–Zhao regime. The Ordos region within the Yellow River bend, directly to the north of Liu Yao's capital at Chang'an, was home to Xiongnu groups that were largely independent of his authority. Farther to the west, in Liang province (that is, the part of modern Gansu west of the Yellow River), a strong Chinese governor named Zhang Gui had defeated local Xianbei groups in battle and sent troops to help defend Luoyang and Chang'an against the Xiongnu. After Zhang died in 320 power remained in the hands of his family, with the governorship passing to two of his sons and then to a grandson. Although they were for all intents and purposes autonomous local rulers, the Zhang governors of Liang province continued to profess allegiance to the Jin court in the south until 323 when military pressure from Liu Yao compelled them to become nominal vassals of Zhao. When Zhao began to show signs of weakness a few years later, Liang province once again proclaimed its allegiance to Jin.[11] South of the Qinling range, in the Sichuan basin, the dominant authority was Li Xiong, the Di leader of refugee groups that had fled from fighting in Guanzhong in the 290s. Li overthrew the local Jin authorities, seized the important city of Chengdu, and proclaimed himself emperor of the new state of Cheng in 306. He remained on the throne for thirty years and fought against the Zhao regime in Guanzhong.[12] By far the most serious threat to Liu Yao's authority, however, was his erstwhile ally Shi Le, who dominated much of the North China plain from his base at Xiangguo (near Ye) in southern Hebei.

Shi Le's background was very different from that of the aristocratic Liu family. The scion of minor tribal chiefs of a branch of the Xiongnu, he had been brought up among the Jie people of southern Shanxi.[13] As a young man he and other barbarians had been seized by agents of the Jin governor of Bing province and sold into slavery in Shandong. Shi eventually gained his freedom and became involved with a group of mounted brigands who supplied themselves with horses stolen from the imperial pastures. Gathering in escaped slaves, outlaws from the mountains and swamps, and herdsmen who included prisoners taken in military actions against the steppe peoples, this mixed force of Chinese and barbarians grew to impressive size and plundered its way along the lower reaches of the Yellow River during the War of the Eight Princes. Shi emerged as one of the leaders, and when the bandit army suffered a defeat at the hands of Jin forces he led the survivors to submit to Liu Yuan.[14] This connection enabled him to rebuild his following and to attract the allegiance of several independent groups of barbarian cavalry. Shi then returned to his old stamping ground on the eastern plain. By the time of the Jin collapse in 311 he dominated the Henan–Hebei–Shandong border region, and he soon extended his authority northward into Hebei and westward into central Shanxi. During this time he remained a vassal of the Han regime at Pingyang, albeit one with tremendous freedom for autonomous action.

Shi Le did not break with the Liu family until 319, when Liu Yao took the throne and moved the capital from Pingyang to Chang'an. Shi then proclaimed himself "King of Zhao." (Since Liu Yao had taken the same name for his own state, historians distinguish between the "Former Zhao" of Liu Yao and the "Later Zhao" of Shi Le.) Bounded by the Yellow River on the south, his realm covered roughly the same territory as the modern provinces of Hebei and Shanxi and included no fewer than twenty-four commanderies.[15] To the south, Henan and Shandong were contested territory where Shi's generals campaigned against forces loyal to the Jin government and many of the local fortress chiefs felt compelled to offer allegiance to both sides at once.[16] The vicinity of Luoyang, meanwhile, was the point where the power of Shi Le confronted that of Liu Yao. Although the city was by this time no more than a shadow of the metropolis that it had been under Western Jin, geography dictated that it was still an extremely strategic location. Located near the end of the line of hills stretching eastward from the mountains at the entrance of the Wei River valley, it was in effect the easternmost outwork for the system of passes leading into the Guanzhong region. And the massive walls of the Jinyongcheng, the citadel of Luoyang, offered a convenient defensive bastion and a secure location to stockpile grain and other military stores. In 328 Liu Yao led a very large army out of the passes to take the former capital from Shi Le's forces. This he succeeded in doing, but only after a siege that lasted one hundred days. Judging that Liu's army had been seriously weakened, Shi Le swept down on Luoyang with the largest force that he could muster, reportedly 27,000 cavalry and 60,000 foot soldiers. Liu Yao was defeated and taken prisoner in a great battle outside the gates of the city, and his state unravelled with shocking speed as Shi Le's troops forced their way into Guanzhong in 329 and killed the heir apparent.[17] The destruction of Former Zhao left Shi Le's Later Zhao in possession of most of North China, including Shanxi, Guanzhong, and the entire central plain south to the line of the Huai River.[18] Despite its military success, however, Shi Le's state did not enjoy nearly the same degree of administrative control over its territory that earlier Chinese dynasties had done; its institutional foundations were extremely weak.

The regimes led by Liu Yuan, Shi Le, and their successors drew very sharp

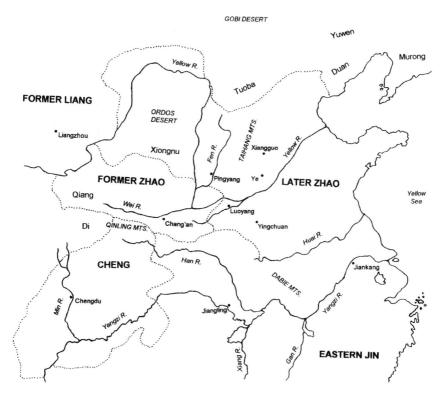

Map 4 North China in AD 327

distinctions between their Chinese and non-Chinese subjects, as did just about all of the later "barbarian" states that were founded in North China during the period of division. Still greatly outnumbered by their Han Chinese subjects in spite of the exodus to the south, the conquerors emphasized their separate identity in order to maintain control and resist absorption into the mass of the indigenous population. The Han–Former Zhao state of the Xiongnu Liu family formally assigned Chinese and non-Chinese to separate systems of administration in 314. In his capacity as emperor of Han, Liu Cong ruled over some 400,000 households of Chinese who were organized into units of 10,000 households. At the same time he gave his heir apparent the title of "Great Shanyu" (ruler) of the Xiongnu, placing him at the apex of a separate hierarchy of some 200,000 encampment groups (*luo*) of steppe origin, split into two great divisions and then into smaller units of 10,000 *luo*. Shi Le's Later Zhao employed a similar organizational scheme. The steppe people were the rulers and the warriors, and they alone bore the proud designation of "compatriots" (*guoren*) which identified them as citizens of the conquest regime. The Chinese, in contrast, were the subjects; they grew the grain, paid the taxes, and provided the labor power to support their barbarian masters.[19]

59

In these northern states the steppe people, who fought mainly as cavalry, formed the backbone of the army. Since all of their men were expected to be warriors, there was not much difference between the "barbarian" side of the administrative structure and the military establishment. The Great Shanyu, normally the designated heir to the imperial throne, commanded the army in the field.[20] The leaders of the groups of ten thousand carried military titles and acted as military commanders, while not just individuals but family groups were placed under the authority of military leaders. Families accompanied warriors when they were transferred from one place to another, and provided a manpower pool from which the strength of a fighting unit could be replenished as the need arose. Like the tribal organization of the steppe, this military structure could be easily expanded. Enemy generals who surrendered were given new titles but continued to lead their old followings and often remained in control of the same territories as before. Although the barbarians were certainly the dominant element in the armies of the various northern regimes, Han Chinese were by no means absent. Armies such as those of Liu Yao and Shi Le incorporated large numbers of Chinese. Some were captives taken in war, while others were conscripts raised from territories and populations under the control of the regime in question. In some armies, such as that which Shi Le led to Luoyang in 328, Han Chinese probably outnumbered the barbarian component. But the majority of the Chinese troops were used for relatively inglorious functions such as hauling supplies or constructing siege works. When they appeared on the battlefield it was almost always as infantry, far less valuable than the barbarian cavalry that constituted the main striking force of a northern army. In contrast to the steppe cavalry, the Chinese footsoldiers were seldom a permanent component of the military establishment. Conscripted only when needed, they were sent home again at the end of the campaign.[21]

As a consequence of the partial depopulation of North China, the various regimes that arose in the region during the age of division often placed greater value on the control of persons than the control of territory. During the fourth and fifth centuries empty cultivable land could be found in abundance in the north, while the labor power to make that land productive was often in short supply. Human populations, therefore, were prominent among the spoils of victory, and successful campaigns were frequently followed by the forcible transfer of thousands or even tens of thousands of people from the newly occupied areas to the core territories of the victor. In some cases military campaigns were little more than gigantic slave-raids, with the occupied territories being abandoned after the population had been removed.[22] Captives taken in this way tended to be concentrated in the vicinity of the victor's capital – such as Liu Cong's Pingyang, Liu Yao's Chang'an, and Shi Le's Xiangguo. Liu Cong, for example, had 80,000 people moved from Chang'an to Pingyang after his forces overran Guanzhong in 316, and when Shi Le captured the same area in 329 he reportedly had no less than 150,000 families of Di and Qiang relocated to the neighborhood of his own capital in southern Hebei. In the second half of the fourth century, the powerful Former Qin state based at Chang'an would reverse the flow and bring large numbers of people *into* Guanzhong from the eastern plains. Populations concentrated in and around the state capital were relatively easy to guard and control, and they were close at hand to provide for the needs of the regular military forces and their families, which were also concentrated in the capital area.[23] Control was much weaker outside of the capital. Outlying areas might be held by detached garrisons of the central army, or by local fortress chiefs who had been compelled or persuaded to offer their allegiance to the conquest regime.

Some authors have claimed that the Han–Former Zhao state founded by Liu Yuan and the Later Zhao state of Shi Le represented very different institutional types: while the well-educated, highly sinicized Liu family sought to establish an imperial dynasty after the Chinese model, Shi Le and his successors were simply the leaders of a bandit gang writ large, plundering and terrorizing the Chinese inhabitants of the north from the great armed camp at Xiangguo that they were pleased to call their "capital."[24] This distinction seems overdrawn. It ignores the many parallels between the institutional structures of the two states and the basic similarity of their modus operandi. Liu Cong's concentration of his forces at Pingyang and his exercise of control over surrounding areas from that base differed very little from what Shi Le was doing at Xiangguo. It is also important to consider the extent to which Shi Le adopted Chinese ritual and ceremonial forms in his rise to power, and the efforts that he made to coopt Chinese elites in the territories under his control. He brought Chinese officials to Xiangguo to set up a rudimentary administration, established schools to train a larger cadre of administrative personnel, and benefited from the wisdom of his Chinese advisor, Zhang Bin. Above all, Shi Le, like his counterparts in Pingyang and Chang'an, relied heavily on the cooperation of Chinese local elites – the fortress chiefs – to make his power effective in the outlying areas of his realm. When he captured forts, he made a point of bestowing appointments as generals or governors on the vanquished fortress chiefs and leaving them in place in the expectation that they would do his bidding in the future.[25]

With their extreme concentration of power at the center and their indirect rule over outlying areas through the Chinese fortress chiefs, both the Former and Later Zhao and most of the other barbarian regimes that were established in parts of North China were extremely fragile. Since the army and the state (or at least the part of the state that really mattered) were basically coterminous, a single catastrophic defeat suffered by the army on the battlefield could easily lead to the immediate collapse of the realm. This is precisely the fate that befall Liu Yao's Former Zhao when his army was destroyed at Luoyang in 328, and his regime would not be the last to end in this way. As conquest regimes established by barbarian chiefs on the basis of naked force, the northern states enjoyed very little legitimacy in the eyes of the Chinese who still constituted the majority of the population (especially when the Jin dynasty was still holding out in the south). Moreover, they were also resented by "captive" non-

Chinese populations who did not belong to the same ethnic group as the state's rulers. This was not necessarily an insurmountable problem as long as the rulers were able to maintain the effectiveness of their coercive apparatus. But should any weakness appear at the center, the outlying regions could easily slip away while captive populations in the vicinity of the capital deserted en masse. The instability of court politics in most of the northern states, and particularly the absence of clear, universally accepted rules regarding succession to the throne, meant that debilitating conflicts could arise quite frequently at the political center, creating the perfect opportunity for powerful centrifugal forces that had been only temporarily held in check.[26] Given these conditions, it should come as no surprise that many of the regimes that arose in North China during the fourth and fifth centuries lasted no more than a dozen years or so, and very few managed to survive for more than two or three generations.

The Later Zhao state saw a relatively orderly transfer of power after the death of Shi Le in 333. However, Shi's son and chosen successor was soon deposed and replaced on the throne by a cousin, Shi Hu, who had been the most successful of Shi Le's generals. The portrait of Shi Hu presented in the seventh-century *History of the Jin Dynasty* is very much in keeping with the traditional Confucian historian's stereotype of the "bad last emperor" who has forfeited Heaven's mandate through his misbehavior.[27] He is depicted as a man of enormous sensual appetites, addicted to the pleasures of the harem and the hunt, a brutal tyrant whose "actions were harsh and cruel." He put vast numbers of peasant labor conscripts to work on his palace complexes at Chang'an, Luoyang, and Ye (whence he had moved the capital from Xiangguo), imposing great hardships on the people, and even dug up the tombs of "the rulers and worthies of former times" to find the treasures that had been buried with them. When he quarrelled with his heir apparent, he had the young man, his consort, and his twenty-six children killed and buried together in a single coffin; then he proceeded to massacre more than two hundred members of the prince's entourage for good measure.[28] Despite the obvious bias, it is quite possible that all of these stories are true. Whatever his failings, however, Shi Hu was also a strong and effective ruler who was able to hold his state together for more than fifteen years.

The same cannot be said of his heirs. The succession struggle was underway even before the ailing Shi Hu had breathed his last in 349. His designated heir apparent lasted only 33 days on the throne; the brother who overthrew and killed him held out for 183 days, and his replacement in turn survived for 103 days.[29] The man who emerged as the kingmaker at the Zhao court during this whirl of palace coups was a certain Shi Min, who held the most important military command in the capital. Shi Min's father was a Chinese of good family who had been captured as a boy and brought up as an adopted son of Shi Hu, and Shi Min himself had been raised as a warrior in the milieu of the barbarian court. Shi Min soon deposed the last of Shi Hu's line and eliminated most of the surviving members of the Shi family, including thirty-eight grandsons of

Shi Hu. In 350 he took the throne for himself, reverting to his original Chinese surname of Ran and changing the name of the state to Wei. Even before this time, he had already asserted a bitter and vengeful Han identity and initiated a genocidal campaign against all of the barbarians in and around Ye. Particular targets were the Jie people, who had been closest to the Shi family and whose alien, Central Asian features made it impossible for them to pass as Chinese. Ran Min offered rewards to Chinese who brought in the heads of slain barbarians. "In the space of a single day, several tens of thousands were decapitated." Ran personally led the Han Chinese to massacre the barbarians, who were killed without regard for wealth, sex, or age. "The dead numbered more than 200,000. Corpses were piled outside the city walls, where they were all eaten by jackals, wolves, and wild dogs."[30] (Ran's ability to carry out this slaughter, incidentally, suggests that by this time a considerable number of Chinese fighting men had been incorporated into the central army of Later Zhao on a more or less permanent basis.) Some of the barbarian troops managed to escape by fighting their way through the gates of the city or jumping from the walls. The survivors rallied in the nearby city of Xiangguo and called for help from the Yan state of the Xianbei Murong clan and other barbarian forces in North China. Soon three armies totalling 100,000 men were converging on Ran Min's base at Ye.

The chaos and bloodshed at the center led very quickly to a complete loss of control over the outlying regions of the empire. Many regional governors declared their allegiance to the Jin emperor in the south, while others defected to the Murong. In Guanzhong, the local magnates killed the officials installed by Zhao, occupied more than thirty forts, raised 50,000 men, and called for help from the Jin armies.[31] The populations that had been forcibly relocated to the capital and other strategic centers of the Zhao state seized the opportunity to abscond en masse in an effort to return to their original homes. When the various groups of Han Chinese, Qiang, Di, and other ethnic groups encountered one another on the roads they turned to robbery and murder. Once the effects of hunger and disease had been added to the equation, perhaps "only two or three of every ten succeeded in reaching their destinations."[32] Against this dismal background of societal collapse, Ran Min was brought to battle, defeated, captured, and put to death by the forces of Murong Jun of Former Yan, who was pushing southward into Hebei from his original base in southern Manchuria.

The Murong took advantage of their victory over Ran Min in 352 to annex core areas of the Zhao state in central and southern Hebei, extending their control as far as the Yellow River. They continued their expansion, now at the expense of Jin, in the years that followed. The capital was moved to Ye in 357, and by the time of Murong Jun's death in 360 his Yan state had spread south of the Yellow River to include Shandong, much of Henan, and parts of northern Anhui. A Yan offensive against Jin reached the Huai River in 364, and Luoyang was captured the following year.[33] The Murong state was by no means the only beneficiary of Zhao's collapse, however. Under a strong and long-lived leader named Shiyijian, the Tuoba people who occupied the steppe margin around today's Datong in northern Shanxi were also extending the territory under their control. Like their fellow Xianbei of the Murong clan, the Tuoba benefited from a strong tribal organization and a relatively clear set of rules governing succession to the throne. Subjugated non-Tuoba groups were easily incorporated into the system as dependent clans and tribes. By about 366, the Tuoba claimed that they commanded several hundred thousand mounted archers and their rich pastures supported a million horses.[34] A third group to benefit from the new situation, the Di people of Guanzhong, did not enjoy the same tradition of political independence as the Tuoba and the Murong. During the chaos of the early fourth century, a Di chief named Fu Hong gathered a strong following among his people. He gave his support first to Liu Yao and then to Shi Hu, who relocated very large numbers of Di and Qiang – including Fu Hong and his followers – from Guanzhong to the plains of Henan and Hebei. After Shi Hu died, Fu and his people, 100,000 strong, resolved to reclaim their homeland in the west. In order to accomplish this they first had to defeat a rival force of Qiang exiles who were marching west with the same intention, and after they had entered the passes they had to evict a renegade Zhao general from Chang'an. With these obstacles overcome, Fu Hong's son proclaimed himself king of Qin in 351 and took the title of emperor the following year. In 354 the nascent Di state in the Wei River valley repulsed an invasion by Jin forces from Henan, and within a few more years this vigorous new power was expanding its control in all directions.[35]

This state, known to historians as "Former Qin," saw both the apogee of its power and a sudden, irremediable collapse under the leadership of Fu Jian, a grandson of Fu Hong and nephew of the Qin founder who seized the throne from a cousin in 357. A vigorous, capable leader with tremendous drive and ambition, Fu Jian subjugated the wandering Qiang groups led by the Yao family in the same year that he took the throne. In 370 he sent his armies to invade the Murong state of Yan. His general and prime minister, Wang Meng, a Han who had risen from humble origins, defeated the Yan army in battle and captured Ye, the Murong capital, before the year was out. The conquest of Yan brought a great increase in the territory and population under Qin control, a gain amounting to 157 districts and a registered population of 2,460,000 households (or 9,990,000 individuals).[36] In 373, Qin forces struck in the opposite direction and seized almost all of Sichuan from the Jin dynasty. Three years later it was the turn of the Liang state northwest of the Yellow River and the Tuoba state of Dai to fall victim to Qin expansion. By 381, Fu Jian had united all of North China under his own rule and was pressing against the Jin empire in the south.[37]

The Di people must at first have seemed unlikely candidates for the role of military hegemon in North China. Unlike the Xiongnu and the Xianbei, the Di did not have a tradition of strong tribal organization under an aristocratic

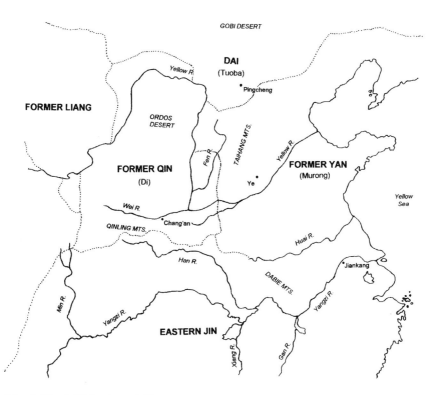

Map 5 North China in AD 366

central leadership, but were accustomed to being governed by a rather large number of independent petty chiefs. While the pastoral economy of the Xiongnu and Xianbei was based to a large extent on horsebreeding, the Di tended to be shepherds and agriculturalists. They were more sedentary in their ways than their neighbors the Qiang, mingled more with the Han Chinese, and readily adoped many Chinese practices. In contrast to most of the other non-Han peoples, many of the Di fought as foot soldiers rather than cavalry.[38] It has been suggested that the weakness of tribal organization among the Di was actually a source of competitive advantage in that it permitted Fu Jian to create a bureaucratic state structure in which appointment and promotion were based on merit.[39] An alternative explanation for the meteoric rise of the Qin regime might point not to the customs of the Di people or the institutions established by Fu Jian and his collaborators, but to the element of contingency in the disorderly period after Shi Hu's death and the power of self-reinforcing feedback loops to perpetuate existing trends once chance has given history a nudge in a particular direction. The initial Di successes in the early 350s may have been the result of superior leadership, luck, or the presence of the Di in superior numbers at the decisive points; thereafter, success built on success as the leaders of Qin incorporated defeated peoples into their own military machine. This process was facilitated by Fu Jian's willingness to assign members of the defeated ruling elites to high military and regional offices within his own power structure, and by the unwillingness of Chinese local officials and fortress chiefs to go to the wall for barbarian rulers who appeared to be losing. "It finally became the rule that as soon as a conquest was complete the loyalty obligations of the subjects to the conquered rulers ceased and went over to the conquerors."[40] All of this worked very well for Fu Jian as long as he continued to be perceived as a winner, but could easily produce a very different dynamic should he suffer a serious and obvious reverse.

The Qin state had a number of deep structural weaknesses, most of which were shared with many of the other non-Han regimes that made transient appearances in North China during the fourth century. Like the rulers of Later Zhao, Fu Jian moved defeated peoples to the vicinity of his capital in very large numbers. There were at least 100,000 households altogether, including the Qiang who had surrendered in 357 and the 40,000 households of Xianbei who were brought from Yan after 370.[41] Though the intention was that they could be more easily controlled in close proximity to the seat of power, they also represented a serious potential threat should the military strength of the Di people begin to wane. Another weakness of the Qin regime was its failure to break the power of the fortress chiefs, who continued to keep large numbers of peasants beyond the reach of the state's taxation and corvée systems.[42] And these local leaders were another potentially hostile force should the center begin to weaken. From time to time there were signs of unrest. In outlying areas, local rebellions arose among the Xiongnu in 366, the Qiang in 367, and the native tribes of Sichuan in 374. All of these risings were put down quickly and without too much difficulty, but at the center of power the ruling Fu clan itself was prone to internal divisions. In 367–8 Fu Jian had to put down an armed revolt by four of his close kinsmen whom he had appointed to regional commands, and another Fu cousin, objecting to a reassignment to Sichuan, rebelled in northern Hebei in 380.[43] The Qin state dealt with these challenges easily enough, but when it suffered a major defeat in a "foreign" war against the Jin dynasty in 383 the entire edifice immediately began to crumble.

Fu Jian's forces had begun to apply serious pressure to the core areas of the Eastern Jin state along the middle and lower reaches of the Yangzi in 378, when the Qin ruler sent his son Fu Pi to besiege the fortress of Xiangyang on the Han River, gateway to the central Yangzi region. After a year-long siege, Xiangyang fell early in 379. About the same time, other Qin forces seized several strongholds along the Huai River and threatened the Jin capital of Jiankang on the lower Yangzi. A Jin counterattack soon drove the Qin armies back to the north side of Huai, but the situation remained precarious. In the summer of 383 a Jin army attempted to recover Xiangyang, but was driven off by a Qin relief column of 50,000 men. Fu Jian responded to this challenge by launching a new military campaign against the southern court. According to the "Chronicle of Fu Jian" in the *History of the Jin Dynasty*, this involved a

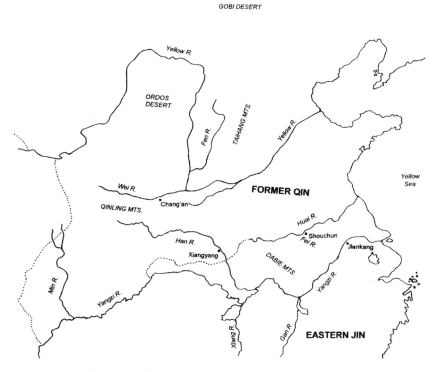

Map 6 North China in AD 383

mobilization on an unprecedented scale. We are told that the army that marched from Chang'an under the command of Fu Jian himself included 270,000 cavalry and 600,000 infantry, obtained by conscripting one out of every ten of the empire's registered adult males; "for a thousand *li* from front to rear, their banners and drums were in each other's view."[44] The army's vanguard was 250,000 strong, and separate columns were to push downstream from Sichuan to the west and advance from the lower reaches of the Huai in the east. "For a myriad *li* from east to west, they advanced together by water and land." The main effort was directed against Shouchun on the Huai River (east of Xiangyang), which fell to the Qin vanguard under Fu Rong in the lunar tenth month of 383. A Qin force of 50,000 men then moved east along the south side of the Huai to take up an advanced position along Luo Creek, a north-flowing tributary of the Huai, in order to block a Jin army of 70,000 approaching from the east. A night attack on this position by only 5000 Jin troops inflicted 15,000 casualties, including the Qin commander, and routed the survivors. The Jin army continued its advance and confronted a much larger Qin force under Fu Rong across the Fei River. Unable to assault this strong position, the Jin commander sent an envoy across the river to suggest that Fu pull back and allow him to cross, on the grounds that it was in the best interest of the invading army to seek a quick decision rather than a lengthy stalemate. Fu Rong consented, but in the expectation that he would be able to attack the Jin army when it was most vulnerable, before it had completed the river crossing. As soon as he signalled the withdrawal, however, his army collapsed in a panic-stricken rout. Fu Rong himself was killed in the stampede. The panic was soon communicated to the main body of the Qin host, which unravelled in short order and joined the flight.

The battle of the Fei River is usually considered one of the most decisive military encounters in all of Chinese history, since it is credited with bringing about the downfall of Fu Jian's empire and ensuring the survival of the émigré regime at Jiankang. However, almost all of our knowledge of the event is drawn from a single text, the "Chronicle of Fu Jian" in the *History of the Jin Dynasty*. As Michael C. Rogers has demonstrated, this is anything but an objective work of history. It contains strong fictional and mythic elements and was written and rewritten so as to serve not one but two distinct political agendas. According to Rogers, the chronicle was not based on authentic archival materials from Former Qin but was fabricated in the south to emphasize the accomplishments of Xie An, the statesman who dominated the court at Jiankang in 383 and claimed credit for the victory, and to promote a mystique of the inviolability of the "legitimate" imperial regime based in the south. A second politically motivated overlay was added in the middle of the seventh century, when the *History of the Jin Dynasty* received its final redaction at the hands of official historians at the court of the second Tang emperor. Seeking to dissuade Tang Taizong from military adventures in the Korean peninsula, these scholar-officials exaggerated both the grandeur of Fu Jian's endeavor and the magnitude of his defeat. Rogers has suggested that the actual clash of arms may have been limited to the relatively small preliminary encounter at Luo Creek, with the Fei River battle presented in the chronicle being no more than a simulacrum of this real – and more or less insignificant – event. Rogers concludes that "there is at least a nucleus of fact that cannot be gainsaid. We have no reason to doubt 1) that a Chin [Jin] counter-offensive in 383 dislodged a Ch'in [Qin] force from Shou-ch'un, which the invaders had occupied for only a matter of days, and drove them back north of the Huai, and 2) that the Ch'in empire fell apart cataclysmically shortly after that event."[45] He chooses to reject the traditional view that there was a direct causal relationship between the battle and the Qin collapse, pointing instead to "internal tensions" as the primary reason for Fu Jian's downfall.[46]

However, even if we discount the evidence of the "Chronicle of Fu Jian," which draws a clear and direct connection between the Fei River battle and the collapse of Former Qin, the fact that so many subject peoples rose in revolt so soon after the military setback on the Huai suggests that the two events were not entirely unrelated. If Fu Jian had indeed taken the field in person, even relatively small reverses such as the Luo Creek engagement and the loss of Shouchun might have damaged the Di ruler's prestige to the extent that the leaders of other ethnic groups were encouraged to rebel against him. And if the losses in these encounters were concentrated among Fu Jian's most loyal and reliable Di troops, as Chen Yinke suggested, the impact would have been even greater.[47] Once subordinate leaders had made up their minds to rebel, Fu Jian's generous policy of appointing the chiefs of defeated peoples to high military commands and allowing them to retain control of forces composed of their own people guaranteed that they would have the means to do so. The first to turn against Fu Jian were members of the Murong family that had ruled the Former Yan state. Murong Chui, who had apparently commanded an independent column west of Shouchun during the 383 campaign, marched into Hebei and succeeded in recovering most of the territory that his family had once ruled; in 386 he proclaimed himself emperor of what came to be known as "Later Yan." In the meantime, other members of the Murong family were operating farther west, in Shanxi and Guanzhong, where they besieged Fu Jian in his capital, Chang'an, in 384–5. Fu managed to escape when the city fell, only to be intercepted and killed by another rebel chief, the Qiang leader Yao Chang, who had once governed Sichuan for the Former Qin. Yao proclaimed himself emperor of Qin in 386 and began to consolidate his control over the whole of Guanzhong. This task was completed by his son Yao Xing, who defeated and killed Fu Jian's last heir in 394. Somewhat farther afield, the Tuoba regained their independence in the Dai region of northern Shanxi, and a Xianbei chieftain named Tufu Guoren established a "Western Qin" state in what is now Gansu. To the northwest of Western Qin, the Later Liang state was founded in the Gansu corridor by Lü Guang, a Di general whom Fu Jian had earlier sent to conquer the oasis states of the Tarim basin. In the aftermath of the collapse of Former Qin, the north was more politically fractured than it had been at any time since the fall of Western Jin.[48]

The Eastern Jin government at Jiankang took advantage of the disorder in the north to recover a large expanse of territory. Xiangyang was taken in 384, and in the following year Jin armies regained all of Sichuan in the west and advanced their northern border to the Yellow River. Some of the southern forces crossed the river into Hebei at this time, but they were soon recalled by a leadership satisfied with the huge gains that had already been made and more intent on the security of the south than the reunification of the empire.[49] This left the field clear for the various Qin successor states to contend for mastery in the north. The two that eventually emerged as the strongest were the Later Yan state founded by Murong Chui and the revived Tuoba kingdom, which had changed its name from Dai to Wei in 386. At first the two states were partners rather than rivals. Under pressure from hostile Xiongnu groups, the youthful Wei leader Tuoba Gui offered his allegiance to Murong Chui and received badly needed military assistance from the more powerful Later Yan state. With Yan backing, Tuoba Gui was able to defeat the Xiongnu challenge and incorporate many of the vanquished tribesmen into his own following. During the next few years, he concentrated on securing the rear of the Wei state by establishing his dominance over the nomadic peoples inhabiting the vast steppe region from the Greater Xingan mountains in the east to the great bend of the Yellow River in the west. In 388–9 he defeated the Kumoxi, Jieru, and Tutulin in the east, and in 390–1 he campaigned north of the Yellow River and defeated the Gaoju, Yuange, Helan, Gexi, Getulin, Chinu, and Chufu. Then, in 391–2, he defeated the Xiongnu who had been dwelling in the Hetao region south of the Yellow River bend and added that valuable territory to the Wei kingdom. These victories over the steppe nomads yielded livestock, slaves, and other booty that could be used to reward the Tuoba warriors and cement their loyalty to the Wei state. And when Tuoba Gui began to contend for control of North China, he was in a uniquely advantageous position as master of the steppe and its resources.[50]

The partnership between the Tuoba of Wei and the Murong of Yan began to turn sour in 391, when the former refused to send the latter a tribute of horses, and by 394 Tuoba Gui was ready to turn his attention away from the steppe to compete with Yan for dominance in North China. According to Kenneth Klein,

> The question late in the year 394 then became whether the Murong were to be able to use their established state power to destroy the Tuoba, as the last marginal power between the cultivated fields of China and the open steppe, or whether the Tuoba were themselves to be able to compete successfully for the rule of a new agrarian empire from their position of dominance over the steppe.[51]

In the summer of 395, Murong Chui sent his heir apparent, Murong Bao, with a powerful army to attack Wei. Rather than confronting this challenge head-on, Tuoba Gui chose to lead his people several hundred miles to the west, into the Hetao region on the other side of the Yellow River. After overrunning the Wei capital region and capturing more than 30,000 families of Tuoba subjects, Murong Bao advanced to the east bank of the Yellow River. For the next several months, the two armies confronted each other across the stream. During this period, the Tuoba leader showed greater initiative by sending strong forces to the opposite bank to cut off segments of the Yan army and threaten its line of communications. With the onset of winter, Murong Bao began to retreat. Tuoba Gui pursued the Yan army with a fast column of cavalry and overtook his quarry at a place called Shenhe Slope, northwest of Horinger in today's Inner Mongolia. The Yan commander had taken few security precautions and was thus caught entirely by surprise when the Wei cavalry stormed into his camp on December 8, 395. The Yan army was routed with very heavy casualties, and Murong Bao was able to get away with only a few thousand men. This defeat was a heavy blow, but the Murong state had by no means reached the end of its strength. In the spring of 396, the aged Yan ruler Murong Chui personally led a new army into Wei's territory. An unwary

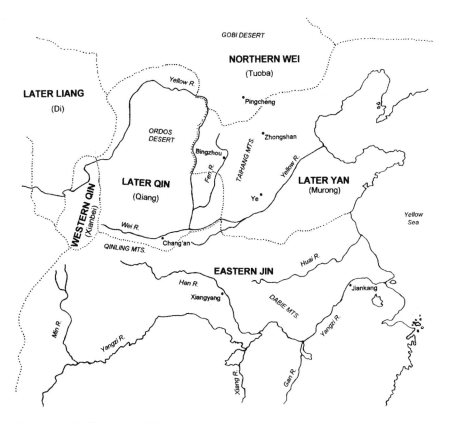

Map 7 North China in AD 395

Tuoba force was defeated near the Wei center of Pingcheng. But the Yan offensive came to an abrupt end when Murong Chui fell ill and died in his camp in the fourth lunar month of 396. It seems to have been the death of the Yan leader, much more than the battle at Shenhe Slope, that turned the tide of the war. From the summer of 396 the initiative clearly belonged to Tuoba Gui. Bingzhou in central Shanxi fell to Tuoba forces in the autumn, even as other Wei armies were crossing the Taihang mountains to invade the core Yan territories in Hebei. The Murong stubbornly defended their major centers, the capital at Zhongshan (modern Dingxian, Hebei) and the great city of Ye farther south, and remained capable of inflicting local reverses on the invaders in 397. Eventually, however, the Wei forces prevailed, with Zhongshan falling into their hands near the end of 397 and Ye at the beginning of 398. Remnants of the vanquished Murong clan kept a rump Later Yan state alive in southern Manchuria, while another group of fugitives founded a "Southern Yan" south of the Yellow River in today's Shandong province.[52]

Wei's expansionist efforts abated for a time after the conquest of Yan, and especially after the death of Tuoba Gui in 409. His son and successor, Tuoba Si, who ruled until 423, was fond of Chinese poetry and literature and seemed to lack the martial drive of earlier Tuoba leaders. During his reign there were no major wars and only two campaigns against the nomadic Rouran in the north.[53] His successor, Tuoba Tao (known posthumously as Emperor Taiwu), was a very different character. According to the great eleventh-century historian Sima Guang,

> The lord of Wei was stalwart and courageous in his behavior. When confronting a fortress wall or an enemy formation he braved the stones and arrows himself. With the men on both sides of him falling dead and wounded one after another, he wore an expression that was no different from usual. On account of this the officers and men stood in awe of him, all of them exerting themselves to the utmost.[54]

Beginning in 430, he undertook a series of campaigns against the remaining independent states in North China. The most important of these were the Xiongnu kingdom of Xia in today's Shaanxi province, which had absorbed many of the territories that had been held by Qiang and Xianbei groups after the fall of Fu Jian's Former Qin; the state of Northern Yan, now ruled by Han Chinese who had supplanted the Murong; and the Xiongnu Northern Liang state in today's Gansu province. The first to fall was Xia, which succumbed to Wei military pressure in 431. The next to go was Northern Yan, which managed to hold out until 436. With the conquest of Northern Liang in 439, Tuoba Tao finally succeeded in uniting all of China north of the Yellow River for the first time since the collapse of Fu Jian's empire more than half a century before.

In addition to good military leadership and a fair amount of good luck, the Wei conquest of Later Yan and the various other states in North China was facilitated by several factors. The first and most obvious of these was the Tuoba's domination of the open steppe, which allowed them to draw upon its considerable resources to support operations elsewhere. Members of defeated tribes were incorporated into the Wei forces, and the steppe also provided the Wei armies with horses in very large numbers. In 391, for example, the Tuoba reportedly acquired 300,000 horses after crushing a single hostile tribe.[55] This number may be an exaggeration, but there can be little doubt that Wei control of the steppe enabled Tuoba Gui and his successors to field cavalry forces that were superior to those of their opponents. The Wei conquests were also facilitated by the timely deaths of a number of elderly leaders in rival states, which left the leadership in the hands of less capable and experienced successors.[56] The most obvious and important example of this was the death of Murong Chui in 396, but Tuoba Tao benefited from the same phenomenon in the 430s. The founder of Xia had died in 424 (or 425), the founder of Northern Yan in 430, and the ruler of Northern Liang in 433. Once their conquests had been accomplished, the Wei leaders proved more skillful than other barbarian rulers in winning the loyalty of the defeated peoples. Like many of their predecessors such as Shi Le, the Wei rulers distinguished between a core element in their state, the so-called "compatriots" (*guoren*), and the mass of ordinary subjects. Almost all military commands and other positions of real power and authority were held by compatriots. Initially the designation seems to have been limited to the ruling clan and closely related groups, but the circle was later widened to include the elites of many of the defeated peoples. The Tuoba carefully cultivated marriage ties with fallen ruling houses, taking women of the Murong, Yao, and other such groups as royal consorts. Members of these families were admitted to the compatriot elite and received titles and government offices. Intermarriage also occurred with important Chinese clans.[57] Gradually, over the course of more than a century, a vigorous mixed-blood elite emerged in North China that could trace its descent not only from the Tuoba and other Xianbei groups, but also from Xiongnu, Qiang, Han Chinese, and many other peoples. It was this stratum that gave birth to the ruling group that reunited north and south under the authority of the Sui dynasty at the end of the sixth century, and its members continued to dominate the empire's political and military leadership for at least the first half of the Tang period.

Notes

1   Yang, "Notes on the Economic History of the Chin Dynasty," pp. 126–7; Chen Yinke, *Wei Jin Nanbeichao shi jiangyanlu*, arr. by Wan Shengnan, pp. 113–14.
2   Wang Zhongluo, *Wei Jin Nanbeichao shi*, vol. 1, p. 223.
3   Wang Zhongluo, *Wei Jin Nanbeichao shi*, vol. 1, p. 228.
4   Yang, "Notes on the Economic History of the Chin Dynasty," p. 127; also see Holcombe, *In the Shadow of the Han: Literati Thought and Society at the Beginning of the Southern Dynasties*, p. 27.
5   For one example, see the biography of Zu Ti in Fang Xuanling et al., *Jin shu*, ch. 62, p. 1694.
6   *Jin shu*, ch. 88, p. 2283; as translated by Holcombe, *In the Shadow of the Han*, p. 49.
7   He Ziquan, *Wei Jin Nanbeichao shilue*, pp. 80–1; Chen Yinke, *Wei Jin Nanbeichao shi jiangyanlu*, p. 135; Tang Changru, "Jindai beijing ge zu 'bianluan' de xingzhi ji Wu Hu zhengquan zai Zhongguo de tongzhi," pp. 173, 181, 183; *Jin shu*, ch. 104, pp. 2711–12.
8   Tang Changru, "Jindai beijing ge zu 'bianluan' de xingzhi ji Wu Hu zhengquan zai Zhongguo de tongzhi," pp. 168, 172–3, 187; and Jin Fagen, *Yongjia luan hou beifang de haozu* (Taipei: Taiwan Commercial Press, 1964), pp. 91–3. For examples of local conflicts, see *Jin shu*, ch. 62, p. 1695.
9   Kenneth Douglas Klein, "The Contributions of the Fourth Century Xianbei States to the Reunification of the Chinese Empire" (Ph.D. dissertation, University of California Los Angeles, 1980), pp. 24–5, 27, 29, 34.
10 Jennifer Holmgren, *Annals of Tai: Early T'o-pa History According to the First Chapter of the Wei-shu* (Canberra: Australian National University Press, 1982), pp. 11, 29–33; Li Tse-fen, *Liang Jin Nanbeichao lishi lunwenji*, vol. 1, p. 132.
11 Li Tse-fen, *Liang Jin Nanbeichao lishi lunwenji*, vol. 1, pp. 113–14.
12 Li Tse-fen, *Liang Jin Nanbeichao lishi lunwenji*, vol. 1, pp. 127–8.

13 *Jin shu*, ch. 104, p. 2707; Tamura Jitsuzo, *Chūgoku shijō no minzoku idō ki*, pp. 34–5. The Jie were a non-Chinese people associated with the Xiongnu. According to some sources, they had Caucasian physical characteristics such as deep-set eyes, high noses, and abundant facial hair, suggesting a Central Asian or Iranian origin. Whether Shi Le was really a Jie or a Xiongnu, and the exact nature of the relationship between the two, is still a matter of disagreement. See David B. Honey, "Lineage as Legitimation in the Rise of Liu Yüan and Shih Le," *Journal of the American Oriental Society*, 110.4 (October–December 1990), pp. 618–20.

14 Tang Changru, "Jindai beijing ge zu 'bianluan' de xingzhi ji Wu Hu zhengquan zai Zhongguo de tongzhi," pp. 153–4.

15 *Jin shu*, ch. 104, p. 2730.

16 *Jin shu*, ch. 105, pp. 2738–9.

17 Dien, "The Stirrup and its Effect on Chinese Military History," p. 39; *Jin shu*, ch. 105, pp. 2744–5; Sima Guang, *Zizhi tongjian*, ch. 94, pp. 2963–5.

18 He Ziquan, *Wei Jin Nanbeichao shilue*, pp. 90–1.

19 For the structure of the northern states, see Chen Yinke, *Wei Jin Nanbeichao shi jiangyanlu*, pp. 108–9; Tang Changru, "Jindai beijing ge zu 'bianluan' de xingzhi ji Wu Hu zhengquan zai Zhongguo de tongzhi," pp. 158–64; and *Zhongguo junshi shi*, vol. 3: *Bingzhi*, p. 175. Kenneth Klein should be credited for the translation of *guoren* as "compatriot."

20 Zhou Weizhou, *Han Zhao guo shi* (Taiyuan: Shanxi renmin chubanshe, 1986), p. 187.

21 *Zhongguo junshi shi*, vol. 3, pp. 176–83.

22 Li Tse-fen, *Liang Jin Nanbeichao lishi lunwenji*, vol. 2, pp. 241–2. For examples of population removals carried out by Shi Le's forces, see *Jin shu*, ch. 104, pp. 2724, 2725, and ch. 105, pp. 2741 and 2745.

23 Chen Yinke, *Wei Jin Nanbeichao shi jiangyanlu*, pp. 110, 128–33; *Jin shu*, ch. 105, p. 2745.

24 See, for example, Wolfram Eberhard, *Conquerors and Rulers: Social Forces in Medieval China*, 2nd edition revised (Leiden: E. J. Brill, 1965), pp. 122–3.

25 He Ziquan, *Wei Jin Nanbeichao shilue*, p. 89. For examples of Shi Le's use of Chinese forms and his promotion of Chinese-style education, see *Jin shu*, ch. 104, pp. 2720, 2729, and ch. 105, p. 2735.

26 For a discussion of the succession problem, see Klein, "The Contributions of the Fourth Century Xianbei States to the Reunification of the Chinese Empire," p. 30.

27 For a discussion of the "bad last emperor" stereotype, see Arthur F. Wright, "Sui Yang-Ti: Personality and Stereotype," in idem (ed.), *The Confucian Persuasion* (Stanford, Ca.: Stanford University Press, 1960), pp. 47–76.

28 *Jin shu*, ch. 106, pp. 2761, 2767, 2772, and ch. 107, pp. 2781–2.

29 This paragraph is based on chapter 107 of the *Jin shu*, especially pp. 2788–94.

30 *Jin shu*, ch. 107, pp. 2791–2.

31 *Jin shu*, ch. 107, pp. 2790, 2796.

32 *Jin shu*, ch. 107, p. 2795.

33 Michael C. Rogers, *The Chronicle of Fu Chien: A Case of Exemplar History*, pp. 7–8; Li Tse-fen, *Liang Jin Nanbeichao lishi lunwenji*, vol. 1, p. 95.

34 Wei Shou, *Wei shu* (Beijing: Zhonghua shuju, 1974), ch. 24, p. 609; Holmgren, *Annals of Tai*, pp. 118–19; Klein, "The Contributions of the Fourth Century Xianbei States to the Reunification of the Chinese Empire," pp. 32–3; He Ziquan, *Wei Jin Nanbeichao shilue*, p. 106.

35 Li Tse-fen, *Liang Jin Nanbeichao lishi lunwenji*, vol. 1, pp. 101–2. Fu Hong died in 350, before his people entered the promised land.

36 Gerhard Schreiber, "The History of the Former Yen Dynasty," *Monumenta Serica*,

15 (1956), p. 117; for Wang Meng, see Li Tse-fen, *Liang Jin Nanbeichao lishi lunwenji*, vol. 1, p. 103.

37 He Ziquan, *Wei Jin Nanbeichao shilue*, p. 95.

38 Eberhard, *Conquerors and Rulers*, p. 124; Richard B. Mather, *Biography of Lü Kuang* (Berkeley and Los Angeles: University of California Press, 1959), p. 11; Jiang Fuya, *Qian Qin shi* (Beijing: Beijing shifan xueyuan chubanshe, 1993), pp. 7–10.

39 Klein, "The Contributions of the Fourth Century Xianbei States to the Reunification of the Chinese Empire," pp. 36–9.

40 Schreiber, "The History of the Former Yen Dynasty," p. 126; also pp. 111 and 123.

41 Wang Zhongluo, *Wei Jin Nanbeichao shi*, vol. 1, p. 276.

42 Jiang Fuya, *Qian Qin shi*, pp. 84–6.

43 For the various revolts, see Rogers, *The Chronicle of Fu Chien*, pp. 122–5, 137, 146–8.

44 Michael C. Rogers, "The Myth of the Battle of the Fei River," *T'oung Pao*, 54 (1968), p. 64. For the earlier Qin operations against Jin, see Lü Simian, *Liang Jin Nanbeichao shi* (Shanghai: Shanghai Guji chubanshe, 1983), p. 226.

45 Rogers, *The Chronicle of Fu Chien*, p. 62.

46 Rogers, "The Myth of the Battle of the Fei River," p. 71; also see *The Chronicle of Fu Chien*, p. 3.

47 Chen Yinke, *Wei Jin Nanbeichao shi jiangyanlu*, p. 233.

48 He Ziquan, *Wei Jin Nanbeichao shilue*, p. 103. For more detailed treatment of the political history of this period, see Li Tse-fen, *Liang Jin Nanbeichao lishi lunwenji*, vol. 1, pp. 96–116. For Lü Guang's career, see Mather, *Biography of Lü Kuang*.

49 Wang Zhongluo, *Wei Jin Nanbeichao shi*, vol. 1, pp. 283–5.

50 Klein, "The Contributions of the Fourth Century Xianbei States to the Reunification of the Chinese Empire," p. 105; also pp. 53–6, 67.

51 Klein, "The Contributions of the Fourth Century Xianbei States to the Reunification of the Chinese Empire," p. 65.

52 For a summary of these events, see Klein, "The Contributions of the Fourth Century Xianbei States to the Reunification of the Chinese Empire," pp. 69–72; a more detailed treatment can be found in Li Tse-fen, *Liang Jin Nanbeichao lishi lunwenji*, vol. 1, pp. 137–44. For the battle of Shenhe Slope, see Sima Guang, *Zizhi tongjian*, ch. 108, p. 3424.

53 Li Tse-fen, *Liang Jin Nanbeichao lishi lunwenji*, vol. 1, pp. 145–6.

54 Sima Guang, *Zizhi tongjian*, ch. 120, p. 3796.

55 Mao Han-kuang, "Bei Wei Dong Wei Bei Qi zhi hexin jituan yu hexin qu," in idem, *Zhongguo zhonggu zhengzhi shi lun* (Taipei: Lianjing, 1990), pp. 40–1.

56 Klein, "The Contributions of the Fourth Century Xianbei States to the Re-unification of the Chinese Empire," p. 93.

57 Klein, "The Contributions of the Fourth Century Xianbei States to the Re-unification of the Chinese Empire," pp. 95, 103. Also see Mao Han-kuang, "Bei Wei Dong Wei Bei Qi zhi hexin jituan yu hexin qu," pp. 42–4.

CHAPTER FOUR

The south under émigré rule

Although they had first been incorporated into the Chinese empire by the first emperor of Qin more than five hundred years earlier, the vast territories south of the Yangzi River confronted northern refugees fleeing the collapse of Western Jin with much that was strange and unfamiliar. In contrast to the densely settled plains through which the Yellow River flowed, the south must have seemed a raw, peripheral, and relatively empty land. Population figures from the middle of the second century AD gave the south only about 35 percent of the registered population of the empire, even though it accounted for considerably more than half of the total land area.[1] The southern population gained ground relative to that of the north over the next two centuries, thanks in large part to successive waves of migration, but the south would long continue to be the less populous half of the Chinese ecumene. The Han Chinese inhabitants of this region were not scattered evenly across the face of the land, but were for the most part tightly concentrated in several major centers of population. One of these centers was the region immediately to the southwest of the mouth of the Yangzi, including the rich, well-watered agricultural lands around Lake Tai and Hangzhou Bay. This was the heart of the Wu kingdom during the Three Kingdoms period, and in earlier times it had been the territory of the ancient states of Wu and Yue. The core of Jin's Yang province, this region had its own landholding elite families and its people spoke a dialect distinct from that of the north. It was here, at Jiankang on the south bank of the great river, that the Jin émigré elite of the early fourth century chose to establish their capital. The other major center was located upstream, where the Han River enters the Yangzi from the north. This region – Jing province for administrative purposes – included a number of important towns such as Jiangling on the Yangzi and Xiangyang on the Han. Also part of Jing province was the well-populated valley of the Xiang River to the south, in what is now Hunan. A lesser center was the area that became known as Jiang province, stretching south from Wuchang and Xunyang (today's Jiujiang) on the Yangzi past the Boyang Lake to the valley of the Gan River. The distant cities of Panyu (Canton) and Jiaozhi (today's Hanoi) on the southern side of the Nanling range were less prominent as centers of Han settlement but played

76

an important role in Chinese trade and other contacts with the peoples of Southeast Asia.

All of these major Chinese settlement areas were situated in low-lying plains and river valleys where the terrain was well suited to the cultivation of rice in flooded paddy fields. Between them lay vast expanses of forested hills and mountains inhabited by aboriginal peoples such as the Man, Liao, Li, and Xi, most of whom had yet to be assimilated to the Chinese way of of life. In this warm, watery, mountainous, and heavily forested environment, so different from the dusty plains of the north, the Yangzi River and its major tributaries such as the Han, Xiang, and Gan rivers were the threads that connected the various Chinese centers of the south to one another. Travel and trade tended to

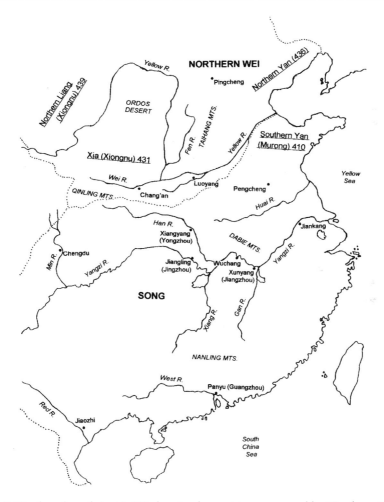

Map 8 North and south in AD 464 showing lesser states conquered by Northern Wei and Song

follow the rivers, and so too did military operations. Ever since the days of the rival kingdoms of Chu, Wu, and Yue, long before the unification of the empire by Qin, the men of the south had specialized in waterborne combat on their lakes and rivers. This tradition was continued in the Three Kingdoms period with much larger and more elaborate vessels outfitted with more sophisticated weapons, and the maintenance and employment of naval forces remained an important element in the warfare of all of the southern dynasties based at Jiankang.

In contrast to North China, which was divided and re-divided among a bewildering profusion of barbarian statelets, the south held together as a single realm for the entire period from the founding of Eastern Jin in 317 to the northern conquest of Chen in 589. From beginning to end the southern state included all of the Chinese territories south of the Yangzi, but its northern and northwestern boundaries varied greatly over time. The Sichuan basin was first incorporated into the southern realm in 347. It was then lost to Fu Jian's Former Qin in 373, recovered in 385, and finally lost to Western Wei in 553. The northern border sometimes ran along the Huai River, about eighty miles north of Jiankang, but this was not always the case. In the first half of the fifth century the southern court was able to extend its control as far as the Yellow River, incorporating most of today's provinces of Shandong and Henan. By 572, on the other hand, it had lost everything north of the Yangzi. From 317 almost down to the fall of Jiankang, the territory between the Yellow River and the Yangzi was the main arena of armed contention between north and south.

While the Chinese of the south managed to retain a semblance of unity, albeit within shifting boundaries, they did not remain subject to the same ruling family for the entire length of the north–south division. There were five southern dynasties, some of which lasted little more than a single generation. In 420 the Eastern Jin dynasty founded by Sima Rui was replaced by the Song dynasty of Liu Yu; in 479 Song in turn gave way to the Qi dynasty, in 502 Qi yielded to Liang, and in 557 Liang was succeeded by the last of the southern dynasties, the Chen. Not all of these dynasties came to power by overthrowing their predecessor directly, but every single one of the transfers of power was made possible by an armed rebellion or civil war. Despite its superficial appearance of unity, the southern realm was riven by a number of deep divisions that gave rise to tremendous political instability. There were tensions between the northern émigrés and indigenous southern elites, between the highest-ranking aristocratic families and lesser elite lineages, and between all of the magnates, both northern and southern, and would-be centralizers at the imperial court. Ministers and high officials from the great families competed to dominate the government, free peasants were hard pressed by the heavy exactions of the imperial state, and aboriginal groups were threatened by the creeping encroachments of Han settlers. The high level of militarization and the decentralization of command authority required by the ongoing confrontation with the barbarian powers of the north made it all too likely that many of these conflicts would be resolved by recourse to violence.[2] In particular, the existence of two widely separated power centers, one at Jiankang and the other at Jingzhou on the middle Yangzi, would have ominous implications for the internal stability of the southern dynasties.[3]

The Eastern Jin regime was vexed by military weakness almost from the moment of its inception. The founder, Sima Rui, was a prince of the imperial house who had commanded the Jin forces in the south from his base at Jiankang since 307. Despite the fact that he held a variety of impressive titles, the military force at his disposal was very limited and he was far from having a monopoly of military power in the Yangzi valley. When he claimed the throne for himself in 317, he did so with the support of powerful members of several great aristocratic families who had retreated to the south after the fall of Luoyang. Particularly prominent in the early years of the Eastern Jin were the Wang family of Langye, the Wang family of Taiyuan, and the Yu family of Yingchuan. All of these families had played a major role at the Western Jin court at Luoyang, and all would provide empresses for the Jin royal family at Jiankang. Two other families, the Huan of Qiaoguo and the Xie of Chenguo, would rise to dominate the court later in the fourth century. The Huan and Xie did not supply empresses and have been described as "a 'new' aristocracy risen from obscure military origins with no history of ties to the Lo-yang court."[4] Most of these aristocratic refugees came south to the Yangzi valley with dependants and armed retainers, and they were eventually able to carve out large estates for themselves, especially in the peripheral frontier districts. Even with the addition of these forces, however, the military support for Sima Rui's regime was extremely weak. In order to survive, the new Eastern Jin court found it necessary to enlist the support of the most powerful native families in the south.[5]

These families were mainly concentrated in the commanderies of Yixing, Wuxing, and Wu by the shores of Lake Tai, the ancient heartland of the lower Yangzi region. They were major landholders, with estates that could survive as self-sufficient enclaves, and they had large numbers of tenants, servants, and other dependants who were capable of bearing arms when the need arose. Some of these families emphasized scholarly accomplishments, but many others, such as the Zhou of Yixing, had strong traditions of military leadership. The southern magnates were never enthusiastic supporters of the Eastern Jin court, dominated as it was by northern émigrés, but in the end the great majority of them did give it their support. Both the court and the magnates wished to maintain order in the lands south of the Yangzi, and both shared a common interest in resisting the inroads of barbarian conquerors such as Shi Le and Shi Hu.[6] An emperor of the Jin royal house served as an important symbol of unity and legitimacy, a role in which a replacement from another family would find it impossible to win acceptance.[7] And the southern elites were ultimately willing to accept a scheme of aristocratic hierarchy that guaranteed their prestige, privilege, and local power even if it did not assign them to the topmost rung. One historian, Kawakatsu Yoshio, has also suggested that southern elites were moved to support and strengthen Sima Rui's government at Jiankang in the hope that it would be able to exert some control over the numerous and often unruly armed bands of northern refugees that had been pouring into the Yangzi valley.[8]

The movement from north to south during the chaos of the early fourth century involved far more than just a handful of aristocrats and their followers. For example, Zu Ti, the scion of an old but much less exalted line of office-holders from southern Hebei, led several hundred families south to the Huai River after the fall of Luoyang.[9] Members of many other lower-ranking provincial elite families also chose to seek safety in the south, and brought with them their slaves, tenants, armed retainers, and neighbors as well as other unrelated commoners who adhered to them for protection. The total numbers involved in this movement must have been substantial. Figures from the middle of the fifth century indicate that at that time there were approximately 900,000 persons in the south who were officially registered as northern migrants or their descendants.[10] Unfortunately, it is not possible to project this number back into the early fourth century. There were several subsequent waves of migration during periods of great disorder in the north (as when Fu Jian's empire fell apart after 383), and we know nothing of the migrants' rate of natural increase or the numbers that had escaped registration. These late figures make it very clear, however, that by far the largest émigré community was located along the banks of the Yangzi not far from Jiankang, and that there were also a substantial number of northerners settled on the middle Yangzi and in the Han River valley. The new arrivals maintained an identity that was quite distinct from their southern neighbors. When the Jin government got around to registering the migrants, it did not incorporate them into the existing southern administrative units, but assigned them to new registration units (often with no actual territory) bearing the same names as the home districts they had left behind in the north. This was a relatively simple administrative task since the usual pattern was for people from a single northern county to migrate as a group and then settle close to one another in the south, and it also allowed the court to create new official posts (as county magistrates and commandery administrators) for the men who led them.[11] Altogether, the Eastern Jin court set up 236 counties and 81 commanderies in exile.[12] Many of the migrants were accustomed to the use of arms, and their leaders of the local elite stratum often came from families that were better known for courage and skill in combat than for cultural accomplishments.[13] These exile communities were an obvious potential military power base for the Eastern Jin regime, but it would be some time before the court was able to organize and utilize them effectively.

The military weakness of the Eastern Jin court during its early days was revealed by the rebellion of Wang Dun, a member of the Langye Wang family who had helped Sima Rui to set up his government at Jiankang. As the leader of one the largest bodies of armed men at the disposal of the new regime, Wang had been sent upriver to establish control over Jing province in 319. However, the emperor and his most trusted officials were not at all comfortable with their dependence on overmighty subjects such as Wang Dun. In 321 one of the centralizers at court, the secretariat director Diao Xie, won the emperor's approval for a scheme to create a strong army directly under central control by confiscating slaves and other dependent retainers (many of whom were already experienced fighting men) from the powerful families, particularly those that were recently arrived from the north.[14] This policy and several personnel appointments that seemed to be aimed at reducing his power prompted Wang Dun to revolt at Wuchang at the beginning of 322. Wang's army descended the Yangzi, defeated Diao Xie's force of ex-slaves at Shitoucheng, an outlying fortress on the shore of the river just northwest of Jiankang, and compelled the now defenseless Jin court to submit to Wang's dictation. Sima Rui was allowed to remain on the throne, and when he died of natural causes near the end of the year, he was succeeded by his son, Sima Shao (known posthumously as Emperor Ming). Wang Dun took the title of "shepherd of Yang province" and established his headquarters at the river port of Gushu, within easy striking distance of the capital. However, his dominance over the Jin court began to unravel when he fell seriously ill in the lunar fifth month of 324. Emperor Ming seized this opportunity to attempt to throw off Wang's tutelage, and Wang sent his army to attack the badly outnumbered defenders of Jiankang. The court was saved from disaster primarily by the timely death of Wang Dun. His less capable elder brother Wang Han not only failed to take Jiankang but was utterly unable to hold Wang's followers together. Within a couple of months Wang Han and his principal associates were dead, in some cases the victims of betrayal by their own subordinates or allies.[15]

This outcome should not, however, be taken as evidence of the strength of the Jin court. In the operations against the rebels, the court had had to rely very heavily on the leaders of a few of the larger northern émigré bands because of the shortage of military forces under its direct control. One of the leaders who played a major role in putting down Wang Dun's rebellion was a man named Su Jun, a native of what is now Shandong province, who had begun his career as a fortress chief in the days of the Western Jin collapse. The court rewarded him with titles and offices for his contribution to the suppression of the Wang Dun rebellion, and with a following now numbering in the tens of thousands he was sent to guard the northern frontier along the Huai River. Like Wang Dun, however, Su quickly came into conflict with officials in the capital who were trying to strengthen the authority of the center and clip the wings of the regional magnates and semi-autonomous military commanders. About to be dismissed from his command, Su rebelled in the tenth lunar month of 327 and marched on Jiankang, taking the city and looting the imperial palace in the second lunar month of 328. The court was able to crush him only after securing the assistance of two upriver military leaders, the more important of whom was the Jing provincial governor Tao Kan.[16] Although he continued to pay lip service to the court's authority and rendered valuable service on occasion, the septuagenarian Tao, a native southerner risen from relatively humble origins, had also set up what amounted to a semi-independent state on the middle Yangzi after the defeat of Wang Dun's forces.[17] In both the Wang Dun and Su Jun affairs, the Jin court had few reliable military forces at its direct disposal and therefore found itself dependent upon the goodwill of men such as Tao Kan. Efforts to concentrate more power at the center, such as the conscription of slaves and retainers advocated by Diao Xie in 321, were likely to trigger rebellions that would leave the court in an even weaker position than before. And the campaigns of Wang Dun and Tao Kan suggested an ominous tendency for regional leaders from Jing province to sweep down the Yangzi to set the affairs of Jiankang in order. In the first half-century or so of its existence, the survival of the Eastern Jin court owed a great deal to its ability to play one warlord against another.

South China was a very highly militarized society, not only at the time of the rebellions of Wang Dun and Su Jun but straight through to the end of the south's independent existence in 589. The most fundamental military problem that the successive southern dynasties faced throughout this period was how to secure enough military manpower, and of sufficient quality, to protect the court against both its northern enemies and its own overmighty subjects. A variety of different solutions were attempted; none was an unqualified success. In the early years of Eastern Jin rule in the south, the government sought to retain the Western Jin system of designating hereditary military households to create a permanent manpower reservoir for the army. These efforts encountered difficulties from the start. The number of military households originally located in the south was extremely small, and serious losses were suffered during the collapse of the Western Jin regime in the north. The most obvious sources of new military households were usually off limits for a variety of reasons. Registered households of taxpaying commoners were relatively few in number due to the fact that powerful families, both southern magnates and northern émigré elites, sheltered large numbers of dependants; to convert commoners to military households would be to diminish a tax base that was already much too small. To claim the dependants as military households, however, was sure to antagonize the powerful families and might even provoke a rebellion. The court was sometimes willing to take this risk, as with Diao Xie's plan in 321 and similar measures introduced by another centralizing Jin statesman at the close of the fourth century, but slaves, "guests," and retainers taken from the estates of the rich could not be the main source of manpower.

In spite of all the difficulties, ways were found to create new military households, with the result that this remained the prevalent form of military service obligation under both the Eastern Jin and Liu Song dynasties. One important source of new military households were the vagrants, vagabonds, and unregistered family groups that did not happen to enjoy the protection of the powerful. Not long after the battle of the Fei River, one Jin general had his troops surround a large marsh in Hailing county, just north of the Yangzi mouth. They set fire to marsh grasses and drove out nearly 10,000 families of vagrants, who were then registered as military households.[18] Convicts might also be consigned to service in the army. According to the letter of the law, the dependants of such convict-soldiers were not supposed to become hereditary military households, but it seems that this provision was honored mainly in the breach.[19] Another source of new military households were the various aboriginal peoples inhabiting the hills and mountains of the south. Conflicts were frequent between the southern governments and the Liao people, who were found mainly in the mountainous regions of southeastern Sichuan, and during the Song and Liang dynasties there was also serious fighting with the Li people who inhabited the mountains separating today's Guangdong province from Hunan and Jiangxi. The most numerous and far-flung of the southern aboriginal groups was the Man, who could be found all the way from the mountains of southwestern Hunan to the hill country of southern Henan. Fighting between the Man people and the Han Chinese was most intense under the Liu Song dynasty, in the middle years of the fifth century.[20] Captives taken in these conflicts were often resettled as military households, and the numbers could be very large. During a single punitive expedition in the winter of 449–50 against the Man living in the mountains north of the Han River, the Song general Shen Qingzhi took 28,000 prisoners; it has been estimated that over the course of his entire career Shen captured more than 200,000 Man who were then enrolled as military households.[21]

This sort of "recruitment" of vagrants, convicts, and tribal peoples provided the southern dynasties with soldiers, but could not guarantee that they would be either reliable or effective. It was surely a contributing factor in the steady decline of the social status and morale of military households. In the Western Jin, military households seem to have enjoyed a status not significantly different from that of ordinary commoners; by the time of the Liu Song dynasty in the fifth century, however, they were regarded as little better than government slaves.[22] The terms of service could be exceedingly harsh. Not every adult male from every military household was called upon for service (the standard rate may have been one in three), but a man who was tapped could remain in the ranks from the age of fifteen or sixteen until he was well into his sixties. If a man had no younger kinsman to replace him, he might be forced to serve to an even more advanced age. If a man fell ill or suffered a debilitating injury, he might find it necessary to substitute an underage family member in order to win his own release.[23] Desertion became a serious problem, and the discontent of the soldiery eventually made the system untenable. During the civil conflicts of the Liu Song period, there were many cases of generals releasing large groups of soldiers (and their families) from their status as members of military households in order to reward them for past service or boost their loyalty and morale at the beginning of a campaign.[24] By the sixth century, under the last of the southern dynasties, the Liang and Chen, hereditary military households were no longer a significant source of manpower.[25]

The government had always found it necessary to supplement the men of the military households with troops drawn from other sources. It had never renounced its authority, dating back to Han times and earlier, to conscript commoners for military service whenever necessary, but this authority was used sparingly by the southern dynasties. Commoners were called for service only in times of special need, and were returned to their homes as soon as the crisis was over. They were often used as laborers or in logistical support roles rather than as combat troops, and military commanders appear to have taken a rather dim view of their fighting quality.[26] Better-quality troops could be gotten by the voluntary enlistment of "recruits" (mubing) who served for a limited term and assumed no hereditary obligations. Fighting men of this sort began to supplant the hereditary soldiers during the Song and Qi dynasties, and were the dominant component in the armies of Liang and Chen.[27] During this period, even the private retainer bands (buqu) of military commanders came to be composed of voluntary recruits rather than servile dependants whose status passed from father to son.[28] At first, a great many of the new recruits were probably freed soldiers from military households who chose to reenlist under better terms of service.[29] There was much that did not change. Just as in the past, under the military household system, it was usual for the families of soldiers to be concentrated in or near military garrisons and to follow the military unit when it was transferred from one location to another.[30] Although the burden of hereditary military service had been lifted from the soldiers and their families, the new system was by no means free of abuses. During the Liang dynasty, for example, it was possible for rich men to enroll themselves as nominal soldiers as a means of gaining the accompanying tax exemption. Troop strength, morale, and fighting power remained serious problems down to the very end of the southern dynasties.[31]

The best soldiers ever raised by the southern dynasties, at least in terms of battlefield effectiveness, were the so-called "Northern Headquarters Troops" (bei fu bing). In 376 Xie An, the dominant minister at the Eastern Jin court, put his kinsman Xie Xuan in command of the forces north of the Yangzi and gave him the authority to recruit and organize a new army. Xie Xuan directed his recruiting efforts at the large number of northern émigré families that had settled along the banks of the Yangzi not far from the capital in the cities of Jingkou, Guangling, and Jinling, and he seems to have achieved considerable success. By the time of Fu Jian's attack on the south in 383 there were 80,000 of the Northern Headquarters troops, and they played the major role in the defeat of the northern invaders. These troops remained an important component of the Eastern Jin military establishment, and were prominent participants in the Jin civil wars in the early years of the fifth century and the suppression of the great rebellion of Sun En and Lu Xun.[32] The founder of the Song dynasty, Liu Yu, used his command of the bei fu bing as a springboard to power. By the time of the major Song campaign against the Northern Wei in 450, however, these very effective troops had all but disappeared from the south's military array.

One possible explanation is that the losses suffered in the fighting of the early fifth century were so heavy that the Northern Headquarters forces could not be reconstructed, especially given that the émigré population from which they had originally been recruited was no longer being reinforced by a flow of new arrivals from the north.[33]

There are a number of other perplexing questions regarding the Northern Headquarters troops. Historians do not agree whether they were voluntary recruits who demonstrated the superiority of *mubing* over soldiers drawn from military households, pointing the way to the new military institutions of the later southern dynasties, or whether they were themselves classified as hereditary soldiery either before or after their recruitment by the Northern Headquarters.[34] The ease and speed with which this powerful force was created is also puzzling, especially in light of the insurmountable obstacles that the Eastern Jin court encountered in its efforts to raise strong, reliable troops during its early years at Jiankang. It is possible that the threat posed by Fu Jian's empire and ambitions in the late 370s persuaded the leaders of the northern émigré bands settled in the neighborhood of Jingkou to cooperate with the Jin court to a much greater degree than had hitherto been the case. And by the 370s, too, the institutional structure of counties, commanderies, and provinces in exile had long been in place to accommodate the northerners within the Jin official system. The leaders of the émigré bands, as we have seen, were made the heads of counties and commanderies. At the same time, they were also incorporated into the official military structure since the units of civil administration doubled as military headquarters. (The "Northern Headquarters" was an alternative name for the military headquarters of the province-in-exile of Southern Xu, based at Jingkou on the Yangzi.[35]) These leaders had their own followings of hereditary military retainers. In other words, by the 370s the means existed for leaders closely associated with the Jin court (in this case, the Xie family) to build a powerful army very quickly by recruiting middle-level officers who could be expected to bring their own subordinates with them.[36] A very similar process appears to have taken place along the Han River in the middle of the fourth century, but there the immediate beneficiary was not the court at Jiankang but the Jing provincial governor Huan Wen and his heirs.[37]

After the death of Xie An in 385, Sima Daozi, the younger brother of Emperor Xiaowu (r. 373–96) and the uncle of Emperor Ming (r. 397–418), emerged as the dominant figure at the Jin court. Like Diao Xie and many others before them, he and his son Yuanxian sought to rein in the provincial governors and increase the power and authority of the center. However, as a result of the personnel changes in Jiankang, the troops of the Northern Headquarters were no longer a reliable asset upon which the centralizers could depend. On the contrary, this force came to pose a deadly threat. It had become the customary practice of Eastern Jin to appoint provincial governors who held important military commands concurrently and were often given control of several adjacent provinces. This practice was well suited to meet the need for effective military command and coordination against the northern threat to the border regions along the Han River and the Huai, but at the same time it left the court at the mercy of the provincial leaders.[38] This was not a problem, of course, when a provincial leader was the kinsman and trusted political associate of the dominant minister at court, as had been the case in the days of Xie An and Xie Xuan. At the end of the fourth century, however, there was no such link between court and camp. The middle Yangzi and Han River valley were in the hands of Huan Xuan, whose father Huan Wen, a powerful northern émigré chief, had been made governor of Jing province in 345. Huan Wen had gone on to reconquer Sichuan for Jin and launch two major offensives against the north. His military might, based on the large northern exile community in the Han River valley and on the fact that this was one of the few places in the southern realm suitable for the breeding of cavalry mounts, was bequeathed to his heir Huan Xuan.[39] Downstream, military power rested mainly in the hands of Wang Gong, a high-ranking aristocrat and elder brother of Xiaowu's empress; as governor of Yan and Qing with headquarters at Jingkou, he had direct command authority over the Northern Headquarters troops.[40]

Tensions between Wang Gong and the Jiankang government led by Sima Daozi prompted the former to flex his military muscle in 397 and force Sima to execute two members of his party. When Sima resumed his political maneuvering against him, Wang marched on the capital in the lunar seventh month of 398. On this occasion Sima Daozi and his party were saved by a bribe paid to Liu Laozhi, the most important of the Northern Headquarters generals, whose defection led in short order to the defeat and elimination of Wang Gong. In the hope of strengthening the court against the provincial governors and freeing it from dependence on the men of the Northern Headquarters, in 399 Sima Yuanxian ordered the conscription of private slaves and agricultural dependants to build up the military forces in the capital. This measure antagonized both its lowly targets and the powerful southern families from whom they were going to be taken, and was a factor contributing to the outbreak of Sun En's rebellion on the southern shore of Hangzhou Bay that same autumn.[41]

Sun En was a large landowner from an aristocratic northern family, but he found common ground with the native southern elite because so many of them were adherents of the "heavenly masters" Daoist sect just as he was. His revolt quickly spread to eight commanderies around Hangzhou Bay and Lake Tai and gathered more than 100,000 adherents.[42] The Jin government sent Liu Laozhi's Northern Headquarters troops to crush the rebels, and a series of seesaw campaigns ensued until Sun finally committed suicide in the spring of 402 after a crushing defeat at the hands of the government forces. The war was note-worthy for Sun En's use of ships, the waterborne mobility of his forces, and their use of island refuges off the coast of Zhejiang; it also saw the emergence of a general named Liu Yu as a key lieutenant of Liu Laozhi.[43] Sun's brother-in-law Lu Xun led the surviving rebels south to Guangzhou, where the government pacified him with the provincial governorship in 405.

At the beginning of 402, Sima Yuanxian and Liu Laozhi prepared to launch an expedition against Huan Xuan, who had made himself the master of all of the upriver territories (including the modern provinces of Hunan, Hubei, Sichuan, and Jiangxi) while the court was distracted by Sun En's rising. Huan struck first, descending the Yangzi from Jiangling to Xunchang (today's Jiujiang) in the second lunar month of 402. At that point Liu Laozhi chose to defect to Huan's side, bringing the Northern Headquarters troops along with him, and with this accession of strength Huan was easily able to occupy Jiankang. Once in possession of the capital, Huan not only killed Sima Yuanxian, but also removed Liu from his troop command, drove him to commit suicide, and then claimed the throne for himself (as the first emperor of the "Chu" dynasty) at the end of 403. This did not sit well with the veterans of the Northern Headquarters. In the second month of 404 Liu Laozhi's former lieutenant Liu Yu, who enjoyed strong support among the officers of the *bei fu bing*, rose at Jingkou and marched on Jiankang.[44] Huan Xuan fled back to his home base at Jiangling, regrouped, and then came down the Yangzi again with a much larger force. The decisive encounter occurred at Zhengrong Island, near today's Echeng, Hubei, on June 10, 404. As the two river flotillas steered into battle, Liu Yu's field commander, a Northern Headquarters general named Liu Yi, took advantage of his upwind position to set fire to many of Huan's vessels.[45] Huan's force collapsed, and Huan himself was soon murdered by an associate while trying to escape to Sichuan. Emperor An was restored to the throne, but from this time forward Liu Yu was the real master of the Jin court. He would devote most of his attention to campaigns against the north, but had to fight twice more in the south before his power was secure. The Guangzhou governor and erstwhile rebel chief Lu Xun took advantage of Liu's absence with the army in the north to strike at Jiankang in 410; frustrated by the hastily recalled northern armies, he was eventually hounded to his death in northern Vietnam. Then, in 412, Liu Yu marched on Jiangling and eliminated his former colleague Liu Yi, who had established himself in Huan Xuan's old power base on the middle Yangzi. It was only in 420, shortly after the death of Emperor An, that General Liu Yu finally took the throne as the first emperor of the Song dynasty.

In order to tie the empire more firmly together and prevent the sort of internal conflict that had torn the Eastern Jin empire apart during its final years, the Song founder established a policy of appointing members of his own family to the major provincial commands; two of his sons, for example, were assigned to control the key upriver garrisons at Jingzhou and Jiangzhou.[46] This arrangement worked well at first, and the thirty-year reign of the second Song ruler, Emperor Wen, was a time of domestic tranquility rarely encountered in the annals of the southern dynasties. The murder of Emperor Wen by the crown prince, Liu Shao, in 453 touched off another round of civil strife. Liu

Shao's brother, Liu Jun, who had been campaigning against the Man people in the Dabie Mountains of Hubei, marched on the capital, defeated and killed the usurper and placed himself on the throne. Jun's subsequent efforts to remove a powerful uncle from his entrenched position as governor of Jing province ignited a new round of fighting that ended in the defeat and death of the uncle. During his ten-year reign, Liu Jun also managed to eliminate several more of his brothers, and in order to keep the surviving princely governors in line he introduced the system of "document clerks" (*dianqian*), assigning relatively low-ranking officials to their staffs to serve as the emperor's spies.[47] But this system could not be effective without a strong hand at the center. The death of Liu Jun in 465 gave rise to yet more internecine violence, the "War of the Uncles and Nephews" that recalled the conflict of the Eight Princes in Western Jin. Local elites were active participants on both sides, and at one point Emperor Ming, the eventual victor, was in firm control of only a single commandery.[48] When Emperor Ming went to join his ancestors in 472 there was, predictably, another flare-up. His last surviving brother, now the governor of Jiang province, rebelled and marched on the capital. The city and the infant emperor were successfully defended by an imperial guard general named Xiao Daocheng. Xiao claimed the southern throne for himself in 479, but only after he had disposed of the Jing provincial governor Shen Youzhi in a bitter campaign on the middle Yangzi in 477–8.[49]

The Qi dynasty founded by Xiao Daocheng was the shortest lived of the southern dynasties, lasting a mere twenty-two years. With regard to domestic peace and tranquility, it did not represent an improvement over its predecessor. Xiao and his successors (he died in 483) followed the Song precedent of appointing imperial princes to control the major provincial commands while sending "document clerks" to control the princes.[50] The system was ultimately no more effective than it had been in the days of Song. The accession of the weak, suspicious, and inexperienced Xiao Baojuan in 498 touched off a string of plots, counterplots, and executions that soon led to revolts by the regional governors. Among them was an imperial cousin named Xiao Yan who happened to be serving as governor of Yong province with his headquarters at Xiangyang on the Han River.[51] Xiao Yan raised 30,000 infantry and 5000 cavalry in his own territory, and began his revolt against Xiao Baojuan near the end of 500. His campaign was greatly assisted by the complete demoralization of most of the forces that might have opposed him. The Jing provincial forces murdered their commander and defected to his side, the governor of Jiang province submitted without putting up a fight, and the town of Gushu also fell without a fight when the commanding general fled. In the twelfth lunar month of 501, disgruntled subordinates killed Xiao Baojuan and opened the gates of Jiankang to Xiao Yan.[52]

The Liang dynasty established by Xiao Yan in 502 survived for fifty-five years, with the reign of the first emperor (known posthumously as Emperor Wu of Liang) accounting for forty-eight of those years. In spite of the idiosyncracies of Emperor Wu, who "donated" himself to a Buddhist monastery as a slave on three occasions and required his ministers to ransom him at tremendous cost to the state treasury, his reign was probably the longest period of general peace and prosperity in the history of the southern dynasties.[53] This golden age was brought to an end in 548 by the rebellion of Hou Jing, a frontier general who had earlier defected to Liang from the north. Hou took Jiankang and then proclaimed himself emperor in 551, but was unable to impose his rule in the face of intense resistance by southern local elites.[54] After the defeat and death of Hou Jing, the south was pulled together again by a former Liang general named Chen Baxian, who established the Chen dynasty in 557. Chen and his successors would rule a much diminished southern realm (with Sichuan, the Han River valley, and everything north of the Huai River having been lost to the north) until their state met its end at the hands of the north's Sui dynasty in 589.

In addition to the obvious observation that the rise and fall of every one of the southern dynasties was a consequence of military action, several other patterns can be discerned in this history. One is that the internal conflicts of the south almost invariably saw the holders of the lower Yangzi power base around Jiankang arrayed against challengers based at one of the upriver centers – at Jingzhou or Jiangzhou on the Yangzi, or at Xiangyang on the Han River. The Song founder Liu Yu and the Qi founder Xiao Daocheng succeeded in extending their power upstream from Jiankang; among those who moved downstream, Wang Dun and Huan Xuan both failed in their efforts to control the capital but the Liang founder Xiao Yan was later successful. Each half of the

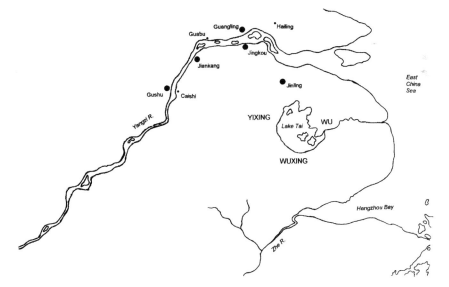

Map 9 The lower Yangzi region under the southern dynasties

southern empire offered an extensive resource base and a large reservoir of northern émigré soldiery, and neither was able to dominate the other consistently and comfortably. Between them, the Yangzi River provided the great military highway that both facilitated and channeled the operations of all of these contenders for power. Armies and their supply trains travelled by water, and many of the most decisive engagements were fought on water rather than on land. Huan Xuan suffered his fatal defeat in a major river battle, as did the rebel leader Lu Xun in 410.[55]

Another pattern evident in the rise and fall of the several southern dynasties is the movement of military leaders from the lower levels of the official hierarchy to occupy the apex of power in Jiankang. The founders of Song, Qi, and Chen were all non-aristocratic military men from relatively humble origins, and they tended to promote others of their own type to the highest government offices once they wielded supreme power. This was a major change from the Eastern Jin, when members of the most prominent and powerful aristocratic families not only tended to monopolize the top offices at court but also held important provincial commands with control over military forces. Examples of the earlier pattern include Wang Dun and later Huan Wen and his son Huan Xuan on the middle Yangzi, and the command of the Northern Headquarters troops first by Xie Xuan and later by Wang Gong. At the same time, however, the highest elites of Eastern Jin were not animated by a martial ethos. Generals such as Huan Wen commanded armies on campaign and issued orders to their subordinate officers, but were not accustomed to leading from the front. Huan could impress other aristocrats with his "martial disposition and vigorous air" and his "rugged and flint-like" manner, to be sure, but this was only a matter of speech and deportment; he does not seem ever to have participated in physical combat himself.[56] It should also be noted that the involvement of members of the Huan and Xie families with military leadership was not typical of the aristocracy as a whole, nor did it impress everyone. From the perspective of some of the most literate and cultured men from the "best" families at the Jin court, Huan Wen could be dismissed as a parvenu and a mere military man. In these elite circles what counted was not only distinguished lineage and the holding of high office, but also a family tradition of cultural superiority, and Huan Wen himself made ample obeisance to the last of these ideals with his "displays of benevolent Confucian administration, learning, and conversational ability."[57]

Liu Yu, the founder of the Song dynasty, was a different sort of military leader. Liu was born in 363 to one of the northern émigré families that had settled at Jingkou on the Yangzi. His great-grandfather had migrated south from the area of Pengcheng (today's Xuzhou, in northern Jiangsu), and the fact that he was appointed a county magistrate after he crossed the Yangzi suggests that he had been a member of the local elite and the leader of a group of migrants. Liu Yu's father was no more than a low-ranking official on the staff of a commandery, and the family was described as "poor." Liu Yu began his military career as a low-ranking officer under a general named Sun Wuzhong, and first emerged to prominence when Northern Headquarters general Liu Laozhi invited him to join his campaign against the rebel leader Sun En. During these operations on the eastern coast, Liu Yu distinguished himself as an officer who put himself in the front line and fought alongside his troops. On one occasion he led a patrol of several dozen men to scout the rebels' where-abouts, and suddenly found himself in a desperate fight with a much larger body of the enemy. "Many of the men he led were dead, but his fighting spirit was still keen; he fought vigorously with a glaive (*changdao*) in his hands, and those he killed and wounded were exceedingly numerous."[58]

With Liu Yu's accession to power in the early years of the fifth century, the composition of the ruling elite began to change from what it had been under Eastern Jin. From this time on, the great majority of top military commands (and provincial posts that included military command) went to men of more humble origins, often men who had made their mark as lower-level military leaders. And it became rare to find aristocrats willing to associate themselves with the armies in any case. When Wang Tanshou of the Langye Wangs joined one of Liu Yu's northern campaigns as a staff officer, Liu saw fit to praise him for his willingness to "bend his ambition to things military."[59] Members of the great aristocratic families continued to hold many of the highest offices at the center, but they were now joined by former military commanders. Real power gravitated to the latter group, who were more dependent upon the emperors for status and position and hence more responsive to the imperial will.[60] Some of these men came from the same class of northern émigrés as Liu Yu, while others were native southerners. Shen Qingzhi, the general who campaigned so effectively against the Man people in the middle years of the fifth century, had almost nothing in common with the old aristocratic elite. He was not an exile from North China, but a native southerner from Wuxing commandery on the south side of Lake Tai. He is supposed to have tilled the land himself, though the fact that he was able to enter the military as a staff aide (*canjun*) – and through the good offices of his brother, who had already served in the same capacity – suggests that he was not from an ordinary peasant family. As a general, Shen was highly critical of the interference of scholars – *shusheng*, in this context perhaps better translated as "bookworms" – in military matters. He himself could neither write characters nor recognize them, and at an imperially-sponsored poetry competition he once had to dictate his entry for another official to write down.[61]

The precedent set by the Song dynasty held true for Qi, Liang, and Chen as well. Xiao Daocheng, the founder of the Qi dynasty, was the son of a Song general descended from northern émigrés who had settled at Jinling on the south bank of the Yangzi. He had some classical education, but became a military officer at an early age. In 442, when he was only fifteen, he was sent with a detached column to attack the Man living near the Han River.[62] The Liang founder, Xiao Yan, had commanded an army in the field, but he arrived at his command because he was a kinsman of the Qi emperors. Chen Baxian came from much more obscure origins. He was the descendant of northern émigrés who had settled at Wuxing, but his father does not seem to have held any office and he began his own career as a minor local sub-official. Thanks to the patronage of a powerful provincial governor from the ruling Xiao family, Chen became first a staff aide and later a troop commander and the administrator of a commandery in the far south. From this base, he eventually went on to found the Chen dynasty. These men continued to appoint military associates from very humble origins to some of the highest posts in the realm. Wang Jingze, a troop commander under Xiao Daocheng, was the son of a shamaness and began his career as a butcher selling dog meat. He was virtually illiterate, spoke only the southern Wu dialect, and had to have documents read aloud to him by aides. These handicaps did not prevent Wang from rising to the very high office of defender-in-chief (*tai wei*). Indeed, Wang once remarked that he never would have risen to such heights if he had known how to write.[63] The Liang general Chang Yizhi also came from a southern family without official antecedents and was said to be able to recognize no more than ten characters.[64] Senior generals of southern origin such as Shen Qingzhi, Wang Jingze, and Chang Yizhi were fairly rare in the Liang dynasty and earlier when northern émigrés predominated, but became the norm under the Chen dynasty. This change has been attributed to the decadence of the northern elites during the first half of the sixth century, to the devastating impact of the Hou Jing rebellion on the émigré power structure based in the neighborhood of Jiankang, and to the fact that Chen Baxian found most of his armed supporters among the southern local elites.[65]

The rise of new elites of military origin did not, however, give rise to a strong martial ethos or a more militarized style of governance at Jiankang. On the contrary, there was a tendency for the newcomers at the center of power to be seduced by the cultural values and lifestyles of the highest aristocratic families.[66] This pattern was especially pronounced during the reign of Xiao Yan (Emperor Wu of Liang) in the first half of the sixth century, moving a northern author to denounce the unmanly qualities of the Liang ruling class in the following terms:

> The Liang scholar-officials usually wore loose garments, along with a wide girdle, a grand hat, and high clogs. When they went out they used carriages or sedan chairs; coming back they had the help of servants. In the suburbs and environs of the city nobody was ever seen on horseback. Chou Hung-cheng was loved by Prince Hsüan-cheng, who granted him a small horse, which he often rode. The whole court considered him unrestrained. If a high state minister [*Shang-shu lang*] rode on horseback, he would be impeached. When the rebellion of Hou Ching occurred, people were so flabby and soft that they were unable to walk, and their bodies so lean and breath so short that they

could not endure cold and heat. It often happened that such people died suddenly. Wang Fu, a magistrate of Chien-k'ang, who was born so weak and gentle, had never mounted a horse. Whenever he saw a horse neighing and galloping, he trembled with fear. He said to somebody, "Really, it is a tiger; why is it called a horse?" Customs had reached such a level![67]

Military forces always had to be raised and maintained to defend the northern frontier and to protect the ruling house against domestic challenges, and military power remained the ultimate arbiter in the rise and fall of dynasties. In the ideological climate that prevailed in the south, however, the essentially civilian cultural and political ideals inherited from Han times retained their hold over men's minds. This did not prevent armed coups and rebellions, but once new men had established themselves at the center of power they and their descendants were easily encouraged to adopt the cultivated lifestyles and pattern of civil officeholding characteristic of the preexisting capital elite. The Confucian state provided not only offices and incomes, but also a powerful aura of legitimacy that obviated the need for coercion in many social and political contexts. This may help to explain why the medieval south never gave rise to a knightly class whose identity was based primarily on the use of arms, even though the various southern and émigré elites were often involved in military leadership.[68]

Notes

1   This calculation is based on the population figures for AD 140 given in Fan Ye, *Hou Han shu* (Beijing: Zhonghua shuju, 1965), chs. 109–13, with the emendations suggested by Bielenstein in "The Census of China during the Period 2–742 A.D.," p. 159. I have taken the Huai River and the Dabie Mountains as the dividing line between north and south; Nanyang and Hanzhong are counted as part of the north, Sichuan as part of the south. Bielenstein's Plate III gives a good sense of the relationship between people and space in the two regions. The calculation of land area is based on the approximate figures for modern Chinese provinces given in *Zuixin shiyong Zhongguo dituce* (Xi'an: Zhongguo ditu chubanshe, 1992).

2   Hamaguchi Shigekuni, *Shin Kan Zui Tō shi no kenkyū* (Tokyo: Tokyo University Press, 1966), p. 379.

3   Zhou Nianchang, "Dong Jin bei fu bing de jianli ji qi tedian," in *Wei Jin Sui Tang shi lunji*, vol. 2 (Beijing: Zhongguo shehui kexue chubanshe, 1983), pp. 152–3; Wang Zhongluo, *Wei Jin Nanbeichao shi*, vol. 1, p. 330.

4   Dennis Grafflin, "The Great Family in Medieval South China," *Harvard Journal of Asiatic Studies*, 41.1 (June 1981), p. 71.

5   Kawakatsu Yoshio, "Tō Shin shizokusei no kakuritsu katei – gunjiryoku to no kanren no moto ni," *Tōhō gakuhō*, 52 (1980), pp. 317–18.

6   Chen Yinke, *Wei Jin Nanbeichao shi jiangyanlu*, pp. 147–9, 155; Wang Zhongluo, *Wei Jin Nanbeichao shi*, vol. 1, pp. 318–20, 323–4, 329.

7   Tang Changru, *Wei Jin Nanbeichao shilun shiyi* (Beijing: Zhonghua shuju, 1983), p. 151.

8 Kawakatsu, "Tō Shin shizokusei no kakuritsu katei," pp. 319–20. Kawakatsu's article also emphasizes the importance of hierarchy-based ideology in securing the acquiescence of southern elites.

9 *Jin shu*, ch. 62, p. 1694.

10 Wang Zhongluo, *Wei Jin Nanbeichao shi*, vol. 1, pp. 345–6.

11 Yasuda Jirō, "Shin–Sō kakumei to Yōshū (Jōyō) no kyōmin – gunsei shihai kara minsei shihai e," *Tōyōshi kenkyū*, 42.1 (June 1983), pp. 130–1. Also see William G. Crowell, "Northern Émigrés and the Problems of Census Registration under the Eastern Jin and Southern Dynasties," in Albert E. Dien (ed.), *State and Society in Early Medieval China* (Stanford, Ca.: Stanford University Press, 1990), pp. 171–209.

12 Holcombe, *In the Shadow of the Han: Literati Thought and Society at the Beginning of the Southern Dynasties*, p. 27.

13 Chen Yinke, *Wei Jin Nanbeichao shi jiangyanlu*, p. 116.

14 Tang Changru, *Wei Jin Nanbeichao shilun shiyi*, pp. 158–60; Kawakatsu, "Tō Shin shizokusei no kakuritsu katei," pp. 328–9. The relevant edict is quoted in Sima Guang, *Zizhi tongjian*, ch. 91, p. 2888, and at greater length in *Jin shu*, ch. 6, p. 154.

15 Fu Lecheng, "Wei Jin Nanbeichao zhanshi," in Zhang Qiyun et al., *Zhongguo zhanshi lunji* (Taipei: Zhongguo wenhua xueyuan chubanbu, 1954; 3rd edition, 1980), pp. 20–1. Also see Sima Guang, *Zizhi tongjian*, ch. 93, pp. 2927–9.

16 He Ziquan, *Wei Jin Nanbeichao shilue*, p. 87; Wang Zhongluo, *Wei Jin Nanbeichao shi*, vol. 1, pp. 331–2.

17 Kawakatsu, "Tō Shin shizokusei no kakuritsu katei," pp. 333–6.

18 The general was Mao Qu; see his biography in *Jin shu*, ch. 81, p. 2126.

19 He Ziquan, "Wei Jin Nanchao de bingzhi," *Bulletin of the Institute of History and Philology of Academia Sinica*, 16 (1947), p. 262.

20 For the tribal peoples of the south, see He Ziquan, *Wei Jin Nanbeichao shilue*, pp. 148–51, and Wang Zhongluo, *Wei Jin Nanbeichao shi*, vol. 1, pp. 468–75.

21 Shen Yue, *Song shu* (Beijing: Zhonghua shuju, 1974), ch. 77, p. 1998. Also see Zhu Dawei, "Wei Jin Nanbeichao nongmin zhanzheng de jige wenti," in *Wei Jin Sui Tang shi lunji*, vol. 2 (Beijing: Zhongguo shehui kexue chubanshe, 1983), pp. 28, 38–9. Zhu estimates that the total number of Man, Liao, and Li at the beginning of Eastern Jin was in the neighborhood of three million.

22 He Ziquan, "Wei Jin Nanchao de bingzhi," pp. 249–50; Hamaguchi, *Shin Kan Zui Tō shi no kenkyū*, pp. 348–9.

23 Hamaguchi, *Shin Kan Zui Tō shi no kenkyū*, pp. 387, 389, 391–2.

24 Lü Simian, *Liang Jin Nanbeichao shi*, p. 1294; Hamaguchi, *Shin Kan Zui Tō shi no kenkyū*, p. 405.

25 Hamaguchi, *Shin Kan Zui Tō shi no kenkyū*, pp. 385–6, 409.

26 He Ziquan, "Wei Jin Nanchao de bingzhi," pp. 255, 257–9; Hamaguchi, *Shin Kan Zui Tō shi no kenkyū*, pp. 417–21; Tang Changru, *Wei Jin Nanbeichao Sui Tang shi san lun*, p. 187. For the weakness of conscript forces and commanders' concerns about them, see Lü Simian, *Liang Jin Nanbeichao shi*, p. 1296.

27 Tang Changru, *Wei Jin Nanbeichao Sui Tang shi san lun*, p. 186.

28 During the later part of the southern dynasties, there were two types of *buqu*. The earlier type of private armed retainer in a hereditary relationship of dependency upon his master's family continued to be found, but in addition there now appeared the new phenomenon of generals enlisting recruits to serve as *buqu*. This development was entirely legal and occurred with the sanction of the government, which might even grant soldiers to the commanders. In the eyes of the law these new *buqu* were not private dependants but rather government soldiers who were, in effect, on long-term loan to the generals. See Tang Changru, "Wei Jin Nanbeichao

shiqi de ke he buqu," in idem, *Wei Jin Nanbeichao shilun shiyi* (Beijing: Zhonghua shuju, 1983), pp. 15–18.

29 Hamaguchi, *Shin Kan Zui Tō shi no kenkyū*, p. 406.

30 Hamaguchi, *Shin Kan Zui Tō shi no kenkyū*, pp. 395–7, 412.

31 Hamaguchi, *Shin Kan Zui Tō shi no kenkyū*, pp. 410–11; Li Tse-fen, *Liang Jin Nanbeichao lishi lunwenji*, vol. 2, pp. 380–1; *Zhongguo junshi shi*, vol. 3: *Bingzhi*, pp. 198–9.

32 Zhou Nianchang, "Dong Jin bei fu bing de jianli ji qi tedian," pp. 156–7, 159.

33 Zhou Nianchang, "Dong Jin bei fu bing de jianli ji qi tedian," pp. 164–7.

34 Zhou Nianchang is convinced that the *bei fu bing* had no connection with the system of hereditary military households; see his "Dong Jin bei fu bing de jianli ji qi tedian," pp. 158, 160. Kawakatsu seems to suggest that the *bei fu bing* were recruited from the members of what were already hereditary military households ("Tō Shin shizokusei no kakuritsu katei," pp. 330–1). Tang Changru is inclined to believe that membership in the force became hereditary, though he admits that no source says this in so many words (*Wei Jin Nanbeichao Sui Tang shi san lun*, pp. 184–5).

35 Zhou Nianchang, "Dong Jin bei fu bing de jianli ji qi tedian," p. 157.

36 Tang Changru, *Wei Jin Nanbeichao Sui Tang shi san lun*, pp. 183–4.

37 Yasuda Jirō, "Shin-Sō kakumei to Yōshū (Jōyō) no kyōmin," pp. 115, 127–8, 130–1.

38 Hamaguchi, *Shin Kan Zui Tō shi no kenkyū*, p. 379.

39 Yasuda, "Shin-Sō kakumei to Yōshū (Jōyō) no kyōmin," pp. 111, 127–8; Yoshimori Kensuke, "Shin-Sō kakumei to Kōnan shakai," *Shirin*, 63.2 (1980), p. 225.

40 *Jin shu*, ch. 84, pp. 2183–4.

41 Wang Zhongluo, *Wei Jin Nanbeichao shi*, vol. 1, pp. 359–60.

42 Yoshimori, "Shin-Sō kakumei to Kōnan shakai," p. 223; Chen Yinke, *Wei Jin Nanbeichao shi jiangyanlu*, pp. 161, 163, 167–8.

43 Wang Zhongluo, *Wei Jin Nanbeichao shi*, vol. 1, pp. 362–3.

44 Wang Zhongluo, *Wei Jin Nanbeichao shi*, vol. 1, pp. 365–6.

45 Sima Guang, *Zizhi tongjian*, ch. 113, p. 3570.

46 *Zhongguo junshi shi*, vol. 3, p. 185.

47 *Zhongguo junshi shi*, vol. 3, p. 186.

48 Yasuda Jirō, "Shinan Ō Shi Kun no hanran ni tsuite – Nanchō monbatsu kizoku taisei to gōzoku dogō," *Tōyōshi kenkyū*, 25.4 (1967), p. 416 and passim.

49 Wang Zhongluo, *Wei Jin Nanbeichao shi*, vol. 1, p. 395. Xiao Daocheng's campaign against Shen Youzhi is described in Fu Lecheng, "Wei Jin Nanbeichao zhanshi," pp. 24–5.

50 *Zhongguo junshi shi*, vol. 3, p. 195.

51 For the character of Xiao Baojuan and the collapse of his government, see Xiao Zixian, *Nan Qi shu* (Beijing: Zhonghua shuju, 1972), ch. 7, especially pp. 98–102, and Wang Zhongluo, *Wei Jin Nanbeichao shi*, vol. 1, p. 397.

52 Fu Lecheng, "Wei Jin Nanbeichao zhanshi," p. 26.

53 He Ziquan, *Wei Jin Nanbeichao shilue*, p. 177.

54 For more on Hou Jing, see Yao Silian, *Liang shu* (Beijing: Zhonghua shuju, 1973), ch. 56, pp. 833–63, and Benjamin E. Wallacker, "Studies in Medieval Chinese Siegecraft: The Siege of Chien-k'ang, A.D. 548–549," *Journal of Asian History*, 5.1 (1971), pp. 35–54.

55 For the defeat of Lu Xun, see Sima Guang, *Zizhi tongjian*, ch. 115, pp. 3640–1.

56 Liu I-ch'ing, *Shih-shuo hsin-yü: A New Account of Tales of the World*, trans. by Richard B. Mather (Minneapolis: University of Minnesota Press, 1976), p. 305. Another anecdote in this fifth-century collection indicates that one of Huan's younger relatives did charge into the enemy ranks on at least one occasion, with

Huan Wen close enough to the front line to be able to direct him to do so (p. 305). An anecdote regarding military leadership as practiced by members of the Xie family can be found on p. 397.

57 Holcombe, *In the Shadow of the Han*, p. 127; also see Grafflin, "The Great Family in Medieval South China," p. 73, and Liu I-ch'ing, *Shih-shuo hsin-yü*, p. 396.

58 *Song shu*, ch. 1, p. 2. The *changdao* was a long, curved blade mounted on a long wooden shaft, resembling the Japanese *naginata* and the European glaive.

59 *Song shu*, ch. 63, p. 1678.

60 Wang Zhongluo, *Wei Jin Nanbeichao shi*, vol. 1, pp. 406–7; Zhu Dawei, "Wei Jin Nanbeichao shi nongmin zhanzheng de shehui houguo," in *Zhongguo nongmin zhanzheng shi luncong*, No. 5 (N.p.: Zhongguo shehui kexue chubanshe, 1987), pp. 9–11.

61 See Shen's biography in *Song shu*, ch. 77, especially pp. 1996, 1998–9, and 2003.

62 Xiao Zixian, *Nan Qi shu*, ch. 1, pp. 1–3.

63 *Nan Qi shu*, ch. 26, pp. 479–81, 484–5; Wang Zhongluo, *Wei Jin Nanbeichao shi*, vol. 1, p. 406. The *tai wei* was one of the Three Dukes (*san gong*), the highest advisors to the throne; see Charles O. Hucker, *A Dictionary of Official Titles in Imperial China* (Stanford, Ca.: Stanford University Press, 1985), p. 399, entry number 4871.

64 Li Yanshou, *Nan shi* (Beijing: Zhonghua Shuju, 1975), ch. 55, p. 1376.

65 Chen Yinke, *Wei Jin Nanbeichao shi jiangyanlu*, pp. 202–6.

66 Chen Yinke, *Wei Jin Nanbeichao shi jiangyanlu*, pp. 186–90.

67 Yen Chih-t'ui, *Family Instructions for the Yen Clan (Yen-shih chia-hsün)*, trans. by Teng Ssu-yü; T'oung Pao Monographs, Vol. 4 (Leiden: E. J. Brill, 1968), ch. 11, p. 116.

68 Holcombe, *In the Shadow of the Han*, p. 72 and passim. In his study of Xiao Zixun's rebellion of 465, Yasuda emphasizes the desire of the militarized local elites on both sides to gain access to the highest, most prestigious civil offices in the capital; see "Shinan Ō Shi Kun no hanran ni tsuite," especially pp. 423–8.

CHAPTER FIVE

From Northern Wei to Northern Zhou

The most fundamental question faced by all of the various conquest regimes established in China by North Asian peoples, from the Xiongnu at the beginning of the fourth century to the Manchus in the middle of the seventeenth century, was that of sinicization. To what extent would the conquerors continue to adhere to their own political, social, and cultural traditions, and to what extent would they adopt Chinese language, dress, and modes of behavior? Would intermarriage be encouraged or discouraged? Would political power be monopolized by the rulers from the steppes, or would it be shared with Han Chinese elites? The recruitment of Han officials and the adoption of Chinese bureaucratic forms and usages certainly made it much easier to govern and extract revenues from the large settled, agricultural population of the North China Plain. At the same time, both the developed literary culture and the luxurious material lifestyle of upper-class Chinese could hold a powerful attraction for men who had been brought up in more impoverished surroundings. Sinicization also had its dangers, however. The conquerors risked losing the toughness and martial prowess that had given them dominion over the Chinese, and they ultimately risked the loss of their separate identity as they merged with the much larger population of Han Chinese.

Like most of the earlier barbarian rulers in North China, the first Northern Wei emperors had adopted some elements of Chinese administration and court ceremonial and had brought some Han Chinese literati into their service.[1] However, for the most part the Tuoba rulers and their Xianbei followers chose to emphasize their separate, North Asian identity. Even after the conquest of most of North China in the middle of the fifth century, they kept their capital at Pingcheng (now Datong, Shanxi), close to the steppe but on the remote northern margin of the Chinese world. Although detribalized and settled on lands around the capital, many of the Xianbei and other northern peoples subject to the Wei rulers continued to speak their ancestral languages and to make their living as herdsmen rather than farmers. The core of the army remained an exclusively North Asian preserve, although Chinese peasants might be called up for major campaigns (often in logistical support roles) or garrison duty (also regarded as akin to corvée labor). After the military subjugation of the north, control was maintained by contingents of Xianbei warriors who occupied the walled cities and lived apart from the Han majority.[2] Some Tuoba rulers and their Han ministers had promoted cautious moves in the direction of greater sinicization from time to time, but such efforts had tended to give rise to political controversy and even violent reaction from Xianbei elites.[3]

Beginning in 493, the Wei Emperor Xiaowen, the son of a Chinese mother, introduced in rapid succession a series of measures amounting to a radical program of sinicization. These included a ban on the wearing of Xianbei clothes, a ban on the speaking of non-Chinese languages at court by officials under the age of thirty, and the replacement of multisyllable Xianbei surnames with single-syllable equivalents in the Chinese style (for example, the royal surname of Tuoba – or Tabgach in its original Altaic form – was changed to Yuan). Xianbei families were ranked in the same manner as the Han Chinese elites, eligibility for office was conditioned on family rank just as among the Chinese, and intermarriage between Han and Xianbei was officially encouraged.[4] The first and most important of all of the reforms was the transfer of the capital to Luoyang, south of the Yellow River. The initial move was accomplished by subterfuge in 493. Emperor Xiaowen mobilized his army for a great campaign against the south and advanced as far as Luoyang, where his ministers "persuaded" him to halt the expedition – and he seized the opportunity to announce the change of capital. The transfer was made effective over the next decade as walls and palaces were built and populations transferred from Pingcheng and other centers in North China. By 495 some 150,000 Xianbei and other northern warriors had been moved south from Pingcheng to fill the ranks of the imperial guards and were granted farmland in the vicinity of the new capital. The total population of the city soon grew to approximately 600,000. This development took place on a site that could boast little more than the small Jinyong Fortress in 493.[5] The transfer did not come without opposition; there was an unsuccessful rebellion of Xianbei nobles and generals in the north in 496, and Emperor Xiaowen forced his crown prince to commit suicide the following year, apparently because of his opposition to the reforms.[6]

Not all of the Xianbei were moved south to Luoyang. Large numbers were left along the northern frontier and in the vicinity of the old capital to guard the Wei realm against the Rouran, a tribal confederacy that had emerged to dominate the northern steppe around the beginning of the fifth century.[7] To counter the Rouran threat, the Wei rulers had established a dozen major garrisons during the first half of the fifth century. These stretched in an arc along the northern frontier from Dunhuang at the end of the Gansu corridor in the far northwest to Yuyi directly north of modern Beijing. The sector of the line that covered Pingcheng and the Dai region of northern Shanxi became known as the "Six Garrisons." These were anchored on the west by Woye garrison on the great northward loop of the Yellow River. To the east of Woye lay Huaishuo (north of modern Baotou), Wuchuan (northwest of Hohhot), Fuming,

Rouxuan, and Huaihuang. These positions commanded the swath of grassland south of the Gobi Desert, where invaders coming from the north would otherwise have been able to pasture their tired and hungry horses before attacking the settled lands to the south.[8] In addition to the headquarters fortress, each garrison controlled a network of lesser outposts (*shu*) and might also have military authority over surrendered tribal groups occupying the nearby grazing lands.[9] The original function of the garrison fortresses and outposts was not as strongpoints for a static defense, but rather as bases from which offensives could be launched to keep the Rouran off balance. In the late fifth century and especially after the move of the capital to Luoyang, however, there was a marked shift to a more passive defensive posture.[10] This was accompanied by other signs of demoralization among the men of the garrisons.

The garrison communities had been built up over time from heterogeneous sources. The core element consisted of Xianbei and other "compatriots" (*guoren*), to which were added large numbers of nomadic, Turkic-speaking Gaoju people who had been captured in the course of various Wei expeditions into the steppe and several hundred thousand Chinese peasants who had been relocated to grow food for the garrisons. Other sources of manpower were captives taken from the Man people along the southwestern fringe of the Wei empire and convicts sent to the garrisons as punishment for a variety of offenses. Leadership within these communities was provided by Xianbei nobles and the descendants of Chinese local elites who had been transferred to the frontier by the Wei rulers. The Xianbei were the dominant group in cultural and linguistic as well as political-administrative terms, and it was usual for garrison families of Chinese descent to adopt the Xianbei language and culture.[11] During the years when the capital was at nearby Pingcheng, the elite families of the northern garrisons occupied a respected place in the Wei state and their members could be promoted to the highest offices. With the transfer of the capital to Luoyang, however, their status took a turn for the worse.

A yawning chasm opened between the Xianbei who remained on the northern frontier and those who had moved south with the emperor and his court. The northerners continued to adhere to old customs and the ancestral tongue, while their cousins in Luoyang were rapidly adopting Chinese ways. The gap was not only cultural but also political and social. The strength of the now-distant garrisons was of much less concern to the government than in the past. Members of the capital elite came to regard garrison commands as hardship posts, with the result that only men of inferior quality and character were willing to accept such appointments. Many of the officials sent from the capital were abusive and corrupt, and they found various ways to feather their own nests at the expense of the people who were subject to their authority.[12] At the same time, the possibility of upward mobility for the garrison elites was closed off. Not only were they excluded from the formal ranking system that established the eligibility of the Luoyang Xianbei for government offices, but they now found themselves officially registered and classified as "garrison households" (*fuhu*) – along with all the other members of the garrison communities, the descendants of convicts among them. They and their families had, in effect, been redefined as members of a hereditary servile status group. For men who prided themselves on the fact that their ancestors had come to the garrisons as the "sons of good families" (*liang jia zi*) rather than captives or convicts, this was an extremely bitter blow.[13] Because of their proximity to the center of power, the Xianbei guardsmen resident in and around Luoyang were able to protect their own interests quite effectively. In 519, for example, a mob of guardsmen set fire to the home of a Han Chinese official who had proposed that military men should be barred from the highest civil posts, the so-called "pure offices," and the idea was quickly dropped.[14] Relegated to the distant frontier, the men of the Six Garrisons found redress of their grievances a much more difficult matter.

When the explosion finally came, it was set off not by the garrison elites but by the most marginal elements of the garrison communities. The steppe frontier had been afflicted by drought and famine, and when the commander at Huaihuang refused to distribute relief grain in the summer of 523 he was murdered by the people of the garrison. Soon afterward, a Xiongnu trooper named Poliuhan Baling led a revolt at Gaoque, an outpost of the Woye garrison, and other disaffected elements swiftly flocked to his banner.[15] Poliuhan's followers seem to have come mainly from the Gaoju, Xiongnu, and other subjugated groups who had been allowed to retain their tribal organization and nomadic way of life, and they may have been encouraged by the raiding of the frontier by hungry Rouran and the complete failure of a Wei army sent up from the south to bring the marauders to bay. Secondary revolts spread along the frontier and into the Ordos region within the great loop of the Yellow River, with many of the garrisons dissolving into chaos. In some of the threatened communities, such as Huaishuo and Wuchuan, members of the garrison elite organized their kinsmen, slaves, and retainers into "loyalist" militias to protect their property and status.[16] The rebellions were put down in the first half of 525 by government armies with considerable assistance from the Rouran khan, who had decided to intervene on the side of the Wei court. By this time large numbers of refugees from the garrisons had already migrated southward into Hebei and Shanxi, and the government chose to move some 200,000 surrendered rebels to the plains of central Hebei on the grounds that it would be easier for them to find food there than on the devastated and drought-stricken steppe frontier. This quickly proved to be a serious miscalculation. Before the end of the year some of the displaced northerners had rebelled again, and during the course of 526 and 527 the various rebels and refugees in Hebei coalesced into a very strong force under the leadership of Ge Rong, a former officer of the Huaishuo garrison.[17]

At this juncture, the most effective military force available to the Wei court was the following of the Shanxi warlord Erzhu Rong. The Erzhu clan were a branch of the Jie people, an eastern Iranian group that had entered China as part of the Xiongnu tribal confederacy and later gave rise to the Shi rulers of Later Zhao in the fourth century. As early supporters of the Tuoba, they had been rewarded with a large grant of territory near the Hutuo River in north-central Shanxi, between Pingcheng and Taiyuan. Here they were allowed to retain their tribal organization and pastoral way of life; by the early sixth century they were said to number 8000 families, with cattle, sheep, camels, and horses in such numbers that they were "counted by the valley" rather than individually. Erzhu Rong and his followers emerged as an important loyalist force after the frontier erupted in rebellion in 523, and they offered a haven for many of the people who had fled southward to escape the chaos in the garrisons. These new adherents included quite a few capable military leaders from among the garrison elite, and the Erzhu used their wealth in livestock to expand their forces further by buying the services of fighting men who had fled from the garrisons.[18] During the chaos in the north Erzhu Rong managed to take control of the city of Taiyuan and make it his headquarters, and it soon became clear that in spite of his opposition to the garrison rebels he was anything but a loyal servant of the Wei court at Luoyang. In the fourth lunar month of 528, he took the poisoning of the young Emperor Xiaoming by Empress Dowager Hu as his pretext to march on the capital and assert control over the court. On May 17, Erzhu Rong ordered his troopers to cut down more than a thousand officials and courtiers who had come out of the city to tender their submission; the Empress Dowager and her three-year-old puppet emperor were flung into the Yellow River.[19]

After enthroning a puppet emperor of his own, Erzhu Rong turned east to confront Ge Rong's rebel swarm on the plains of Hebei. Debouching rapidly from the Fukou Pass in the Taihang Mountains with a force of 7000 picked cavalry in the ninth lunar month of 528, Erzhu smashed the much larger rebel army which was spread over the space of a dozen miles north of the city of Ye.[20] This victory resulted in the relocation of thousands of the defeated warriors to Taiyuan to swell the ranks of the Erzhu forces, and it left Erzhu Rong as the strongest power in what remained of the Wei empire. His hegemony was short-lived, however. In the ninth lunar month of 530 the puppet emperor Xiaozhuang eliminated the dictator in a carefully contrived palace ambush, landing the first blow with his own saber. Erzhu Rong's heir Erzhu Zhao responded by sacking the capital, killing Emperor Xiaozhuang, and installing yet another candidate on the Wei throne.[21] In spite of this brutal and decisive action, the new leader of the Erzhu was unable to secure his clan's hegemony. The new emperor and his court remained surprisingly recalcitrant, kinsmen sent to govern outlying regions of the empire tended to disregard Erzhu Zhao's authority, and, most serious of all, the former followers of Ge Rong who had been subordinated to the Erzhu escaped from Shanxi to Hebei and once again challenged the Erzhu hegemony.[22] The leader of this movement was a general named Gao Huan.

Gao's grandfather was a Han Chinese official in the service of Wei who had

101

been sent to the Huaishuo garrison as punishment for an offense. Gao himself grew up in poverty on the frontier, not even owning a horse until he married the daughter of a wealthy Xianbei cattleman. This marriage apparently opened the door to minor office in the garrison, with Gao serving first as a subaltern (*duizhu*) and then as a dispatch courier. After the outbreak of the rebellions in the Six Garrisons in 523, Gao was one of the many frontiersmen who ended up in the plains of Hebei, where he moved from one rebel group to another before defecting from Ge Rong's camp to that of the Erzhu.[23] He was given positions of great responsibility first by Erzhu Rong and then by Erzhu Zhao, who made the fatal mistake of putting him in command of what was left of Ge Rong's host. Gao promptly decamped from Shanxi and began to establish an independant regime in Hebei in 531. Although Gao's own cultural and linguistic identity, thanks to his family's experience in the "melting pot" of the Six Garrisons, was very much that of a Xianbei and his closest associates were fellow frontiersmen from Huaishuo, he nevertheless succeeded in winning support from some of the aristocratic Han families of Hebei.[24] These families had, of course, raised strong militia forces from among their retainers and tenants as was the usual practice in unsettled times. When the showdown between Gao Huan and Erzhu Zhao occurred at the Hanling ridge near Ye in the late spring of 532, Gao commanded a strong army that included both frontier cavalry and Han Chinese elements.[25] The Erzhu forces were decisively defeated, and in the space of less than a year Gao was able to reduce the Erzhu strongholds in Shanxi, incorporate the defeated troops into his own army, and install a Wei prince of his choosing on the imperial throne in Luoyang.

Gao Huan's control of the empire was still far from complete, however. His intended puppet emperor, Xiaowu, soon showed that he had a mind of his own, and, what was worse, he could look to the west for military support. Back in 530 Erzhu Rong had sent an armed expedition to establish control over the Wei River valley and adjacent regions, and by 534 the leaders of that expedition were well on their way to establishing an independant regional regime. The man who emerged as the central figure in this venture was a young general named Yuwen Tai. For the next sixteen years he would be Gao Huan's deadly rival, and his descendants would eventually destroy the state ruled by Gao's heirs.

While Gao Huan was a man of the Huaishuo garrison, Yuwen Tai hailed from the Wuchuan garrison sixty-five miles to the east. He was descended from a Xiongnu group that had adhered to the Wei state in its early days and received "compatriot" status. His great-great-grandfather had gone out to join the Wuchuan garrison in the early years of the fifth century, and his family clearly belonged to the garrison elite. When the rebellions broke out in the Six Garrisons in 523, his father organized a loyalist militia to resist the rebels. Yuwen Tai was perhaps eighteen years old at the time.[26] Like many other refugees from the garrisons, Tai and his father eventually sought shelter with one of the rebel groups in Hebei. After the father was killed in battle Tai adhered to Ge Rong, and after Ge's defeat in 528 he entered the service of the Erzhu. At this point he benefited from the fact that other members of the Wuchuan elite had already found shelter with Erzhu Rong at Taiyuan, where they had acquired a modicum of authority. One such was Heba Yue, the son of an old comrade of Tai's father, who was selected by Erzhu Rong to be the principal troop commander of the expedition to recover the Wei River valley.[27] Heba brought Yuwen Tai along as one of his officers. When Heba was murdered by another general at the beginning of 534, the senior officers of the army elected Yuwen Tai, still not yet thirty years old, to be their new leader. The manner of his elevation may help to explain the relatively informal, collegial style of decisionmaking that seems to have been characteristic of the regime over which he presided. Yuwen Tai was clearly superior to his fellows in political authority and his power grew with the passage of time, but he seems to have dealt with the other generals as social equals and permitted a fair amount of give-and-take.[28] This situation may have been facilitated by the fact that most of Yuwen Tai's close associates were products of the same Xianbei cultural milieu in the frontier garrisons. At least eight of the twelve generals he commanded in 537 were Xianbei, and six of the twelve were from the Wuchuan garrison.[29]

After he assumed command of Heba Yue's army, Yuwen Tai maneuvered to consolidate his position in the northwest and encouraged the Wei court's defiance of Gao Huan. When the exasperated Gao marched on Luoyang in the summer of 534, Emperor Xiaowu fled westward to take refuge with Yuwen Tai and was installed in the other ancient Han-period capital, Chang'an. Gao responded by placing yet another puppet emperor on the throne, transferring the capital to his own base at Ye in southern Hebei, and forcing the entire population of Luoyang to move there. The former capital quickly turned into the desolate ruins described by a former inhabitant who visited the site thirteen years later:

> The city walls had collapsed, palaces and houses were in ruins; Buddhist and Taoist temples were in ashes; and shrines and pagodas were mere heaps of rubble. Walls were covered with artemisia, and streets were full of thorns. The beasts of the field had made their holes in the overgrown palace steps, and the mountain birds had nested in the courtyard trees. Wandering herdsmen loitered in the highways, and farmers had planted millet between the ceremonial towers before the palace.[30]

The flight of Emperor Xiaowu in 534 marked the beginning of the division of North China into two rival states, a division that would hold for more than forty years. Both states were ruled by figurehead emperors of the Wei house until 550, when Gao Huan's heir deposed the last ruler of "Eastern Wei" and made himself the first emperor of the (Northern) Qi dynasty. Seven years later

Yuwen Tai's successors did the same, and "Western Wei" became (Northern) Zhou, ruled by the house of Yuwen. From first to last the two states were bitter enemies; the fondest ambition of each was the conquest of the other. In the early days the initiative rested with Gao Huan in the east, who commanded by far the larger resource and population base and by far the greatest number of North Asian fighting men. The western regime was at first hard pressed to survive. Gradually, however, it would develop the institutional and strategic means to turn the tables decisively against the easterners.

Gao Huan made his first large-scale effort to conquer Guanzhong at the beginning of 537. Gao himself led one column and threw three pontoon bridges across the Yellow River at Puban to cross over from Shanxi, while a second column advanced by way of the Tong Pass south of the Yellow River and a third column even farther south moved through the mountain passes from southwestern Henan. This attempt came to naught when Yuwen Tai concentrated 6000 cavalry, his main force, against the Eastern Wei column in the Tong Pass and succeeded in crushing it, prompting Gao Huan to beat a hasty retreat.[31] A second effort came in the autumn, when Gao again advanced on Puban and prepared to cross the Yellow River with an enormous army that was said to number more than 100,000 men. Gao's approach precipitated the withdrawal of Yuwen Tai's army from an advanced position in western Henan to confront the invaders in Guanzhong. The badly outnumbered defenders, only 7000 strong by one report, deployed at a place called Shayuan on the north bank of the Wei River, where their position backed up against a bend of the river that would have protected the army's flanks and rear.[32] Yuwen Tai took advantage of the tall reeds growing by the riverbank to conceal his flank units. When the Eastern Wei army arrived on the afternoon of November 19, its attack dissolved into a disorderly rush to close with the weak-looking western formation. It charged directly into the trap that Yuwen Tai had set, and was quickly cut in half by a heavy cavalry charge from the right wing of the Western Wei army. Gao Huan's army was routed, and the westerners claimed to have taken 6000 heads and 70,000 prisoners, of whom all but 20,000 were soon allowed to return to the east.[33] The fight was fairly typical of a great many medieval Chinese battles in that it revolved around a cleverly baited trap leading to a devastating ambush. The deployment of the Western Wei troops with their backs to the river illustrates another common motif, as generals would occasionally place their troops in such desperate positions to solidify fighting spirit and eliminate all hope of survival by flight.

The victory at Shayuan all but guaranteed the survival of Yuwen Tai's regime. The easterners would never again penetrate Guanzhong in force, and fence-sitting local elites were encouraged to throw their support to the victors. Among the other spoils of victory, Western Wei was able to establish lasting control over the Hongnong area in western Henan and the southwestern corner of Shanxi, between the Puban ford and the lower course of the Fen River.[34] Probably at the insistence of the emperor and his advisors, Western

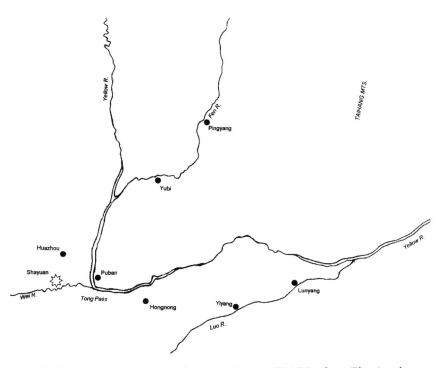

Map 10 The zone of confrontation between Western Wei (Northern Zhou) and Eastern Wei (Northern Qi)

Wei forces followed up this victory almost immediately by advancing east to the vicinity of Luoyang.[35] There, however, they were badly defeated by an eastern army at the battle of Heqiao (the Yellow River bridge) on September 13, 538, and driven back to Guanzhong in disarray.[36] The initiative shifted again to Gao Huan, who moved down the Fen River from Taiyuan to attack the fortress of Yubi in the late autumn of 542. Located on the Fen about twenty-five miles above its confluence with the Yellow River, Yubi – the "jade rampart" – had been built by Western Wei in 539 to cement its hold on southwestern Shanxi and block the invasion route into Guanzhong by way of the Puban ford. After a furious assault that went on without interruption for nine days and nights, Gao Huan withdrew because of a snowstorm that claimed the lives of many of his exposed soldiers.[37] In the following year, 543, Yuwen Tai marched east to Luoyang once again, and just as in 538 Gao Huan brought his main army south from Taiyuan to deal with him. The eastern and western armies met in the Mang hills between Luoyang and the Yellow River in the third lunar month, and a series of engagements spread over several days ended in another costly defeat for Yuwen Tai, who again withdrew to the west.[38]

In 546 Gao Huan made another attempt on Yubi. The siege probably began in the ninth lunar month and lasted for approximately fifty days. In contrast to the stone walls of late Roman and Byzantine cities and fortresses, fortifications in North China during this period were normally built by the *hangtu* or rammed-earth method that had been in use since very early times. A thin layer of earth was spread between wooden frames and pounded until it was hard, more earth was spread on top of that and pounded, and so the wall was built up layer by layer. It was usual for cities to be protected by solid, massive *hangtu* ramparts between ten and thirty feet thick, and the walls were often surrounded by a deep ditch or moat.[39] If the walls were in good repair and the fortress held by a strong garrison with adequate provisions, it could be extremely difficult to capture. In China as in the Mediterranean world and the Latin West during the Middle Ages, the technologies of fortification and siege-craft tended to give the defenders of strongholds a significant edge over their attackers. Sieges could drag on for many months, and fortresses were more likely to fall as a result of starvation rather than assault, sapping, or battery. The attackers sometimes ran out of food before the defenders did.[40]

Gao Huan's siege of Yubi illustrates the difficulties faced by an army trying to take a strong fortress. Gao's men began by building an earthen mound to overlook the south wall of the fortress, but the defenders were able to counter by adding to the height of their towers. The attackers then tried tunnelling, but the defenders intercepted the tunnels by digging a deep trench inside and parallel to the south wall. When the attackers tried to weaken the wall with a sort of battering ram, the defenders lowered a cloth screen from the top of the wall to soften its impact. Gao Huan's men eventually succeeded in undermining the wall and causing a small section to collapse, but the Western Wei defenders quickly filled the gap with a makeshift palisade. After spending thousands of lives to no avail, Gao abandoned the siege and withdrew to Taiyuan. He died only a few weeks later.[41]

After 546, the conflict settled into a low-intensity, decades-long stalemate, with few major initiatives undertaken by either side.[42] With Gao Huan's passing the cast of characters had begun to change, and both regimes now seemed more concerned with internal developments and advances in other directions.[43] Moreover, the ten-year war from 537 to 546 seemed to demonstrate to both sides the futility of offensive operations. Eastern Wei's most promising avenue of advance into Guanzhong, from Taiyuan by way of the Puban ford, was blocked by the adamantine walls of Yubi, while Western Wei's preferred invasion route on the south side of the Yellow River led only to the ruins of an abandoned capital. The new eastern capital of Ye was another 170 miles to the northeast (as the crow flies) and on the other side of the Yellow River, while it was at Taiyuan in central Shanxi that Gao Huan had established his military headquarters and concentrated the bulk of his North Asian soldiery. Any western army operating in the vicinity of Luoyang was badly exposed to an attack launched from Taiyuan to the north, as happened in 538 and 543.[44]

In their battles in the 530s and 540s, both Gao Huan and Yuwen Tai led armies that were composed mainly of Xianbei, Gaoju Turks, and other North

Asian warriors. Although the numbers given in the sources cannot always be trusted, it seems that the Western Wei armies were consistently smaller than those of Gao Huan, who was often credited with forces of 100,000 or more. As a result of his victory over the Erzhu and his dominance of Hebei, Shanxi, and Henan, Gao's following included not only the Six Garrison rebels from Hebei, but also the vast majority of the former Erzhu forces and the Wei imperial guards from Luoyang as well as tribal groups from the northern frontier.[45] Although Gao won the support of powerful Han Chinese families in Hebei and made use of their private militias when he defeated the Erzhu at Hanling in 532, he had little faith in the fighting quality of Chinese soldiers. On the eve of the battle of Hanling, he had said to one of the militia leaders, "The troops under your command are Han. I fear they will be of no assistance. Now what you ought to do is take a thousand or more Xianbei troops and mix them in with the others."[46] In Gao's view, fighting was the responsibility of the Xianbei while the function of the Chinese was to feed and cloth the North Asian warriors. He sought to defuse ethnic tensions within his realm by pointing to the benefits of this division of labor. To the Xianbei he would say, "The Han are your slaves. The men till for you; the women weave for you. They provide you with grain and silk so that you are warm and well-fed. For what reason do you bully them?" Han Chinese were treated to a different speech. "The Xianbei are your retainers [ke]. For a single measure of your grain and a single length of your silk they attack the bandits so that you are safe. For what reason do you regard them as a scourge?"[47] Despite Gao's views, the military of Eastern Wei and Northern Qi did not remain the exclusive preserve of North Asians. During the 550s an effort was made to recruit Chinese "braves" (yongfu) whose courage, strength, and martial skills were up to Xianbei standards, and some Han peasants were eventually conscripted for military service as an extension of their corvée obligation during the last few years of Northern Qi.[48] The large reservoir of North Asian fighting men, however, meant that from first to last there was very little incentive for the government of Gao Huan and his successors to experiment and innovate, let alone introduce sweeping changes in its military institutions.

For Yuwen Tai, the situation was very different. The original Erzhu expedition that had brought him to Guanzhong was only a thousand strong, with two thousand reinforcements following soon after. To these may be added the several thousand Xianbei guardsmen who accompanied Emperor Xiaowu on his flight to the west, assorted herdsmen and refugees from the Six Garrisons recruited on the edge of the Ordos region, and possibly some of the captives taken at the battle of Shayuan in 537. From these elements, however, must be deducted the heavy losses incurred during the disastrous Luoyang campaigns of 538 and 543. Given the severe shortage of North Asian cavalry and the obvious inferiority to Gao Huan in this regard, Yuwen Tai and his associates had little choice but to recruit Han Chinese and other elements of the ethnically mixed population of Guanzhong to fill out the ranks of their army.[49]

An obvious source of fresh manpower was the private militias that had been raised by members of the local elite in Guanzhong and other regions, such as western Henan and southwestern Shanxi, that were accessible to Yuwen Tai's forces. Local strongmen had organized these militias, which became known as *xiang bing* or "local troops," from among their kinsmen, dependants, and neighbors during the disorder that followed the Six Garrisons rebellion, and the Western Wei regime enjoyed a great deal of success in wooing the leaders with grants of titles and offices.[50] One such leader was Wang Yue, a man of Lantian near Chang'an, who was admired by the people of the district for being "spirited and capable." He was made a county magistrate, and later led more than a thousand men from his community to fight for Yuwen Tai at Luoyang in 538.[51] Another was Pei Xia, a former commandery administrator from a prominent family of southwestern Shanxi, who brought a contingent of "local troops" to fight at Shayuan.[52] Chen Yi, a man of Yiyang in the mountains of western Henan, did not come from a family with an official background, but was known for his spirit of knight-errantry. After Emperor Xiaowu fled to the west, Chen gathered several dozen brave youths to carry out raids against Gao Huan's supporters. He was made county magistrate of Xin'an (near Yiyang), and led local troops to participate in both of the great Luoyang campaigns.[53] In addition to bestowing certain titles indicative of military command authority on the leaders of existing local militias, the Western Wei government apparently made an effort in the late 540s to organize the *xiang bing* into a hierarchical command structure headed by its own appointees. The men chosen to head the local troops in each prefecture (*zhou*) were carefully selected. They were men who not only enjoyed the trust of the Western Wei leaders, but also possessed local prestige sufficient to command the respect and obedience of lower-level militia bosses. One such appointee was Su Chun, a man from the town of Wugong in Qizhou, west of Chang'an, who was the son of a commandery administrator and the younger brother of one of the most important officials of the Western Wei regime. At the time of his appointment in 548, he had already served as a commandery administrator himself and could claim considerable military experience.[54] Yuwen Tai and his associates, most of whom were newcomers to Guanzhong, could use men such as Su Chun to forge links with lesser members of the local elite and draw them into the state structure.

The local troops provided a very significant addition to the military strength of Western Wei, especially in the perilous early years of the regime, and they were still a part of the military establishment as late as 580, just before Northern Zhou was replaced by Sui.[55] They were not, however, the central military institution of Western Wei and Northern Zhou. That position belonged to the "Twenty-four Armies," which are first mentioned in connection with the western command structure as of the year 550. Just exactly where these armies came from, how they were organized, and how they evolved over time are all matters of intense debate and deep disagreement. Many of the relevant arguments skate on very thin evidence, but the subject is one of great importance since the Twenty-four Armies played the central role in Zhou's conquest of Northern Qi in 576 and were the institutional ancestor of the celebrated system of "territorial soldiery" (*fubing*) that formed the backbone of the Sui and early Tang military.[56]

The Twenty-four Armies were clearly distinguished from the much smaller imperial guard. Their leaders reported not to the emperor, but to the headquarters that Yuwen Tai had set up at Huazhou (modern Dali, Shaanxi, guarding the eastern edge of Guanzhong) in his capacity as chancellor (*chengxiang*) of Western Wei.[57] The command structure in 550 was based on multiples of six. At the top were six close associates of Yuwen Tai who were designated as "pillars of the state" (*zhu guo*). Below these most senior commanders were twelve major-generals, each of whom had under his authority two armies (*jun*) commanded by "cavalry major-generals." Making up each of the armies was an indeterminate number of battalions (*tuan*), each of which was led by two "chariot-and-horse major-generals."[58] After 550 the number of "pillars" and major-generals increased considerably, and these most senior posts probably became sinecures unconnected with the actual command of troops. The number of *jun* under the "cavalry generals" held stable, however, and this seems to have become the key level of military command.[59] We do not know how large each of these units was, but there is reason to believe that the entire force consisted of about 50,000 men in 550 and well over 100,000 in the 570s.[60] Even in 550, this would have been a far larger force than Yuwen Tai's original following of Xianbei cavalry.

Where did all of these new soldiers come from? One school of thought holds that the Twenty-four Armies were built up through the incorporation of local troops, though there is no consensus regarding the mechanism by which this was accomplished or the role that local elites played in the leadership of these forces after they were "regularized." Another view downplays the contribution of the *xiang bing* and points to direct recruitment (or even conscription) of individual farmers by the state as the principal source of new manpower.[61] The evidence for both positions is very limited, and some of the sources are maddeningly ambiguous. Much of the debate has revolved around the interpretation of just a few key passages. One appears in the Zhou annals immediately after the notice of the defeat at the Mang hills near Luoyang in 543: "Subsequently there was a widespread recruitment of locally powerful men [*hao you*] in Guanlong in order to augment the armies."[62] Should this be taken as a reference to individuals, or to local strongmen leading bands of followers?

Another brief snippet, a quote from a lost history of the Wei dynasty preserved in a thirteenth-century encyclopedia, tells us that in 550 "strong and able commoners [*min*] were registered as soldiers of the headquarters [*fu bing*]."[63] The context makes it clear that the "headquarters" in question are those of the chariot-and-horse major-generals commanding the various battalions (*tuan*) under the Twenty-four Armies. This passage would seem to suggest that the Western Wei state was now able to induct individual farmers into the regular army for the first time, but there are still unanswered questions. It is not entirely clear whether these men were conscripts or volunteers, nor do we have any indication of the numbers involved or whether this now became the primary means of military recruitment.

The long-term trend, however, does appear to have been in the direction of incorporating larger numbers of individual commoners into the system without the mediation of local elites. In 574, on the eve of a new offensive against Northern Qi, Emperor Wu of Zhou initiated another great military buildup. Ordinary people (*bai xing*) were recruited to fill the ranks of the regular army, and those who joined were removed from the household registers in their home districts. Since this implied freedom from normal tax and corvée obligations, it was reported – no doubt with some exaggeration – that "after this half the Chinese became soldiers."[64]

There has been disagreement as to whether Chinese recruits who were re-registered as soldiers under the Twenty-four Armies became full-time fighting men who followed their units from garrison to garrison, or whether they continued to reside in their home communities and were called up only for rotational guard duty and military campaigns. A passage in the seventh-century *History of the Northern Dynasties* gives the impression that soldiers had no time for farming, since they were supposed to alternate fifteen days on guard duty at the palace with fifteen days off duty learning flag signals and practicing combat.[65] On the other hand, there is also textual evidence to support the farmer–soldier model, and we may reasonably question whether the relatively poor western realm would have been able to dispense entirely with the productive labor of more than 100,000 cultivators.[66] One way to resolve this debate would be to recognize that the sources may well be describing two different systems that existed side by side, one for Chinese peasant recruits and another for Xianbei and other highly professionalized elements within the army. This view is lent credence by the fact that in the early years of the Sui dynasty a clear distinction was made between rural residence units of territorial soldiers (*xiang tuan*) and those based within walled cities (*jun fang*).[67]

In spite of all the disagreement over the early *fubing* system as it existed within the framework of the Twenty-four Armies, there are a few basic points about the military establishment of Western Wei and Northern Zhou that can be asserted with some confidence. The first is that the armies grew dramatically over time, and did so to a considerable extent by incorporating ordinary Chinese farmers. The great majority of the new soldiers were surely infantry rather than cavalry.[68] They (and possibly also their families) were removed from the civilian household registers and re-registered by the military authorities. Theirs was not, however, a base or servile status (as with the military households under the Wei, Jin, and southern dynasties), but an honorable position that carried tangible rewards such as exemption from taxes and corvée. The army was also multiethnic. It continued to include units of Xianbei, and grew not only by incorporating Chinese but also people of many other ethnic groups, such as the Qiang who were especially numerous in some districts of Guanzhong north of the Wei River.[69] Although it is difficult to argue that the army was simply a congeries of private militias that were brought under nominal state authority when their leaders were given official titles, it does seem that local elites continued to play a leadership role at the middle and lower levels.[70] The success of the new military system was due in part to the fact that it exploited rather than challenged the preexisting structure of local society – an observation that is borne out by the fact that the rulers of Western Wei and Northern Zhou were never seriously troubled by grassroots rebellions. At the same time, the system also prevented the concentration of independant and potentially destabilizing military power in the hands of the most senior commanders. Most of the "pillars" and major generals came from outside Guanzhong, while the great majority of the troops and lower-level officers were locally recruited and had no personal ties to top-echelon leaders. Warlordism was never a problem in Western Wei and Northern Zhou.[71]

An important additional element seems to have been added to the Twenty-four Army system during the final decade of Northern Zhou. For most of the history of the western regime founded by Yuwen Tai, the emperors had little real power and the imperial guard was a relatively small force composed mainly of Xianbei. The dictatorship that Yuwen Tai had exercised in the name of the Yuan (Tuoba) rulers of Western Wei was continued after his death in 556 by his nephew and political heir Yuwen Hu, who inaugurated the Zhou dynasty by installing a son of Yuwen Tai as his puppet emperor. The third kinsman that Yuwen Hu placed on the throne, the shrewd and capable Emperor Wu of Zhou, finally succeeded in eliminating his overbearing cousin in a palace coup in 572. During the years when he had reigned but not ruled, Emperor Wu had taken care to cultivate his connections with the army, making tours of inspection and holding great military reviews. Once he held the reins of power in his own hands, he moved quickly to establish direct imperial control over the Twenty-four Armies. In effect, these forces were incorporated into the imperial guard. In 574 all of their soldiers were given the title of "officer in attendance" (*shiguan*), a term that had previously been reserved for men of high rank and status who served in direct attendance upon the emperor. This measure must surely have added to both the prestige of the soldiers in their home communities and their feelings of loyalty to the sovereign. And it may have been at this time that soldiers of the Twenty-four Armies first began to perform guard duty by rotation in the environs of the imperial palace, an important feature of the *fubing* system under the Sui and Tang dynasties.[72]

Despite – or perhaps because of – his years in the shadow of Yuwen Hu, Emperor Wu proved to be an ambitious and aggressive ruler. Shortly after taking power in his own right, he began to make preparations for a renewal of the war against Northern Qi which had been in a state of suspended animation for several decades (with the exception of a brief flurry of activity in 562–4). In the summer of 575, he mobilized an army of 170,000 men for another

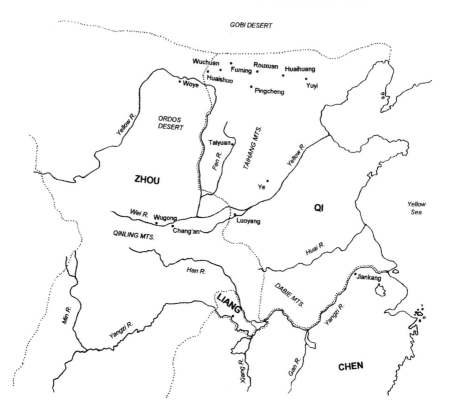

Map 11 North China in AD 572, also showing the old Northern Wei garrisons

offensive eastward to the vicinity of Luoyang. In spite of some initial successes, the 575 effort fared little better than Yuwen Tai's Luoyang campaigns more than thirty years earlier. The Zhou army failed to capture the Jinyong Fortress, the emperor fell ill at a critical moment, and once again – as in 538 and 543 – the main army of the eastern regime came south from Taiyuan to strike the exposed westerners. These circumstances prompted a withdrawal to the safety of Guanzhong after only 18 days of active campaigning.[73] In the autumn of 576, Emperor Wu resolved upon a new strategic approach. Instead of taking the well-trodden path to Luoyang, he would "grasp the throat" of Northern Qi by advancing directly up the valley of the Fen River to attack Taiyuan itself. If a decisive victory could be gained over the enemy's principal army on its home turf, the eastern regime might be expected to unravel of itself. The emperor forced the adoption of this plan over the objections of his generals, who considered it much too risky.[74]

The campaign began on November 10, 576. The first objective was the Qi border fortress of Pingyang, located near the point where the Fen turns westward toward its confluence with the Yellow River. Emperor Wu invested the fortress with his main army, probably 60,000 strong, while eight smaller contingents totalling 85,000 men (and ranging in strength from 5000 up to 20,000) fanned out in an arc to the north and east to cover the besiegers against a possible relief effort.[75] The emperor directed the siege operations himself, and the town fell in early December through the treachery of one of the Qi commanders. By this time the Qi ruler, Gao Wei, was approaching from Taiyuan with a large army. The Zhou emperor chose to throw a 10,000–man garrison into the town he had just taken and withdraw the rest of his army to the vicinity of Yubi.[76] Now it was Qi's turn to besiege Pingyang. The siege lasted nearly a month, until Emperor Wu returned with the main Zhou army. On the morning of January 10, 577, he deployed 80,000 men in battle formation on a front several miles long and rode along the line with a small retinue to strengthen the morale of his troops. He was prevented from getting at the Qi army, however, by a protective ditch that they had dug south of Pingyang, between Mount Qiao and the Fen River. It was not until mid–afternoon that Gao Wei, persuaded by the eunuchs in his entourage that it was unbecoming for an emperor to take refuge behind a ditch, finally filled in the obstacle and crossed over to join battle. Soon after the fighting began the Qi left wing was pushed back a short distance, prompting the nervous Gao Wei to flee the field. The outcome had been in doubt up to this point, but the flight of the emperor led in short order to the demoralization and collapse of the Qi army. The Zhou forces took more than 10,000 prisoners and broke the siege of Pingyang.[77]

Once again cautious generals tried to persuade Emperor Wu to halt the campaign, but he would have none of it. "Let go of the enemy and troubles will arise. If you gentlemen have doubts, I will go after them alone." The advance elements of the Zhou army reached Taiyuan on January 17, with the emperor following two days later.[78] On the 20th some 40,000 Qi troops came out to offer battle. They were driven back, and Emperor Wu exploited the situation by leading a small force of cavalry through the east gate to create a lodgement within the walls of the city. The fight was not over, however. That night, a determined Qi counterattack eliminated the bridgehead and nearly took the emperor himself – he had to cut his way out of the east gate, and was only able to make good his escape because there were so many corpses on the ground that the Qi troops could not get the gate to shut completely. The next morning, January 21, the Zhou army directed its full strength against the east gate and carried the city, the main center of the Gao family's military power since the early 530s.[79] After this, the rest of the campaign seems anticlimactic. Emperor Wu descended from the Shanxi highlands to the eastern plain by way of the Fukou pass, arriving beneath the walls of Ye, the seat of the civil administration of Northern Qi, on February 21, 577. The city fell the next day.[80] All that remained were mopping-up operations. The feckless Qi ruler Gao Wei, who had fled from Taiyuan to Ye and from Ye to Shandong, was captured and eventually put to death near the end of the year. Northern Qi had ceased to exist, and for the first time since the revolt of the

Six Garrisons a genuinely unified political order was imposed on all the people of North China.

Many factors contributed to the fall of Northern Qi. On a personal level, Gao Wei was clearly outclassed by Emperor Wu of Zhou, who did not flinch from battle and worked assiduously to present himself to his soldiers as a great captain, even dressing in martial attire rather than an emperor's flowing robes when at home in his capital.[81] The Qi leader, in contrast, forgot his lines and started to laugh when he tried to harangue the troops who had been assembled for the defense of Ye, prompting the soldiers to ask one another whether this was a man worth risking their lives for.[82] It was not simply a matter of leadership style but also of political and strategic acumen. After his failure in 575 the Zhou ruler made the shrewd decision to march on Taiyuan rather than Luoyang the following year, while his eastern rival chose to accept battle at Pingyang when it was clearly not in his interest to do so. Emperor Wu had also taken steps to weaken and distract the Qi regime by negotiating an alliance with the southern state of Chen that led to a major Chen offensive against Qi forces in the Huai River valley in 573.[83] The Qi army, meanwhile, was demoralized and disaffected as a result of Gao Wei's unjust execution of the popular North Asian general Hulü Guang in 572; in the opinion of one contemporary observer, this was *the* decisive factor shaping the outcome of the east–west struggle.[84]

There were also deeper, long-term influences at work. One was the new military structure that had been developed by Western Wei and Zhou. The army that conquered Qi was composed of many different contingents, including irregular forces raised by local elites, tribal auxiliaries from the steppe margin of the empire, and even volunteers recruited from among the young gallants of the capital.[85] It is generally agreed, however, that the most important component of the Zhou army, both qualitatively and quantitatively, was the Twenty-four Armies. This force was much larger, better trained, and more reliable than the armies that Yuwen Tai had commanded in the 530s. Another element contributing to the growth of the western armies was the campaign of expansion westward and southward undertaken during the late 540s and 550s, when the war with Qi was largely in abeyance. Western Wei forces subdued the Gansu corridor, a major trade route and an important source of horses, in the late 540s. With the collapse of the Liang dynasty, they moved south to take the Sichuan basin in 553. The Han River valley, too, was brought under control between 549 and 554, with a scion of the Liang royal house left in possession of a tiny client kingdom around Jiangling on the Yangzi. These conquests opened new sources of grain and manpower that helped to offset the original gross imbalance in favor of the east.[86]

While the western state was getting stronger, the eastern regime did not see any comparable gains. Despite their larger population base, the Eastern Wei and Northern Qi rulers were generally less effective when it came to mobilizing resources for state purposes.[87] One reason for this was the local power of the Chinese great families, especially in Hebei, and this in turn pointed to a fundamental weakness of the Qi polity. In the populous east, the dominant Xianbei were a small minority in a sea of Han Chinese. As the descendants of garrison soldiers who had not looked favorably upon the sinicizing reforms of the Wei Emperor Xiaowen, they sought to preserve their language, customs, and identity (Xianbei was not only the language of command for the army but the primary tongue of the Qi court). They were fearful and suspicious of the Han majority and jealously guarded their hold on political power, with the result that bloody purges of Chinese officials were not infrequent occurrences.[88] Under these circumstances, real cooptation of Chinese elites was out of the question, as was the incorporation of Chinese leaders into the regular military establishment.[89] The hostility of the Xianbei toward the majority population was fully reciprocated, and when the crisis came in the 570s few Chinese were willing to exert themselves on behalf of their alien masters.

A very different development occurred in Guanzhong. There, as we have seen, Yuwen Tai and his relatively small group of Xianbei had little choice but to forge links with the Chinese population in order to survive. This process was probably also facilitated by the more variegated ethnic environment of the western region and by the fact that the leading Han families of the region were much weaker than their counterparts in the east. The leaders of Western Wei and Northern Zhou had less reason to fear that they might be submerged in a sea of Han Chinese.[90] Instead of excluding Chinese from government offices and military commands, Yuwen Tai and his successors sought to draw them in through such devices as the regularization of the local troops (*xiang bing*) and the expansion of the Twenty-four Armies. They continued to use the Xianbei language and were no less proud of their heritage than were their eastern cousins; however, they did not seek to exclude Chinese elites from their circle but to incorporate them and create a sense of common identity. One means by which this was done was the bestowal of multisyllable Xianbei surnames on Han and Qiang as a way of making them honorary Xianbei; the *xiang bing* leader Su Chun, for example, was granted the surname of Helan. This practice began in the 530s and reached a peak in the 550s.[91] Another trend, not so much a matter of public policy but probably more effective in the long run, was intermarriage between Xianbei, Han, and Qiang families. By the time of the conquest of Northern Qi, a new ruling elite was taking shape in Guanzhong, a hybrid aristocracy that combined Chinese cultural elements with many of the values and customs of the garrison Xianbei. The martial skills and outlook characteristic of Yuwen Tai's original North Asian following were adopted by many members of the Chinese elite, with the result that the new northwestern aristocracy came to be made up of "tough, ruthless men of action, skilled in horsemanship and archery" and "resourceful military leaders, experienced in the politics of their time."[92] Hunting, itself an important form of training for the real business of war, was their favorite pastime. However, they cannot easily be dismissed as mere barbarians. Many of the first generation of Xianbei to occupy Guanzhong, and perhaps even Yuwen Tai himself, were illiterate, but members of the second generation were better educated and much more likely to have at least a rudimentary knowledge of the Confucian classics.[93] It came to be the ideal for a gentleman to be skilled in both the martial and literary arts, so that he was equally capable of serving as either a general or a minister. Out of this new northwestern aristocracy came the first emperor of the Sui dynasty, who completed the reunification of China that had been begun by Emperor Wu of Zhou, and the founders of the Tang dynasty, who created an imperial order that would endure for almost three hundred years.

Notes

1 Li Tse-fen, *Liang Jin Nanbeichao lishi lunwenji*, vol. 1, pp. 145–6.
2 Tang Changru, *Wei Jin Nanbeichao Sui Tang shi san lun*, pp. 192–3, 195–6.
3 Rogers, *The Chronicle of Fu Chien*, p. 14; Chen Yinke, *Wei Jin Nanbeichao shi jiangyanlu*, pp. 251–2.
4 W. J. F. Jenner, *Memories of Loyang: Yang Hsüan-chih and the Lost Capital (493–534)* (Oxford: Clarendon Press, 1981), p. 58; He Ziquan, *Wei Jin Nanbeichao shilue*, pp. 164–5.
5 The Jinyong Fortress was a rectangle 1086 meters north to south and 255 meters east to west; see *Zhongguo junshi shi*, vol. 6: *Bing lei* (Beijing: Jiefangjun chubanshe, 1991), p. 141.
6 Jenner, *Memories of Loyang*, pp. 42, 61–2, 104, 117–18.
7 Very little is known about the Rouran, who are sometimes equated with the Avars of early medieval Europe; see Denis Sinor (ed.), *The Cambridge History of Early Inner Asia* (Cambridge: Cambridge University Press, 1990), pp. 291–7.
8 Jenner, *Memories of Loyang*, pp. 81–2; for the location of the Six Garrisons, see Scott A. Pearce, "The Yü-wen Regime in Sixth-Century China" (Ph.D. dissertation, Princeton University, 1987), p. 59, and Tan Qixiang, *Zhongguo lishi dituji* (Shanghai: Cartographic Publishing House, 1982), vol. 4, maps 50 to 55.
9 For the administration of the garrisons, see Zhou Yiliang, "Bei Wei zhen shu zhidu kao ji xu kao," in idem, *Wei Jin Nanbeichao shi lunji* (Beijing: Zhonghua shuju, 1963), pp. 199–219; and Mao Han-kuang, "Bei Wei Dong Wei Bei Qi zhi hexin jituan yu hexin qu," pp. 39, 54, 71.
10 Pearce, "The Yü-wen Regime in Sixth-Century China," pp. 65–7; Mao Han-kuang, "Bei Wei Dong Wei Bei Qi zhi hexin jituan yu hexin qu," p. 66.
11 For a thorough discussion of the ethnic and social composition of the garrisons, see Pearce, "The Yü-wen Regime in Sixth-Century China," pp. 70–82.
12 Mao Han-kuang, "Bei Wei Dong Wei Bei Qi zhi hexin jituan yu hexin qu," pp. 71–2; Jenner, *Memories of Loyang*, pp. 69, 82.
13 Pearce, "The Yü-wen Regime in Sixth-Century China," pp. 155–71.
14 Jenner, *Memories of Loyang*, pp. 74–5.
15 Sima Guang, *Zizhi tongjian*, ch. 149, pp. 4674–5.
16 Pearce, "The Yü-wen Regime in Sixth-Century China," pp. 98, 183–91.
17 Pearce, "The Yü-wen Regime in Sixth-Century China," pp. 192–9.
18 For the Erzhu, see Pearce, "The Yü-wen Regime in Sixth-Century China," pp. 114, 123, 201–2, 206; Jenner, *Memories of Loyang*, pp. 86–9; and Wei Shou, *Wei shu*, ch. 74, p. 1644.
19 Jenner, *Memories of Loyang*, pp. 89–91.
20 Sima Guang, *Zizhi tongjian*, ch. 152, pp. 4751–2; *Wei shu*, ch. 74, pp. 1649–50; Pearce, "The Yü-wen Regime in Sixth-Century China," p. 208.

21 See Jenner, *Memories of Loyang*, pp. 95–7, 160–1; and Sima Guang, *Zizhi tongjian*, ch. 154, p. 4783.

22 Pearce, "The Yü-wen Regime in Sixth-Century China," pp. 212–15; Jenner, *Memories of Loyang*, pp. 97–8.

23 For Gao Huan's background and early career, see Li Baiyao, *Bei Qi shu* (Beijing: Zhonghua shuju, 1972), ch. 1, pp. 1–3; He Ziquan, *Wei Jin Nanbeichao shilue*, p. 186; and Pearce, "The Yü-wen Regime in Sixth-Century China," pp. 83–4, 119–20.

24 Mao Han-kuang, "Bei Wei Dong Wei Bei Qi zhi hexin jituan yu hexin qu," pp. 89–90; Zhou Yiliang, "Beichao de minzu wenti yu minzu zhengce," in idem, *Wei Jin Nanbeichao shi lunji* (Beijing: Zhonghua shuju, 1963), pp. 125, 128–9; Pearce, "The Yü-wen Regime in Sixth-Century China," p. 64.

25 For a description of the battle, see Sima Guang, *Zizhi tongjian*, ch. 155, pp. 4818–20.

26 The most important source for Yuwen Tai's ancestry and early life is Linghu Defen, *Zhou shu* (Beijing: Zhonghua shuju, 1971), ch. 1, pp. 1–3. Also see He Ziquan, *Wei Jin Nanbeichao shilue*, p. 186, and Pearce, "The Yü-wen Regime in Sixth-Century China," pp. 2–33. Note that there is conflicting evidence regarding Yuwen Tai's age; I have chosen to follow *Zhou shu*, ch. 2, p. 37, which indicates that he died at the age of fifty-two *sui* in 556. This would mean that he was born in 505.

27 For the relationship between Yuwen and Heba, see Pearce, "The Yü-wen Regime in Sixth-Century China," pp. 98–9, 101–3, 107.

28 The collegiality of Yuwen Tai's "junta" – and its limits – is discussed in Pearce, "The Yü-wen Regime in Sixth-Century China," pp. 394–403.

29 Albert E. Dien, "The Role of the Military in the Western Wei/Northern Chou State," in Albert E. Dien (ed.), *State and Society in Early Medieval China* (Stanford, Ca.: Stanford University Press, 1990), p. 346. For an extremely detailed analysis of the origins and possible factional affiliations of Yuwen Tai's associates, see Mao Han-kuang, "Xi Wei fubing shi lun," in idem, *Zhongguo zhonggu zhengzhi shi lun* (Taipei: Lianjing, 1990), pp. 169–94.

30 Yang Xuanzhi's "Luoyang qielan ji," translated by Jenner in *Memories of Loyang*, p. 142. Jenner also describes the events leading to the abandonment of Luoyang on pages 99–102.

31 *Zhou shu*, ch. 2, p. 22; Pearce, "The Yü-wen Regime in Sixth-Century China," pp. 301–2; Zhao Wenrun, "Lun Xi Wei yu Dong Wei zhijian de ji ci zhanyi," *Bei chao yanjiu*, 1996, No. 2, pp. 11–12.

32 The figure of 7000 is from Wang Yinglin, *Yu hai* (rpt. of 1337 edn; Taipei: Huawen shuju, 1964), ch. 138, p. 18b, quoting Li Fan's *Ye hou jia zhuan*.

33 *Zhou shu*, ch. 2, pp. 23–4; Sima Guang, *Zizhi tongjian*, ch. 157, pp. 4884–6; Pearce, "The Yü-wen Regime in Sixth-Century China," pp. 306–7; Zhao Wenrun, "Lun Xi Wei yu Dong Wei zhijian de ji ci zhanyi," pp. 12–13.

34 For the establishment of the Western Wei position in Shanxi, see Mao Han-kuang, "Beichao Dong Xi zhengquan zhi Hedong zhengduo zhan," in *Zhongguo zhonggu zhengzhi shi lun* (Taipei: Lianjing, 1990), pp. 137, 165, and passim.

35 Pearce, "The Yü-wen Regime in Sixth-Century China," pp. 309–12. This was not Emperor Xiaowu, but another Wei prince, known posthumously as Emperor Wen, who came to the throne after Xiaowu died (probably poisoned by Yuwen Tai) at the end of 534.

36 *Zhou shu*, ch. 2, pp. 25–6; Sima Guang, *Zizhi tongjian*, ch. 158, pp. 4894–6.

37 *Zhou shu*, ch. 18, p. 295; Sima Guang, *Zizhi tongjian*, ch. 158, p. 4912; Zhao Wenrun, "Lun Xi Wei yu Dong Wei zhijian de ji ci zhanyi," pp. 16–17.

38 *Bei Qi shu*, ch. 2, pp. 21–2; Sima Guang, *Zizhi tongjian*, ch. 158, pp. 4914–17;

Pearce, "The Yü-wen Regime in Sixth-Century China," p. 316; Zhao Wenrun, "Lun Xi Wei yu Dong Wei zhijian de ji ci zhanyi," p. 17.

39 Otagi Hajime, "Tōdai shū ken jōkaku no kibo to kōzō," in *Di yi jie guoji Tangdai xueshu huiyi lunwenji* (Taipei: Zhonghua minguo Tangdai xuezhe lianyihui, 1989), pp. 648–82. For general background on fortification and siegecraft in China, see Joseph Needham and Robin D. S. Yates, *Science and Civilisation in China*, vol. 5, pt. 6: *Military Technology: Missiles and Sieges* (Cambridge: Cambridge University Press, 1994), pp. 241–485, and *Zhongguo junshi shi*, vol. 6: *Bing lei*.

40 For medieval Western sieges, see John Beeler, *Warfare in Feudal Europe, 730–1200* (Ithaca and London: Cornell University Press, 1971), pp. 44–5, 57; J. F. Verbruggen, *The Art of Warfare in Western Europe during the Middle Ages*, trans. by Sumner Willard and S. C. M. Southern (Amsterdam and New York: North-Holland Publishing Company, 1977), pp. 285, 289; and Haldon, *Warfare, State, and Society in the Byzantine World, 565–1204*, pp. 183–5.

41 Wallacker, "Studies in Medieval Chinese Siegecraft: The Siege of Yü-pi, A.D. 546," pp. 789–802.

42 The major exception was Yuwen Hu's advance to Luoyang in 564, which was no more successful than the efforts in 538 and 543. See Sima Guang, *Zizhi tongjian*, ch. 169, pp. 5246–8.

43 Pearce, "The Yü-wen Regime in Sixth-Century China," p. 318 and passim.

44 Mao Han-kuang, "Beichao Dong Xi zhengquan zhi Hedong zhengduo zhan," p. 162. In Tang times, the "official" road distance from Luoyang to Ye was 606 *li*, approximately 200 miles; Liu Xu et al., *Jiu Tang shu*, ch. 39, p. 1492.

45 Hamaguchi Shigekuni, *Shin Kan Zui Tō shi no kenkyū*, pp. 149, 162–6, 224–5.

46 Sima Guang, *Zizhi tongjian*, ch. 155, p. 4819.

47 Sima Guang, *Zizhi tongjian*, ch. 157, p. 4882.

48 He Ziquan, *Wei Jin Nanbeichao shilue*, pp. 198–9; Tang Changru, *Wei Jin Nanbeichao Sui Tang shi san lun*, p. 199.

49 Hamaguchi, *Shin Kan Zui Tō shi no kenkyū*, pp. 225–9; also see Dien, "The Role of the Military in the Western Wei/Northern Chou State," pp. 337–45.

50 Kikuchi Hideo, "Hokuchō gunsei ni okeru iwayuru kyōhei ni tsuite," in *Shigematsu sensei koki kinen Kyūshū Daigaku tōyōshi ronsō* (Fukuoka: Kyushu University, 1957), pp. 121–2, 125. Also see the treatment of *xiang bing* in Pearce, "The Yü-wen Regime in Sixth-Century China," pp. 543–61.

51 *Zhou shu*, ch. 33, pp. 578–9.

52 *Zhou shu*, ch. 35, p. 618.

53 *Zhou shu*, ch. 43, pp. 777–8.

54 *Zhou shu*, ch. 23, pp. 395–6; for another example, see the biography of Guo Yan in the same work, ch. 37, p. 666.

55 Gu Jiguang, *Fubing zhidu kaoshi*, p. 323.

56 This literature is conveniently summarized by Kegasawa Yasunori, "Zenki fuheisei kenkyū josetsu – sono seika to ronten o megutte," *Hōseishi kenkyū*, 42 (1992), pp. 123–51.

57 Hamaguchi, *Shin Kan Zui Tō shi no kenkyū*, p. 235.

58 For more on the Twenty-four Army structure, see Li Yanshou, *Bei shi* (Beijing: Zhonghua shuju, 1974), ch. 60, pp. 2153–5; *Zhou shu*, ch. 16, pp. 272–3; Dien, "The Role of the Military in the Western Wei/Northern Chou State," pp. 352–5; Pearce, "The Yü-wen Regime in Sixth-Century China," pp. 382–4; and Gu Jiguang, *Fubing zhidu kaoshi*, pp. 43–4 and 73, n. 59.

59 Pearce, "The Yü-wen Regime in Sixth-Century China," pp. 388–9, 425, 664; Gu Jiguang, *Fubing zhidu kaoshi*, p. 54.

60 Gu Jiguang, *Fubing zhidu kaoshi*, p. 61; Wang Zhongluo, *Wei Jin Nanbeichao shi*, vol. 2, pp. 614, 619; Wang Yinglin, *Yu hai*, ch. 138, p. 18b.

61 For more on these debates, see Kegasawa, "Zenki fuheisei kenkyū josetsu – sono seika to ronten o megutte," pp. 144–5; and Pearce, "The Yü-wen Regime in Sixth-Century China," pp. 599–611.

62 *Zhou shu*, ch. 2, p. 28. The translation follows Pearce's ("The Yü-wen Regime in Sixth-Century China," p. 543) with slight modification.

63 Wang Yinglin, *Yu hai*, ch. 137, p. 1a. Pearce discusses this source in "The Yü-wen Regime in Sixth-Century China," pp. 597, 736–46.

64 Wei Zheng et al., *Sui shu* (Beijing: Zhonghua shuju, 1973), ch. 24, p. 680; Gu Jiguang, *Fubing zhidu kaoshi*, pp. 56–7.

65 *Bei shi*, ch. 60, p. 2155; translated by Dien in "The Role of the Military in the Western Wei/Northern Chou State," p. 354. It is worth noting, however, that this passage can also be interpreted as describing rotational service by part-time soldiers who will return home after the second fifteen-day period. See Gu Jiguang, *Fubing zhidu kaoshi*, p. 65.

66 Unfortunately the key textual evidence is in a surviving fragment of Li Mi's *Ye hou jia zhuan*, considered to be an unreliable source. See Wang Yinglin, *Yu hai*, ch. 138, p. 19a, and Albert E. Dien, "The Use of the *Yeh-hou chia-chuan* as a Historical Source," *Harvard Journal of Asiatic Studies*, 34 (1974), pp. 221–47.

67 *Sui shu*, ch. 28, p. 778. One such multisystemic explanation of apparent contradictions in the materials on the early *fubing* is offered by Zhang Guogang, "Tangdai fubing yuanyuan yu fanyi," *Lishi yanjiu*, 1989, No. 6, pp. 150–1. Also see Tang Changru, "Wei Zhou fubing zhidu bianyi," in idem, *Wei Jin Nanbeichao shi luncong* (Beijing: Sanlian, 1955), pp. 277–9; and Mao Han-kuang, "Xi Wei fubing shi lun," pp. 263–4.

68 Pearce, "The Yü-wen Regime in Sixth-Century China," p. 654.

69 Mao Han-kuang, "Xi Wei fubing shi lun," pp. 212–13.

70 Mao Han-kuang, "Xi Wei fubing shi lun," pp. 258–9.

71 This point is developed in Dien, "The Role of the Military in the Western Wei/Northern Chou State," p. 332 and passim.

72 *Zhou shu*, ch. 5, p. 86; Gu Jiguang, *Fubing zhidu kaoshi*, p. 65; Tanigawa Michio, "Fuheisei kokka ron," *Ryūkoku daigaku ronshū*, 443 (December 1993), p. 20; Kikuchi Hideo, "Tō setsushōfu no bunpu mondai ni kansuru ichi kaishaku," *Tōyōshi kenkyū*, 27 (1968), pp. 138–9.

73 *Zhou shu*, ch. 6, p. 93; Sima Guang, *Zizhi tongjian*, ch. 172, p. 5346.

74 *Zhou shu*, ch. 6, p. 94; Sima Guang, *Zizhi tongjian*, ch. 172, pp. 5352–3.

75 *Zhou shu*, ch. 6, pp. 95–6. The main Zhou army in the 575 campaign had numbered 60,000, organized in six divisions just as in 576.

76 It is not clear why the Zhou ruler chose to pull back. Perhaps he wanted the Qi army to exhaust itself attacking Pingyang. The byzantine politics of the Zhou court may also have been a factor, since Emperor Wu paid a flying visit to Chang'an after his withdrawal from Pingyang. See Pearce, "The Yü-wen Regime in Sixth-Century China," pp. 708–10.

77 *Zhou shu*, ch. 6, pp. 94–7; Sima Guang, *Zizhi tongjian*, ch. 172, pp. 5357–9.

78 *Zhou shu*, ch. 6, p. 97; Sima Guang, *Zizhi tongjian*, ch. 172, p. 5363.

79 *Zhou shu*, ch. 6, p. 98; Sima Guang, *Zizhi tongjian*, ch. 172, pp. 5363–4.

80 *Zhou shu*, ch. 6, p. 100; Sima Guang, *Zizhi tongjian*, ch. 173, p. 5369.

81 *Zhou shu*, ch. 5, p. 83.

82 Sima Guang, *Zizhi tongjian*, ch. 172, p. 5366; Pearce, "The Yü-wen Regime in Sixth-Century China," p. 712.

83 Pearce, "The Yü-wen Regime in Sixth-Century China," pp. 704–5; for an account of the Chen offensive, see Fu Lecheng, "Wei Jin Nanbeichao zhanshi," p. 35.

84 Yen Chih-t'ui, *Family Instructions for the Yen Clan*, p. 50; Sima Guang, *Zizhi*

tongjian, ch. 171, p. 5308; Pearce, "The Yü-wen Regime in Sixth-Century China," p. 705.

85 See Arthur F. Wright, "The Sui Dynasty," in Denis Twitchett (ed.), *The Cambridge History of China*, vol. 3: *Sui and T'ang China, 589–906, Pt. 1* (Cambridge: Cambridge University Press, 1979), pp. 99–100; Pearce, "The Yü-wen Regime in Sixth-Century China," pp. 571–2; *Zhou shu*, ch. 5, p. 86; *Sui shu*, ch. 56, p. 1389.

86 Pearce, "The Yü-wen Regime in Sixth-Century China," pp. 318–28.

87 He Ziquan, *Wei Jin Nanbeichao shilue*, p. 195.

88 See Qi Zebang, "Lun Dong Wei-Bei Qi de daotui," in *Wei Jin Nanbeichao shi yanjiu* (Chengdu: Sichuan sheng shehui kexue yuan chubanshe, 1986), pp. 383–403.

89 Mao Han-kuang, "Xi Wei fubing shi lun," pp. 259–60.

90 Zhou Yiliang, "Beichao de minzu wenti yu minzu zhengce," p. 176.

91 Pearce, "The Yü-wen Regime in Sixth-Century China," pp. 411–12 and, for the use of the Xianbei language, pp. 443–4. Albert E. Dien provides a more detailed examination of the surname question in "The Bestowal of Surnames under the Western Wei–Northern Chou: A Case of Counter-Acculturation," *T'oung Pao*, 63 (1977), pp. 137–77. For Su Chun, see *Zhou shu*, ch. 23, p. 395.

92 Arthur F. Wright, *The Sui Dynasty* (New York: Alfred A. Knopf, 1978), pp. 94–5. Also see Pearce, "The Yü-wen Regime in Sixth-Century China," pp. 427–30, 447–8, 451–3, and passim.

93 Pearce, "The Yü-wen Regime in Sixth-Century China," pp. 444–7.

CHAPTER SIX

North versus south

The Northern Zhou dynasty survived for only four years after Emperor Wu's triumph over Northern Qi. It was not brought down by any revolt in the newly conquered eastern plain, nor was any failure of policy to blame. Instead, the house of Yuwen fell victim to the grim actuarial odds facing all human beings – even the best fed, clothed, and sheltered of them – in the sixth century, and to the bad luck that brought a young child to the throne when a very capable adult was needed to maintain control over powerful and ambitious ministers. Emperor Wu, Yuwen Yong, died in the sixth lunar month of 578 as he was preparing to lead a punitive expedition against the Turks, who had replaced the Rouran as the dominant power on the northern steppe. He was not yet thirty-six years old. His heir was a violent and unstable teenager who himself died of a sudden illness in the fifth month of 580. The throne then went to a six-year-old child, and real power fell into the hands of the late emperor's father-in-law, a senior official named Yang Jian who was the son of one of Yuwen Tai's generals. After liquidating much of the Yuwen clan and defeating an armed challenge from Zhou loyalists based in Hebei, Yang inaugurated the Sui dynasty, with himself as the first emperor (known post-humously as Emperor Wen), on March 4, 581.[1] Even as he moved to consolidate his power in the north, he also began to take steps to prepare for the conquest of the Chen state in the south. In 585 he dispatched one of his closest associates, an especially ruthless general named Yang Su, to Sichuan to begin building a great fleet that would sweep down the Yangzi to overwhelm the southern heartland.[2]

With this move, Yang Jian was following in the footsteps of the Jin dynasty, which had conquered the southern kingdom of Wu in 279–80. The Jin emperor had ordered his governor in Sichuan, Wang Jun, to begin building a river fleet in 272. That fleet, led by Wang himself, descended the Yangzi in the eleventh lunar month of 279, overwhelmed the Wu fortresses along the river, and joined land forces that had marched down from the north to capture Wuchang. From there Wang raced down the Yangzi to take the Wu capital of Jianye (which would be known as Jiankang under the southern dynasties), slipping in ahead of a more cautious overland column that had reached the north bank of the river. The Jin victory owed much to the fact that Wang Jun's fleet was more powerful than the southern water forces.[3] And it clearly provided the model for the Sui campaign against Chen. No other northern attack on the south in the intervening years had involved the descent of a strong waterborne force from Sichuan, and no other northern offensive had succeeded in taking the southern capital. For most of the period from the founding of Eastern Jin to the reunification of the north in 577, a rough military balance had prevailed between north and south. During periods of division and weakness in the north, southern armies were sometimes able to press as far as the Yellow River and even into Guanzhong, while the stronger and more unified of the northern regimes were able to occupy Sichuan and push all the way down to the north bank of the Yangzi. Neither side, however, had ever succeeded in making serious inroads into the core territories of the other. The reasons for this prolonged stalemate are worth exploring in some detail since they reveal much about the military techniques of the age and the ways in which military operations might be constrained by technology, resources, and political priorities. Let us begin with the south's campaigns to drive out the "barbarians" and recover the ancient heartland of Chinese civilization.

In the early years of the Jiankang regime, many of the émigré leaders showed a strong interest in reconquering the north. In 313, four years before the formal establishment of Eastern Jin, one of those leaders, Zu Ti, moved north with a small force consisting of a couple of hundred retainers and another 2000 volunteers he had recruited himself. The government, led by the future Emperor Yuan, provided so little support that Zu's men even found it necessary to forge their own weapons, yet after seven years of campaigning Zu had recovered all of Henan for Jin and was poised to cross to the north side of the Yellow River. The offensive came to an abrupt end when Zu died in 321 (disheartened, it was said, by his knowledge of the tensions within the Jin leadership group that would shortly give rise to Wang Dun's rebellion), and the territory that had been recovered was soon lost again.[4] A grandiose scheme proposed by another émigré leader in the 330s also failed to yield concrete results, and in 353 a major expedition led by a militarily inexperienced scholar resulted in disaster when the Jin army was betrayed by its Qiang allies.[5] The latter campaign was undertaken to exploit the chaos in North China following the collapse of the Zhao regime of Shi Le and Shi Hu, and conditions were propitious enough that a second expedition was launched in 354. The prime mover in this effort was Huan Wen, the powerful governor of the middle Yangzi region. Huan took his fleet up the Han River, then advanced overland through the Wu Pass and into the Wei River valley. There he was confronted by the forces led by the Fu clan of the Di people, who were then in the process of establishing the Former Qin regime. Huan fought two battles with the Qin forces, winning the first and losing the second, but his offensive was brought to an end by logistical difficulties rather than defeat on the battlefield. Huan had timed his entry into Guanzhong for late spring in the expectation that he would be able to feed his army, originally 40,000 strong, from the harvest of the local winter wheat crop, and his calculations were completely upset by Qin's decision to pursue a scorched-earth strategy and burn the standing crops in the fields. The hungry Jin army beat a hasty retreat in the sixth lunar month of 354, losing some 10,000 men to Qin pursuers.[6]

In 369 Huan Wen, now the dominant figure at the Jin court, made another attempt to recover the north. This time he began his advance from the eastern end of the frontier in the fourth lunar month, moving northwestward across the Henan plain by way of tributaries of the Huai River so that his army of 50,000 men could be supplied by water – although this required a great deal of engineering work due to dry weather and low water levels. Disregarding advice to establish a base in the north, accumulate supplies, and continue the campaign the following year, Huan crossed the Yellow River and confronted the army of the Murong Xianbei state of Former Yan at Fangtou. After suffering several reverses at the hands of the Yan forces, Huan learned that a Former Qin army was coming to aid Yan and that his own army's food supplies were about to give out (Yan raiders having cut the Jin supply line in Henan). He burned his boats and retreated southward by land, but was overtaken by pursuing Yan cavalry at Xiangyi, where his army was smashed in a battle that reportedly cost Jin some 30,000 men.[7]

The next major "northern expedition" came in 409, when Liu Yu, the new strongman of the Eastern Jin court after his victory over Huan Xuan, launched a large-scale invasion of the Murong state of Southern Yan in what is now Shandong province. Liu began his advance by water in the late spring, moving up the Si River from the Huai, but at Xiapei he left his boats and baggage train behind and took his army directly northward across the mountainous base of the Shandong peninsula. The Murong king failed to send troops to block the mountain passes, but stationed a large army at Linqu, a day's march to the south of his capital (Guanggu, today's Yidu). This force was met and defeated by the Jin army, which moved on to besiege Guanggu, capturing it and eliminating the Southern Yan state in the spring of 410. Liu Yu's success owed much to the fact that he was able to feed his army with grain harvested in the territory of the Southern Yan, whose leaders had not taken the trouble to "clear the fields" as the Former Qin had done in Guanzhong in 354.[8] After an intermission caused by internal struggles in the south, Liu Yu directed his attention to the Wei River valley, where the Qiang state of Later Qin held sway, in 416. The Jin armies began their advance in the eighth lunar month by several different routes. In the west, a land force moved directly on Guanzhong by way of the Wu Pass. In the center, another overland column marched through Xuchang to Luoyang, while in the east the largest of the Jin forces were moved by boat along the Bian and Si rivers and then to Luoyang by way of the Yellow River. After Luoyang was taken in the tenth lunar month several columns joined forces to advance up the Yellow River to force the Tong Pass, and from there they continued up the Wei River to Chang'an, still accompanied by the Jin

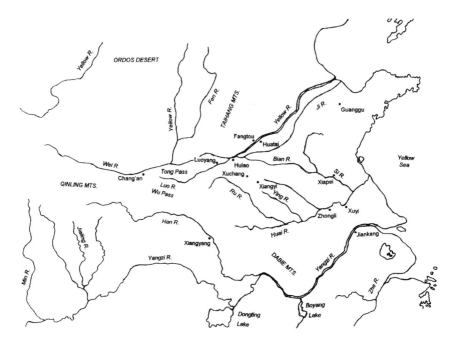

Map 12 The zone of confrontation between north and south, *ca.* AD 400

river fleet. The Qin army was defeated in a battle at the Wei River bridge north of Chang'an in the seventh lunar month of 417, leading to the surrender of the Qin ruler. The southern presence in Guanzhong could not be sustained, however. Liu Yu returned to the south in the eleventh month after the sudden death of the trusted lieutenant he had assigned to keep an eye on the court at Jiankang. The small garrison that he left behind, only about 10,000 men, suffered from divided command and was easily smashed by a Xiongnu warlord pressing south from the Ordos region in 418.[9]

When southern forces came north again, this time dispatched by Liu Yu's son, Emperor Wen of the Song dynasty, their goal was to recover territory on the south side of the Yellow River that had recently been lost to the rising power of the Tuoba Wei. In 430 some 100,000 Song troops came north in several columns, again including a water force that entered the Yellow River from the river system of Henan. The Wei forces initially withdrew to the north bank of the river, but in the tenth lunar month they counterattacked, retaking Luoyang and several other strategic points and laying siege to Huatai on the south bank (near today's Jixian, Shandong). Early in 431 a Song relief column was forced to withdraw because of supply problems, and the 10,000-man garrison of Huatai soon capitulated.[10] Emperor Wen made a second attempt to recover northern Henan in 450. Operations began in the seventh month, and Song forces quickly laid siege to Huatai and occupied other positions on the south side of the Yellow River. The Wei ruler, Emperor Taiwu, had already been planning an offensive of his own when Song attacked. He waited until the ninth month to march to relieve his garrison at Huatai, then caught and crushed the besieging army as it was retreating. News of the defeat at Huatai prompted the Song emperor to order another column that had almost taken the Tong Pass to fall back to Xiangyang on the Han River.[11] The Wei offensive that followed reached all the way to the Yangzi, and is sometimes identified as the key turning point when the balance of power shifted decisively in favor of the north.[12]

Southern armies marched north again in the days of Liang and Chen, but they had little to show for their efforts. A Liang campaign in 505 went no farther north than the Huai River. Later, in 528, a Liang army was able to take advantage of the chaos in the Wei realm after the Six Garrisons revolt to march north and occupy Luoyang, but it was very soon expelled from the city by the veteran warriors of the Erzhu clan.[13] The gains from the very last southern offensive, Chen's recovery of the land between the Huai River and the Yangzi from Northern Qi in 573, were quickly lost to Northern Zhou. When Sui aimed its knock-out blow at Chen in 588, an offensive could be launched from the north bank of the Yangzi just a few miles from the southern capital.

There were many reasons for the south's failure to recover all of the lost territories, or even to make lasting conquests in the north. Most obvious was the tactical asymmetry of northern and southern armies during the period of division. The northern regimes, most of which had access to either the pasture lands of northwestern China or the steppe itself and were led by peoples of steppe origin, had little difficulty raising large forces of highly skilled horsemen and mounted archers. With little pasture and relatively few horses, southern armies were made up mainly of infantry with only a very small cavalry component.[14] On the battlefield, southern armies lacked both mobility and offensive shock power. When they were victorious they lacked the means for a rapid pursuit of mounted foes, and when they were defeated by such a mobile opponent they had no hope of escape. Southern armies were driven to adopt various expedients to compensate for their weakness in cavalry. One, employed with considerable success by Liu Yu during his conquest of Southern Yan in 409–10, was to bring a large number of wheeled vehicles with the army. These do not seem to have been war chariots modeled on those of antiquity, and there is no evidence that they differed at all from the ordinary two-wheeled baggage carts of North China, more likely to be drawn by oxen than by horses. The carts could be deployed to create instant field fortifications to cover the army's flanks or buttress an infantry formation about to be attacked by cavalry.[15] Since the southern armies were often tied to waterways because of their logistical needs, boats could also be used to support and assist infantry forces. In particular, they could serve as protected, mobile firing platforms from which archers, crossbowmen, and the operators of various types of missile-throwing engines might harrass the enemy – much like the armored trains employed by twentieth-century Chinese warlords.

As should already be clear from the brief recitation of failed "northern expeditions" given above, the southern armies were also hamstrung by logistical difficulties. The failure of Huan Wen in Guanzhong in 354 demonstrated that a southern army campaigning in the north could not count on being able to live off the land, and the campaign could not continue if the troops could not be fed. Liu Yu's success against Southern Yan owed much to his opponents' failure to adopt the same scorched-earth strategy as Former Qin. Because of the uncertainty involved in trying to provision an army from local sources, most southern campaigns in the north relied on food supplies brought up from the south. And this, in turn, tied the southern armies to the network of waterways in the North China Plain, especially streams such as the Bian and the Si that rose not far from the Yellow River and then flowed southeastward into the Huai. In all economies before the coming of the railroad, water transport represented by far the cheapest and most efficient means of moving bulk commodities such as grain over long distances. Chinese river boats could carry very large loads, as much as 60,000 liters by some accounts; a typical cart-load was less than one-sixtieth of this. More important, however, was the fact that a boat's crew required rations equivalent to a much smaller percentage of total payload than was the case with draft animals and teamsters, pack animals and drivers, or human porterage. A wagon drawn by two oxen carrying 500 kilograms of grain would be empty at the end of twelve days if the draft animals were fed entirely from the payload.[16] These relationships were well understood by medieval Chinese logisticians, and choices were made accordingly.[17] Reliance on water transport, however, led to serious vulnerabilities. The movement of supplies could be impeded by drought conditions, a difficulty faced by Huan Wen in 369, and the advance of an army could be held up by enemy forces occupying key points on the network of waterways. This situation, too, was faced by Huan Wen when his army failed to take Biankou and was therefore unable to divert water from the Yellow River to raise the level of the Bian River and other waterways in Henan. Southern armies dependent on long riverine supply lines were also vulnerable to attacks on those arteries by fast-moving northern cavalry forces since, given the size of the armies, the nature of their weaponry, and the lack of modern communications technology, there was no possibility of maintaining and defending a continuous front more than a few miles long. As we have seen, Huan Wen had to call off his 369 campaign when Former Yan forces succeeded in cutting his supply line.

Not only did the southern regimes encounter great difficulty in supplying their forces operating in the north, but they were also at a disadvantage in terms of total resources available for mobilization. In the primarily agricultural economy of medieval China, the military power of the state was largely a function of the number of registered farming households from which it could claim taxes (in the form of grain and homespun fabric) and corvée labor. The grain and fabrics were needed to feed, clothe, and reward soldiers, while corvée laborers performed many necessary noncombatant functions such as building and repairing fortifications, digging canals, and hauling supplies – and might also be called upon to fight. Few figures for registered population survive from the period of division, but those that do consistently indicate that the southern rulers commanded a much smaller resource base than their rivals in the north. In 464, for example, the Song dynasty recorded 906,870 households containing a total of 4,685,501 individuals, and there is reason to believe that by the time the Chen dynasty fell in 589 the registered population had fallen to approximately 500,000 households and 2,000,000 individuals. In the north, on the other hand, a single regional regime, the Former Yan state that confronted Huan Wen's northern expedition of 369, could claim 2,458,969 households and 9,987,935 individuals.[18] When the north was united as a single realm, the imbalance was even greater. On the eve of the Six Garrisons revolt, Northern Wei had a registered population of approximately 5,000,000 households and 32,000,000 individuals.[19] There is no question that the numbers for the south are far below the actual population of the region, especially in light of the waves of migration from the north and the many signs of a vibrant and growing regional economy. The important point, however, is that the southern rulers did not have full access to this population for purposes of tax and corvée because so many people were sheltered as the tenants or dependants of powerful families.[20]

This was not the only way in which the southern regimes were handicapped by their political and social environment. The competition of great families for power and influence at court, the tensions between northern émigrés and native southern elites, and the struggles between centralizing court officials and provincial magnates all tended to hinder the south's efforts to recover northern territories. One reason that Zu Ti's operations in Henan received so little support from the Eastern Jin government was the suspicion and hostility of members of the Wang family who formed the dominant element at the court in Jiankang. Similarly, the court made every effort to restrain Huan Wen's drive to launch a northern expedition in the early 350s for fear that it would make him too strong to manage. From very early on in Eastern Jin, there was a tendency to subordinate irredentist desires to the immediate demands of southern politics, and this tendency became ever stronger with the passage of time.[21] There is no reason to doubt the genuineness of Zu Ti's zeal for a *reconquista*. With Huan Wen in the middle years of the fourth century, the issue is murkier; he was accused of seeking to use the recovery of the north as a springboard to usurpation.[22] When we come to Liu Yu in the early fifth century, however, there is little doubt that northern campaigns were intended to serve political ambitions. The conquest of Southern Yan in 409–10 increased Liu's prestige and strengthened his hand at court, while the Guanzhong campaign of 416–17 was supposed to pave the way for his establishment of the Song dynasty. It is significant that Liu abandoned the campaign and rushed back to Jiankang as soon as his position there appeared to be in jeopardy, and that he did not bother to renew operations in the north after taking the southern throne for himself in 420.[23] The native southern elites had never had much interest in recovering the north. After the passage of a couple of generations, the émigré families came to share this attitude. Despite ritualistic pronouncements to the contrary, they regarded the south as their home and were concerned primarily with safeguarding their position there.[24] Risky, large-scale offensive campaigns held little attraction. From the middle of the fifth century down to the last days of the Chen dynasty, the south's northern campaigns were generally aimed at restoring or securing threatened borders and making limited territorial gains. Reconquest had all but disappeared from the agenda.

Although they were influenced by rather different concerns, northern rulers, too, were seldom able to make the conquest of the south a priority. When the north was divided among two or more states, their leaders were concerned primarily with their rivalry with one another. If there was energy and attention to devote to the south, it was usually channelled into the conquest of border regions whose annexation served to increase the strength of the state vis-à-vis its principal northern rival. Northern Zhou expansion in Sichuan and the valley of the Han River conformed to this pattern, to give one example. Even when the north was united under a single government, ethnic conflicts and tensions between Han Chinese, North Asians, and proto-Tibetan groups such as the Qiang could be a major cause of weakness and instability. We have already seen how a military setback in his great southern campaign of 383 triggered the rapid collapse of Fu Jian's Former Qin empire as his Qiang and Xianbei subjects turned against him.[25] The apparently all-out effort launched by Fu Jian had no real parallel in the years between the Jin conquest of Wu in 280 and the Sui conquest of Chen in 588–9. For most of the period of division, northern regimes were content with limited offensives to achieve incremental gains at the expense of the south. This pattern was a reflection not only of internal conflicts and other distractions, but also of material and logistical difficulties comparable to those which hampered the south's offensive campaigns. The fierce, mobile northern cavalry forces enjoyed a tremendous advantage in the open field, but were often frustrated by the many towns and cities, fortified and strongly garrisoned, that dotted the borderlands. In 422–3, for example, the 10,000 Song defenders of Hulao, just south of the Yellow River, were able to hold up a much larger Wei army for some 200 days. Another Wei army that attacked Zhongli on the Huai River in 507 was even less successful; the 3000 Liang defenders held out for three months until a relief army arrived to drive off the besiegers.[26] Nor were northern armies free of the logistical vulnerabilities that dogged their southern opponents. In 379 the Northern Headquarters general Liu Laozhi forced the retreat of a Qin army by destroying its baggage train and capturing its supply vessels.[27]

The way in which a daring northern offensive could be contained by a combination of geography, enemy fortifications, and supply problems is nicely illustrated by the southern campaign of the Wei Emperor Taiwu in the winter of 450–1. This followed hard on the heels of the defeat of the Song forces that had advanced to the Yellow River earlier in 450. Emperor Taiwu opted to bypass the Song garrisons along the Huai River and make a lightning thrust to the Yangzi with his cavalry. He reached Guabu, on the north bank of the river not far from Jiankang, on February 1, 451, only ten days after crossing the Huai. This move created alarm in the Song capital; troops and war vessels were stationed along the south bank of the river over a distance of more than a hundred miles and the river fleet was placed under the overall command of the crown prince. The Wei ruler made noises about crossing the river, but this was surely bluff since his men had neither the vessels nor the skills they would need to overcome the Song fleet. With both men and horses now beginning to suffer from a shortage of provisions, Taiwu withdrew northward on February 18. En route, he laid siege to the town of Xuyi on the Huai in order to capture grain supplies that would feed his army on its retreat across Henan to the Yellow River. The defenses of Xuyi held firm for several weeks, however, and when sickness broke out in the Wei camp and reports arrived that a Song fleet was ascending the Huai River from the sea, Emperor Taiwu abandoned the siege and withdrew into Henan to avoid being trapped by the enemy warships. He had laid waste to half a dozen Song provinces and led some 50,000 captives back to the north, but had also suffered heavy losses himself and had no real territorial gains to show for his efforts.[28] Even though he took care to launch his campaign in the winter, Emperor Taiwu found the south to be an inhospitable environment. Summer operations would have been even more difficult, as the Wei statesman Cui Hao had pointed out many years earlier:

> The southern soil is low-lying and damp, and the summer months are steamy and hot; this is precisely the season that torrential rains are frequent and the vegetation is dense and deep. Sicknesses will surely arise. . . . Moreover, the enemy will make strict preparations in advance; he will certainly make his walls strong and defend them stoutly. If you encamp the army to assault them, provisions will not be supplied; and if you divide your troops to pillage, you will have nothing left with which to counter the enemy.[29]

An element of the southern scene that Cui did not mention, but one that had an important effect on the outcome of Emperor Taiwu's campaign, was the presence of many rivers and other waterways. These presented serious obstacles to northern cavalry, while at the same providing avenues for the rapid movement of southern water forces. In their defensive operations on the Yangzi and the Huai just as in their offensive forays into Henan, the southern regimes relied heavily on warships and waterborne mobility. The vessels used were of many types and sizes, ranging from towering, multiple-decked warships carrying hundreds of sailors and marines to small patrol boats and skirmishing craft with only a handful of men on board. Although there seem to have been many differences in design, most of these vessels surely shared certain basic features that were almost ubiquitous in traditional Chinese shipbuilding. These included a flat-bottomed, carvel-built hull lacking keel, stempost, and sternpost, with transoms at stem and stern and hull planking attached to solid transverse bulkheads rather than frame or ribs.[30] Most war vessels were powered both by sails, usually of rattan and matting construction, and by oars. A variety of tactics were used in battle. In contrast to traditional Mediterranean naval warfare, Chinese river battles do not seem to have involved the use of large numbers of vessels as rams. This situation may have been influenced by the fact that the Chinese craft lacked the keels that provided the structural basis for Mediterranean rams, though there was no reason why separate ram-like devices could not have been attached to the front of Chinese warships. The capture of vessels by boarding, though by no means unheard-of, also seems to have been less common in China than in the West. The most common tactics involved the use of missiles to damage enemy vessels and kill or injure members of their crews.[31] Most vessels carried archers and crossbowmen, and the larger warships deployed lever-operated trebuchets on their topmost decks. The outcome of a battle could be greatly influenced by a difference in the size and range of the crossbows used by the two sides, as happened when Liu Yu defeated Lu Xun's rebel fleet on the Yangzi at the end of 410.[32] As protection against missiles, some vessels had their upper decks roofed over or their sides "armored" with ox hides. Crewmen took refuge behind wooden battlements or shot their weapons through loopholes in the sides of the ships. The heavy emphasis on missile combat tended to favor defense over offense in naval actions and made it rather difficult to eliminate sturdily built enemy ships (as opposed to simply killing crewmen). The major exception to this general rule was an attack with fireships, which could do great damage to an unwary opponent under the right conditions.[33] Operations on the rivers of southern China differed from naval warfare in several significant ways. Battles were almost always fought in tightly enclosed spaces with little room for maneuver, and the direction of an enemy's approach was seldom uncertain. River currents gave the advantage to an attacker coming from upstream, but this was linked to the danger that the attacker might have difficulty escaping in the event of a defeat. Above all, river fleets usually had to cooperate very closely with land forces, and often carried large numbers of soldiers that could be disembarked to capture cities and forts or attack enemy armies.[34]

During the 600-year span from Western Jin to the fall of Tang, the usual – indeed, almost the only – use for Chinese naval forces was on the country's rivers and inland waterways. During the great conflicts between north and south, war fleets were used to transport armies of invasion across or along rivers – or to prevent hostile forces from getting across the major rivers. Coastal waters, on the other hand, tended to be neglected. China was not threatened by forces coming from the sea in this period, and there were few tempting targets for overseas expansion. The only major seaborne expeditions were those launched by Sui and Tang rulers against the states of the Korean peninsula during the seventh century. This overall situation was in stark contrast to the more aggressive use of naval forces by Byzantines, Arabs, and Norsemen at the other end of the Eurasian landmass, but it was a logical response to China's peculiar geography and strategic environment.

During the country's prolonged division between north and south, southern mastery of the tools and techniques of riverine warfare conferred a huge defensive advantage. Northern regimes were more accustomed to cavalry warfare and were not in the habit of maintaining strong water forces. The drier north produced fewer individuals with the necessary skills, and northern shipbuilders tended to produce smaller vessels suitable for the relatively shallow northern rivers.[35] Northern armies were usually at a loss when confronted with a wide river patrolled by a southern fleet. Emperor Taiwu spoke of cutting reeds to construct rafts that would float his men and horses across the Yangzi, but wisely chose not to attempt the crossing.[36] If a northern power wished to conquer Jiankang, it had little choice but to build a real fleet of its own that would be capable of wresting control of the Yangzi away from the southerners – as Jin had done in 279–80.

This was precisely the path followed by the Sui founder Yang Jian in the late 580s. By this time, he enjoyed several advantages that had not always figured in earlier northern campaigns against the south. A unified north was now able to

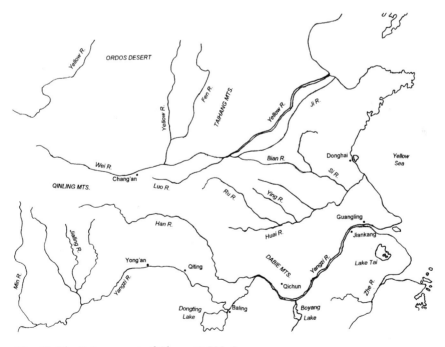

Map 13 The Sui conquest of Chen, AD 588–9

131

bring overwhelming force to bear against Chen, and earlier conquests made by Northern Zhou meant that this force could be launched from very near at hand. Sui forces did not have to worry about reducing enemy fortresses on the Huai River or maintaining long supply lines since they already controlled all the north bank of the Yangzi, and possession of the Sichuan basin on the upper Yangzi made it possible for Sui to send a great fleet down the river as Jin had done in 279. Preparations for a Sui attack on Chen began in earnest in 587. War vessels were built in large numbers at several locations, including the coastal Donghai commandery just south of the Shandong peninsula, Qichun in today's Hubei province, and the Han River valley. The largest shipbuilding effort was at Yong'an, on the Yangzi in southwestern Sichuan, where Yang Su, to judge from the reported size of the fleet he later commanded, must have constructed thousands of new craft. The largest of these were the great Five-Banner warships. These had five decks, were capable of accommodating 800 men, and were outfitted with six 50-foot-long, spike-bearing booms (*paigan*) that could be dropped from the vertical to damage enemy vessels or pin them in a position where they would be raked by close-range missile fire. A second class of vessels called Yellow Dragons could carry 100 men each, and there seem to have been other types of smaller craft as well.[37]

By the late autumn of 588, eight Sui armies totalling 518,000 men were in position on the north side of the Yangzi from Sichuan to the sea. In addition to Yang Su's force at Yong'an, these included a mixed land and water force based at Xiangyang on the Han River under the nominal leadership of Yang Jian's third son Yang Jun, Prince of Qin, the flotilla at Qichun, and four land armies along the lower Yangzi under the overall authority of Yang Jian's second son, Yang Guang. The eighth force was the fleet that had been built on the seacoast at Donghai; under the leadership of Yan Rong, it was supposed to move by sea to invade the coastal area near Lake Tai. It is worth noting that three of the eight Sui commands were composed entirely or primarily of water forces, while a fourth, that of Yang Jun on the Han River, also had a significant naval component.[38] Facing the Sui forces were perhaps 100,000 Chen troops to cover the entire distance from the Yangzi gorges to the sea; the largest concentrations were stationed at the western end of the line and near Jiankang itself.[39] The basic Sui strategy was to use Yang Su's forces on the upper Yangzi to pin the Chen fleet there and thereby create favorable conditions for Yang Guang's armies to cross the lower Yangzi. If this plan failed and the upstream Chen forces broke away to help defend Jiankang, it would still be possible for Yang Su to sweep down the river and assist the Sui armies in taking the Chen capital.[40]

The Sui offensive was opened by Yang Su's river fleet. In the twelfth lunar month of 588 (December 24 to January 21, 589) Yang led his force downstream through the Yangzi gorges. Most of the ensuing combats took place along a fifty-mile stretch of the Yangzi above and below the modern city of Yichang, Hubei.[41] The first Chen resistance was encountered at the Wolf's Tail rapids, where a hundred warships of the Green Dragon class, supported by several thousand men in palisade forts built on the precipitous terrain of the north and south banks, contested passage of the river. Fearing that his ships would be vulnerable to attack if they attempted to negotiate the rapids in daylight, Yang launched a three-pronged attack on the Chen position under cover of darkness. While he himself led a large portion of his fleet downstream past the forts (with crewmen and marines biting on sticks to guarantee noise discipline), two land columns made simultaneous attacks on the Chen positions north and south of the river. The operation was a complete success, and almost all of the Chen troops were taken prisoner.[42] Yang Su encountered the next obstacle about twenty miles downstream at Qiting, where the Chen general Lü Zhongsu had stretched three iron chains across the river to bar the passage of the Sui fleet. Once again, Yang found it necessary to land troops to capture the enemy positions on the shore. After a large number of unsuccessful attacks in which more than 5000 Sui soldiers were lost (with their opponents cutting off the noses of Sui dead in order to claim rewards from their commander), the Chen forts were finally carried in another night attack, enabling Yang's men to remove the chains. Lü Zhongsu withdrew his fleet to Yan Island beneath Mount Jingmen. Yang Su now sent four of his massive Five-Banner warships, crewed by a thousand Man aborigines from southeastern Sichuan, to lead the attack on the Chen fleet. They destroyed a dozen or more of the Chen vessels with their spiked booms, and this led to the destruction of the enemy fleet and the capture of more than two thousand prisoners. After the battle at Yan Island, all the Chen defenses east of Baling (at the mouth of Dongting Lake) collapsed as garrisons abandoned their posts and fled. Chen Huiji, the garrison commander at Gong'an, attempted to bring 30,000 men and over a thousand ships down the Yangzi to reinforce the defenses of Jiankang, but he was blocked by the Sui forces of Yang Jun, Prince of Qin, who had descended the Han River to its confluence with the Yangzi. By this time, however, Jiankang had already fallen.[43]

On January 22, 589, the first day of the new year by Chinese reckoning, Heruo Bi, an army commander under Yang Guang, brought his troops across the Yangzi from Guangling. This surprise move was facilitated by a long period of preparation and deception. Heruo had hidden all of his serviceable boats while exposing derelict junks in plain view by the river bank. When his men returned to Guangling from guard duty along the river, he had them march in with flags flying and set up new encampments as if they were fresh troops arriving. The Chen forces on the south side of the river were initially deceived by this and made ready to repel an imminent attack, but when they saw through Heruo's ruse (as they were meant to do) they relaxed their guard. Heruo also conducted large hunts near the river bank, so that Chen sentries came to regard any commotion on the opposite shore as nothing out of the ordinary.[44] Heruo's sudden offensive move was also aided greatly by the fact that Chen had concentrated all of its war vessels from the lower Yangzi at Jiankang, with infighting among court officials preventing their redeployment to patrol stations along the river.[45] Heruo was able to take the important city of Jingkou on January 27. Meanwhile, a smaller Sui force of only 500 men under Han Qinhu had slipped across the Yangzi upstream of Jiankang to capture the town of Caishi. Their task was made easier by the drunkenness of the Chen garrison. Reinforced to 20,000 men, Han's column advanced on Jiankang from the south while Heruo's troops closed in from the northeast. Disregarding advice from one of his generals that he avoid battle while sending warships to cut off the Sui forces operating south of the river, the Chen ruler sent his army out to attack Heruo Bi's troops on February 10, 589.[46]

The battle took place on the high ground a few miles east of Jiankang. The five contingents that made up the Chen army deployed along a front of more than six miles, with the result that they were unable to support one another effectively. Only the southernmost Chen division under Lu Guangda showed any initiative in attacking Heruo Bi's army of 8000, which was pushed back several times with the loss of 273 men. Heruo finally escaped from this onslaught by pulling back behind a smokescreen (probably created by setting fire to the grass), then turned around to attack another of the Chen divisions. This unit had little stomach for a fight and soon turned tail and fled; as soon as the rest of the Chen army became aware of what had happened, the rout became general. While Heruo Bi was fighting east of the city, Han Qinhu's army was approaching the southern gate. Some of the Chen troops stationed there fled, while a general who had just surrendered persuaded others to lay down their arms. Han proceeded to the palace and made the Chen ruler his prisoner before Heruo, who had encountered more resistance, was able to enter the city through the northern gate. The two Sui generals would later squabble over their relative merit in the taking of Jiankang, until the emperor stepped in to declare their contributions to be of equal value.[47]

The submission of the rest of the Chen empire followed very quickly after the fall of Jiankang. Yang Guang had the captured Chen ruler write letters instructing his remaining upriver commanders to surrender, an instruction that almost all of them chose to obey. Having already defeated a Chen force at the mouth of the Qi River, Wang Shiji's flotilla from Qichun moved south to receive the surrender of the administrative units in what is now Jiangxi province.[48] The only significant resistance anywhere in the south came from the governor of Wu commandery, by the shore of Lake Tai. He was attacked by an overland column dispatched from Yang Guang's army at Jiankang, and by Yan Rong's fleet, which made its way from the sea into Lake Tai. By the end of the second lunar month, resistance in this region had been crushed.[49] With the help of a powerful aboriginal leader, the far south was also brought into line with little difficulty.[50] During the campaign of 588–9, Sui commanders made real efforts to win the southerners over. Heruo Bi imposed severe measures to prevent his troops from looting, while Yang Su made a point of releasing the Chen soldiers that he captured. This was a striking contrast with the earlier behavior of Western Wei and Northern Zhou armies, which had dragged off tens of thousands of southern captives to slavery in the north.[51] From the perspective of 589, the south had been pacified with surprising ease and the Sui policy of restraint appeared to be an unqualified success.

Toward the end of the following year, however, an extremely violent anti-Sui rebellion began in the Lake Tai area and northern Zhejiang and spread south along the coast as far as present-day Vietnam. Newly appointed Sui officials in the affected areas were killed by the rebels; some of them were disemboweled or even cut up and eaten. How are we to account for the sudden change from the behavior of the southerners in 589? The Sui officials do not seem to have been especially cruel, oppressive, or exploitative. The difference was that the men who had yielded so quickly the year before were senior officials of the Chen dynasty, while those who led the new uprising represented a much broader stratum of local elites who suddenly found their interests adversely affected by the new administration. In particular, the Sui administrators seem to have challenged the time-honored privileges of the southern magnates, which would have included such things as immunity from taxation and the ability to conceal families of tenants and retainers from the state authorities with impunity. The revolt was sparked by a rumor, very likely spread by local elites, that the Sui government was planning the forced relocation of hundreds of thousands of southerners to new homes in the north.[52]

The Sui emperor named Yang Su to command an expeditonary army against the rebels; Yang crossed the Yangzi near Jingkou and defeated several rebel forces, and then carried the campaign into what is now Zhejiang. He sent one of his subordinate commanders, Shi Wansui, with 2000 men to campaign against other rebel groups in the mountainous coastal regions further to the south. It is reported that Shi marched more than 300 miles and fought more than 700 engagements, and that his whereabouts were unknown to Yang Su's headquarters for more than a hundred days. Yang eventually put an end to the rebellion by persuading one of the two principal rebel leaders remaining in the field to turn on his colleague and hand him over to Sui in exchange for his own life.[53] From this time on, the south seems to have been firmly under Sui control. Southern separatism would not assert itself again until the Sui dynasty began to lose its grip on the entire country in the second decade of the seventh century.

Notes

1 These events are described in much greater detail in Wright, *The Sui Dynasty*, pp. 58–63, 110–13.
2 Sima Guang, *Zizhi tongjian*, ch. 176, p. 5483; *Sui shu*, ch. 48, pp. 1282–3.
3 Fu Lecheng, "We Jin Nanbeichao zhanshi," pp. 14–15. Also see the analysis in Zhang Tieniu and Gao Xiaoxing, *Zhongguo gudai haijun shi* (Beijing: Bayi chubanshe, 1993), pp. 54–6.
4 For Zu Ti, see *Jin shu*, ch. 62, pp. 1695–7; and Sima Guang, *Zizhi tongjian*, ch. 88, p. 2801, and ch. 91, p. 2889.
5 The leader in the 330s was Yu Liang; see *Jin shu*, ch. 73, p. 1923. The 353

campaign was led by Yin Hao; see Wang Zhongluo, *Wei Jin Nanbeichao shi*, vol. 1, p. 334.

6 Fu Lecheng, "Wei Jin Nanbeichao zhanshi," p. 30.
7 Fu Lecheng, "Wei Jin Nanbeichao zhanshi," pp. 30–1; Sima Guang, *Zizhi tongjian*, ch. 102, pp. 3214–18.
8 Fu Lecheng, "Wei Jin Nanbeichao zhanshi," pp. 31–2.
9 Wang Zhongluo, *Wei Jin Nanbeichao shi*, vol. 1, pp. 378–83; Fu Lecheng, "Wei Jin Nanbeichao zhanshi," pp. 32–3; He Ziquan, *Wei Jin Nanbeichao shilue*, p. 118.
10 Fu Lecheng, "Wei Jin Nanbeichao zhanshi," p. 33.
11 Fu Lecheng, "Wei Jin Nanbeichao zhanshi," p. 34.
12 Xu Hui, "Nanbeichao zhanzheng tedian tanxi," *Jiang hai xuekan*, 1991, No. 3, p. 119.
13 Wang Zhongluo, *Wei Jin Nanbeichao shi*, vol. 1, p. 445.
14 Chen Yinke, *Wei Jin Nanbeichao shi jiangyanlu*, pp. 227–8, 236–7; Lü Simian, *Liang Jin Nanbeichao shi*, pp. 1202–3, 1306–7.
15 Lü Simian, *Liang Jin Nanbeichao shi*, p. 1307. One pundit blames the defeat of the Song army near Huatai in 449 on their failure to bring carts as Liu Yu had done; see Fu Lecheng, "Wei Jin Nanbeichao zhanshi," p. 34. For more on Chinese carts, see Joseph Needham, *Science and Civilisation in China*, vol. 4: *Physics and Physical Technology*, pt. 2: *Mechanical Engineering* (Cambridge: Cambridge University Press, 1965), pp. 250, 319–20, and plates 189 and 213.
16 Graff, "Early T'ang Generalship and the Textual Tradition," pp. 103–17. For a comparison of the cost of various forms of transport based on modern data and expressed in terms of kilograms of grain or grain-equivalent expended to move one ton a distance of one kilometer, see Colin Clark and Margaret Haswell, *The Economics of Subsistence Agriculture*, 4th edition (London: St Martin's Press, 1970), Table 47, pp. 196–8.
17 See, for example, the arguments presented by Diao Yong in Wei Shou, *Wei shu*, ch. 38, pp. 868–9.
18 Chen Yinke, *Wei Jin Nanbeichao jiangyanlu*, pp. 226–7.
19 Zhu Dawei, "Wei Jin Nanbeichao shi nongmin zhanzheng de shehui houguo," in *Zhongguo nongmin zhanzheng shi luncong*, vol. 5 (n.p.: Zhongguo shehui kexue chubanshe, 1987), p. 32.
20 Tang Changru, *Wei Jin Nanbeichao Sui Tang shi san lun*, pp. 88–90.
21 Ochi Shigeaki, "Tō-Shin chō chūgen kaifuku no ichi kōsatsu," *Tōyō gakuhō*, 38.1 (June 1955), pp. 76, 80–2.
22 Wang Zhongluo, *Wei Jin Nanbeichao shi*, vol. 1, pp. 333, 338; but also see Rogers, *The Chronicle of Fu Chien*, p. 60.
23 Ochi, "Tō-Shin chō chūgen kaifuku no ichi kōsatsu," pp. 83–4; Wang Zhongluo, *Wei Jin Nanbeichao shi*, vol. 1, pp. 367, 381.
24 Ochi, "Tō-Shin chō chūgen kaifuku no ichi kōsatsu," pp. 84–5; Rogers, *The Chronicle of Fu Chien*, pp. 52–3, 65, 60.
25 Many scholars have identified ethnic tension as a fundamental weakness in the northern polity, and one that imposed limits on the ability of northern rulers to coerce the south. See, for example, Chen Yinke, *Wei Jin Nanbeichao shi jiangyanlu*, p. 229, and Xu Hui, "Nanbeichao zhanzheng tedian tanxi," p. 120.
26 Xu Hui, "Nanbeichao zhanzheng tedian tanxi," p. 120.
27 Zhou Nianchang, "Dong Jin bei fu bing de jianli ji qi tedian," p. 161.
28 A summary description of the campaign can be found in Fu Lecheng, "Wei Jin Nanbeichao zhanshi," p. 34; a more detailed account can be found in Sima Guang, *Zhizhi tongjian*, ch. 125, pp. 3957–60, and ch. 126, pp. 3961–7.
29 *Wei shu*, ch. 35, p. 819.

30   Joseph Needham, *Science and Civilisation in China*, vol. 4: *Physics and Physical Technology*, pt. 3: *Civil Engineering and Nautics* (Cambridge: Cambridge University Press, 1971), p. 391. Needham discusses the different types of warships on pp. 424–5 and 685–6. Also see Li Tse-fen, *Liang Jin Nanbeichao lishi lunwenji*, vol. 2, pp. 261–3, and Rafe de Crespigny, *Generals of the South: The Foundation and Early History of the Three Kingdoms State of Wu*, Faculty of Asian Studies Monographs, New Series No. 16 (Canberra: The Australian National University Faculty of Asian Studies, 1990), pp. 277–80.

31   For discussions of Chinese naval tactics, see Needham, *Science and Civilisation in China*, vol. 4, pt. 3, pp. 449, 678–85 and 690, as well as de Crespigny, *Generals of the South*, pp. 278–81.

32   Lü Simian, *Liang Jin Nanbeichao shi*, p. 1308; Sima Guang, *Zizhi tongjian*, ch. 115, p. 3640.

33   De Crespigny, *Generals of the South*, pp. 281–2.

34   De Crespigny, *Generals of the South*, p. 281.

35   Lü Simian, *Wei Jin Nanbeichao shi*, p. 1217.

36   Sima Guang, *Zizhi tongjian*, ch. 125, p. 3959.

37   Sima Guang, *Zizhi tongjian*, ch. 176, p. 5494; *Sui shu*, ch. 48, p. 1283; Zhang Tieniu and Gao Xiaoxing, *Zhongguo gudai haijun shi*, pp. 62–4. My understanding of the *paigan* and their function is based on Joseph Needham, *Science and Civilisation in China*, vol. 4, pt. 3, p. 690.

38   Sima Guang, *Zizhi tongjian*, ch. 176, pp. 5497–8; Zhang Tieniu and Gao Xiaoxing, *Zhongguo gudai haijun shi*, p. 64.

39   Sima Guang, *Zizhi tongjian*, ch. 176, p. 5499. This number does not seem reliable, and is contradicted by another number (ch. 177, p. 5506) that seems equally unreliable. More than 30,000 Chen troops appear to have been stationed near the Yangzi gorges (ch. 177, p. 5512).

40   Sima Guang, *Zizhi tongjian*, ch. 176, p. 5494.

41   This follows the placement of battle sites in Tan Qixiang (ed.), *Zhongguo lishi dituji*, vol. 5, maps 26–7.

42   *Sui shu*, ch. 48, p. 1283; Sima Guang, *Zizhi tongjian*, ch. 176, p. 5499.

43   Sima Guang, *Zizhi tongjian*, ch. 177, pp. 5511–12; *Sui shu*, ch. 48, p. 1283.

44   Sima Guang, *Zizhi tongjian*, ch. 177, p. 5504.

45   Sima Guang, *Zizhi tongjian*, ch. 176, pp. 5500–1.

46   Sima Guang, *Zizhi tongjian*, ch. 177, pp. 5505–7.

47   Sima Guang, *Zizhi tongjian*, ch. 177, pp. 5507–9, 5518.

48   Sima Guang, *Zizhi tongjian*, ch. 177, pp. 5506, 5512–13.

49   Sima Guang, *Zizhi tongjian*, ch. 177, pp. 5513–14; *Sui shu*, ch. 61, pp. 1463–4.

50   See Wright, *The Sui Dynasty*, pp. 150–3.

51   Sima Guang, *Zizhi tongjian*, ch. 177, p. 5505; *Sui shu*, ch. 48, p. 1283.

52   Sima Guang, *Zizhi tongjian*, ch. 177, pp. 5529–30.

53   These campaigns are described in Sima Guang, *Zizhi tongjian*, ch. 177, pp. 5530–2.

CHAPTER SEVEN

The Koguryŏ War and the
fall of the Sui dynasty

The Sui conquest of Chen in 589 restored a political unity to all of the Chinese cultural area, north and south, that had not been seen since the early years of the fourth century. This reunification was accomplished by military means, but the Sui rulers Yang Jian (Emperor Wen) and his son and successor Yang Guang (Emperor Yang) did not rely entirely on force of arms to hold their new empire together. The first Sui emperor introduced a more centralized system for the recruitment of government officials, one that brought new talent into government service and began to make systematic use of written examinations to evaluate candidates for office. Although the top echelon of the Sui administration continued to be dominated by men of the same northwestern aristocracy that had run the Northern Zhou state, men from all regions of the empire occupied lower-level offices and came to identify their own interests with the new dynasty. Emperor Wen promulgated new legal and ritual codes for the entire empire, and engaged in various forms of symbolic and ideological propaganda to build support for his regime. He expressed support for traditional Confucian norms of virtuous behavior and promoted Confucian scholarship, and gave limited encouragement to Daoism as well. Above all, however, Emperor Wen, himself a devout Buddhist, sought to use the Buddhist faith shared by his subjects in both north and south to knit the realm together and legitimate his own rule. He appealed to Buddhist principles, sponsored the establishment of a large number of new Buddhist temples, and sought to present himself to his people as a Ćakravartin king – a divinely-ordained Buddhist ruler – all while establishing tight government control over the Buddhist clergy.[1]

Some of the measures that the Sui rulers adopted to promote imperial unity and internal tranquility involved adjustments in the military system they had inherited from Northern Zhou. On June 16, 590, very shortly after the conquest of Chen, Emperor Wen issued the following decree:

At the end of Wei there was chaos and loss, and the empire's territory was divided like a melon. Mobilization for military service occurred every year, and there was no time for rest. Soldiers and men of the

138

armies were placed under the authority of wards [*fang*] and head-quarters [*fu*], campaigning to the north and attacking to the south with no fixed place of residence. Their dwellings did not have complete walls, and seldom did their land possess mulberry trees. They were always wandering lodgers, without the identifying label of hometown or neighborhood. We pity them deeply! All military men [*junren*] shall be subordinated to the prefectures and counties. Their cultivation of the land and household registration shall be the same as for ordinary subjects [*min*]. As for control and leadership by the headquarters, it is appropriate that this should be according to the old pattern. The newly established military headquarters [*junfu*] in Shandong, Henan and the lands along the northern frontier shall be abolished.[2]

The last measure announced in the edict appears to have been aimed primarily at new local military units that had been set up in the southern part of the former Qi realm as part of Sui's preparations for the attack on Chen, and it is congruent with other post-conquest policies of Emperor Wen that aimed at the demilitarization of eastern and southern China. On April 12, 595, for example, it was decreed that all the weapons of the empire were to be gathered by the authorities, and that henceforth anyone who dared to engage in the private fabrication of arms would be subject to prosecution. Several years later another decree ordered the confiscation of all boats in the south that were more than thirty feet long – long enough, that is, to be useful in warfare. These measures were clearly aimed at the recently-conquered territories of Qi and Chen, and in fact the edict of 595 explicitly exempted the Sui heartland of Guanzhong from the weapons ban.[3]

The bulk of the 590 edict, however, addresses somewhat different concerns. It appears that during the course of the campaigns that brought about the fall of Northern Qi in 578 and the conquest of Chen in 589, many military units were moved from their original homes in Guanzhong to new locations in the eastern plain. The soldiers were often accompanied by their dependants, but they were unable to establish lasting settlements because of frequent redeployments dictated by the needs of imperial strategy. They and their families were subject to their military commanders rather than to local civil authorities, and Sui at first continued the established Zhou practice of registering military households separately from ordinary commoners who had fixed places of residence and were in most cases farmers. With the reunification of the empire it became possible for these people to settle down on a more permanent basis, and this appears to have been the main object of Emperor Wen's edict. Henceforth soldiers and their families were to be registered by the local civil authorities together with the rest of the population. They would now receive grants of land from the government under the long-established land distribution (and tax collection) scheme known as the "equal-field" system just as ordinary farm families did, which would no doubt allow them to better provide for their own upkeep and thereby reduce the army's demands on state resources. At the same time, however, the soldiers continued to be listed in registers kept by the local military authorities and were expected to fulfill their military obligations as before. All of this clearly served Emperor Wen's unifying and centralizing agenda. The military effectiveness of the troops was not impaired, but the hold of military commanders over their subordinates was considerably weakened.[4]

These provisions of the edict of 590 are generally understood to have been directed at the forces descended from the old Twenty-four Armies of Northern Zhou, that is, the troops that later came to be known as the "soldiers of the headquarters" (fubing). Their organization had evolved considerably by the early years of the Sui dynasty. The number of "cavalry generals" had greatly increased over the twenty-four recorded back in 550, and their rank had declined. Instead of commanding "armies," they now appear as the leaders of local headquarters (fu) controlling units of regimental size that were the basic building blocks of the Sui military structure. The "chariot-and-horse generals" experienced a comparable increase in numbers and decline in status. Some continued to have their own headquarters and command regimental-sized units of their own, but most became deputy commanders in the headquarters of the cavalry generals.[5] Some (but apparently not all) of the local regiments led by the cavalry generals and chariot-and-horse generals were under the authority of local area commanders (zong guan), and some (but apparently not all) were subordinated to the imperial guard commands in the capital. Emperor Wen expanded the number of guard commands to twelve from the four that had existed under Northern Zhou.[6] In early Sui, soldiers from the local regiments seem to have performed rotational service in the capital under the guard command with which their unit was affiliated. This system may well have been based on the established model of corvée labor, under which adult male peasants were required to perform approximately one month of service each year on a rotational basis.[7] Among the various regiments, a distinction was maintained between those descended from the (mainly Xianbei) imperial guards of Western Wei and Zhou and those that had been raised from among the farming population, and in addition there were also small units of imperial bodyguards composed of sons and other young kinsmen of the ruling elite.[8] This elaborately divided command structure worked to the emperor's advantage in that it prevented individual officers from disposing of enough military power to threaten the throne. Guard generals would have had little opportunity to forge personal ties with soldiers doing their brief tours of rotational service in the capital.

Soon after his succession to the throne in 604, Yang Guang began introducing significant changes in the Sui military system to further tighten central control. At the beginning of 605, he ordered the abolition of all of the thirty-nine remaining area commands (zong guan fu). The area command was the Northern Zhou variant of a widespread institutional practice already several centuries old by the beginning of the sixth century, namely the granting of both civil and military authority to local administrators. An area commander was responsible for the civil administration of the prefecture (*zhou*) in which he had his headquarters, while exercising military command authority over the forces of several neighboring prefectures. The area commands in some ways resemble the Byzantine "themes" (*themata*) that appeared after the Arab onslaught in the middle of the seventh century, and like them evolved in response to military needs.[9] The system provided a flexible tool for dealing with the frequent military crises of the age of division, but it was considerably less useful under the new, unified imperial order that obtained after 589. The number of area commands was reduced after the early years of the dynasty, and those that remained were located mainly in places important for covering the capital, maintaining a hold on the south, or guarding the empire's external frontiers. This arrangement, however, seems to have left greater concentrations of military power in the provinces than Emperor Yang was willing to tolerate. When the area commands were abolished, their military units were subordinated to the various guard commands in the capital and began to perform service there by rotation. This meant a large increase in the total number of regimental-size units reporting to the imperial guards.[10]

Two years after the abolition of the area commands, Emperor Yang introduced further reforms in the military system. The number of guard commands was expanded from twelve to sixteen, and the structure of the local units that supplied them with soldiers was streamlined and rationalized. The "cavalry regimental headquarters" and "chariot-and-horse regimental headquarters" were reorganized on a single pattern as "soaring hawk regimental headquarters" (*yingyang fu*); their deputy commanders were now clearly designated as such and no longer shared their title with the leaders of independant units.[11] About this time, probably because they were so much more numerous than in the past, the regimental headquarters became known by geographical identifiers instead of their original numerical designations. For example, a unit that had once been known as the "Third Valiant Cavalry of the Right Martial Guard" might now be called the "Dragon Spring Regimental Headquarters." We do not know the total number of regimental headquarters or the standard size of the individual unit.[12] It is generally agreed, however, that Emperor Yang greatly increased the number of units over what had existed in his father's day, and that he created new regiments in the eastern and southern parts of the empire – territories that had been part of Qi or Chen only a few years earlier. He was no less avid a centralizer than his father had been, but his methods were different. Instead of concentrating military power in the northwest to dominate the more recently conquered regions, he apparently sought to coopt the local elites of the south and east by assigning them rank and office within the framework of a military system centered on the capital.[13] One man who was drawn into the Sui leadership structure by these means was Chen Leng, the leader of a unit of irregular local troops (*xiang bing*) in Lujiang, north of the Yangzi in today's Anhui province. He was made a cavalry general in the early years of Emperor Yang's reign, and later rose to a leadership position with one of the guard commands in the capital.[14]

There were many others like Chen Leng.[15] It is also worth noting, however, that the Sui military system did not perform its integrative function simply by drawing local powerholders into the service of the dynasty, as important as this was. Biographies of military leaders in the early seventh-century *History of the Sui Dynasty* indicate that promotion was often based on merit acquired in the field, and that military leadership positions were not the exclusive preserve of existing elites. Military service offered the prospect of career advancement and upward mobility to men from humble backgrounds. Wang Bian, the son of a merchant from Fengxiang in Guanzhong, began his military career as a junior officer under Northern Zhou and rose to become a regimental commander under Emperor Yang.[16] The most striking example of upward mobility, however, must be Zhang Dinghe. A man of Wannian, one of the two districts making up the Sui capital, Zhang was a poor but ambitious youth. He began his military career as an ordinary guardsman (*shiguan*) under one of the regimental headquarters. When the army was mobilized for the great offensive against Chen, Zhang was too poor to be able to provide for his own rations and tried (without success) to persuade his wife to sell her trousseau for that purpose. He participated in the campaign nevertheless, gained military merit, and was eventually promoted to valiant cavalry general, commandery governor, and major-general of the Left Garrison Guard.[17]

The restoration and maintenance of imperial unity, accomplished by means of both military campaigns and institutional arrangements, was clearly the central task of the early Sui military. There were also other problems to be dealt with, however. Most prominent of these was the challenge posed by the nomadic Turks, who received the main attention of the Sui armies for several years before preparations could begin in earnest for the attack on Chen. In 552, the Turks had supplanted their erstwhile masters, the Rouran, as the dominant power of the northern steppes, and they swiftly established control over a vast territory stretching from Manchuria west to the Aral Sea, and from Lake Baikal south to the Chinese frontier. The Turks easily gained the upper hand over the warring northern regimes of Zhou and Qi, extorting concessions from each of the two by threatening to ally with its rival. Qi responded to the rising power of the Turks by building new defensive walls, some 900 *li* (300 miles) in 555 and another 400 *li* in 556. The Qi walls had small forts or outposts (*shu*) every ten *li*, and major forts to guard the most important strategic points.[18] These fortifications, however, bore little resemblance to the much later Ming "Great Wall" north of Beijing. Instead of being built of stone or fired bricks, they were constructed rather hastily by corvée laborers using the tamped earth (*hangtu*) method and were liable to deteriorate rapidly unless considerable further effort were put into maintaining them.[19]

The Turks met Yang Jian's establishment of the Sui dynasty with hostility. This may have had something to do with the belief of the new Turkish ruler,

Shabolue Qaghan, that the Sui founder had not shown him sufficient respect, and with the fact that Shabolue's consort was a woman of the Yuwen family that Yang had just ousted from the throne of Northern Zhou.[20] It is also possible that the qaghan wished to impede the consolidation of the Sui regime for fear that the balance of power in eastern Asia would soon tip decisively in favor of a united China. At the end of 582, Shabolue launched large-scale raids on the commanderies north and west of the Wei River valley. Several Sui armies were beaten by the Turks, who plundered six commanderies and made off with large numbers of livestock.[21] The next spring, Sui forces counterattacked and defeated Shabolue himself at the Baidao Pass, near today's Hohhot, Inner Mongolia. But at other points on the frontier, the Turks still seemed to have the upper hand; in the sixth month, for example, they were able to defeat and kill the Sui area commander for Youzhou.[22] Repeatedly, during the course of the 580s, Sui mobilized corvée laborers to repair sections of the long walls that had been built by Northern Qi.[23]

Sui soon managed to turn the tables on the Turks, not by means of wall-building or punitive expeditions, but because of deep divisions that emerged in the Turk polity in the second half of 583. Fighting broke out between Shabolue and his first cousin Apa, an important regional leader and the son of a former qaghan, and Apa asserted his own claim to supreme rulership of the Turks. The Turkish leadership structure was prone to such fissures, since there was no clear, agreed-upon rule for the transfer of political authority from one generation to the next. Succession to the rulership normally went laterally from brother to brother, but when a series of siblings was exhausted disputes over precedence could easily arise between first cousins.[24] This was what happened in 583. Apa was backed by Tardu, the regional ruler of the western portion of the Turk empire, while Sui now provided military support to its former enemy Shabolue. Defeated by Shabolue in the east, Apa turned on his ally Tardu and established an independant qaghanate embracing all of the Turkish territory from Yiwu (Hami) west to the Aral Sea.[25] This marked the beginning of the lasting division of the Turks into feuding eastern and western realms. Their power was greatly reduced, and with the eastern qaghan Shabolue now beholden to Sui, it became possible for Yang Jian to concentrate on the conquest of Chen without fear for the safety of his northern borders. In later years, Sui actively sought to foster divisions within the Turkish leadership. A conflict erupted between Shabolue's son and successor, Dulan Qaghan, and a younger brother after Emperor Wen favored the latter with a woman of the Sui imperial family as his bride in 597. The Sui ruler provided his new Turkish client with strong military backing and installed him as Qimin Qaghan with headquarters in a fortress on the Sui border.[26] Within a few years, Qimin's forces prevailed and he established himself as the undisputed leader of the Eastern Turks. Under the leadership of Qimin and his successor Shibi, they remained largely subservient to Sui until 615. In the late summer of 605, a force of 20,000 Turks directed by a Sui officer carried out a surprise attack on another steppe people, the Khitan of southern Manchuria, who had been raiding the northeasternmost sector of the Chinese frontier.[27]

Sui's taming of the Eastern Turks was more a consequence of the cunning promotion and exploitation of splits within the Turkish leadership than the result of direct military action. Sui armies were not well equipped to deal with the Turks. They usually consisted of both infantry and cavalry, with the cavalry component made up largely of armored warriors riding armored horses. The horse armor was normally composed of small, rectangular sections (lamellae) of leather or metal, heavy enough to slow down the movement of the horse.[28] This sort of cavalry enjoyed a tactical advantage in fighting within China, where battles were fought in relatively confined spaces and one of the most important functions of mounted troops was to break infantry formations through shock action. On the open steppe, however, facing the much more mobile light cavalry of the Turks and other nomadic peoples, the heavily armored Sui horsemen must have found it difficult to come to grips with the enemy. At the operational level, this difficulty was compounded by logistical limitations. Chinese armies campaigning on the steppe normally carried their own provisions with them, using either pack animals or supply carts, which imposed limits on both the distances over which those armies could operate and the speed at which they could move. The logistics of the Turks and other steppe peoples were much more flexible. As long as they were moving through grasslands, the nomads' animals could feed on the grass and the soldiers could eat the animals. It was usual for each warrior of a steppe army to bring several additional horses, some to serve as remounts and others to be killed and eaten by the army as the need arose.[29] Sui armies campaigning against nomads were also limited by what might be called a cautious tactical doctrine. Fearing that their troopers would be surprised or ambushed by the more maneuverable foe, most Sui generals were reluctant to use their cavalry aggressively against the Turks. They tended to move in large, square formations with infantry, cavalry, and carts positioned to provide mutual support; the usual position of the cavalry was in the center of a hollow square formed by infantry and carts, where they were available for a counterattack but could not be used for more pro-active moves against the enemy. One of the few generals willing to break this mold was Yang Su, who had commanded the great Sui river fleet during the conquest of Chen. Campaigning against a hostile Turkish leader in 599, Yang complained that the square formation "is the way to make oneself secure, but is not sufficient to obtain victory." He deployed his cavalry in separate formations capable of offensive action and smashed the Turkish army.[30] His success does not seem to have had a great influence on other commanders. When Emperor Yang made a great progress along the northern frontier in 607, the square formation was once again the order of the day.[31]

The conquest of the south and the successful management of relations with the Turks left China's rulers free to move in other directions. Both Sui emperors sought to dominate neighboring states and peoples and recapture the glory of Han times – an agenda that had ominous implications for northern Vietnam and the Korean peninsula, which were now organized as independant states but had once been integral parts of the Han empire. Jiaozhou, the area around today's Hanoi, was easily recovered from a local ruler in 602. In the spring of 605, a Sui army pushed even farther south and invaded the coastal kingdom of Champa (known to the Chinese as Linyi), which had its capital near modern Danang. This particular expedition had less to do with the reconstruction of Han glories than with Emperor Wen's desire to lay hands on the fabled (and largely imaginary) riches of this southern land.[32] After the Sui army under Liu Fang crossed the Duli River, it was attacked by Champan troops on war elephants. Following initial reverses, Liu dug a number of pits, covered them with grass, and used a feigned flight to lure the elephants into the traps. The Sui troops also employed crossbows against the elephants, causing many of them to turn around and trample their own army. Liu then ordered his men to charge hard on the heels of the stampeding elephants, causing the collapse of the Champan army. He went on to occupy and loot the Champan capital, but on the return march his army was stricken by disease and suffered heavy losses, with Liu himself among the dead.[33] This denouement was almost to be expected. Until quite recent times armies operating in all climes were vulnerable to epidemic disease, but the danger was especially great when soldiers from temperate areas moved south into the tropics and came into contact with a lush profusion of unfamiliar microbes.

In the north, Sui hegemony was resisted by the Korean kingdom of Koguryŏ. This state had its capital at Pyongyang in the northern part of the Korean peninsula, and extended westward into southern Manchuria as far as the Liao River. It shared the peninsula with the kingdoms of Paekche in the southwest (including everything from today's Kwangju almost up to Seoul) and Silla in the southeast around modern Pusan. Both Koguryŏ and Paekche had been founded in the fourth century by warlike tribes moving down from Manchuria.[34] Koguryŏ showed scant respect for Sui authority; early in 598, its king joined forces with the Malgal, a Tungusic people from eastern Manchuria, to raid Sui territory west of the Liao River. This move infuriated Emperor Wen, who ordered an invasion of Koguryŏ by forces totalling 300,000 men. The land army marched from Linyuguan, near today's Qinhuangdao, Hebei, on August 4, but soon encountered torrential rains that interfered with the transport of provisions to the troops. Food supplies ran short, sickness broke out, and the army was withdrawn at the end of October, having suffered huge losses and accomplished nothing. A Sui fleet sailing from the Shandong peninsula to attack Pyongyang fared no better; it encountered storms in the Yellow Sea and many of the vessels were lost.[35] The entire operation seems to have been planned in complete ignorance of the climate and seasonal weather patterns of southern Manchuria, where the rainy season of July and August turned roads to mire and could bring military operations to a standstill.[36] In spite of this spectacular show of ineptitude, the king of Koguryŏ was alarmed enough to apologize to

Emperor Wen, who readily accepted this face-saving gesture and made no further moves against the Korean kingdom for the remainder of his reign.

Relations between Sui and Koguryŏ took a turn for the worse in 607, when Emperor Yang discovered that the Koreans had been engaged in secret negotiations with the Eastern Turks. After the king of Koguryŏ refused his summons to appear in person at the Sui court, Emperor Yang began to make deliberate preparations for another northeastern campaign. "The authority of the Central Kingdom had been flouted, and sooner or later the response would have to be the application of overwhelming force against the miscreant."[37] War preparations moved into high gear toward the end of 610, when Emperor Yang imposed a new tax on the wealthy families of the empire in order to purchase horses for the army. On April 14, 611, he officially decreed that there would be a punitive expedition against Koguryŏ. Construction of a fleet of 300 seagoing vessels began at Donglai on the northern side of the Shandong peninsula, and 10,000 watermen were brought up from the Yangzi and Huai valleys to crew the fleet, along with 30,000 javelin-men – probably aborigines – from Lingnan in the far south and 30,000 crossbowmen. On June 1 the emperor himself arrived at Zhuo commandery, just south of today's Beijing, which would be the principal jumping-off point for the Sui land army.[38] This location was the northeastern terminus of the Yongji canal, constructed in 608–9, which joined the Yellow River near Liyang. Only a few miles upriver from Liyang was the entrance of the Tongji canal, begun in 605, which ran southeastward across the Henan plain to connect with the Huai River and the Yangzi. This transportation system linking the richest and most populous parts of the empire with the northeastern frontier region greatly facilitated the buildup of military resources for the Koguryŏ campaign, and the need to wait for its completion may help to explain the rather long hiatus between the original *casus belli* and the real commencement of war preparations.[39]

All through the seventh year of the "Great Enterprise" reign period of Emperor Yang of Sui, the year known in the West as AD 611, troops, horses, grain, and military equipment poured into Zhuo commandery. The seventh-century *History of the Sui Dynasty* and Sima Guang's eleventh-century *Comprehensive Mirror for Aid in Government* report that the logistical preparations were on a grand scale. Craftsmen in Henan and the lower Yangzi region were ordered to produce 50,000 carts to convey clothing, armor, and tents. The common people of Henan and Hebei were mobilized to "provide for the needs of the army," and boats and crews were requisitioned from the south to transport grain supplies from the huge state granaries at Liyang and Luokou (near Luoyang) up to Zhuo commandery. A reported 600,000 men were conscripted to convey "deer carts," each crewed by two men and laden with 180 liters of grain, to forward supply bases at Luhe garrison (near today's Jinzhou) and Huaiyuan garrison (close to the Liao River), more than 250 miles northeast of Zhuo commandery.[40] These "deer carts" were really Chinese wheelbarrows, differing from the Western variety in that the wheel is located directly in the center and bears most of the weight, permitting a much heavier load. As Joseph Needham, the great historian of Chinese science and technology, pointed out, the Chinese wheelbarrow design was "conceived as a substitute for a pack animal." Tradition has it that the first such contraption was devised by the great Three Kingdoms strategist Zhuge Liang expressly for the purpose of supplying his troops in the early years of the third century, though there is ample evidence that single-wheel carriers were already in use well before his time.[41]

The troops who gathered at Zhuo commandery included both the men of the "soaring hawk regimental headquarters" (*yingyang fu*) and male commoners, mostly farmers, called up for temporary military service as an extension of their corvée obligation. We have no way of knowing what percentage of the total force fell into each of these categories, though there are reports that Emperor Yang established a large number of new regimental headquarters (*fu*) on the North China Plain in the years immediately preceding the Korean expedition.[42] The host gathering at Zhuo commandery also included some units that belonged to neither category, such as the 500 Turkish horsemen following Chuluo Qaghan, a Western Turk leader who had taken refuge at the Sui court.[43] Its largest portion was organized into twenty-four "armies," each under the command of a "major-general" and with apparently identical organization. The nucleus of each army was forty companies (*dui*) of heavy cavalry. These companies were supposed to number 100 men, with ten companies forming a battalion (*tuan*). Each army had eighty companies of infantry, presumably also 100 strong, organized into four battalions of twenty companies. In addition, an army had a baggage train accompanied by an unspecified number of "dispersed" soldiers that was also organized into four battalions, plus a single company of 200 mounted archers who seem to have been under the direct command of the major-general himself, perhaps to serve as scouts.[44] To these twenty-four armies must be added the "six armies of the Son of Heaven" that accompanied the emperor into the field, making a grand total of thirty armies. With Emperor Yang would travel a mobile replica of his government from the capital city of Daxingcheng (Chang'an), with all the major administrative agencies represented. The many civil officials present at Zhou commandery had been ordered to discard their flowing robes and dress in military attire for ease of movement in the field.[45]

The *History of the Sui Dynasty*, written when the campaign was still a living memory, offers a description of the dress and equipment of the soldiers of the twenty-four armies. Different units were carefully distinguished by banners and differences in uniform colors and equipment. The first cavalry battalion of each army wore "bright-brilliant" (*mingguang*) armor joined with dark green (*qing*) cords; they had iron horse armor with dark green tassels and were distinguished by lion banners.[46] The second battalion wore armor of vermillion leather joined with deep red cords; its horse armor had an "animal pattern" and red tassels, and the unit flag depicted a panther-like beast. The third and fourth battalions, too, had their distinguishing colors. The infantry were provided with banners, one for each company, and of a different color for each battalion of the army. Each army had not one but two military bands. The first, of ninety-four pieces, consisted mainly of different types of drums, while the second, of thirty-seven pieces, included bells, flutes, whistles, and horns.[47] Given the large size of the Sui expeditionary force and the relatively short time in which it was assembled, one may reasonably question whether all of the soldiers in all of the armies were really outfitted in accordance with such a high and uniform standard. If they are not entirely fanciful, this and other passages may represent the plans and intentions of the Sui leaders rather than what was actually accomplished.

The *History of the Sui Dynasty* reports that the total strength of the forces mobilized for the expedition against Koguryŏ was 1,133,800 combat troops, with approximately twice that number serving in logistical support roles.[48] These figures are open to question on several grounds. First, the number of combat troops is difficult to reconcile with the organizational structure and unit strengths outlined above. Emperor Yang's host at Zhuo commandery consisted of thirty armies, each composed of 4000 cavalry and 8000 infantry plus musicians, mounted archers, and an unspecified number of personnel attached to the baggage train; since this last group was also organized into four battalions, it seems likely that it did not greatly exceed 8000 men. The strength of each would then have been in the neighborhood of 20,000, making a total of 600,000. When the men who appear to have been assigned to the fleet are added to this figure, we are left with a grand total of 670,000.[49] The figures reported in the *History of the Sui Dynasty* are doubly suspect because they represent such a high proportion of the registered population of the Sui empire recorded in 609: 46,019,956 individuals of all ages, both male and female.[50] One adult male from every forty-one registered individuals would have been called to serve as a combat soldier for this campaign, and if we include the men reportedly summoned as corvée laborers to transport grain from one place to another, the ratio rises to an incredible one in fourteen. In an agricultural society where many lived at or near the subsistence level, the price of putting too many farmers into the army would have been a sharp drop in agricultural output leading to the inability to feed the large armies thus created. In the late Roman empire, the ratio of men serving in the army to overall population (the "military participation ratio" – MPR – to use the term coined by the sociologist Stanislav Andreski) was probably in the neighborhood of 1:100. In England in 1298 the ratio was 1:139; in 1710 it was 1:150 in England and 1:66 in France. Ratios higher than this were sometimes achieved, but this was usually accomplished by the mobilization of militia forces for very short periods and was done most easily in relatively simple, undifferentiated societies where every adult male was expected to serve as a soldier when necessary and was equipped with the skills to do so effectively.[51]

In the case of Emperor Yang's army of 612, there is a special reason why the number of troops may be exaggerated. The official history of the Sui dynasty was written by scholars in the service of the succeeding Tang dynasty, men who had a strong interest in portraying Emperor Yang as a "bad last emperor" whose downfall reflected the will of Heaven.[52] By adding to the size of his army, they would also have increased the apparent magnitude of his eventual failure and the aura of cosmic retribution that surrounded it. Even if the early Tang historians did not "cook the books" in this way, it is likely that the figure of 1,133,800 combat soldiers given in the *History of the Sui Dynasty* represents the total number of men that the government *summoned* for service in 611, rather than the number that actually arrived at Zhuo commandery and Donglai and then participated in the campaign against Koguryŏ the following year. An army roughly half this size, the figure suggested by addition of the reported strengths of the contingents that made up the Sui host, is much more plausible and is also in line with the reported size of the Sui force that moved against Chen in 588. Such a force would have been much too large to march, camp, and fight together as a single army, but, as we have seen, the masses gathered at Zhuo commandery were divided into thirty much more manageable "armies" – each roughly the size of a Napoleonic *corps d'armée* – that would march separately and occupy separate camps.[53]

On February 8, 612, Emperor Yang ordered the lead elements of his army to begin their march eastward from Zhuo commandery.[54] The timing of the beginning of the campaign, and the elaborate preparations made over the course of the preceding year, indicates that the emperor and his advisors had drawn the appropriate conclusions from Emperor Wen's failure of 598 and were determined to set their forces in motion as early in the year as the weather permitted in order to provide adequate time to reduce Koguryŏ's border fortresses before the arrival of the summer rains.

About the time that his troops were setting out, Emperor Yang conducted a series of elaborate ceremonies near his palace at Zhuo commandery.[55] The Chinese "Son of Heaven" was not simply a political leader but also a sacral ruler, the ritual intermediary between human society, nature, and the cosmos, and war was regarded as a significant disruption of the natural order that called for special observances. This was especially true when the emperor himself set out on campaign. On this occasion Emperor Yang had an altar of the soil (*she*) constructed on the bank of the Sanggan River and, after a period of seclusion and abstinence, he dressed in special vestments and rode to the altar in a carriage of state to perform the *yi* sacrifice. Then, on another day and at another location south of his palace, he performed the *lei* ceremony, in which he made offerings of meat, jade, and silk to the Lord-on-High (Shang Di). The meat was distributed to the soldiers, and the other items burned on a great pyre.[56] The final imperial ceremony, a burnt offering to Ma Zu, the original progenitor of horses (identified with four stars in the constellation Scorpio sometimes called the "Heavenly Team"), was conducted at an altar erected to the north of the commandery city.[57] A further recognition of the importance of the equine contribution to military undertakings occurred that same day, when the emperor had functionaries make additional sacrifices to the horse spirit Ma Bu and the first domesticator of horses. During the course of the campaign the emperor would arrange for offerings to be made to the spirits of the mountains and rivers that his army passed, and the ritual code also stipulated another round of ceremonies to follow the ruler's victorious return from the field.[58]

The main Sui army moved eastward through the sparsely-populated mountains and plains of southeastern Manchuria, reaching the Liao River on April 19, 612. Here it was confronted by Koguryŏ troops drawn up on the east side of the stream. An initial attempt to construct three pontoon bridges failed because the bridges were just a little too short and Sui troops trying to struggle the rest of the way through the water were at a terrible disadvantage vis-à-vis the defenders of the eastern bank. A second attempt several days later was a success, however, and the main Sui army was able to cross to the opposite side and inflict a severe defeat on the enemy forces. Emperor Yang moved forward to besiege Ryotongsŏng (Liaodongcheng, near modern Liaoyang city), Koguryŏ's principal fortress in the valley of the Liao River. While these events were transpiring on land, the Sui fleet under Lai Huer set sail from Donglai, entered the estuary of the Taedong River, and reached a point about twenty miles downstream from Pyongyang by the middle of July. After an initial victory, Lai was emboldened to press on to the Koguryŏ capital, rejecting advice from his second-in-command that he should wait for the arrival of the Sui land army in order to make a concerted attack. Lai led 40,000 men up to Pyongyang, where the Korean defenders feigned defeat in a battle outside the city and lured the Sui troops into the outer walls in pursuit. As they scattered to seize plunder and captives, Lai's men were attacked by a fresh Korean force that had been concealed in an empty Buddhist temple and were driven back to their ships with heavy losses. After this unpleasant experience Lai kept his remaining forces in a secure position on the coast southeast of Pyongyang, where they would not find it easy to make contact with other Sui armies approaching from the north.[59]

Along the Liao River several hundred miles to the northwest, Ryotongsŏng and the other Koguryŏ fortresses held firm against Sui attack. Emperor Yang, who was no doubt keenly aware that the campaigning season was slipping away, decided to send nine of his thirty armies directly to Pyongyang without waiting for the fall of the fortresses. The soldiers were issued 100 days' supply of grain for the operation from the forward depots at the Luhe and Huaiyuan garrisons, but by the time they reached the Yalu River most of their provisions had either been consumed or discarded. In this case the distance to be covered exceeded the carrying capacity of the troops; when extra-large loads of grain were added to the shields, armor, weapons, clothing, tents, and other military equipment with which the soldiers were already burdened, the entire load came to more than a man could carry. Threatened with decapitation if they threw away any of the grain, the troops took to burying it inside their tents during the night.[60]

A disagreement arose between the Sui generals when the army reached the Yalu River. One of the army commanders, Yuwen Shu, argued that the supply situation necessitated a withdrawal, but Yu Zhongsheng, who had been placed in overall command of the strike force by Emperor Yang, insisted on driving forward to Pyongyang in spite of the shortage of food. In this he was encouraged by Korean commanders who deliberately fought losing skirmishes in order to draw him in deeper. Yu penetrated to within ten miles of the enemy's capital, but here the hungry Sui army was daunted by the strength of the city's defenses and failed to make contact with Lai Huer on the other side of Pyongyang, whose ships were loaded with grain precisely for the purpose of reprovisioning the Sui land forces at this juncture. The defenders refused to join battle with them, and there was apparently little food to be gleaned from the Korean countryside. The Sui army soon began to retreat northward in a square formation, under almost constant harassment from the Koreans. It reached the Sa River (today's Ch'ŏngch'ŏn River), about midway between Pyongyang and the Yalu, in the second half of August. There, just as the army was in the midst of its crossing, the units remaining on the south bank were hit by a strong Korean attack. Most of the Sui force collapsed in a panic-stricken rout, with some elements (no doubt cavalry) reaching the Yalu River in the space of a single day and night. The vast majority of the troops of the nine armies that had been sent across the Yalu were lost.[61]

On August 27, almost immediately after receiving word of the debacle at the Sa River, Emperor Yang ordered what remained of his army to withdraw from the Liao frontier. He had nothing to show for his efforts beyond the acquisition of a single Koguryŏ outpost on the western side of the Liao River.[62] The cost included not only the loss of tens of thousands of soldiers, but also unrest and instability within the Sui empire itself. In the summer of 611, during the preparations for the Korean campaign, a large area along the lower reaches of the Yellow River had been inundated by flooding, and in 612 the same region was hit by drought and epidemic disease. It was against this background that troops were mobilized and grain, animals, and labor service exacted from the population. The government's requisitioning drove the already high price of grain even higher, and the great distance between Hebei and the Liao River meant that large numbers of farmers, with their draft animals and carts, were removed from their homes and fields for a much longer period than the standard annual exaction for corvée labor. Many did not return at all. And the burden was made even heavier when men were punished for failing to meet expectations that were already unrealistic; it was reported, for example, that tranport laborers who delivered spoiled grain were required to make good the loss at their own expense.[63] Many of the men called up by the state as soldiers or laborers never arrived at Zhuo commandery or the Liao River, but deserted and turned to banditry, swelling the population of certain relatively inaccessible tracts of hill country, forest, and wasteland that had long been the haunt of fugitives and outlaws.[64] Among these areas were the Wagang hills in

Dong commandery, the "Long White Mountain" in Qi commandery south of the Yellow River, and the Douzikang salt marshes on the north side of the river in Bohai commandery. In 611 Dou Jiande, a relatively wealthy and locally influential farmer of Zhangnan county near the Yongji Canal in Qinghe commandery, was put in a charge of a group of 200 local men conscripted for the Korean expedition. Instead of proceding to Zhuo commandery, Dou led his charges to take refuge in the Gaojibo, a marshy area to the west of Zhangnan. There he joined forces with an existing bandit gang that was already more than a thousand strong, and eventually became a major threat to Sui authority in central Hebei.[65] In 611 and 612 there were numerous reports of unrest and banditry in the areas that had been devastated by the Yellow River flood and most severely affected by the demands of the Korean expedition. By the spring of 613, disorders had been reported in the commanderies of Beihai, Qinghe, Pingyuan, Hejian, Bohai, Jiyin, Jibei, Lingwu, and Qi.[66] With the exception of Lingwu in the far northwest, all of these locations lay along the Yongji Canal or the lower course of the Yellow River.

The spreading disorder notwithstanding, Emperor Yang resolved to renew the campaign against Koguryŏ in the new year. On January 28, 613, he issued an edict ordering the troops of the empire to gather again at Zhuo commandery. Efforts were made to better prepare for the logistical support of the forces in Manchuria. A new forward supply base was established on the west side of the Liao River, and grain was moved by ship from the large state granaries near Luoyang down the Yellow River and across the Gulf of Bohai to the small port of Wanghaidun on the Manchurian coast.[67] In recognition of the opportunities that were lost in 612 when all the army commanders attacking Ryotongsŏng had been required to clear their moves with the emperor in advance, the generals were now to be allowed much greater scope for autonomous decisionmaking.[68] There was also a change in the composition of the Sui army. Perhaps because he was disappointed with the performance of his troops in 612, Emperor Yang ordered the recruitment of a new class of soldier for the 613 campaign. Designated as *xiaoguo* – or "brave and determined" warriors – these troops were organized into locally based units along much the same lines as the men of the existing "soaring hawk regimental headquarters." Unlike the *fubing* of the older regiments who were by now mostly men designated by the state rather than volunteers, the *xiaoguo* were raised by voluntary recruitment. In some ways these units may be understood as a throwback to the local elite forces formerly recruited by Western Wei and Northern Zhou; many of the soldiers seem to have been ambitious men, with a modicum of wealth, power, and influence in their home communities, who had held no government office in the past but hoped to rise on the basis of military merit and perhaps even catch the eye of the emperor himself. In some cases, local strongmen brought their personal followers with them into the *xiaoguo* units. The direct connection of the *xiaoguo* with the emperor was underlined by the subordination of their regiments to the imperial guard headquarters that was responsible for supervising the elite corps of imperial bodyguards as opposed to the ordinary *fubing*.[69] In spite of all of these efforts to strengthen morale, troop quality, command control, and logistical support, there were ominous signs that the army of 613 was not as well provided for as the one that had marched the year before: due to a shortage of horses, units were authorized to use donkeys in place of the usual pack horses.[70]

Emperor Yang arrived at his advanced base on the Liao River on March 30, 613, and crossed to the east bank on May 21. The plan of campaign was essentially the same as in 612. The main army, accompanied by the emperor himself, laid siege to Ryotongsŏng, while a subsidiary column attacked the fortress of Sinsŏng (Xincheng), farther to the north near today's Fushun. Another force under generals Yuwen Shu and Yang Yichen was sent toward Pyongyang, though it is not clear whether they were instructed to move forward more cautiously than Yu Zhongsheng had in the previous year. Lai Huer was again ordered to sail from Donglai and threaten Pyongyang from the seaward side. Perhaps because of the need to coordinate his movements with those of the land army, he had not yet sailed as of the end of June.[71] Ryotong-sŏng proved no easier to capture than in 612. This time we are told that the Sui forces attacked day and night from all four directions, both tunneling under the walls and employing battering rams and wheeled assault vehicles mounting segmented, extensible ladders. The Korean defenders were able to counter all of these moves, however, and Emperor Yang eventually turned to building a great earthen ramp up to the top of the city wall, with eight-wheeled wooden overlook towers positioned alongside so that Sui archers could sweep the wall top in preparation for the great assault. At this point, when the siege had been underway for nearly two months, word arrived that Yang Su's son Yang Xuangan, who had been stationed at Liyang on the Yongji Canal to supervise the transport of supplies, had rebelled against Emperor Yang. The rising began on June 25, but it took until July 20 for the news to reach the imperial camp outside Ryotongsŏng.[72]

Yang Xuangan was an ambitious man with reason to dislike the emperor, who had compelled his father to take poison several years earlier. Emperor Yang's defeat in the campaign of 612 apparently encouraged him to believe that Heaven had withdrawn its mandate from the Sui royal house, and the emperor's absence in the remote northeast seemed to offer a golden oppor-tunity. Even before he went into open rebellion, Yang had been delaying the shipment of supplies northward through Hebei on the pretext that bandit activity had blocked traffic on the Yongji Canal.[73] By late June he was confi-dent enough to arm the transport workers under his control at Liyang, rally other disaffected elements, and march on Luoyang, the secondary capital of the empire. The news of Yang's rising brought the Koguryŏ campaign of 613 to an abrupt end. The emperor withdrew his army from before Ryotongsŏng under cover of darkness, leaving behind mountains of equipment in his abandoned camp. Fearing a trap, the Koreans waited two days before setting out in pursuit, and even then they followed the much larger Sui army at a respectful distance and limited themselves to the easiest pickings, massacring several thousand Sui stragglers at the Liao River crossing. The Sui troops who had been gathered at Donglai for another sea voyage to Korea were instead dispatched in the direction of Luoyang.[74]

Although Yang was able to defeat a Sui force that attempted to block his path to the "eastern capital" of Luoyang, the city itself defied his efforts to take it. After several fruitless weeks, and with Sui armies converging from several directions, Yang raised the siege of Luoyang in early August and moved westward toward Guanzhong in what was more a flight than an advance. His army was overtaken and crushed by Sui pursuers, and Yang himself was killed.[75] The entire affair had lasted less than two months, but the consequences were dire. They were not limited to the abrupt termination of the 613 campaign against Koguryŏ. Yang Xuangan was the first member of the ruling circle of powerful northwestern families to turn against the Sui, and his rebellion was on a much larger scale – and much more threatening to the dynasty – than any of the other outbreaks that had occurred thus far. His action appears to have inspired a considerable number of secondary risings in many different regions, and it was at this time that the tide of rebellion began to spread beyond the areas in Henan and Hebei that had been most adversely affected by flood, drought, famine, and the exactions for the Koguryŏ campaigns. In the late summer and autumn of 613, several new revolts broke out in the lower Yangzi region, Zhejiang, and Guangdong, and before the end of year there were also risings in the Huai valley and in the western part of Guanzhong, where a rebel leader had the temerity to proclaim himself emperor.[76] Some of these rebellions were crushed, but new disturbances continued to occur and the harried imperial forces were unable to reestablish order across vast expanses of territory.

Against this backdrop of spreading chaos, Emperor Yang remained obsessed with the need to bring distant Koguryŏ to heel. On April 4, 614, he ordered the mobilization of troops for a third campaign. This time, however, many of the soldiers were not able to make their way to the rendezvous point on schedule – which may explain why the emperor did not reach the Liao River until August 27, four months after his arrival at Zhuo commandery. By this time it was much too late in the season to lay siege to the Korean fortresses east of the Liao. A more effective blow, however, was struck by Lai Huer, who had again crossed the Gulf of Bohai to the Korean coast. He defeated an enemy army and advanced to threaten Pyongyang, prompting the king of Koguryŏ to sue for peace and hand over a Sui general – an associate of Yang Xuangan – who had defected the year before.[77] It was clear that the king was simply playing for time, but his gesture made it possible for Emperor Yang to declare victory and withdraw his army from the Liao frontier before the onset of winter. When the Korean king failed to come to the Sui court as he had been commanded to do, the emperor ordered preparations for another campaign in 615. By this time, however, the situation in the Sui empire had degenerated to such an extent that further foreign adventures were out of the question.[78] In the summer of 615 Emperor Yang's prestige suffered yet another devastating blow when, in the course of an effort to "show the flag" on the northern frontier, he was surrounded for a month at the town of Yanmen by the now-hostile Eastern Turks. In 616 he withdrew to Jiangdu in the Yangzi valley as disorder continued to reign in the north, and it was there that he met his end at the hands of disaffected guardsmen (*xiaoguo*) in the spring of 618.

Emperor Yang's downfall was closely linked to the Korean campaigns, which imposed additional heavy burdens on regions already suffering from floods, drought, famine, and epidemic disease, and thereby fanned the flames of peasant unrest, banditry, and rebellion. The emperor's continuing fixation on the punishment of Koguryŏ greatly impeded his government's capacity to deal with the disorders. The two most important tools of pacification were military power and the distribution of relief grain. Yet the majority of the empire's soldiers were sent against Koguryŏ year after year, while the wheat, rice, and millet that filled the great state granaries located at key nodes along the water transportation network were hoarded for the purpose of feeding the soldiers fighting in the northeast. Perhaps most damaging of all, however, was the blow to the emperor's prestige. Chinese emperors rarely led their armies in person. When the monarch organized a military undertaking on such a massive scale and took the field himself at the head of his army, he could not afford to fail; his defeat would be a signal to all the ambitious men of the empire that he was vulnerable, that he had lost Heaven's mandate and was destined to fall. At least one of Emperor Yang's officials tried to dissuade him from accompanying the army for precisely this reason.[79]

Historians have pointed to many reasons for the failure of the Sui campaigns against Koguryŏ.[80] The greatest emphasis has been given to the short campaigning season in southern Manchuria, where military operations were all but impossible during the cold months from October to March and could also be brought to a halt by the rains of July and August. In the space of only about four months, the Chinese armies had to cover hundreds of miles and overcome the strong fortresses that Koguryŏ had established on the east side of the Liao River. The coordination of the Sui forces over great distances was also a serious problem, most notably in 612 when the land army and the fleet failed to make contact in the vicinity of Pyongyang. And the huge size of the Sui army must be considered a source of weakness as well as strength, since it slowed the army's movements, contributed to difficulties of command and control, and increased the burden on the logistical system to the breaking point.[81]

Problems of logistics lay at the heart of the Sui failure. The attempt to capture Pyongyang in 612 was unsuccessful not because the Sui army was absolutely unable to penetrate the screen of fortresses east of the Liao River, but because that army could not be fed once it had advanced into the deep interior of Koguryŏ. There was little or nothing to be found locally (the Koreans having presumably gathered their grain in the walled cities and fortresses), the Sui troops were separated from their supply bases by mountains, rivers, hostile inhabitants, and hundreds of miles of bad roads, and the soldiers could not carry enough grain to sustain themselves in the field for any length of time. Again and again, Sui military planners seem to have underestimated the distances to be covered, while overestimating the speed at which they could cover them and the carrying capacity of their forces.[82] A case in point is the story of the thousands of two-man wheelbarrows ("deer carts") that were dispatched to transport grain from Zhuo commandery to the forward supply bases near the Liao River in 611. Each vehicle was loaded with 180 liters of grain, enough to feed its crew for seventy-five days. Moving through rugged, sparsely populated country, the wheelbarrow-men took much longer than expected to cover the 400 miles to the Liao River; many of them ended up consuming all or most of the grain they were carrying and, fearing punishment, absconded to join the swelling ranks of the outlaw bands.[83] In this case, the miscalculation not only contributed to the failure of the Sui campaign, but also helped to fan the flames of popular unrest. No Chinese ruler could be confident of subjugating Koguryŏ unless and until he found reasonable solutions to the daunting logistical problems of campaigning in such difficult country so far from home.

Notes

1　For Emperor Wen's efforts to promote imperial unity and ideological legitimation, see Arthur F. Wright, "The Formation of Sui Ideology, 581–604," in John K. Fairbank (ed.), *Chinese Thought and Institutions* (Chicago: University of Chicago Press, 1957), pp. 71–104, and idem, *The Sui Dynasty*, chs. 4 and 5.

2　*Sui shu*, ch. 2, pp. 34–5.

3　*Sui shu*, ch. 2, pp. 39, 43. Wright, "The Sui Dynasty," p. 102.

4　This analysis follows that of Gu Jiguang, *Fubing zhidu kaoshi*, pp. 99, 104–7.

5　Gu Jiguang, *Fubing zhidu kaoshi*, pp. 111–12, 114–15.

6　Kikuchi Hideo, "Fuhei seido no tenkai," in *Iwanami kōza: Sekai rekishi*, vol. 5 (Tokyo: Iwanami shoten, 1970), pp. 415–16.

7　Zhang Guogang, "Tangdai fubing yuanyuan yu fanyi," *Lishi yanjiu*, 1989, No. 6, pp. 150–1.

8　Gu Jiguang, *Fubing zhidu kaoshi*, pp. 110, 119.

9　For the Byzantine themes, see Haldon, *Warfare, State, and Society in the Byzantine World, 565–1204*, pp. 71–85, and Treadgold, *Byzantium and Its Army, 284–1081*, pp. 21–7.

10　Kegasawa Yasunori, "Zui Yōdai ki no fuhei sei o meguru ichi kōsatsu," in *Ritsuryō-sei: Chūgoku, Chōsen no hō to kokka* (Tokyo: Kyūko shoin, 1986), pp. 453–5, 470.

11　*Sui shu*, ch. 28, pp. 793–4; Kikuchi Hideo, "Tō setsushōfu no bunpu mondai ni kansuru ichi kaishaku," pp. 148–9.

12　Gu Jiguang, *Fubing zhidu kaoshi*, pp. 117–18.

13　Kegasawa, "Zui Yōdai ki no fuhei sei o meguru ichi kōsatsu," pp. 473–5.

14　*Sui shu*, ch. 64, pp. 1518–19.

15　Gu Jiguang, *Fubing zhidu kaoshi*, p. 102.

16　*Sui shu*, ch. 64, p. 1520.

17　*Sui shu*, ch. 64, p. 1509.

18　Sima Guang, *Zizhi tongjian*, ch. 166, p. 5130; Li Baiyao, *Bei Qi shu*, ch. 4, p. 63.

The eastern state had earlier built walls against the Ruoruan (*Bei Qi shu*, ch. 2, p. 22) and Western Wei as well (*Bei Qi shu*, ch. 4, p. 56). Northern Wei had also engaged in wall-building in the first half of the fifth century; see *Wei shu*, ch. 3, p. 63, and ch. 4B, p. 101.

19 Waldron, *The Great Wall of China: From History to Myth*, pp. 26–7. This work challenges the entrenched notion that there was a single, massive Great Wall with an uninterrupted existence from the third century BC to the present.

20 *Sui shu*, ch. 84, p. 1865.

21 Sima Guang, *Zizhi tongjian*, ch. 175, pp. 5458–9; *Sui shu*, ch. 84, p. 1866.

22 Sima Guang, *Zizhi tongjian*, ch. 175, p. 5463, 5466.

23 *Sui shu*, ch. 1, pp. 15, 23, 25.

24 Barfield, *The Perilous Frontier*, p. 133.

25 *Sui shu*, ch. 84, pp. 1868–9; Sinor, "The Establishment and Dissolution of the Türk Empire," pp. 305–6.

26 *Sui shu*, ch. 84, pp. 1872–3.

27 Sima Guang, *Zizhi tongjian*, ch. 180, pp. 5621–2.

28 For more on Chinese heavy cavalry and armor, see Albert E. Dien, "A Study of Early Chinese Armor," *Artibus Asiae*, 43 (1982), pp. 5–66; and Yang Hong, *Zhongguo gu bingqi luncong*, especially pp. 103–12.

29 For a discussion of steppe logistics, see John Masson Smith, Jr., "Ayn Jālūt: Mamlūk Success or Mongol Failure?" *Harvard Journal of Asiatic Studies*, 44.2 (December 1984), especially pp. 331–9.

30 Sima Guang, *Zizhi tongjian*, ch. 178, p. 5564. Also see ch. 175, p. 5463.

31 Sima Guang, *Zizhi tongjian*, ch. 180, p. 5631.

32 Wright, "The Sui Dynasty," pp. 107, 109.

33 Sima Guang, *Zizhi tongjian*, ch. 180, p. 5619.

34 Korean histories have traditionally placed the founding of these kingdoms several centuries earlier, but modern scholarship points to the fourth century. See Gina L. Barnes, *The Rise of Civilization in East Asia: The Archaeology of China, Korea and Japan* (London: Thames and Hudson, 1999), p. 222, and Gari Ledyard, "Galloping Along with the Horseriders: Looking for the Founders of Japan," *Journal of Japanese Studies*, 1.2 (Spring 1975), pp. 217–54.

35 Sima Guang, *Zizhi tongjian*, ch. 178, pp. 5560–2.

36 Chen Yinke, *Tangdai zhengzhi shi shulun gao* (Beijing: Sanlian, 1956), p. 140. Shenyang receives nearly half its annual rainfall of 28 inches in the two months of July and August; see *People's Republic of China Atlas* (N.p.: U.S. Central Intelligence Agency, 1971), pp. 54–5.

37 Wright, "The Sui Dynasty," p. 142.

38 Sima Guang, *Zizhi tongjian*, ch. 181, pp. 5653–4; *Sui shu*, ch. 24, pp. 686–7.

39 For more information on the Sui canal system, see Wright, "The Sui Dynasty," pp. 134–7, 144.

40 Sima Guang, *Zizhi tongjian*, ch. 181, pp. 5654–6. For the location of the two garrisons, see Tan Qixiang, *Zhongguo lishi dituji*, vol. 5, maps 19–20.

41 Needham, *Science and Civilisation in China*, vol. 4: *Physics and Physical Technology*, pt. 2: *Mechanical Engineering*, pp. 260–3; the quote is from pp. 270–1.

42 Asami Naoichirō emphasizes the role of the conscripts in his "Yōdai no dai ichi ji Kōkuri enseigun: sono kibo to heishu," *Tōyōshi kenkyū*, 44.1 (June 1985), pp. 23–44, while Kegasawa Yasunori stresses the centrality of the "troops from the headquarters" (*fubing*) in his "Gyōkasei kō," *Ōryō shigaku*, 11 (1986), pp. 61–63. With regard to the creation of new regiments, see Sima Guang, *Zizhi tongjian*, ch. 181, p. 5655, and *Sui shu*, ch. 24, p. 686.

43 Sima Guang, *Zizhi tongjian*, ch. 181, p. 5658.

44 *Sui shu*, ch. 8, pp. 160–1; Sima Guang, *Zizhi tongjian*, ch. 181, pp. 5659–60. Asami ("Yōdai no dai ichi ji Kōkuri enseigun," p. 27) suggests that the infantry companies were 200 strong, but this is little more than a guess.

45 *Sui shu*, ch. 8, p. 162; Sima Guang, *Zizhi tongjian*, ch. 181, pp. 5652, 5660.

46 *Sui shu*, ch. 8, p. 160. Albert E. Dien identifies the *mingguang* as armor made from decarburized steel; see his "Study of Early Chinese Armor," p. 16. Chinese archeologists, however, tend to associate the term with a different type that Dien prefers to call placque armor.

47 *Sui shu*, ch. 8, pp. 160–1. Underneath the armor, yellow was the standard color for Sui military dress; see Peter A. Boodberg, "Marginalia to the History of the Northern Dynasties," in *Selected Works of Peter A. Boodberg*, comp. Alvin P. Cohen (Berkeley and Los Angeles: University of California Press, 1979), p. 268.

48 *Sui shu*, ch. 4, p. 81.

49 Working from the assumption that each infantry company was 200 strong, and placing great emphasis on one report that two armies together totalled 50,000 men, Asami comes out with 750,000 – plus another 50,000 for the fleet. This is still well below 1,133,800. See "Yōdai no dai ichi ji Kōkuri enseigun," pp. 27–8.

50 *Sui shu*, ch. 29, p. 808.

51 Contamine, *War in the Middle Ages*, pp. 12, 117, 307. For the definition of MPR, see Stanislav Andreski, *Military Organization and Society* (Berkeley and Los Angeles: University of California Press, 1971), p. 33.

52 See Wright, "Sui Yang-Ti: Personality and Stereotype," pp. 47–76.

53 For a more thorough discussion of these issues, see Graff, "Early T'ang Generalship and the Textual Tradition," pp. 46–9.

54 Sima Guang, *Zizhi tongjian*, ch. 181, p. 5659.

55 These are described in *Sui shu*, ch. 8, p. 160.

56 This appears to have been very similar to the sacrifice to Shang Di described in a Tang ritual text from the first half of the eighth century. See Howard J. Wechsler, *Offerings of Jade and Silk: Ritual and Symbol in the Legitimation of the T'ang Dynasty* (New Haven: Yale University Press, 1985), pp. 118–20.

57 For Ma Zu, see the entry in Morohashi Tetsuji, *Dai Kan Wa jiten* (Tokyo: Taishūkan, 1966). The "Heavenly Team" was an alternative name for Fang, the fourth of the twenty-eight "lunar mansions" (*xiu*) of traditional Chinese astronomy; see Joseph Needham, *Science and Civilisation in China*, vol. 3: *Mathematics and the Sciences of the Heavens and the Earth* (Cambridge: Cambridge University Press, 1959), p. 235 and fig. 94 opposite p. 250.

58 *Sui shu*, ch. 8, pp. 159–60. When the emperor left his capital to begin a military campaign and returned to it after the campaign was over, there were rites in the imperial ancestral temple.

59 Sima Guang, *Zizhi tongjian*, ch. 181, pp. 5661–3.

60 Sima Guang, *Zizhi tongjian*, ch. 181, pp. 5663–4.

61 Sima Guang, *Zizhi tongjian*, ch. 181, pp. 5664–6. For the intended role of the Sui fleet in feeding the land army near Pyongyang, see *Sui shu*, ch. 24, pp. 687–8.

62 Sima Guang, *Zizhi tongjian*, ch. 181, p. 5666.

63 Sima Guang, *Zizhi tongjian*, ch. 181, pp. 5654, 5656, 5667; *Sui shu*, ch. 24, p. 688.

64 Huang Huixian, "Sui mo nongmin qiyi wuzhuang qianxi," in *Tang shi yanjiuhui lunwenji* (Xi'an: Shaanxi renmin chubanshe, 1983), pp. 175–6.

65 Liu Xu et al., *Jiu Tang shu*, ch. 54, pp. 2234–5; Ouyang Xiu, *Xin Tang shu*, ch. 85, pp. 3696–7; Sima Guang, *Zizhi tongjian*, ch. 181, pp. 5656–67; Hu Rulei, "Lue lun Li Mi," in *Zhongguo nongmin zhanzheng shi yanjiu*, vol. 2 (Shanghai: Shanghai renmin chubanshe, 1982), p. 55.

66 Sima Guang, *Zizhi tongjian*, ch. 182, pp. 5669–70; Woodbridge Bingham, *The*

Founding of the T'ang Dynasty (rpt. New York: Octagon Books, 1970), pp. 43, 130–1.

67 Sima Guang, *Zizhi tongjian*, ch. 181, p. 5666; ch. 182, p. 5668.

68 Sima Guang, *Zizhi tongjian*, ch. 181, p. 5662; ch. 182, p. 5671.

69 For the *xiaoguo*, see Kegasawa, "Gyōkasei kō," especially pp. 64–7 and 75–7. Kegasawa believes that their total number eventually reached 100,000 to 150,000 men.

70 *Sui shu*, ch. 24, p. 688.

71 Sima Guang, *Zizhi tongjian*, ch. 182, pp. 5669–72.

72 Sima Guang, *Zizhi tongjian*, ch. 182, pp. 5671, 5672, 5676–7.

73 Sima Guang, *Zizhi tongjian*, ch. 182, pp. 5672–3.

74 Sima Guang, *Zizhi tongjian*, ch. 182, pp. 5676–8.

75 Sima Guang, *Zizhi tongjian*, ch. 182, pp. 5678–81.

76 Bingham, *The Founding of the T'ang Dynasty*, pp. 45, 131–2.

77 Sima Guang, *Zizhi tongjian*, ch. 182, pp. 5689–91.

78 Sima Guang, *Zizhi tongjian*, ch. 182, pp. 5691–2; Wright, "The Sui Dynasty," p. 146.

79 Sima Guang, *Zizhi tongjian*, ch. 181, p. 5659.

80 Summaries are offered in Wright, "The Sui Dynasty," pp. 145–7 and John Charles Jamieson, "The Samguk Sagi and the Unification Wars" (Ph.D. dissertation, University of California at Berkeley, 1969), pp. 33–4. For in-depth analyses, see Chen Yinke, *Tangdai zhengzhi shi shulun gao*, p. 140, and Li Tse-fen, *Sui Tang Wudai lishi lunwenji*, pp. 217, 227–8.

81 Li Tse-fen, a former military officer, is especially sensitive to the disadvantages of large numbers; see his *Sui Tang Wudai lishi lunwenji*, p. 217. For a general discussion of the impact of numbers on speed and maneuverability, see Delbrück, *Numbers in History*; for the logistics of premodern warfare, see Donald W. Engels, *Alexander the Great and the Logistics of the Macedonian Army* (Berkeley and Los Angeles: University of California Press, 1978), especially pp. 18–22, and the articles by Walter E. Kaegi and Bernard S. Bachrach in John A. Lynn (ed.), *Feeding Mars: Logistics in Western Warfare from the Middle Ages to the Present* (Boulder, Colo.: Westview Press, 1993), pp. 39–78.

82 See Sima Guang, *Zizhi tongjian*, ch. 182, p. 5669.

83 Sima Guang, *Zizhi tongjian*, ch. 181, p. 5656. Grain consumption is figured at the rate of two *sheng* (approximately 1.2 liters) per man/day, the standard ration according to an eighth-century military handbook; see Li Quan, *Taibai yinjing*, pp. 556, 558. The distance of 400 miles is as the crow flies; Tang sources indicate that more than 700 miles of *road* separated Zhuo commandery from Xincheng on the Liao River; see *Jiu Tang shu*, ch. 39, pp. 1516, 1526–7.

CHAPTER EIGHT

Li Shimin and the military consolidation of the Tang dynasty

During the nearly three centuries from the collapse of the Western Jin to the reunification of China under the Sui, both north and south had given rise to a bewildering profusion of dynastic regimes. Dynasties replaced one another in rapid succession, sometimes by means of an internal military revolt or coup d'état (the usual pattern in the south) and sometimes through the conquest of one state by another (more common in the north). The fall of the Sui dynasty and its replacement by the Tang followed a different script, one that had first been acted out at the end of the third century BC, when the Qin dynasty had given way to Western Han. A similar performance occurred early in the first century AD, when the short-lived regime of Wang Mang was replaced by the Eastern Han, and some elements could be found in the Eastern Han collapse – though in this case it took nearly a century for a unified successor state to appear. After the founding of the Tang dynasty, the pattern would be repeated at least two more times, in the transitions from Tang to Song and Yuan to Ming (with the Ming–Qing transition also showing many of the same features). The typical sequence was a combination of natural disasters (floods, droughts) and government exactions stimulating grassroots "peasant" rebellions, sometimes of a sectarian nature, which brought down the old dynasty and gave rise to a number of regional warlord regimes. Eventually one of these regimes would succeed in crushing its rivals, establishing a new imperial government, and unifying the country. In the case of the transition from Sui to Tang, this process lasted a little more than ten years, from the first stirrings of revolt against Sui rule to the elimination of the last serious military challenge to the authority of the new dynasty. Tang success owed much to diplomatic efforts and the adroit manipulation of imperial ritual, supernatural portents, and other time-honored symbols of political legitimacy.[1] It also helped that the Tang founders emerged from the northwestern aristocracy that constituted the core of the Sui political elite, and therefore enjoyed a very substantial advantage in attracting the support of other members of the same class. Above all, however, the initial consolidation of Tang rule was a military process; the Tang founders attracted support because they were able to overcome their rivals on the battlefield. This chapter will examine the military process and the role of Li Shimin, second son

160

of the first Tang ruler and later emperor himself, who was the principal Tang field commander and one of the most celebrated military leaders in all of Chinese history.

The rapid decline of Sui authority in the years after 612 was accompanied by the rise of disorderly and violent conditions at the local level. The principal actors there can be sorted into three categories: bandit–rebels whose activities were of a "predatory" nature, local elites who organized forces to protect their communities from the depredations of the bandits, and local Sui officials, who now enjoyed unaccustomed freedom of maneuver as a result of the weakness of the center.[2] The first type began as deserters and outlaws who took refuge from the authorities in the hills, marshes, and forests. As their numbers grew, they ventured out to attack and plunder the walled towns. In many cases, their leaders were not ordinary peasants, but minor local officials or men of substance in their communities. Dou Jiande, who emerged from the Gaojibo marshes to become the principal rebel leader in central Hebei, came from a relatively wealthy farming family and had once been a village head, while Zhai Rang, the leader of the Wagang rebels south of the Yellow River, had been a minor official dealing with judicial affairs in Dong commandery. Both men had difficult relationships with authority, however. Dou admired the spirit of the *xia*, local strongmen and gangsters who had resisted the authority of earlier dynasties while meting out their own brand of extra-legal justice; he had once had to flee for his life because of an offense he committed, but was later able to return home under an amnesty. Zhai, too, took up the life of an outlaw after he was condemned to death for an offence.[3] Their activities made survival even more difficult for those who remained in the towns and villages. One of the worst offenders was a bandit leader named Zhu Can, formerly a clerk in a county office in what is now northern Anhui, whose followers ravaged southern Henan and the valley of the Han River.

> The prefectures and counties taken by Can were all made to yield their grain stores to provision the army, which wandered aimlessly. When they departed from a place they burned whatever remained and destroyed the inner and outer walls. Nor did they work at planting and harvesting, but made pillage and robbery their occupation. The people were starving, the corpses piled up, and many turned to cannibalism.[4]

At one time there were between twenty and thirty bandit armies operating in Hebei alone.[5]

To protect themselves and their communities against the bandits, local elites organized their kinsmen and neighbors into militia forces. Many also followed another time-honored response to troubled times and relocated to forts built on hilltops or in other easily defensible locations.[6] One leader of protective forces was Lu Zushang, a man from Le'an in Yiyang commandery, south of the Huai River. He was the son of a Sui general, and his family was wealthy and locally influential. Though still a teenager Lu recruited "stalwart warriors" and pursued the bandits, with the result that before long they no longer dared to enter his district. He eventually established himself as governor of Yiyang.[7] Another such leader was Su Yong of Xindu commandery in central Hebei, who led several thousand local men against the rebels in support of the Sui authorities. When Su died, the commandery governor asked his son to take over command of these troops.[8] In many areas local power remained in the hands of regular Sui appointees, but they were often cut off from higher authority and thown back upon their own resources. One such official was Li Xizhi, the deputy governor of Shian commandery in the far south (today's Guilin), who used his own family fortune to recruit 3000 fighting men to defend the headquarters town of the commandery.[9] Many of these men continued to uphold the appearance of loyalty to the Sui house even after the assassination of Emperor Yang in the spring of 618, but in effect they had already become autonomous political actors.

Over the course of several years, the confusing mosaic of local violence resolved into a simpler pattern of regional conflict among a relatively small number of major warlords. Some of the local contenders for power proved to be more ambitious, capable, and successful than others; they were able to incorporate many armed bands of various stripes into their political–military organizations, and with these larger forces they came to dominate territories more extensive than one or two commanderies. These new regional leaders included both bandit chiefs and men who had been Sui officials. The ones who had begun their careers as bandits showed an ability and willingness to accommodate the interests of the "protective" groups by establishing more or less stable regional governments. Once this had been accomplished, it became quite easy to gain the support of local elites, since these men were generally more interested in preserving their own wealth and power than in defending the Sui dynasty.[10] Where local elites or former Sui officials were the ones establishing a regional regime, they were able to use their opposition to Sui rule as a basis for winning over the bandit leaders.[11] In the course of 617 and 618, most of the emerging regional leaders asserted claims to sovereignty over the whole of China by assuming imperial titles, performing imperial rituals, and giving court offices to their key followers.

By the summer of 618, there were nine major contenders for power. The one-time bandit Dou Jiande now dominated central Hebei and had assumed the style of "King of Changle" in 617; he would soon extend his power southward to the Yellow River and change his title to "King of Xia." At a time when many of the other rebel leaders in Henan and Hebei were carrying out an indiscriminate *jacquerie* against Sui officials and members of the educated classes in general (it being the policy of one Meng Haigong of Jiyin to kill anyone he came across who could quote from the Confucian classics or the histories), Dou was one of the few who recognized the usefulness of these people and made efforts to conciliate them and recruit them into his service. Sui officials began to go over to him in large numbers, bringing whole commanderies with them, and with their assistance Dou began to set up a regular administrative structure.[12]

South of the Yellow River in Henan, the dominant rebel leader was Li Mi. Li was a prominent member of the northwestern aristocracy who had participated in Yang Xuangan's rebellion in 613 and then taken refuge with the bandit group led by Zhai Rang. Zhai initially put Li forward as a figurehead, but Li gradually accumulated real power in his hands and was able to eliminate Zhai in a bloody coup near the end of 617.[13] Li's following consisted of an uneasy coalition of peasant rebels and former Sui troops, and his strength rested to a very large extent on his control of the great Sui granary at the confluence of the Luo River and the Yellow River, which enabled him to feed a very large number of followers and helped to attract the allegiance of other rebel leaders in Henan and Shandong.[14] Li took the relatively modest title of "Duke of Wei," but his pronunciamento of June 6, 617, left little doubt that he had his eye on the imperial throne.[15] Li's principal opponent was Wang Shichong, a Sui general based at Luoyang. Wang was the son of a Sui official, but came from a somewhat lower social stratum than Li Mi; his father was apparently an Iranian-speaking Sogdian from the far northwest (*Xi Yu hu ren*). Wang was initially subject to the authority of a Sui regency committee in Luoyang, but became the effective ruler of the city – albeit still nominally loyal to Sui – after a coup on August 11, 618. Li Mi had the upper hand in his conflict with Wang Shichong, and from the early spring of 618 his army occupied key positions just outside Luoyang and threatened to starve the city into surrender.[16]

Farther south, between the Huai River and the Yangzi, the most powerful figure was Du Fuwei. Du came from a very poor peasant family and began his career as a teenage brigand on the "Long White Mountain" in Qi commandery, south of the Yellow River in today's Shandong province. He led a band of followers south across the Huai River to escape pressure from Sui forces, came to dominate the region, and began to extend his power to the south side of the Yangzi.[17] Du's ambitions seem to have been more modest than those of many other leaders, and he did not assume an imperial title. A very different approach was taken by Xiao Xian, the other major rebel leader in the south. Xiao had been a Sui county magistrate, but, more significantly, he was also a scion of the ruling house of the Liang dynasty, which had fallen only sixty years before. He was initially put forward as a figurehead by a cabal of middle-ranking officers from a "soaring hawk regimental headquarters" in Baling commandery in northern Hunan. Manuevering dexterously to establish himself as a real ruler rather than a puppet, Xiao moved his capital to Jiangling, brought almost all of the territory south of the Yangzi under his control, and proclaimed himself emperor of a revived Liang state in 618.[18]

An important contender in the northwest was Xue Ju, a member of the local elite of Jincheng commandery (modern Lanzhou) and a battalion commander of the local "soaring hawk" regiment. On May 13, 617, he sent his troops to

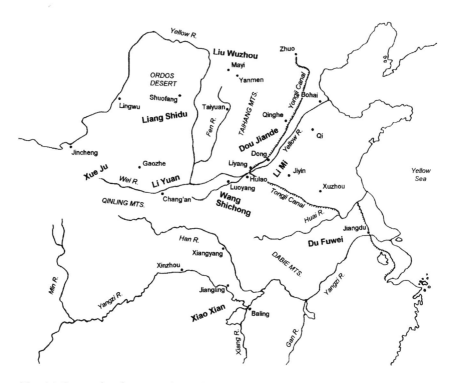

Map 14 Contenders for power in AD 618

arrest the local Sui officials, threw open the state granaries to feed the poor, and proclaimed himself "Hegemon King of Western Qin." He soon brought all of eastern Gansu under his control and upgraded his title to emperor.[19] Two other Sui regimental officers also seized power at different points on the northern frontier in the spring of 617. Liang Shidu, a former regimental commander from a prominent family of Shuofang commandery on the southern edge of the Ordos, seized power from the commandery officials and declared the establishment of the "Liang" state with himself as emperor.[20] Only a week later, a battalion commander named Liu Wuzhou murdered the governor of Mayi commandery (southwest of Datong in modern Shanxi province). He too opened the granaries, brought the surrounding territory under his control, and adopted an imperial title. Both Liu and Liang received strong backing from Shibi Qaghan of the Eastern Turks, who was eager to play the game of divide and rule in the crumbling Sui empire.[21]

At Jincheng, Shuofang, and Mayi, local elites who held commands in the Sui regimental system were able to "privatize" the soldiers of their local units. These men were, however, relatively minor competitors when compared with

Li Yuan, the Sui viceroy of Taiyuan with direct administrative control over five commanderies in northern and central Shanxi. Li belonged to a prominent northwestern family that had intermarried with the ruling houses of Sui and Northern Zhou, and his grandfather had been a close associate of the great Yuwen Tai. When he turned against Emperor Yang in the summer of 617, Li Yuan was able to build a powerful army from the "soaring hawk" regiments under his command supplemented by thousands of recruits raised from the large population of Taiyuan commandery.[22] This force marched on the Sui capital of Daxingcheng (soon to be renamed Chang'an) in the late summer and autumn of 617, defeating two Sui armies en route and capturing the city near the end of the year.[23] This move gave Li Yuan control of both the Wei River valley and the most valuable and populous sections of what is now Shanxi province, and established him as a major contender for empire-wide power. He initially adopted the guise of a Sui loyalist and enthroned a grandson of Emperor Yang as a puppet ruler, then dispensed with this pretense and took the throne himself as the first emperor of the Tang dynasty on June 18, 618.

At the end of the summer of 618, the most formidable of the emerging regional powers were Li Mi in Henan, Dou Jiande's Xia regime in Hebei, and Li Yuan's Tang state in Guanzhong and Shanxi. While most of the regional leaders seem at this point to have been concerned primarily with the consolidation of their territorial bases and managed to avoid major conflicts with their neighbors, there were two large-scale wars in progress where major powers happened to be competing for the same geographical niche. In the northwest, the Xue forces directly threatened Tang control of the Wei River valley. Li Yuan dispatched a number of military and diplomatic missions to win over uncommitted forces on the eastern plains, but the major Tang military effort in 618 was directed westward into Gansu. In the east, the principal conflict was between Li Mi and Wang Shichong. Wang was fighting for survival, while Li would not be able to cement his hold over Henan until he disposed of the remnant Sui forces and captured Luoyang. The stakes here were extremely high, since the victor would be left in possession of the most populous region of the Sui empire and could expect to receive the allegiance of many of the smaller armed factions.

By the early autumn of 618, the defenders of Luoyang were faced with starvation. Wang Shichong decided to march out and offer battle to Li Mi in the hope of inflicting enough damage to break Li's grip on Luoyang and perhaps even drive him from the granary at the mouth of the Luo River. From among the much larger garrison, Wang selected a relatively compact force of 20,000 "elite troops" of whom about 1000 were cavalry. Many if not all of them seem to have been troops recruited south of Huai River who had been following Wang against various rebel armies for several years.[24] To arouse the enthusiasm of his troops for the coming battle, Wang erected a shrine to the Duke of Zhou, the ancient statesman who had founded the city of Luoyang in the eleventh century BC, and had shamans announce the Duke's intention: if the soldiers went out to fight Li Mi they would certainly win great merit, but if they refused they would all die of a pestilence.[25] (Wang had a keen interest in divination and was fond of invoking unseen powers; one of his generals once complained that Wang "likes to make oaths and incantations, just like a shaman or an old witch."[26]) In this case Wang's ploy seems to have achieved the intended effect, and on October 4, 618, he led his picked force out of Luoyang. They advanced eastward along the south bank of the Luo River to bypass Li Mi's forward positions, then crossed to the north bank and continued their advance with a canal parallel to the river protecting their left flank. On the afternoon of October 5, the Sui army made camp just southwest of the walled county town of Yanshi, about twenty miles from Luoyang. Immediately in front of them, to the north, was the canal. To their right the canal flowed into the Luo River just above Yanshi; on their left, the land between the river and the canal stretched like a causeway all the way back to Luoyang. Farther to the north, on the other side of a plain several miles across, rose the long ridge of the Mang hills, an extension of the Long Mountains that passed north of Luoyang and continued all the way to the mouth of the Luo River. Behind them flowed the Luo River. Wang and his men were deep behind rebel lines, and in the event of defeat escape would be all but impossible.[27]

When the Sui army column issued from Luoyang on October 4, Li Mi was encamped with his main field army at the Jinyong Fortress, about six miles east of the city. Leaving one of his generals to hold the fortress, Li took his best troops, probably numbering about 40,000, and marched east to Yanshi. There he camped on the heights of Mangshan and summoned his generals to a council of war.[28] The discussion centered on a single question: should the rebels join battle with Wang Shichong's army, or should they seek to avoid an engagement? Li Mi argued that they should avoid battle. Wang's men were a picked, elite force, and they had plunged deep into hostile territory and would be sure to fight desperately. Moreover, the fact that their food supplies were exhausted made it imperative for them to seek a quick resolution through battle. Under these circumstances, Li averred, all the rebels had to do was sit tight. Wang had gotten himself into a situation from which he could not retreat, and his provisions would soon be used up. But this plan was not to the liking of the majority of Li's generals. They argued that Wang's good troops were few in number and had been demoralized by repeated defeats, and pointed to the numerical advantage enjoyed by their own side. Some of these men were former bandit chiefs and others defectors from the Sui forces, but all were potentially autonomous warlords who commanded the personal loyalty of their own subordinates. In spite of his misgivings, Li had no choice but to yield to the majority.[29]

The rebels apparently decided to wait for Wang Shichong to make the first move. Li Mi remained in his main camp on top of Mangshan, while one of his generals named Shan Xiongxin established a separate camp in the plain just north of the walls of Yanshi. Li's dispositions were better suited for defense than for offense. His two camps were close enough to provide mutual support, and may be visualized as an inverted letter "L" running east along the mountain and then turning sharply south across the plain to Yanshi. Should Wang be foolish enough to attack Li's camp on Mangshan, he would soon have Shan Xiongxin charging into his right flank and rear; if he attacked Shan, Li could apply the same treatment on the left. Relying on these dispositions and the natural strength of his hilltop position, Li did not bother to fortify his camp. When Wang Shichong brought his army across the canal, Li would descend into the plain to crush him.[30]

The first clash between the two armies occurred late on October 5. Wang sent several hundred of his cavalry across the canal to attack Shan Xiongxin's camp, and Li Mi responded by sending a force to succor Shan. The skirmish was soon brought to a close by darkness, and both sides returned to their respective camps. Wang's attack on the eastern end of Li's line was probably intended to draw his opponent's attention away from the other flank. Under cover of darkness, Wang sent a detachment of 200 horsemen up into the hills, where they concealed themselves in a ravine behind Li's position.[31]

The Sui general had already put bridges across the canal, and in the pre-dawn darkness of October 6 he led his main force over to the other side and managed to deploy his men in battle formation very close to the enemy camp. Li's pickets – if indeed there were any – failed to detect the approach of the Sui army. It was only at daybreak that the rebels became aware of their peril and began to pour out of their unfortified camp and deploy for battle. But by then it was already too late as Wang's army surged forward to strike them before they had completed their deployment. This alone may have been sufficient to decide the outcome, but Wang also had a second surprise for the rebels. Hardly had the two armies clashed when, in accordance with his prearranged plan, the 200 cavalry who had made their way around behind Li's position charged down into the camp from the north and began to set fire to the tents and huts. When the rebels saw the flames rising from their camp, their collapse was immediate and complete. Several large contingents surrendered en masse on the field of battle, while Li made his escape with about 10,000 men.[32] This battle marked the end of Li Mi's power. His followers still held many strong positions, but he could no longer count on their loyalty. Instead of trying to rally his forces, he fled westward to surrender to Li Yuan in Guanzhong. Most of Li's army and territories promptly submitted to Wang Shichong, who became the new master of Henan. It was reported that Wang "gathered in all of Li's multitudes. East to the sea and south as far as the River Yangzi, all came to adhere to him."[33]

Wang Shichong's defeat of Li Mi at Yanshi well illustrates the swift reversal of political fortunes that could follow from the outcome of a single major battle, as subordinate commanders promptly transferred their allegiance to the victor who now appeared to have received Heaven's seal of approval. This episode also underlines the fragility of the political–military factions that were competing for power in a divided China. The various regional leaders and would-be emperors all presided over diverse coalitions of lesser leaders of various stripes – ranging from former Sui officials to ex-bandits – who commanded the immediate loyalty of their followers and were concerned primarily with guaranteeing their own wealth, power, and status by aligning themselves with the ultimate winner. Leadership was to a large extent a matter of intra-coalitional diplomacy; subordinates could sometimes overrule their chief, as at Li Mi's council of war, and a disgruntled follower could have a decisive impact in a crisis. Li's subordinate Shan Xiongxin occupied a position from which he should have been able to make a devastating attack on Wang Shichong's flank when the Sui general attacked the main rebel camp on the morning of October 6, yet no such riposte is recorded. It is possible that Shan's men were as surprised as the main body under Li, and therefore unable to mount an effective response. Another possibility is that Shan sat on his hands and deliberately failed to intervene. Shan was one of the original bandit followers of the murdered Zhai Rang, and his relations with Li Mi were badly strained. Within a few days of the defeat at Yanshi he brought his command over to Wang Shichong.[34]

The battle at Yanshi also points to the central place of stratagems and psychological considerations in traditional Chinese warfare. Accounts of medieval Chinese battles are filled with ambushes, feigned flights, and all sorts of surprises, tricks, and traps. This literature indicates that the goal of commanders in battle was not simply to overpower their opponents, but somehow to achieve a psychological effect that would trigger the collapse and panic-stricken flight of the opposing army.[35] This approach was recommended by the ancient treatises on the art of war, and by the numerous precedents recorded in earlier histories, such as Sima Qian's *Historical Records* and Ban Gu's *History of the Han Dynasty*. Both Li Mi and Wang Shichong were educated men who are supposed to have had some familiarity with this literature.[36] This seems to be borne out by their actions. Wang Shichong could have precipitated a decisive battle with Li Mi simply by marching out of the gates of Luoyang and advancing a short distance toward the Jinyong Fortress; instead, he chose to move more than twenty miles east of the city and fight with his back to a river, making escape all but impossible in the event of defeat. His battle plan very closely resembles that adopted by the great Han general Han Xin at the battle of Jingxing in 205 BC and recorded by Sima Qian. The army of the kingdom of Zhao, many times larger than that led by Han Xin, occupied a strong fortified camp at the mouth of the Jingxing Pass. Han led his army out of the pass and deployed for battle with the Zhao camp in front of him and a river at his back. After the Zhao soldiers had all swarmed out to attack Han's main body, 2000 cavalrymen that he had secretly sent into the mountains behind the Zhao position charged into the empty camp and replaced the Zhao banners with their own. The sight of this triggered the collapse of the Zhao army.[37] After the battle was won, Han Xin explained his risky deployment in terms of the need to solidify his soldiers' morale and cited the ancient military treatise attributed to Sunzi on the galvanizing effect of terrain from which there is no escape save through victory: "Throw them into a place from which there is nowhere to go, and they will die rather than flee. When they are facing death, how could one not obtain the utmost strength from the officers and men? When soldiers have fallen in deep, they have no sense of fear."[38] The deliberate occupation of "fatal terrain" (si di) was seen as a psychological trigger by which a commander could stimulate a sort of primal savagery in men who were otherwise no more than indifferent soldiers. This idea would have been familiar to both Wang Shichong and Li Mi; and it helps to explain both Wang's odd choice of position and Li's reluctance to join battle with him.[39]

At the same time that Wang Shichong was disposing of Li Mi, the principal Tang field army was in the midst of a prolonged confrontation with the forces of the Xue family on the northwestern periphery of the Wei River valley. The focus of this conflict was the upper course of the Jing River, a tributary of the Wei, in the area that is now on the border of the two provinces of Shaanxi and Gansu. The Tang founder had sent his second son, Li Shimin, to command the army facing the Xue forces. At this time Shimin was only nineteen years old, but he had already demonstrated his martial prowess in several battles and had held a major independent command during the latter part of the Tang advance on Chang'an in 617.[40] Although Shimin was surely not the prime mover of the Tang founding, as is asserted in the traditional histories which are based on sources compiled after his usurpation of the throne in 626, he was still an extremely capable military and political leader in spite of his youth. Like other members of his class, Li Shimin was trained in both the literary arts needed to run a civil administration and the martial skills needed to lead men in battle. He was fully literate and must have had some acquaintance with the histories and the Confucian classics; he was also an accomplished (if not outstanding) poet and calligrapher.[41] On the other hand, he was trained in horsemanship, archery, and swordplay, and was accustomed to taking a very active role in the rough-and-tumble of close combat, fighting until his sword was broken and his sleeves filled with blood.[42] During the period when his father was the principal Sui commander in what is now Shanxi, he would have had ample opportunity to become acquainted with both administrative procedures and military techniques. The magnitude of Shimin's accomplishment, however, was such that it is difficult to attribute it to his upbringing alone. His is one case where the use of the word "genius" does not seem at all inappropriate.

Li Shimin's northwestern campaign did not get off to a smooth start. Xue Ju inflicted a serious defeat on the Tang army in the first battle of Qianshuiyuan, fought on August 6, 618. Although it is not entirely clear whether the fiasco was the fault of Shimin himself or of subordinates who failed to heed his instructions, the result was a Tang retreat all the way back to Chang'an.[43] When Shimin returned to the Jing valley in September, he faced a new opponent. Xue Ju had just died, apparently of natural causes, and leadership of the Qin forces had passed to his son Xue Ren'gao. This time Shimin occupied a strong fortified camp near the town of Gaozhe. He sent units out to fight small engagements with the enemy, but resolutely refused to commit his main body to a major battle. After a confrontation lasting some sixty days, Xue's army ran short of provisions and became increasingly disaffected – with several generals soon bringing their troops over to the Tang side. Having received an unmistakable signal that the enemy was now vulnerable, Shimin sent out two detachments one after another to invite attack. Once Xue's army had worn itself out assailing these decoys, Shimin approached from an unexpected direction with his main body and scored a decisive victory at the second battle of Qianshuiyuan on November 29. A vigorous cavalry pursuit carried him to the walls of the town that was serving as the enemy base, and induced Xue Ren'gao's capitulation on November 30.[44]

Shimin's next major campaign took place in Hedong, today's Shanxi, where he was sent to counter the forces of Liu Wuzhou. Liu and his principal field commander, a former bandit leader named Song Jin'gang, had pushed south from their base at Mayi in the late autumn of 619 to drive the Tang garrison from Taiyuan and overrun almost all of the Fen River valley. After marching into Hedong over the frozen Yellow River at the end of 619, Shimin's first move was to construct a strong fortified camp at Bobi (some six miles southwest of today's Xinjiang, Shanxi), avoid a major engagement, and wait for the enemy to weaken. As he analyzed the situation, the formidable army under Song Jin'gang had a serious weakness in that it was at the end of a long supply line and heavily dependent upon plundering the countryside in order to feed itself. For this reason it was in Song's interest to seek a decisive engagement as soon as possible, and Shimin was determined to deny him this opportunity. But even while the main Tang army kept to its defenses, its commander led smaller columns to attack isolated enemy detachments. He also sent troops by a roundabout route to harass the enemy supply line, which descended the Fen River valley from Taiyuan. In the middle of May 620, after a confrontation that had lasted some five months, Song's provisions were finally exhausted and he had no choice but to retreat northward toward his base. At this moment, with the opposing army strung out along the the roads, Shimin finally unleashed his counterattack. Song Jin'gang's army was overtaken and destroyed piecemeal in a series of clashes along the Fen River south of Taiyuan between May 21 and June 1.[45] Just as after the battle at Qianshuiyuan, but on a much larger scale, Shimin pushed his cavalry pursuit to the utmost and gave his opponents no opportunity to rally. Song's master Liu Wuzhou abandoned Taiyuan to seek refuge with his Turkish sponsors.

This campaign recovered Shanxi for Tang and eliminated a major threat; it also freed the Tang armies to push eastward into the plains of Henan, where Wang Shichong had eliminated his Sui puppet and proclaimed himself emperor of Zheng. In early August 620, Li Shimin began his advance on Wang Shichong's Luoyang with an army of 50,000 men. By the end of the month, he had occupied the heights of the Mang hills and was beginning to establish a chain of fortified camps to command the approaches to the city.[46] At the same time, subsidiary Tang columns advanced to occupy territories farther to the north and south of Luoyang. In the early autumn, a Tang force seized the strategic pass of Huanyuan in the Songshan massif, about twenty-five miles east of the city.[47] These successes apparently triggered the defection to the Tang camp of a large number of local leaders who had previously adhered to Wang Shichong. By the end of the year, virtually all of the local magnates, garrison commanders, and bandit chiefs of central Henan had switched their allegiance to Tang, affecting a vast area roughly corresponding to the Sui commanderies of Xingyang, Ru'nan, Huai'an, Nanyang, Yingchuan, Huaiyang, Qiao, Han-dong, and parts of Liang and Dongping.[48] Not only was Wang Shichong's supply line to the east effectively severed, but he had lost almost his entire territorial base except for distant strongholds at Xiangyang and Xuzhou from which he was now completely isolated.

Defeated in several engagements outside the walls of Luoyang, Wang Shichong now faced the slow, inevitable strangulation of his capital by the Tang blockade. By the spring of 621, conditions within the stricken city were if anything even worse than in the days of Li Mi's encirclement.

> The millet in the granaries was nearly gone, and people in the city were eating one another. Some took dirt and put it in vessels to separate out the impurities. The sand and pebbles having settled to the bottom, they skimmed off the mud that was left floating on the sur-face, threw scraps of rice into it, formed it into cakes and ate them.[49]

Wang tried to bring in grain from the few outlying towns under his control, but this was an extremely difficult undertaking with so many Tang troops roaming the area.[50] After the loss of several thousand men in another battle outside the walls on March 11, 621, there was little Wang could do except hope for the speedy arrival of the Hebei warlord Dou Jiande, who had earlier promised to come to his assistance.[51]

Near the end of 620, Dou had been persuaded to heed Wang's appeals for help by the arguments of his advisor Liu Bin. Liu pointed out that before Li Shimin's advance on Luoyang there had been a three-way balance of power between Tang in Guanzhong, Zheng in Henan, and Dou's own Xia state in Hebei. Now, however, Tang had clearly gained the advantage over Zheng, and once Zheng fell Xia would be endangered, he said, citing the ancient proverb, "when the lips are gone, the teeth will become cold."[52] Balance-of-power considerations, therefore, lay at the heart of Dou's decision to rescue Wang Shichong, but his attitude toward his new ally was not without complexities. In the same speech in which he urged an alliance with Wang, Liu Bin also pointed out that the desperate, damaging struggle between Tang and Zheng would create the conditions for Dou's future annexation of the badly weakened Zheng state. This "laughing third" approach was a recurring theme in China's multi-cornered internal conflicts, and may help to explain why Dou postponed his expedition to relieve Luoyang for several months while he subjugated local bandit leaders south of the Yellow River in what is now Shandong.[53] It was not until April of 621 that Dou began his advance on Luoyang with a force reportedly numbering 100,000 men. The Xia army moved west along the south bank of the Yellow River, accompanied by boats and barges laden with supplies.[54]

As Dou's huge army moved ever closer to Luoyang, Li Shimin rejected suggestions that he abandon the siege and retreat to the safety of Guanzhong. Instead, he left the bulk of the Tang army to continue the siege while he led a light column to block Dou's advance at the strategic pass of Hulao, about sixty miles east of Luoyang.[55] A Western sinologist who visited the site in the early 1930s described it as a "Chinese Thermopylae":

> Fifty miles east of Lo Yang, the confused loess hills which stretch eastward along the south bank of the Yellow river from the Shensi border end abruptly at the stream of Ssu Shui. The stream flows in a flat valley about a mile broad, bordered to the west by the loess hills which end in a steep slope. To the east the stream has in past ages scoured out a low, vertical cliff, on top of which the great plain begins; flat, featureless, dotted at intervals with villages in groves of trees. The stream itself, receding from the cliff in the course of time, now flows in the centre of the sunken valley, with a stretch of flat land on either bank. The road from the east to Lo Yang and Shensi descends into the ravine, crossing the stream at the little city of Ssu-shui, before entering the hills by a narrow defile among precipices.[56]

After occupying the town and the hills above the pass on April 22, Shimin refused to bring his army out for a general engagement with the Xia forces. The natural strength of his position decreed that a battle could not occur there without his consent, and he had no reason to risk a decision right away since each passing day brought the starving defenders of Luoyang closer to surrender. Dou's army camped on the plain about ten miles east of Hulao. There it remained for more than a month. Dou made no effort to bypass the Hulao position by marching to the north or south, perhaps because such a move would have taken him away from his grain barges and riverine supply line.[57] Toward the end of May, the Tang commander took steps to draw Dou into a decisive battle in front of Hulao. He sent cavalry forces out to raid the Xia supply line, while at the same time positioning his troops at the Hulao Pass in such a way as to give an impression that the place was weakly held.[58] The sources do not say why Li Shimin chose to provoke a battle at this particular time. It is possible that he believed the morale of Dou's men had deteriorated, and it is very likely that he did not wish to allow the exposed Xia army to withdraw to safety in Hebei after Luoyang had fallen. A decisive victory over Dou in Henan might save Tang the trouble of conquering Hebei later on, and we can be certain that Shimin understood that the terrain before Hulao was a potential death trap for the Xia army.

Whatever Li Shimin's reasons for precipitating a battle, his opponent did not fail to snap at the proffered bait. By the early morning hours of May 28, Dou Jiande had set a large portion of his army in motion across the plain toward Hulao. His men descended into the valley of the Sishui by several paths and deployed along the east bank of the stream, their line stretching from the Yellow River on the north to "Magpie Mountain" (a high point along the eastern escarpment) on the south, a distance of perhaps a mile and a half. Before them on the opposite bank was the walled town of Sishui, which guarded the entrance to the narrow defile of Hulao.[59] At this point, they must have discovered that the town and the precipitous heights behind it were much more strongly held than they had been led to expect.

Li Shimin did not immediately deploy his army into a line of battle to face Dou's formation on the opposite side of the stream, but held his troops back in positions that were all but unassailable. The Tang commander ascended a height to observe the Xia army, then explained his plan to his officers: they would remain within their defenses until the enemy troops, tired and hungry after a long, fruitless wait in formation, began to withdraw. At this point, they would rush out and fall upon the by now demoralized and disorganized Xia army. Under these circumstances, he said, victory would be certain.[60] Punctuated by skirmishes between small units of cavalry, the standoff continued from 7 or 8 AM, when the Xia army had first completed its deployment, until the noon hour. Tired, hungry, and thirsty, Dou's soldiers now struggled with one another for drinking water, and many of them simply sat down in the ranks or milled about in confusion. Perceiving the discomfort and disorganization in the enemy's ranks, Li Shimin now ordered a detachment of 300 cavalry to ride along the front of their formation and test their reaction. When the Xia troops wavered and drew back, the Tang commander ordered some of his cavalry units to move south and then east in order to turn the enemy's left flank.[61] Dou's response to the developing threat to his exposed left was to attempt to withdraw his army from the narrow valley of the Sishui to the much stronger defensive position atop the eastern escarpment.[62] But this operation meant the disruption of his army's linear formation, thereby providing the opening for the second phase of Li Shimin's attack. Personally leading a strong force of light cavalry, the Tang prince charged across the Sishui to cut into the retreating Xia troops, with the main body of the Tang army following in echelon behind him.[63] In the course of the ensuing melee, Shimin's cousin Li Daoxuan is supposed to have cut his way completely through the Xia mass, forced his way back through the same way he had come, then repeated the operation several more times; by the time the battle was over, he had so many arrows sticking out of his armor that he looked like a porcupine.[64] According to most of the surviving narrative accounts, the final collapse of the Xia army came after Li Shimin and a small party of horsemen cut their way through to the top of the eastern escarpment and unfurled the Tang banners for all to see, though it is possible that the arrival of the Tang flanking column from the south was also a contributing factor.[65]

The Xia collapse was total. Three thousand of Dou Jiande's soldiers were dead on the field or slain during the pursuit; another 50,000 were reportedly taken prisoner. Most of these must have fallen into Tang hands because their escape was blocked by the eastern cliffs. Among the prisoners was Dou himself, who had been wounded by a lance thrust during the fighting and was trying to make his escape by way of an islet in the Yellow River when he was intercepted and captured by two Tang officers.[66] The pursuit continued for a distance of ten miles, right up to walls of the Xia camp. Dou and the other high-ranking captives from Hulao were paraded beneath the walls of Luoyang on June 3, and Wang Shichong, realizing that his situation was hopeless, capitulated the next day.[67] Dou's wife and his closest political associates escaped from the camp on the Yellow River and made their way back to Hebei with a small cavalry escort. There some Xia officials wanted to enthrone Dou's adopted son and continue the struggle, but the most senior leaders were of the opinion that the magnitude of the Tang victory allowed only one conclusion – that Li Yuan had received Heaven's mandate, in the face of which further resistance would be futile. On June 10 they surrendered Dou's core prefectures to the Tang, and within a few days all of the remaining Xia territories also submitted.[68]

Li Shimin's victory at Hulao conformed to essentially the same formula as his earlier victories over Xue Ren'gao and Liu Wuzhou. In all of these cases he avoided a general engagement by occupying a strong defensive position or fortified camp, while sending out smaller detachments to harass the enemy forces or raid their supply lines. It was only after the enemy had begun to weaken or had made themselves vulnerable by initiating a withdrawal that Li Shimin would unleash a ferocious attack by his main force. His aim was not simply to defeat his opponent on the battlefield but to completely eliminate the enemy regime, and it was his practice to continue a relentless cavalry pursuit until this aim had been accomplished. This pattern was characteristic of most of the major engagements in which Li Shimin exercised battlefield command; it was, so to speak, his strategic trademark.[69] Success was usually facilitated by the fact that the enemy had already advanced a great distance and stood at the end of a long and tenuous supply line when confronted by the Tang prince, whose own supply line was shorter or at least more secure.

Although the Tang histories contain no clear statement that Li Shimin had studied the ancient military treatises as a youth, his operational style was very much in accord with the precepts of Sunzi's *Art of War*.[70] The author of this text seems to have been well aware that delay and the avoidance of decision by battle could often be the best means of staving off immediate defeat and thereby preserving the possibility of eventual victory: "In former times those who were adept at war would first make themselves impossible to defeat, thereby to await the opportunity when it would be possible to defeat the enemy."[71] The second part of the strategy was to watch for an opening, wait for the enemy to tire or make a mistake, then fall upon him at the moment of his greatest vulnerability. "One who is adept at war first positions himself where he cannot be defeated, and then never misses any possibility of defeating the enemy. For this reason, the victorious army will first make certain of victory and only afterwards seek to engage in combat."[72] A show of timidity or weakness was, of course, ideal for lulling the enemy into letting down his guard and thus creating an opening for the decisive blow: "For this reason, at first be like a virgin, so the enemy will open his door; afterward be as fast as a fleeing hare, so the enemy won't have time to resist."[73] These teachings would have been known to many military leaders, but Li Shimin – if indeed he was familiar with them at all – did far better than most when it came to translating these rather abstract directives into concrete operational plans. It seems unlikely that his success was based entirely on book-learning. In later years, he would attribute his ability to evaluate the strength of the enemy – an essential element in deciding when to attack – to the fact that he had grown up in the midst of armies and war.[74]

In addition to his care in ensuring that his major battles occurred on his terms and at the time of his choosing, Li Shimin's practice of the military art was also marked by a distinctive tactical pattern. This typically involved the use of preliminary infantry or cavalry attacks to engage and pin down sections of the enemy battleline, preparing the way for the main assault – a cavalry charge that aimed at cutting through the line on a relatively narrow front, then hitting it from behind to cause the complete collapse of the enemy formation. When he fought Song Jin'gang at Jiexiu (south of Taiyuan) on June 1, 620, he sent detachments to engage the northern and southern ends of the enemy line before leading his elite cavalry to strike the decisive blow in the center. In a battle fought just outside Luoyang on March 11, 621, he first sent a force of 5000 infantry to engage Wang Shichong's army before he charged down from the northern heights with the cavalry.[75] And at Hulao, as we have seen, he first sent horsemen south to threaten the Xia left before he led the main body forward to the attack. The details might change, but the basic pattern rarely varied.

Two elements of Li Shimin's battle plan are worth noting. The first is his own role on the battlefield. While the Tang prince's favored strategy was extremely cautious, his personal behavior in combat was very much the opposite. In almost every engagement in which he participated before he became emperor in 626 (and a different set of rules applied), Li Shimin placed himself at the head of the final, decisive cavalry charge and played a very active role in the cut and thrust of the melee. At Hulao he led his light cavalry in a charge against Dou Jiande's wavering host, then cut straight through the hostile mass with a small party of horsemen to display the Tang banner on a crest behind the enemy position. He later claimed that in all of his campaigns he had killed more than a thousand men by his own hand.[76] Li Shimin may have been especially promiscuous in this regard, but he was by no means unique. Li Mi was twice wounded by arrows, and there was a story that another rebel leader, Du Fuwei, once plunged into the ranks of the opposing army to seize a man who had just hit him with an arrow.[77] Dou Jiande was wounded by a lance thrust in the fighting at Hulao. And Yang Xuangan, the high-ranking official who had revolted against Emperor Yang in 613, "was valiant and very strong; each time he fought, he personally wielded the long lance and put himself at the front of his troops."[78] Military leaders of this period were trained to fight with bow, sword, and lance. Once battle had been joined, they tended to perform in a "motivational" rather than "coordinating" role by exposing themselves to danger in the front ranks. Leaders who did not behave in the right way risked losing the loyalty of their followers.[79]

Also noteworthy is the role of cavalry in Li Shimin's battles. Horses – and skilled horsemen – were often in short supply in agrarian China, and cavalry were a distinct minority in most Sui and Tang armies.[80] Despite their relatively small numbers, however, mounted troops usually played the decisive role on medieval Chinese battlefields. Their superior mobility enabled them to maneuver to attack the flank or rear, or to quickly exploit any openings that might appear in the enemy line; their height advantage made it easy for them to intimidate the opposing infantry, to throw them into panic-stricken flight with a sudden charge, or bull their way into and through the dense throngs of foot soldiers. Before the battle cavalry were needed for scouting and could be used for raids on the enemy's supply convoys; after the battle, they were essential for an effective pursuit.[81] In virtually all of Li Shimin's major engagements the decisive blow was struck by cavalry, and when the Tang prince joined the fray himself it was at the head of his elite corps of 1000 horsemen dressed in black clothing and black armor.[82] In contrast to the heavily armored cavalry of the Sui dynasty and earlier, the horsemen led by Li Shimin and other Tang com-manders are often described as "light cavalry" – meaning that the rider was still armored but the horse was not.[83] It is possible that this change was due to the fact that the Tang army began as a Sui frontier force confronting the highly mobile light cavalry of the Eastern Turks; well before he plunged into China's internal conflict, the Tang founder Li Yuan selected 2000 of his mounted troops, equipped them in Turkish fashion, and trained them to fight in the Turkish manner.[84] Whatever its historical origin, the greater speed and mobility of the Tang light cavalry must have contributed to the success of Li Shimin's raids and pursuits.

The great victory at Hulao was the single most decisive engagement of the civil wars that separated the Sui collapse from the consolidation of Tang authority. At one stroke, Li Shimin eliminated the two most dangerous rivals of the Tang regime, cemented Tang control over Henan, and – if only briefly – brought Hebei into the fold as well. After Hulao, the ultimate outcome of the civil wars was not seriously in doubt. As great as Li Shimin's contribution was, however, it did not bring an immediate end to the conflict. Other Tang foes remained active on the steppe frontier and in the south, and Tang armies continued to campaign on a number of fronts. Li Shimin could not be everywhere at once. Significant contributions were also made by other generals, among whom two of the most prominent were Li Xiaogong and Li Jing.

Li Xiaogong, a second cousin of Li Shimin, was one of the many kinsmen that Li Yuan appointed to major military commands or sent on important diplomatic missions after taking control of the capital at the end of 617. His assignment was to Sichuan, where no major rebel leader had emerged and the Sui officials holding the urban centers had been persuaded to submit to Tang envoys in 618. Possession of Sichuan then provided the Tang with a strategic base from which to launch an attack on the Liang revivalist Xiao Xian, who was then holding the middle Yangzi region and the far south. Li Xiaogong was made area commander of Xinzhou in southeastern Sichuan in 619, and in the following year he was ordered to build warships and practice water combat in preparation for a descent through the Yangzi gorges on the model of Yang Su's campaign of 588–9.[85] Since he had no prior military experience, another officer named Li Jing was made chief of staff for the expeditionary army. The son of a Sui commandery governor, Li Jing was also the nephew of the great Sui general Han Qinhu, one of the conquerors of Chen in 589, and was said to have been a remarkably clever youth who was well acquainted with the contents of the ancient military treatises. He had been the deputy governor of a Sui commandery before he was accepted into the Tang ranks. It was apparently his idea to launch the campaign against Xiao Xian in the autumn of 621, when the Yangzi was in spate and the Liang ruler had temporarily sent most of his soldiers back to their homes because he believed himself safe from attack during the season when the gorges were most difficult to navigate.[86] The Tang fleet led by the two Lis disposed of Xiao's upriver flotilla in a battle at the mouth of the Qing River, and descended swiftly to Jiangling before the dispersed Liang forces could be brought back to defend their capital. After all of the troops that he had on hand were defeated in a battle outside the walls, Xiao Xian capitulated on November 10, 621. Li Xiaogong and Li Jing would spend the next few years extending and consolidating Tang control over vast territories in the far south, including the modern provinces of Hunan, Guizhou, Guangxi, and Guangdong as well as the northern part of Vietnam.[87]

On the plains of North China, sporadic fighting continued for nearly two years after the battle of Hulao. Before the end of June 621, the Tang execution of Dou Jiande in the marketplace of Chang'an provoked a group of his former generals to rise against the victors on the assumption that the same fate was being prepared for them. They put forward Dou's cavalry commander Liu Heita as their new leader, and Xu Yuanlang, a Shandong bandit chieftain who had earlier submitted to Tang, now threw in his lot with the rebels.[88] This new anti-Tang coalition quickly reclaimed the territories that had been controlled by Dou Jiande. It was not until the end of 622, after the Tang armies had fought three more major campaigns, that Hebei was finally pacified, and Xu Yuanlang was not defeated and killed until the spring of 623. In the south, the last major fighting occurred along the lower Yangzi in the spring of 624, when Li Xiaogong and Li Jing crushed the rebellion that had been started by Du Fuwei's lieutenant Fu Gongshi the previous autumn. Along the northern frontier, some opponents of Tang rule managed to hold out even longer because of strong backing from the Eastern Turks. Liang Shidu, the master of Shuofang in the Ordos region south of the Yellow River bend, was not eliminated until June 3, 628. His demise marked the end of overt, armed resistance to Tang authority in China proper, but it would take much longer to repair the damage that had been done by the civil wars of the Sui–Tang transition.

Notes

1 This subject is addressed in Howard J. Wechsler, *Mirror to the Son of Heaven: Wei Cheng at the Court of T'ang T'ai-tsung* (New Haven: Yale University Press, 1974), pp. 31–2, and idem, *Offerings of Jade and Silk*, pp. 55, 68–9.

2 Elizabeth Perry has pointed to the distinction between "predatory" and "protective" strategies in rural China in the nineteenth and twentieth centuries; see her *Rebels and Revolutionaries in North China, 1845–1945* (Stanford, Ca.: Stanford University Press, 1980), pp. 3–4. Tanigawa Michio adopts essentially the same typology as Perry in his article, "Zui matsu no nairan to minshū: hyōraku to jiei," *Tōyōshi kenkyū*, 53.4 (1995), pp. 173–92.

3 For Dou Jiande, see *Jiu Tang shu*, ch. 54, p. 2234; *Xin Tang shu*, ch. 85, p. 3696; Sima Guang, *Zizhi tongjian*, ch. 181, pp. 5656–7; and Hu Rulei, "Lue lun Li Mi," p. 55. For Zhai Rang, see *Jiu Tang shu*, ch. 67, p. 2483, and *Zizhi tongjian*, ch. 183, p. 5707.

4 *Jiu Tang shu*, ch. 56, p. 2275.

5 Zang Rong, "Lun Dou Jiande de chenggong yu shibai," in *Zhongguo nongmin zhanzheng shi yanjiu jikan*, No. 3 (Shanghai: Shanghai renmin chubanshe, 1983), p. 69.

6 For more on these local protective forces, see Huang Huixian, "Lun Sui mo Tang chu de 'Shandong haojie,'" in *Zhongguo nongmin zhanzheng shi luncong*, vol. 5 (n.p.: Zhongguo shehui kexue chubanshe, 1987), pp. 61–77, and idem, "Sui mo nongmin qiyi wuzhuang qianxi," pp. 190, 196.

7 *Jiu Tang shu*, ch. 69, p. 2521.

8 *Jiu Tang shu*, ch. 83, p. 2777.

9 *Jiu Tang shu*, ch. 59, pp. 2330–1.

10 Huang Huixian, "Lun Sui mo Tang chu de Shandong haojie," p. 116.

11 Qi Xia, "You guan Sui mo nongmin qiyi de jige wenti," in Li Guangbi et al. (eds), *Zhongguo nongmin qiyi lunji* (Beijing: Sanlian, 1958), p. 109.

12 For Dou Jiande, see *Jiu Tang shu*, ch. 54, pp. 2236–7; Sima Guang, *Zizhi tongjian*, ch. 183, p. 5715; ch. 185, pp. 5804–5; and Zang Rong, "Lun Dou Jiande de chenggong yu shibai," p. 69. For Meng Haigong, see *Zizhi tongjian*, ch. 182, p. 5669.

13 See Li Mi's biographies in *Sui shu*, ch. 70, pp. 1624–32; *Jiu Tang shu*, ch. 53, pp. 2207–24; and *Xin Tang shu*, ch. 84, pp. 3677–84. The development of Li Mi's political-military organization is covered in some detail in Graff, "Early T'ang Generalship and the Textual Tradition," pp. 245–60 and 269–80.

14 Sima Guang, *Zizhi tongjian*, ch. 183, p. 5722.

15 Sima Guang, *Zizhi tongjian*, ch. 183, p. 5727; the full text of Li's manifesto can be found in *Jiu Tang shu*, ch. 53, pp. 2212–18.

16 For Wang's background and early life, see *Sui shu*, ch. 85, p. 1894, and *Jiu Tang shu*, ch. 54, p. 2227. The struggle between Li Mi and the Sui forces under Wang Shichong is covered in some detail in Graff, "Early T'ang Generalship and the Textual Tradition," pp. 260–80.

17 *Jiu Tang shu*, ch. 56, pp. 2266–8; also see Qi Xia, "You guan Sui mo nongmin qiyi de jige wenti," pp. 103–5.

18 *Jiu Tang shu*, ch. 56, pp. 2263–5.

19 *Jiu Tang shu*, ch. 55, pp. 2245–6; Bingham, *The Founding of the T'ang Dynasty*, p. 139.

20 *Jiu Tang shu*, ch. 56, p. 2280.

21 *Jiu Tang shu*, ch. 55, pp. 2252–3, 2280; Bingham, *The Founding of the T'ang Dynasty*, p. 138.

22 See Nunome Chōfū, "Ri En no kigi," in idem, *Zui Tō shi kenkyū* (Kyoto: Tōyōshi kenkyūkai, Kyoto University, 1968), pp. 101–49, especially pp. 112, 125, 132, and 141.

23 One of these battles is analyzed in David A. Graff, "The Battle of Huo-i," *Asia Major* (third series) 5.1 (1992), pp. 33–55.

24 This follows *Sui shu*, ch. 85, p. 1897. Some sources such as Sima Guang, *Zizhi tongjian*, ch. 186, p. 5809 give 2000 cavalry, but the smaller number seems more plausible in light of the short commons inside Luoyang.

25 Again following *Sui shu*, ch. 85, p. 1897, rather than the more elaborate variants in *Xin Tang shu*, ch. 85, p. 3692, and Sima Guang, *Zizhi tongjian*, ch. 186, p. 5809.

26 *Jiu Tang shu*, ch. 68, p. 2503; also see *Sui shu*, ch. 85, p. 1894.

27 For Wang's advance to battle, see *Sui shu*, ch. 85, p. 1897; *Jiu Tang shu*, ch. 54, p. 2230; and Sima Guang, *Zizhi tongjian*, ch. 186, p. 5809. The canal is described in Xu Song, *Tang liang jing chengfang kao*, ch. 5, p. 40b, in Hiraoka Takeo (ed.), *Tōdai no Chōan to Rakuyō* (Kyoto: Jimbunkagaku kenkyūsho, Kyoto University, 1956), and Gu Zuyu, *Du shi fangyu jiyao* (1879 Sichuan Tonghua shuwu edition; rpt. Taipei: Xinxing shuju, 1967), ch. 48, pp. 16b and 27b.

28 *Sui shu*, ch. 70, p. 1632; *Zizhi tongjian*, ch. 186, p. 5809. Graff, "Early T'ang Generalship and the Textual Tradition," pp. 298–9, deals with the size of Li Mi's army.

29 The council of war is described in *Sui shu*, ch. 70, pp. 1633–4, and *Zizhi tongjian*, ch. 186, pp. 5809–10.

30 *Sui shu*, ch. 70, p. 1632, and ch. 85, p. 1897; *Jiu Tang shu*, ch. 68, p. 2503; *Zizhi tongjian*, ch. 186, p. 5810.

31 Sima Guang, *Zizhi tongjian*, ch. 186, pp. 5810–11.

32 This account of the battle is based on Sima Guang, *Zizhi tongjian*, ch. 186, pp. 5810–11, checked against the earliest accounts in *Sui shu*, ch. 70, p. 1632, and ch. 85, p. 1897. The *Zizhi tongjian* attributes yet another stratagem to Wang Shichong: he had a man who looked like Li Mi trussed up and, when the battle was at its most intense, had him led out in front of the army to convince his men that Li had been captured. This story is not very plausible and does not appear in the *Sui shu*. For a more thorough examination of the evidence, see Graff, "Early T'ang Generalship and the Textual Tradition," pp. 306–12.

33 *Sui shu*, ch. 85, p. 1898.

34 *Sui shu*, ch. 70, p. 1632, and Sima Guang, *Zizhi tongjian*, ch. 186, p. 5812. The modern historian Wang Qian pointed to the tensions within Li Mi's leadership group as the key to understanding his defeat; see *Wang Qian Sui Tang shi lungao*, ed. Tang Changru (Beijing: Zhongguo shehui kexue chubanshe, 1983), pp. 245–6, 265–7.

35 Peter A. Boodberg, "The Art of War in Ancient China" (Ph.D. dissertation, University of California, 1930), pp. xix–xx.

36 *Sui shu*, ch. 70, p. 1624; ch. 85, p. 1894; *Jiu Tang shu*, ch. 54, p. 2227.

37 Sima Qian, *Shi ji*, ch. 92, pp. 2615–17, translated by John DeFrancis in "Biography of the Marquis of Huai-yin," *Harvard Journal of Asiatic Studies*, 10.2 (Sept. 1947), pp. 189–94. For further analysis of the battle, see Kierman, "Phases and Modes of Combat in Early China," p. 56 ff.

38 *Sunzi jiao shi*, ed. Wu Jiulong (Beijing: Junshi kexue chubanshe, 1990), p. 197. This is my translation from Chapter 11 of the *Sunzi* ("Jiu di"). Here and elsewhere my rendering of passages from the classic has been influenced by earlier translators such as Lionel Giles, Ralph Sawyer, and Kidder Smith's "Denma Translation Group."

39 For a more extensive discussion of these issues, see Graff, "Early T'ang Generalship and the Textual Tradition," pp. 317–41.

40 For Li Shimin's age, see Bingham, *The Founding of the Tang Dynasty*, p. 124; for his role in 617, see Sima Guang, *Zizhi tongjian*, ch. 184, p. 5756, and Graff, "The Battle of Huo-i."

41 For a somewhat speculative discussion of Li Shimin's youthful reading, see Huang Yongnian, *Tang Taizong Li Shimin* (Shanghai: Shanghai renmin chubanshe, 1987), p. 6. For a discussion of the exaggeration of Li Shimin's contribution to the Tang founding and the reasons for it, see Wechsler, *Mirror to the Son of Heaven*, pp. 8–32.

42 Graff, "The Battle of Huo-i," especially pp. 51–2; Sima Guang, *Zizhi tongjian*, ch. 184, p. 5748; and ch. 188, pp. 5902–3. There are many other examples.

43 Sima Guang, *Zizhi tongjian*, ch. 185, p. 5801. Almost all the traditional accounts place the blame on Shimin's subordinates, but some modern scholars suspect a cover-up; see Huang Yongnian, *Tang Taizong Li Shimin*, pp. 17–18.

44 Sima Guang, *Zizhi tongjian*, ch. 186, pp. 5820–2; Du You, *Tong dian*, ch. 155, p. 3972.

45 The campaign is described in Sima Guang, *Zizhi tongjian*, ch. 188, pp. 5872–5, 5880–1. Also see Wang Qian, *Wang Qian Sui Tang shi lungao*, p. 253 ff.

46 Sima Guang, *Zizhi tongjian*, ch. 188, pp. 5885–8.

47 Sima Guang, *Zizhi tongjian*, ch. 188, pp. 5889, 5895–6; Wang Qinruo et al., *Cefu yuangui* (Taipei: Taiwan Zhonghua shuju, 1967), ch. 19, pp. 10b–11a.

48 This overview is a composite assembled from Sima Guang, *Zizhi tongjian*, ch. 188, pp. 5888–91, 5893–5, and 5897; *Jiu Tang shu*, ch. 2, p. 26; *Cefu yuangui*, ch. 19, pp. 11a–12a, and ch. 164, pp. 11b–12a; and Li Fang et al., *Taiping yulan*, ch. 109, p. 3a, in *Guoxue jiben congshu* (Taipei: Xinxing shuju, 1959).

49 *Jiu Tang shu*, ch. 54, p. 2233.

50 Sima Guang, *Zizhi tongjian*, ch. 188, p. 5902; *Xin Tang shu*, ch. 92, p. 3808, and ch. 94, p. 3837.

51 The battle is described in Sima Guang, *Zizhi tongjian*, ch. 188, pp. 5902–3.

52 Sima Guang, *Zizhi tongjian*, ch. 188, pp. 5896–7.

53 Huang, *Tang Taizong Li Shimin*, p. 28; also see Harro von Senger, *The Book of Stratagems* (New York: Viking Penguin, 1991), pp. 125, 130.

54 Sima Guang, *Zizhi tongjian*, ch. 188, p. 5905, ch. 189, p. 5908; *Jiu Tang shu*, ch. 54, p. 2241.

55 Sima Guang, *Zizhi tongjian*, ch. 189, pp. 5909–10; for analyis of Shimin's decision, see Graff, "Early T'ang Generalship and the Textual Tradition," pp. 372–81.

56 C. P. Fitzgerald, *Son of Heaven: A Biography of Li Shih-min, Founder of the T'ang Dynasty* (Cambridge: Cambridge University Press, 1933), p. 80. I visited Sishui myself in May 1993. The only way in which I would emend Fitzgerald's admirable description is to say that the eastern escarpment is more than twenty meters even at its lowest point and did not strike me as being the least bit "low."

57 Dou's camp was located very close to the point where the Yongji Canal from Hebei entered the Yellow River. The influence of logistics on Dou's choices is considered in Graff, "Early T'ang Generalship and the Textual Tradition," pp. 387–95.

58 For the raids, see *Jiu Tang shu*, ch. 54, p. 2241; Sima Guang, *Zizhi tongjian*, ch. 189, p. 5913; and *Cefu yuangui*, ch. 420, p. 19a. For Li Shimin's efforts to give an impression of weakness, see *Jiu Tang shu*, ch. 2, p. 27; *Tong dian*, ch. 159, p. 4084; and Zhao Dongjie et al., *Sishui xian zhi* (Rpt. Taipei: Chongwen chubanshe, 1968), ch. 10, p. 4a, which gives the text of a Tang stele erected on the battlefield.

59 This reconstruction of Dou's deployment is based on evidence presented in Graff, "Early T'ang Generalship and the Textual Tradition," pp. 402–5. Accounts of the battle are found in Sima Guang, *Zizhi tongjian*, ch. 189, pp. 5913–15; *Jiu Tang shu*, ch. 2, p. 27, and ch. 54, p. 2242; *Xin Tang shu*, ch. 85, p. 3702; *Cefu yuangui*, ch. 19, pp. 12b–13a; *Tong dian*, ch. 155, p. 3978, and ch. 159, p. 4084; *Taiping yulan*, ch. 107, p. 12a, ch. 109, p. 4a–b, ch. 289, pp. 3b–4b, and ch. 331, p. 11a–b; and the 659 stele inscription preserved in Zhao Dongjie, *Sishui xian zhi*, ch. 10, pp. 3a–5a.

60 *Jiu Tang shu*, ch. 2, p. 27.

61 Here I follow *Tong dian*, ch. 155, p. 3978, and the 659 stele inscription in *Sishui xian zhi*, ch. 10, p. 4b.

62 Following *Tong dian*, ch. 155, p. 3978; *Taiping yulan*, ch. 289, p. 4a; *Cefu yuangui*, ch. 19, p. 13a; and *Jiu Tang shu*, ch. 2, p. 27.

63 *Jiu Tang shu*, ch. 2, p. 27; *Tong dian*, ch. 155, p. 3978; *Cefu yuangui*, ch. 19, p. 13a; and *Taiping yulan*, ch. 289, p. 4a.

64 *Jiu Tang shu*, ch. 60, p. 2353; *Xin Tang shu*, ch. 78, p. 3518.

65 The stele incription hints at the arrival of the southern column; see *Sishui xian zhi*, ch. 10, p. 4b.

66 Sima Guang, *Zizhi tongjian*, ch. 189, p. 5914; *Jiu Tang shu*, ch. 54, p. 2242; *Xin Tang shu*, ch. 85, p. 3702.

67 Sima Guang, *Zizhi tongjian*, ch. 189, pp. 5915–16.

68 *Jiu Tang shu*, ch. 54, p. 2242, ch. 63, p. 2408; Sima Guang, *Zizhi tongjian*, ch. 189, pp. 5918–20.

69 Others have made much the same observation. Perhaps the earliest was the Southern Song commentator Hu Sanxing (see Sima Guang, *Zizhi tongjian*, ch. 188, p. 5882). To Hu can be added C. P. Fitzgerald, *Son of Heaven*, pp. 83, 101; Shi Suyuan, "Cong san da zhanyi kan jiechu junjia Li Shimin," *Renwen zazhi*, 1982, No. 3, p. 97; Wan Jun, *Tang Taizong* (Shanghai: Xuexi shenghuo chubanshe, 1955), pp. 17–18; and Zhao Keyao and Xu Daoxun, *Tang Taizong zhuan* (Beijing: Renmin chubanshe, 1984), pp. 55–6.

70 Li Shimin did quote from the military classics later in life, after he became emperor in 626. For a detailed consideration of the evidence, see Graff, "Early T'ang Generalship and the Textual Tradition," pp. 424–9.

71 *Sunzi jiao shi*, p. 53. My translation from Chapter 4 of the *Sunzi* ("Xing pian").

72 *Sunzi jiao shi*, pp. 60–1. My translation from Chapter 4 of the *Sunzi*. This idea is also expressed elsewhere in the text, as, for example, in Chapter 11 ("Jiu di"), p. 214: "When the enemy opens the gate, one must swiftly enter."

73 *Sunzi jiao shi*, p. 216. My translation from Chapter 11 of the *Sunzi*.

74 Sima Guang, *Zizhi tongjian*, ch. 198, p. 6253.

75 For these battles, see *Jiu Tang shu*, ch. 2, p. 25, and Sima Guang, *Zizhi tongjian*, ch. 188, pp. 5902–3.

76 Dong Hao (comp.), *Quan Tang wen* (Taipei: Jingwei shuju, 1965), ch. 4, p. 25a.

77 Li Fang, *Taiping guangji* (Beijing: Renmin wenxue chubanshe, 1959), ch. 191, p. 1431.

78 *Sui shu*, ch. 70, p. 1618.
79 For the distinction between motivation and coordination, see Martin van Creveld, *Command in War* (Cambridge, Mass.: Harvard University Press, 1985), p. 43. In *The Mask of Command* (New York: Viking, 1987), John Keegan argues that the effectiveness of military commanders is in large measure dependant on their ability to play the culturally determined roles expected by their followers. Wang Shichong, who is not known to have participated in combat, was detested by many of his subordinates; see *Xin Tang shu*, ch. 54, pp. 2231–3; ch. 68, p. 2503.
80 Graff, "Early T'ang Generalship and the Textual Tradition," pp. 170–5.
81 The many functions of Tang-period cavalry are explored in Li Shu-t'ung, "Tangdai zhi junshi yu ma," in idem, *Tang shi yanjiu* (Taipei: Taiwan Commercial Press, 1979), pp. 231–76.
82 Sima Guang, *Zizhi tongjian*, ch. 188, p. 5901.
83 See Yang Hong, *Zhongguo gu bingqi luncong*, pp. 58–9, and idem, *Gudai bingqi shihua* (Shanghai: Shanghai kexue jishu chubanshe, 1988), pp. 144–5, 153–5.
84 See Wen Daya, *Da Tang chuangye qi ju zhu* (Shanghai: Shanghai Guji chubanshe, 1983), ch. 1, p. 2; Dien, "A Study of Early Chinese Armor," p. 41; and David A. Graff, "Strategy and Contingency in the Tang Defeat of the Eastern Turks, 629–630" (forthcoming).
85 *Jiu Tang shu*, ch. 60, pp. 2347–8.
86 *Jiu Tang shu*, ch. 67, pp. 2475–6.
87 *Jiu Tang shu*, ch. 67, pp. 2476–7; Sima Guang, *Zizhi tongjian*, ch. 189, pp. 5934–5.
88 *Jiu Tang shu*, ch. 55, pp. 2258, 2261.

CHAPTER NINE

The early Tang military and the expeditionary armies

The contrast between the population figures recorded by the Sui government and those dating from the early period of Tang rule is startling. In 609, before Emperor Yang's Korean campaigns and the great rebellions, the officially registered population of the empire stood at 8,907,546 households and 46,019,956 individuals. Approximately three decades later, in an unspecified year between 634 and 643, the corresponding figures were only 2,874,249 households and some 12 million individuals.[1] Banditry remained a serious problem in some parts of China long after the defeat of Tang's last major military rivals, and there were reports of widespread devastation, with vast areas said to be almost devoid of human habitation. In 632, the Tang minister Wei Zheng painted the following picture of conditions in Henan, formerly one of China's most populous regions: "From the Yi and Luo rivers east to the seacoast, there is an immense wasteland of weeds and rushes. The crowd of humanity has disappeared; the sounds of chickens and dogs are no longer heard."[2] This was, however, a considerable exaggeration, crafted for maximum rhetorical effect within the context of policy advocacy. While flood, drought, famine, banditry, and war had all taken their toll in the intervening years, the actual population of China could not have been reduced by nearly three-quarters. For the most part, the discrepancy between the Sui and early Tang figures is thought to reflect not mortality but the state's loss of administrative control over its people.[3] During the preceding years of chaos, people left their homes in large numbers and local government records must surely have been destroyed in many places. Cleaning up this mess would have been difficult enough under any circumstances, but in early Tang the situation was further complicated by the fact that in some parts of China the authority of the imperial court did not penetrate to the local level.

In the course of their struggle with the various other contenders for imperial power, the Tang leaders had found it not just expedient but essential to make deals with local powerholders. Whether bandits, local elites, or former Sui officials, when these local strongmen came over to the Tang side they were almost invariably granted titles and offices that allowed them to retain control of their existing territories and military forces. When necessary, the Tang founder created new units of local government to accommodate his new supporters, with the result that the number of prefectures and counties in early Tang was said to be twice that of Sui.[4] Many of the leaders who were thus rewarded retained their local power for some years after the Tang victory. They were in a position to prevent the re-registration of population (thereby reserving for themselves revenues that would otherwise have been claimed by the center), and also had the ability to mobilize armed men in their territories. This was certainly the case in Henan and Hebei, the regions that had been most fought over during the civil wars. Early in 626, as the power struggle between Li Shimin and his elder brother Jiancheng, the heir apparent, intensified, Shimin sent one of his trusted followers to Luoyang with ample funds to buy the support of such local leaders, who were referred to as the "heroes east of the mountains."[5] It is possible that they continued to block the court's access to local resources well into the second half of the seventh century.[6] Their continued existence must have been tolerated by the center for a variety of reasons. All of them accepted the legitimacy of Tang rule, and very few (if any) were strong enough to present a serious military challenge to the new dynasty. Moreover, toleration facilitated economic recovery and the restoration of social order if only because it obviated the need for further military campaigns.

The most powerful of the local leaders were neutralized in various ways during the 620s. Some were executed on charges of treason or killed in the course of abortive rebellions, while many others were transferred to official posts outside of their home areas. Safely away from their old power bases, the latter generally became faithful servants of the new dynasty. Some of these men came from quite humble origins and represented an infusion of new blood into the aristocratic ruling elite of Sui times. One such figure was Zhang Shigui. Originally a leader of mountain bandits in the westernmost corner of Henan, Zhang submitted to Tang in 618 and was made prefect of his native Guozhou. He provided supplies for Tang forces on their way to fight in the Luoyang area, and was soon brought to court as a general of the imperial guards. He was then sent to Sichuan as a prefect, campaigned against the Liao people of the upper Yangzi highlands, and eventually served as chief administrator of the important prefectures of Youzhou (today's Beijing) and Yangzhou (the metropolis of the lower Yangzi region).[7] Zhang's literacy was apparently far below the aristocratic standard; on one occasion when he presented a passable entry at a court poetry contest, it was widely believed that he had engaged the services of a ghost writer.[8] An even more important figure than Zhang was Li Shiji. Born Xu Shiji, he came from a wealthy but uneducated farm family in eastern Henan. He was an early lieutenant of the bandit leader Zhai Rang and then Li Mi, and when he surrendered an important granary and a number of commanderies to Tang after Li's defeat in 618, he was rewarded with the imperial surname. Li went on to play an important role in many of the military campaigns of the Tang consolidation, and later spent sixteen years as chief administrator at Bingzhou (Taiyuan), keeping a watchful eye on developments among the steppe peoples. In spite of his admitted illiteracy, Li ended his career as a chief minister under the third Tang emperor.[9]

After Li Shimin came to the throne in 626 by means of a coup in which he eliminated two of his brothers (including Jiancheng, the heir apparent) and forced his father Li Yuan to abdicate, he took steps to weaken the remaining local leaders. In the spring of 627, the new emperor (who would be known posthumously as Tang Taizong) ordered an administrative reorganization that abolished many of the new prefectures and counties that had been created to accommodate local strongmen who had submitted to Tang during the civil war period.[10] The grants of office that had been handed out so liberally a few years before were now being taken back. Men who had been prefects were demoted to county magistrates, and men who had been county magistrates lost their official standing entirely. From this time on, the center began to exercise greater control over local appointments.[11] The fact that there is no evidence of rebellion may be taken as either a measure of the degree of military control attained by the new dynasty, or a sign that the state continued to turn a blind eye toward the exercise of informal power by local strongmen at the sub-bureaucratic level.

Taizong's efforts to repair the damage that the civil wars had done to the centralized structure of imperial government were paralleled by measures to heal the spiritual and psychological scars of the conflict. Despite the widespread acceptance of the Buddhist faith by the people of medieval China, Buddhist teachings enjoining non-violence and the avoidance of killing do not appear to have mitigated the ferocity of the fighting; some of the uprisings of the period were, in fact, led by Buddhist monks, and there is evidence that at least some monks participated in combat.[12] Once the conflict was over, however, the faith was enlisted by the state to help bring about closure. In the third month of 628 the new emperor held a Buddhist memorial service for those who had perished, and at the end of 629, on the advice of the monk Mingchan, he ordered the construction of monasteries on the sites of seven of his battles, so that monks would be able to offer prayers for the dead.[13] The name chosen for the one erected on the Hulao battlefield, "Temple of Equality in Commiseration" (deng ci si), clearly indicates that the fallen of both sides were to receive equal solicitude, thus helping to heal the divisions engendered by the civil war.

The Tang empire was not, however, in a position to put aside arms and warfare. Although the country was now at peace internally, conflicts continued along the borders. At the time that the battlefield temples were being constructed, Tang armies were engaged in a major offensive campaign against the Eastern Turks. Back in 617, when their qaghan, Shibi, was supporting a number of different rebel leaders in order to keep China weak and divided, the Turks had provided Li Yuan with 2000 horses for his advance on the Sui capital.[14] Once the Tang founder had grown in strength and began to look like a winner, however, the Turks had thrown their support to Tang foes such as Liu Wuzhou in Shanxi (619) and Liu Heita in Hebei (622). After the elimination of the major Tang rivals within China, the Turks, now led by Shibi's younger brother Xieli, entered the lists themselves and launched massive plundering expeditions against Shanxi and the northern borders of Guanzhong year after year from 623 to 626, perhaps in the hope of encouraging anti-Tang uprisings.[15] The great incursion of 626 carried all the way to the north bank of the Wei River only a few miles from Chang'an. Li Shimin, who had taken the throne only three weeks earlier, rode out to parley with Xieli on September 23. He put on a great show of bravado, but probably had to make a large payment to the Turks in order to secure their withdrawal.[16] In the immediate aftermath of the confrontation at the Wei River, the new emperor introduced a crash program of military training for his guardsmen in the capital; before the end of the year, he had issued another edict calling for military drills and maneuvers in the agricultural slack season after the autumn harvest and made inquiries about the possibility of increasing the size of the army by selecting underage males for military service.[17]

In the end, Taizong's revenge upon the Turks was made possible less by his own preparations than by a series of events that laid bare all of the weaknesses of the Turk polity. Xieli's expedition of 626 may have yielded a great deal of booty, but its failure to spark an uprising within China probably damaged the qaghan's prestige among his own people and especially among the subject tribes.[18] To this situation was added unusually severe weather on the Mongolian steppe at some point before the middle of October 627; possibly in the spring or early autumn of that year. Heavy snows covered the ground to a depth of several feet, preventing the nomads' livestock from grazing and causing a massive die-off among the animals. It is not clear whether tribal revolts against Xieli were already in progress by this time, but the natural catastrophe surely contributed to political unrest. According to one Chinese source, losses to his herds prompted the qaghan to make new demands on subject tribes that were themselves hard-pressed, and this in turn pushed the hungry nomads into rebellion.[19] Whatever the exact sequence of events, the snowstorms and famine of 627 dramatically demonstrated the ecological vulnerability of even the strongest steppe empire, dependant as it was on the survival of its herds and unable to store surpluses from one year to the next in the manner of agrarian China.

By the summer of 628, many of the subordinate peoples of the Turk empire were in open revolt. Especially threatening to Xieli's Turks were the Xueyantuo, the most powerful of the Turkic Tiele tribes that inhabited the territory north of the Gobi Desert. Failure to put down these uprisings led to a fatal division within the Turks' ruling Ashina clan. Xieli sent his nephew Tuli, a subordinate qaghan ruling over the tribes of eastern Mongolia and southwestern Manchuria, to put down the rebels. When Tuli returned in defeat, Xieli had him confined for ten days and flogged. The next time that Xieli tried to levy troops from his following, Tuli refused to provide them – which prompted Xieli to attack him in the spring of 628. The civil war within the

Ashina clan was made possible and even likely because of the ambiguous succession system practiced by the Turks. Rule was normally passed from brother to brother, but there was no clear standard for adjudicating the competing claims of members of the next generation. As the son of Shibi Qaghan, Xieli's elder brother and predecessor, Tuli was in a position to claim the throne as "the representative of the genealogically senior line who was now of age."[20] And Tuli had the wherewithal to challenge Xieli because of the Turks' practice of creating "subordinate qaghans" to rule as satraps over vast portions of the empire precisely as a means of placating the offspring of previous qaghans who had been passed over for the succession.[21] The Tang emperor was apparently well aware of the fissiparous nature of the Turk polity, and did not miss opportunities to promote and exploit divisions. When Tuli requested Taizong's support in the fourth lunar month of 628, the emperor ordered one of his frontier commanders to give direct military assistance to Tuli and sent another general to Taiyuan to begin preparations for a major offensive against Xieli.[22]

By the autumn of 629, the preparations appear to have been complete, and Taizong may also have been encouraged by diplomatic communications with the Xueyantuo, who now dominated the territory north of the Gobi Desert. On September 11, he appointed his minister of war, Li Jing, to be commander-in-chief of the expeditionary army that would march against the Turks, and on December 13 he gave the order for the offensive to begin.[23] The Tang forces advanced in six major columns, with a distance of no less than 720 miles separating the easternmost and westernmost columns. Most of these efforts probably aimed to pin down regional Turkish leaders so they would not be able to come to Xieli's assistance. The main blow was to be struck by the central column directly under the control of Li Jing, working in very close cooperation with another column under Li Shiji.[24] Li Jing advanced northward from Mayi toward the frontier town of Dingxiang, around which Xieli and his followers were camped. In a move that took the Turks completely by surprise, Li advanced with 3000 light cavalry to occupy a ridge south of Dingxiang. When the Tang troops made a night attack on the town and penetrated the outer wall, Xieli retreated northward to a place called Iron Mountain. His decision to abandon Dingxiang was probably influenced by the approach of Li Shiji's column from the east and the threat that this force posed to his path of retreat.[25]

Li Jing and Li Shiji joined forces at the Baidao Pass, between Dingxiang and Iron Mountain, and a lull ensued in the campaign as Xieli sued for peace and Taizong responded by sending an envoy from Chang'an to the Turkish camp to negotiate the terms of his submission.[26] During this time, the two Tang generals hit upon the idea of making a surprise attack on the Turks now that they had let down their guard. They did not seek authorization from the emperor (who was more 600 miles away by road), nor did they attempt to inform the Tang ambassador of their plan.[27] Li Jing set out for the Turkish camp with a force of 10,000 cavalry, while Li Shiji took a separate column to block the route that the Turks would have to take if they wanted to escape northward across the desert. As Li Jing's men neared Xieli's camp on March 27, 630, a mist screened their approach until they were only a short distance away from their quarry. When the Turks finally became aware of their plight, it was too late to organize an effective defense. The Tang vanguard charged directly toward the qaghan's tent, cutting down dozens of Turks and throwing the entire camp into confusion. Xieli chose to make his escape on a fast horse, accompanied by just a few followers. With him went all hope of resistance. The "battle" at Iron Mountain was apparently little more than a one-sided slaughter. Chinese accounts report that some 10,000 of the nomads were killed and more than 100,000 men and women submitted to the victors.[28] Many of these survivors probably surrendered when they ran into Li Shiji's blocking position at the southern end of the path across the Gobi.[29] Li Jing later faced charges for allowing his troops to plunder the Turkish camp, but was never punished for taking military action – apparently in contravention of the emperor's wishes – while negotiations were in progress.[30] Taizong was clearly delighted with the outcome, regardless of the means by which it had been obtained. It is also noteworthy that the Tang victory over the Eastern Turks had been won by fast-moving forces of light cavalry resembling those of the Turks themselves. Had the Chinese relied upon their more numerous infantry forces, it would have been all but impossible to surprise the Turks, catch up with them, or prevent their escape.

The Iron Mountain campaign spelled the end of the Eastern Turk qaghanate and marked the beginning of half a century of Chinese dominance over the Mongolian steppe. Most of the remaining Turk leaders soon surrendered to Tang, and one of them delivered the fugitive Xieli into the hands of Tang officers on May 12, 630.[31] A few groups of Eastern Turks continued to hold out in the far northwest, but the major power north of the Gobi was now Taizong's ally, the qaghan of the Xueyantuo. After considerable debate at the Tang court, a decision was made to settle the surrendered Turks on marginal lands along the northern border, with the majority apparently concentrated in the Ordos region south of the Yellow River bend.[32] The surrendered Turks were treated with great care. Although nominally organized into prefectures and protectorates within the Chinese administrative system, the tribesmen actually remained under the authority of their own chiefs, who received official appointments and other honors from the emperor. "Those of their chieftains and leaders who came to submit were all appointed to be generals, generals of the palace gentlemen, and other officers. More than one hundred of them were arrayed at court as officials above the fifth rank, and as a result several thousand families of Turks came to dwell in Chang'an."[33] Their presence contributed to the exotic, cosmopolitan flavor of the Tang capital, which was renowned for drawing people, goods, and fashions from many parts of Asia.[34] They also made a major contribution to the military power of Tang China. A number of the Turk leaders who had been made generals of the imperial guards later commanded

Tang armies on campaign and played a major role in the subjugation of peoples farther to the north and west. The armies they commanded would include large numbers of their fellow Turks.[35]

The sources do not provide us with many details regarding the composition of the Tang army that defeated the Eastern Turks, but it must certainly have included a large number of soldiers from the regimental headquarters (*fubing*).[36] The system of locally based territorial regiments, the mainstay of the Northern Zhou and Sui military, had collapsed together with the Sui dynasty, as various contenders for power "privatized" the units under their command, but the Tang leaders began to reconstruct it in Guanzhong as early as 619 and then extended the system to other regions. This task was nearly complete by the early 630s. The Tang *fubing* system probably differed very little from the Sui system under Emperor Yang, but far more is known about the workings of the Tang system.[37] The structure rested on several hundred military units of approximately 800 men each, based in designated prefectures and locally recruited. After a great many changes in nomenclature, these units, which had been known as "soaring hawk regimental headquarters" under Emperor Yang, received the lasting designation of "assault-repulsing regimental headquarters" (*zhechong fu*) in 636, when their commanders became "assault-repulsing colonels" (*zhechong duwei*). Each regiment was affiliated with one of the twelve imperial guard commands in the capital, where its men were supposed to perform one-month tours of guard duty according to a complex schedule of rotation. The more distant a unit from the capital, the greater the number of shifts into which it was divided and, consequently, the less often each individual soldier's turn would come up. Regiments within 166 miles of the capital were divided into five shifts, for example, while those between 166 and 333 miles away were formed into seven shifts. The number of "guardsmen" (*weishi*) present in the capital at any given time may have been in the neighborhood of 50,000.[38] Guardsmen might also be sent to frontier garrisons for periods of up to three years, but this sort of duty was neither as universal nor as systematic as the regular rotational service in Chang'an.[39]

When not on guard duty or campaign, the soldiers were expected to support themselves through farming. In exchange for limited exemption from taxes and corvée, they were supposed to furnish all of their own provisions and much of their own equipment. Men were enlisted as *fubing* at the age of twenty-one and continued to serve until sixty. The local civil authorities selected new soldiers every three years from among the eligible males in the community on the basis of the three criteria of wealth, strength, and number of adult males in the household. The intention was evidently to place the burden of military service on those who could best afford it. However, some prefectures had so many regiments that it would have been impossible for them to meet their quotas had they not been able to induct young men from poor families. Surviving Tang household registers from the northwestern frontier area of Dunhuang indicate that guardsmen from the lowest socioeconomic strata far outnumbered those from better-off families.[40] Nevertheless, service as a *fubing* must have had some attraction for ambitious men from wealthy families. In addition to the local prestige and status that came from serving the emperor as guardsmen, they also had the opportunity to acquire honorific ranks through their exploits on the battlefield, ranks which entitled them to hold more land than would normally be allotted them by the state under the "equal-field system" of land tenure.[41]

Due to the fact that they combined military service with farming, the *fubing* have sometimes been characterized as a "militia" by Western authors. With its connotations of low quality and ineffectiveness (especially on account of the implied contrast with a "professional" soldiery), this term is rather misleading when used in connection with the *fubing*. Given their life-long military service and the training they received over that period, it would be more accurate to view them as a special type of professional soldier.[42] Each man is supposed to have been fully equipped with a panoply that included armor, bow and arrows, saber, and lance. He was expected to practice certain martial skills, such as archery, on a daily basis, and every winter, during the agricultural slack season, he would join his comrades for an intensive period of organized drill during which the regimental commander would deploy the men in battlefield formations, hold mock combats, and teach cooperation and coordination by leading them on large-scale hunts.[43] There is little doubt that the *fubing* were highly effective on the battlefield during the seventh century.[44]

The number of *fubing* regimental headquarters changed over time. The maximum of 633 regiments (approximately 600,000 soldiers) was attained in the early years of the eighth century, when the system was already in decline. A modern authority on the *fubing* has argued that only 353 regiments had been created by the year 636.[45] The great majority of these were concentrated in areas close to the capital, while vast stretches of central, eastern, and southern China were almost entirely without regimental headquarters. Of the 353 regiments, no less than 261 were located in the Guanzhong region, and many of the remaining 92 were probably situated in nearby areas such as Hedong (modern Shanxi province), the original base of the Tang founder Li Yuan. Of the more than 320 prefectures that made up the Tang empire, more than two-thirds never contained as much as a single regiment of *fubing*. Those that did, however, were often home to a great many of them. This was especially true in Guanzhong, where the metropolitan prefecture around Chang'an eventually contained 131 regiments and several other nearby prefectures were also very heavily burdened.[46] Even in regions with relatively few regiments, those units tended to be geographically concentrated. All of the regiments in Henan, for example, were located in Luoyang or adjacent prefectures, with none established in the plains to the east. The burden of service was thus very unevenly distributed. Inhabitants of prefectures without regiments were never called upon to serve as *fubing*, while in some of the more highly militarized prefectures in the northwest it would seem that almost every able-bodied adult male was a soldier.[47]

No Tang source provides a clear rationale for this highly imbalanced distribution of *fubing*. Explanations proposed by modern scholars include the necessity of protecting the approaches to the capital and the need to make sure that enough troops were available within a reasonable distance to provide an adequate pool of manpower to support the system of rotational guard duty.[48] It has also been argued that this pattern was simply a historical legacy of the Tang regime's origin in the northwest; most of the men of the original Tang armies came from Guanzhong and Hedong, and regimental headquarters were set up in their home communities to accommodate them when they returned from the civil war.[49] Continued adherence to this pattern even decades later, however, suggests that the Tang founders – northwestern aristocrats and the political heirs of Yuwen Tai's Guanzhong-based regime of the sixth century – simply did not trust the people of the eastern plain.[50] This impression is reinforced by the distribution of the few regiments that *were* set up in the east and south. There is a very high correlation between the locations of the regiments and areas that were early centers of support for the Tang cause or served as headquarters for Tang regional commanders during the pacification of the east and south.[51] In other words, these were relatively loyal and reliable forward bases from which the surrounding areas – with no regularly established military units of their own – could be dominated and policed.

This would not have been the only respect in which the early Tang military system placed a strong emphasis on control. The mechanism of rotational service itself guaranteed that the generals of the imperial guards would have no opportunity to establish lasting personal ties with the guardsmen passing through the capital on their one-month tours of duty, and therefore would not have the means to pose a threat to the dynasty. Other checks and safeguards were established to insure that the local regiments could not be used against the center by local leaders. The mobilization and deployment of troops from one of the "assault-repulsing regimental headquarters" normally required the dispatch of tallies from the capital. The tally was made of copper, in the shape of a fish, and carried the name of the regiment and its parent guard command. One half was kept by the Credentials Office of the imperial Chancellery, the other was kept by the regimental headquarters. When the tally arrived from the capital it was matched with the local half in the presence of both the regimental commander and the prefect, and only then were troops sent out in accordance with the accompanying imperial order. A commander who moved as few as ten men without permission was subject to one year of penal servitude, while a colonel who mobilized an entire regiment of 1000 men might face death by strangulation.[52]

The method of forming campaign armies also worked to prevent generals from turning the troops under their command into personal followers. When the situation demanded, ad hoc "expeditionary armies" (*xingjun*) were assembled from the local regiments and various other troop sources and placed under the command of generals dispatched from the imperial guard headquarters at Chang'an; once the emergency was over, the troops returned to their prefectures and the generals to the capital.[53] Expeditionary armies ranged in size from about 3000 men to upwards of 100,000, depending upon the anticipated difficulty of their assignments. The largest such forces consisted of several separate columns, each with its own "expeditionary army commander" (*xingjun zongguan*). One of them would be designated as "expeditionary army commander-in-chief" (*xingjun da zongguan*) with overall authority to coordinate the operations of his fellows (it was in this capacity that Li Jing was sent against the Eastern Turks in 629).[54] The soldiers of the expeditionary armies were drawn from several sources. The "assault-repulsing regimental headquarters" were one of these sources, but too much use of *fubing* threatened to disrupt the schedules of rotation and weaken the garrison of the capital. For this reason, the *fubing* were often supplemented with short-term conscripts. These troops, known as "conscript-recruits" (*bingmu*), were usually drawn from those prefectures without regimental headquarters, which helped to spread the burden of military service a little more evenly among the population. They represented a far more flexible form of military manpower than the *fubing* since they could be called up in any numbers desired, often from areas nearest the scene of hostilities, and served only for the duration of the campaign.[55] A third major source of manpower for the expeditionary armies were tribal allies and auxiliaries, including the surrendered Eastern Turks. These warriors served under their own leaders, retained their own form of organization, and were responsible for their own equipment and supplies.[56] They were especially valuable – even essential – in campaigns against other steppe peoples, and accounted for the great majority of some expeditionary armies. In 651, for example, 30,000 Chinese soldiers and 50,000 Uighur tribesmen were mobilized to attack the qaghan of the Western Turks.[57]

An invaluable source of information on the functioning of the expeditionary armies and early Tang military practices in general is a treatise written by the great Li Jing himself. It no longer exists as a complete work, but large extracts have survived through their incorporation into the *Tong dian* (*Comprehensive Canons*), an encyclopedia of institutional history compiled by the scholar-statesman Du You in the second half of the eighth century.[58] The relevance of this material is not limited to the second quarter of the seventh century, since Li was almost certainly describing many practices that were not new in his own time and continued to be followed long afterward. Part of Li's work consisted of rather general advice on strategy; here he included many quotes and paraphrases from the military classics of antiquity, and seems to have been operating entirely within the intellectual framework established by Sunzi. For example, great emphasis is placed on determining when the enemy is most vulnerable, in order to be able to choose just the right moment to engage him in a decisive battle. More interesting, because of their uniqueness and the unimpeachable authority of their source, are the passages that provide detailed information on army organization, combat drills, battlefield formations, scouting, signalling, basic tactics, march orders, and camp layouts.

According to Li Jing, a typical expeditionary army might consist of 20,000 men, broken down into seven divisions (*jun*) of between 2600 and 4000 men each. Only about two-thirds of the soldiers in each division – 14,000 for the entire army – are to be used as combat troops, with the balance left behind to guard the army's camp or baggage train. All of the divisions contain the same mix of specialized troops and weapon types, including archers (a total of 2200), crossbowmen (2000), and cavalry (4000). Li Jing's descriptions of infantry drills suggest that the remainder of the troops are probably supposed to be footsoldiers armed with spears.[59] Perhaps 60 percent of the total force of 20,000 is provided with armor.[60] At the time that Li was writing, the *fubing* regiments were divided into three to five battalions (*tuan*) of 200 men, each of which was further subdivided into two companies (*lü*) of a hundred men, four platoons (*dui*) of fifty men, and twenty squads (*huo*) of ten men.[61] The only one of these units that plays a meaningful tactical role in Li's treatise is the *dui*, which suggests that most levels of the *fubing* organizational hierarchy – including the regiment itself – were used mainly for personnel management rather than battlefield command and control.

For Li, the fifty-man platoon is the fundamental, irreducible unit for all deployment and maneuver. It has a full complement of five officers (commander, deputy, standard-bearer, and two color guards), and it is the smallest unit to be provided with a flag. It has a fixed battle formation five ranks deep in which each man has his assigned place; led by the flag, it is expected to advance, retreat, and maneuver as a body.[62] Though capable of independant manuever, a single *dui* of infantry was clearly too small to operate effectively by itself. Hence, it was brought together with other *dui* to create larger formations on the battlefield. While Li Jing's standard drill formation calls for the deployment of two lines of *dui* in a loose checkerboard pattern, he also gives instructions for joining varying numbers of *dui* more tightly together to form larger groupings of 150, 250, 450, and 500 men.[63] Six *dui* made a 300–man tactical unit called a *tong*; with one *dui* told off to guard the baggage, the remaining five could be deployed in several different configurations and assigned different combat roles on an ad hoc basis.[64] When the entire army was deployed in a standard battle formation, the infantry was formed in two lines or echelons of equal strength while the cavalry was positioned to cover the flanks.[65] According to Li Jing, the cavalry were the army's "eyes and ears" and could also be used to pursue fugitives, exploit openings, and ride down dispersed enemy troops, while the infantry formed the stable core around which the cavalry could maneuver.[66]

Tactical commands were relayed to the troops by means of drums, horns, bells or gongs, and flag signals. Just as in antiquity, the beating of drums was the signal for an advance, while gongs or other metallic instruments signaled a halt or withdrawal. Li Jing provides the following example of signaling in his description of a military drill:

At the end of the fourth sounding of the horn, the men of all the *dui* simultaneously draw in their spears and kneel on the ground. Their eyes watch the great yellow standard of the commander-in-chief, their ears listen for the sound of the drum. The yellow flag points forward, and the drum begins to beat; they shout in unison, "Wu-hu! Wu-hu!" and move forward together to the center line . . . When they hear the gong sound, they must stop shouting and fall back, carrying their spears on their shoulders.[67]

The commander of a Tang expeditionary army was supposed to have five flags, one in the color of each of the five directions, with which he could direct the movements of his troops. When two flags were crossed, for example, the *dui* were supposed to respond by combining into larger formations.[68]

Some sections of Li Jing's work touch on prohibitions and punishments. These could be extremely harsh, with many offenses punished by decapitation. The soldiers of Tang expeditionary armies were forbidden, on pain of death, from spreading superstitious rumors or bringing women into the army's camp. A standard bearer who damaged his unit's morale by failing to hold his flag straight was subject to decapitation, and any soldier who failed to advance when the signal was given was to be killed immediately by the man behind him. The first men to begin plundering after a battle was won also faced execution.[69] This last prohibition dovetails with the concern, repeated many times in Li Jing's work, that the army never relax its guard and expose itself to surprise, ambush, or sudden counterattack. In battle, troops were often divided into two echelons, with one assigned to attack the enemy while the other was held back to maintain a secure defensive position should the attack go awry. When the enemy retreated in battle, the Tang infantry were allowed to advance only a short distance. Then, if the retreat appeared genuine and not a ruse, the cavalry would be ordered to continue the pursuit.[70] When a Tang expeditionary army was campaigning in hostile territory, mounted scouts were sent out to the front, rear, and both flanks. In each of these directions, there were two men at a distance of five *li*, two more at ten *li*, and so on – out to a distance of thirty *li* (or ten miles).[71] These vedettes were to use flags to signal the approach of the enemy, a method that would have been quite effective in the open grasslands of the north and west where so many of the early Tang expeditionary armies campaigned against a variety of peoples including Turks, Tuyuhun, and Xueyantuo.

The contents of Li Jing's manual are remarkably similar to what we find in Byzantine military treatises such as the *Strategikon* traditionally attributed to the Emperor Maurice (r. 582–602) and the *Tactica* of Emperor Leo VI (r. 886–912). The *Strategikon*, believed to have been written between 592 and 610, possibly by Maurice or a close associate, is a near contemporary of Li Jing's military writings.[72] It shows the same concern with battle formations, marching order, camp layouts, scouting, and discipline. Some prescriptions are almost exactly the same. For example, both Li Jing and the author of the *Strategikon* recommend the execution of soldiers who break ranks to engage in plundering.[73] Also noteworthy is the overall approach to battle. Like Li Jing and his intellectual antecedents, the author of the *Strategikon* urges caution when deciding whether or not to join battle: "To try simply to overpower the enemy in the open, hand to hand and face to face, even though you might appear to win, is an enterprise which is very risky and can result in serious harm."[74] Raids, ambushes, and all manner of tricks and stratagems are recommended instead. The Byzantine author of the *Strategikon* is if anything more cautious than Li Jing, suggesting that battle should be avoided entirely if one's aims can be accomplished by other means.[75]

For several decades after the defeat of the Eastern Turks in 630, Tang expeditionary armies won victory after victory. In 635 several columns operating under the overall command of Li Jing broke the power of the Tuyuhun, a nomadic people of mixed Xianbei and Tibetan stock who occupied the territory on the northeastern corner of the Tibetan plateau that is now the province of Qinghai.[76] In 641, after the Tang empire and the Xueyantuo had fallen out over Taizong's plan to return the surrendered Eastern Turks to the open steppe, Li Shiji inflicted a major defeat on these former allies in a battle at the Nuozhen River.[77] Another round of campaigning in 645–6 led to the flight and death of the Xueyantuo qaghan and his successor's submission to Tang. In 648, an expeditionary army led by the Turkish general Ashina She'er conquered the Indo-Iranian oasis kingdom of Kucha in the Tarim basin.[78] In the 650s, the focus of Chinese military operations shifted north and west, to the Western Turks and the lands around the Ili valley and Issyk-kul. There, in 657, a Tang army smashed the forces of the Western qaghan Shaboluo and – for the space of a few years, at least – extended Tang authority into Central Asia as far as the northeastern border of Persia.[79] Most of these campaigns were fought over vast distances remote from the borders of China proper, and involved nomad allies and auxiliaries as well as Chinese troops. The Tang expeditionary forces typically launched relentless, long-range pursuits of defeated steppe leaders that drove them to death or oblivion, with no opportunity at all to recoup their losses. The campaigns were usually both short and decisive, and thus very well suited to the temporary, ad hoc nature of the expeditionary army organization.

It was only in the northeast that Tang arms met with a serious setback. In 641, no doubt encouraged by successes elsewhere and by the recovery of the empire from the devastation of the civil wars, Taizong began to contemplate the conquest of Koguryŏ on the grounds that its territory had once been an integral part of the Han empire. As the historian Howard Wechsler has suggested, his motives were probably much more complex; they may have included an ambition to outdo Emperor Yang of Sui, pragmatic concerns that Koguryŏ not be allowed to dominate the Korean peninsula and thereby pose a threat to northeastern China, and perhaps even an aging emperor's desire to escape from problems at court by getting back in the saddle and reliving the military triumphs of his youth.[80] He found a suitably righteous pretext for action the following year, when one of the great nobles of Koguryŏ, a man named Yŏn Kae-so-mun, killed the king and placed another member of the royal family on the throne as his puppet. Preparations for a major campaign began in earnest in 644. A great fleet of 500 ships was constructed on the southeastern coast and along the Yangzi River to transport 40,000 conscript-recruits and 3000 gentleman volunteers (drawn from the elite of the two capitals, Chang'an and Luoyang) across the sea from the Shandong peninsula to the Korean coast. At the same time, an army of 60,000 Chinese soldiers plus an unspecified number of tribal auxiliaries gathered at Youzhou on the north-eastern frontier. This force, under the command of Li Shiji, would advance overland to the Liao River. Li's main body would eventually be reinforced by some 10,000 armored cavalry led by the emperor himself.[81] The relatively small size of these forces, with the sources mentioning no more than 113,000 combat troops traveling by both land and sea, suggests that Tang strategists had learned

Map 15 The Liao River valley and the Korean peninsula in the seventh century AD

from Emperor Yang's mistakes and had no wish to court disaster by bringing more men than they could feed. The road ahead, however, was no easier than it had been three decades before. Not only would the Tang troops face the same obstacles of climate, weather, and terrain that had hindered Sui efforts, but the manmade defenses east of the Liao River were even more formidable since Koguryŏ had spent nearly ten years erecting a strong new belt of fortifications along a front of several hundred miles from Puyŏsŏng (Fuyucheng; modern Siping) to the Liaodong peninsula.[82]

Li Shiji's army marched from its advanced base at Yingcheng (modern Chaoyang) in April of 645. On May 1, he surprised his opponents by crossing the Liao River farther north than they had expected. His first objective, the fortress of Kaemosŏng (Gaimoucheng), was invested on May 16 and fell after a siege of only eleven days, yielding 20,000 people and more than 100,000 *shi* (or six million liters) of grain. He then turned southwest toward Ryotongsŏng (Liaodongcheng), the stronghold that had successfully defied Emperor Yang in 612 and 613. On June 7, he defeated a Korean army of 40,000 marching to the relief of the city, and a few days later he was joined by the emperor and his cavalry escort. Like Kaemosŏng, Ryotongsŏng was taken with surprising ease. On June 16, a favorable wind enabled the besiegers to set the entire city ablaze with incendiary projectiles, opening the way for a successful assault on the walls. The Tang army then advanced to Paekamsŏng (Baiyancheng), a short distance to the east of Ryotong, arriving under the walls on June 27. Here the commandant delivered the place into Tang hands. Taizong refused to permit his troops to loot the town and enslave its inhabitants, and when their leaders protested this departure from established military practice he undertook to reward the most deserving soldiers from his own purse. The emperor arrived outside Ansisŏng (Anshicheng), the next major fortress to the south, on July 18.[83] The following day, he was apprised of the approach of a large relief army of Koreans and Malgal. Deploying 15,000 men under Li Shiji as a bait to draw the Koreans, while concealing another force of comparable size in a position from which it could debouch into the enemy rear, Taizong inflicted a crushing defeat in the battle fought on July 20. The remnants of the Korean army retreated to a nearby hilltop where they were surrounded by the Chinese. The next day Taizong received the surrender of 36,800 men; the total bag also included 50,000 horses, 50,000 head of cattle, and 10,000 suits of iron armor. Of the prisoners, 3500 officers and chieftains were sent back to China, 3300 Malgal tribesmen were put to death, and the remainder of the ordinary Korean soldiers were freed and allowed to return to their homes.[84]

After this great victory, however, the Tang campaign began to encounter difficulties. Ansisŏng put up a more stubborn resistance than any of the other towns that Taizong had attacked. As the days and weeks passed and the end of the campaigning season drew closer, the Tang emperor several times considered the possibility of bypassing the fortress and either seeking softer targets or pressing deeper into Koguryŏ. Each time the scheme was rejected on account of the threat that the bypassed stronghold would pose to the Tang army's rear and its supply line to the grain stored at Ryotongsŏng.[85] Here, it seems, Taizong was paying the price for the relatively small size of his army which, unlike that of Emperor Yang, could not effectively mask the border fortresses at the same time as it moved deeper into the interior. Nor was the force that had gone to attack Koguryŏ from the sea of very much help at this juncture. Its commander had captured Pisasŏng (Beishacheng) on the Liao-dong peninsula on June 1 and threatened several points along the coast, but he failed either to cooperate effectively with the land army or to strike directly at Pyongyang.[86] The Tang army at Ansisŏng eventually staked everything on the construction of a huge mound to command the southeastern corner of the city wall. When a sudden sortie by the defenders took the mound – and three days of frantic assaults by Tang troops failed to dislodge them – Taizong decided to order a withdrawal on October 13. It was high time. His soldiers were already suffering from the cold weather, and the grain stocks at Ryotongsŏng were nearly exhausted. The sources do not mention the numbers lost by the Tang army, but its retreat so late in the season was a severe ordeal. The troops had to improve their road through the waterlogged Liao marshes with fascines and even sunken army carts, and bitter winds and snow near the end of October claimed many lives.[87]

In the wake of this fiasco, the Tang emperor briefly adopted a new strategy of sending generals with small, mobile forces to make harassing attacks on the Koguryŏ frontier, with the aim of wearing down the enemy by forcing them to maintain strong defenses and a high level of vigilance at all times. This approach achieved some success in the spring and summer of 647, when a ship-borne force of 10,000 men menaced the coastline while Li Shiji raided across the Liao River.[88] In the following year, however, Taizong ordered preparations for another large-scale campaign against Koguryŏ, preparations that were cut short only by his death in the sixth lunar month of 649.[89]

This did not mark the end of the conflict. Tensions between the Tang empire and Koguryŏ continued through the 650s. In the winter of 654 the Khitan people of southern Manchuria, then Tang clients, were attacked by Koguryŏ and the Malgal. The following spring, a Tang army crossed the Liao River and defeated a defending force near Sinsŏng. Further clashes occurred on the Liao frontier in 658 and 659. In 660, however, the pattern changed, as China again dispatched a major force to the Korean peninsula with the aim of landing a decisive blow. This move was prompted by a call for help from the kingdom of Silla, which occupied the southeastern portion of the Korean peninsula and had just suffered the loss of some of its frontier territories to incursions by both Koguryŏ and Paekche, the third of the Korean states.[90] The initial blow was aimed at the weaker partner, Paekche, which lay on the western coast of the peninsula. Su Dingfang, the officer who had led the Tang vanguard into Xieli's camp in 630, now brought a large army across the Yellow Sea to Paekche in the eighth lunar month of 660. He defeated a Paekche force at the mouth of the Kum River, then ascended the river to take the capital (near today's Kongju) and capture the ruling family. The kingdom of Paekche, with its thirty-seven commanderies, 200 walled towns, and 760,000 households, was divided into five area commands and annexed to the Tang empire.[91]

The next blow was aimed at Koguryŏ itself, which was now exposed to attack from several directions. The Tang government raised 44,000 conscript-recruits from sixty-seven prefectures in the North China Plain and sent them across the sea, again under Su Dingfang, to strike at the heart of Koguryŏ. Su ascended the Taedong River to lay siege to Pyongyang in the seventh lunar month of 661. Meanwhile, a second Tang column advanced overland from the Liao River. Led by Qibi Heli, who was both a Tang general and a Tiele chieftain, it penetrated as far as the Yalu, where it defeated a Koguryŏ army in the ninth lunar month. Su Dingfang's siege of Pyongyang continued until the spring of 662, when the defeat of a subsidiary Tang force prompted him to raise the siege and withdraw from enemy territory.[92]

While Su's army was struggling to subdue Koguryŏ, the Tang garrison units that had been left to hold Paekche also found themselves in a difficult situation. The people of the kingdom were not yet resigned to accepting Chinese rule, and there was a major rising against the occupiers in the winter of 660–1. Liu Renyuan, the principal Tang commander in Paekche, was besieged in the capital until one of his colleagues, Liu Rengui, organized a relief column composed of both Chinese garrison troops and contingents from Silla and stormed the stockades that the rebels had erected to control the mouth of the Kum River. The standoff that followed, with the Tang forces holding some walled towns and the Paekche rebels controlling many others, lasted from the spring of 661 to the autumn of 663. During this time both sides called for reinforcements. Liu Renyuan received more troops from Silla and some 7000 conscript-recruits mobilized in the coastal prefectures of Shandong, while the Paekche leaders sent a mission to the island power of Wa (as Japan was called at this time) to request military assistance. In the autumn of 663 the Tang and Silla forces launched a major campaign to capture Churyusŏng, the principal base of the Paekche leadership. While the main army, accompanied by the king of Silla, advanced overland, Liu Rengui brought the Tang fleet and supply ships to the mouth of the Kum River. There he encountered and destroyed the Japanese fleet in a series of naval actions, reportedly sinking no fewer than 400 of the enemy vessels. Churyusŏng was in Chinese hands by October 14, 663, the rebellion apparently crushed.[93]

In 666 Tang was again ready to focus its attention on Koguryŏ. By this time, the strategic situation was very different. Not only were Chinese (and Sillan) forces in a position to threaten Koguryŏ from both north and south, but the iron-handed dictator Yŏn Kae-so-mun had died at the beginning of the summer. His sons immediately fell to feuding among themselves, creating an ideal situation for Tang strategists to exploit. Chinese forces began to attack the Liao frontier in the summer and autumn of 666, but the major effort was launched early in 667 with the aged Li Shiji as commander-in-chief of the Liaodong expeditionary army. Li's first objective, the fortress of Sinsŏng, was handed over by its demoralized defenders on October 6, and this success was followed by the prompt submission of sixteen other walled towns. These gains, together with assistance from one of the contending Koguryŏ factions, must have made it possible for Li to feed and shelter a large army on the east side of the Liao River through the winter, a feat that had eluded earlier Chinese expeditions against Koguryŏ. Li's advanced position in southeastern Manchuria then enabled him to press forward into the heartland of Koguryŏ in the spring of 668. The important fortress of Puyŏsŏng was taken in the second lunar month, and many other walled towns submitted without resistance. Pyongyang itself fell to Li Shiji on October 22 after a siege of little more than one month, betrayed by a fifth column among the defenders. Koguryŏ now shared the fate of Paekche as it was divided into a number of area commands and annexed to the Tang empire.[94]

The primary reason for the Tang triumph of 668, coming after a long series of failures dating back to 599, was the violent dissension within Koguryŏ in the wake of Yŏn Kae-so-mun's death. Not only was China now able to find many willing collaborators within a divided Koguryŏ, but a pervasive demoralization seems to have taken hold among the once-stalwart defenders of the walled towns. Another important factor contributing to the Tang success was that from the late 650s onward it became possible to apply pressure to Koguryŏ not only from the sea and the Liao River frontier, the traditional lines of advance, but also along the kingdom's southern land border in the Korean peninsula. This was partly a consequence of Tang's widening the conflict to include the subjugation of Paekche, but even more important was the alliance with Silla. The military cooperation of the southeastern kingdom preceded the conquest of Paekche and helped to make it possible by providing both a nearby supply base and a significant infusion of manpower. Had it not been for support from Silla, it seems likely that the Tang garrison forces would have been swept away in the great uprising of 661. Silla's armies also applied pressure on Koguryŏ directly and played a major role in provisioning the Chinese forces that besieged Pyongyang in 661–2.[95]

With regard to the longer term, however, China and Silla were working at cross purposes. As the events of the 660s made abundantly clear, the Tang goal was to turn the Korean peninsula into an integral part of the empire – though the king of Silla would apparently be allowed to enjoy a local autonomy similar to that granted to other vassal chieftains who had accepted Tang official titles. Silla, on the other hand, harbored the ambition of unifying the entire peninsula under its own rule. In the end, it was Silla that emerged victorious.

Already in 669 there was unrest and rebellion in the newly-conquered territory of Koguryŏ. Tang efforts to remove tens of thousands of people to exile in China only exacerbated the situation.[96] In the early 670s the Tang general Gao Kan inflicted repeated defeats on the resisters, whose leaders simply took refuge in Silla and returned to fight another day. Before the end of 672 troops from Silla had taken the field in open support of the Koguryŏ rebels, and by the beginning of 674 Silla had managed to occupy all of the territory that had once belonged to the kingdom of Paekche.[97] In 674 and 675 Tang forces under Liu Rengui attacked Silla itself. Chinese histories record that Liu was victorious and forced the king of Silla to sue for peace, while Korean historians report the defeat of the Chinese armies.[98] The fact that the Tang government found it necessary to withdraw the headquarters of its Korean protectorate to the Liao River valley in the early months of 676 suggests that the Korean version is probably closer to the truth.[99] Silla was left in uncontested control of almost the whole of the Korean peninsula, and there was no great Tang campaign to recover what had been won with such difficulty and so quickly lost. China's decision to write off the Korean venture was surely influenced by the appearance of serious threats in other quarters. In 670 a large Chinese army was severely defeated by the Tibetans along the Dafei River in what is now Qinghai province, and in 679 the Eastern Turks revolted against Chinese suzerainty and began to rebuild their old empire on the Mongolian steppe. These developments required the Tang empire to assume an unaccustomed defensive posture, and set in motion major changes in its military institutions and imperial strategy.

Notes

1 The 609 population is reported in *Sui shu*, ch. 29, p. 808; note that a commandery-by-commandery count of household figures in the same work yields 9,075,791 (p. 831, n. 4). For the early Tang figures, see E. G. Pulleyblank, "Registration of Population in China in the Sui and T'ang Periods," *Journal of the Economic and Social History of the Orient*, 4 (1961), pp. 290, 293.

2 Wu Jing, *Zhenguan zhengyao* (Shanghai: Shanghai Guji chubanshe, 1978), p. 70. For other contemporary testimony in the same vein, see Wu Feng, *Sui Tang Wudai shi* (Beijing: Renmin chubanshe, 1958), pp. 59–60. Banditry is mentioned in Sima Guang, *Zizhi tongjian*, ch. 192, p. 6025.

3 Pulleyblank, "Registration of Population in China in the Sui and T'ang Periods," pp. 292–5.

4 *Jiu Tang shu*, ch. 38, p. 1384. For the Tang treatment of local leaders, see Sima Guang, *Zizhi tongjian*, ch. 188, p. 5890, and Wechsler, *Mirror to the Son of Heaven*, p. 32.

5 Sima Guang, *Zizhi tongjian*, ch. 191, p. 6004.

6 Robert M. Somers, "Time, Space, and Structure in the Consolidation of the T'ang Dynasty (AD 617–700)," *Journal of Asian Studies*, 45.5 (1986), pp. 971–94.

7 See Zhang's biography in *Jiu Tang shu*, ch. 83, p. 2786, and his epitaph in Mao Han-kuang, *Tangdai muzhiming huibian fukao*, vol. 4, p. 141.

8 *Cefu yuangui*, ch. 388, p. 11a.

9 For Li Shiji's biographies, see *Jiu Tang shu*, ch. 67, p. 2483, and *Xin Tang shu*, ch. 93, p. 3817; his origins are discussed in Huang Huixian, "Sui mo nongmin qiyi wuzhuang qianxi," pp. 186–7. For his illiteracy, see *Cefu yuangui*, ch. 320, p. 11a; and Li Fang, *Taiping guangji*, ch, 176, p. 1309.

10 Sima Guang, *Zizhi tongjian*, ch. 192, p. 6033.

11 For indications of the new personnel situation, see *Jiu Tang shu*, ch. 2, p. 35; Sima Guang, *Zizhi tongjian*, ch. 192, pp. 6043, 6044, 6054–5, and ch. 193, pp. 6058, 6061.

12 Paul Demiéville's "Le Bouddhisme et la guerre," in idem, *Choix d'études bouddhiques (1929–1970)* (Leiden: E. J. Brill, 1973), pp. 261–99, explores the rationalizations that Buddhists found for fighting, and mentions the rebel-monks (pp. 274–5) and military activities of the clergy (pp. 276–7).

13 Weinstein, *Buddhism under the T'ang*, pp. 12–13.

14 Sima Guang, *Zizhi tongjian*, ch. 184, p. 5749.

15 Andrew Eisenberg, "Warfare and Political Stability in Medieval North Asian Regimes," *T'oung Pao*, 83 (1997), pp. 320–1.

16 See Graff, "Early T'ang Generalship and the Textual Tradition," pp. 451–4.

17 *Jiu Tang shu*, ch. 2, pp. 30–1; Song Minqiu, *Tang da zhao ling ji* (Beijing: Commercial Press, 1959), ch. 107, p. 552; Sima Guan, *Zizhi tongjian*, ch. 192, pp. 6026–7.

18 Eisenberg, "Warfare and Political Stability in Medieval North Asian Regimes," pp. 323–4.

19 Sima Guang, *Zizhi tongjian*, ch. 192, p. 6037. Two other passages (*Jiu Tang shu*, ch. 194A, p. 5158, and *Zizhi tongjian*, ch. 192, pp. 6045–6) seem to place the outbreak of rebellion before the snowstorms.

20 Barfield, *The Perilous Frontier*, p. 143; also see p. 133.

21 See Michael R. Drompp, "Supernumerary Sovereigns: Superfluity and Mutability in the Elite Power Structure of the Early Türks," in Gary Seaman and Daniel Marks (eds.), *Rulers from the Steppe: State Formation on the Eurasian Periphery* (Los Angeles: Ethnographics Press, 1991), pp. 92–115.

22 Sima Guang, *Zizhi tongjian*, ch. 192, p. 6049; *Jiu Tang shu*, ch. 194A, p. 5158.

23 Sima Guang, *Zizhi tongjian*, ch. 193, pp. 6065–6.

24 For these arrangements, see *Jiu Tang shu*, ch. 194A, p. 5159, and Sima Guang, *Zizhi tongjian*, ch. 193, p. 6066.

25 For detailed reconstruction of these events and a discussion of the sources, see Graff, "Early T'ang Generalship and the Textual Tradition," pp. 489–92.

26 Sima Guang, *Zizhi tongjian*, ch. 193, p. 6072.

27 The sources disagree as to which general first came up with the plan; see *Jiu Tang shu*, ch. 67, pp. 2479 and 2485, and my attempt to reconcile these divergent accounts in "Early T'ang Generalship and the Textual Tradition," pp. 494–7.

28 Sima Guang, *Zizhi tongjian*, ch. 193, pp. 6072–3.

29 *Jiu Tang shu*, ch. 67, pp. 2485–6.

30 See Sima Guang, *Zizhi tongjian*, ch. 193, p. 6078; *Jiu Tang shu*, ch. 67, p. 2480; and *Xin Tang shu*, ch. 93, p. 3814.

31 Sima Guang, *Zizhi tongjian*, ch. 193, p. 6074.

32 See Sima Guang, *Zizhi tongjian*, ch. 193, pp. 6075–7; the debate is summarized in Pan Yihong, *Son of Heaven and Heavenly Qaghan* (Bellingham, Wash.: Western Washington University, 1997), pp. 183–7.

33 *Jiu Tang shu*, ch. 194A, p. 5163.

34 See Edward H. Schafer, *The Golden Peaches of Samarkand: A Study of T'ang Exotics* (Berkeley: University of California Press, 1963).

35 For the use of Turk and other nomad auxiliaries by the Tang, see Kang Le, *Tangdai qianqi de bianfang* (Taipei: National Taiwan University, 1979), pp. 38, 47, 52.

36 The charge into Xieli's camp at Iron Mountain was led by Su Dingfang, commander of a regiment based in Chang'an; see *Xin Tang shu*, ch. 111, p. 4137.

37 The following description of the early Tang *fubing* system is based mainly on *Xin Tang shu*, ch. 50, pp. 1324–6, translated with copious annotation by Robert des Rotours in *Traité des fonctionnaires et Traité de l'armée* (Leiden: E. J. Brill, 1947), and on the classic studies of Hamaguchi Shigekuni, "Fuhei seido yori shin heisei e,"

Shigaku zasshi, 41 (1930), pp. 1255–95, 1439–1507, and Gu Jiguang, *Fubing zhidu kaoshi*. The most thorough treatment in English is the first chapter of Swee Fo Lai, "The Military and Defense System under the T'ang Dynasty" (Ph.D. dissertation, Princeton University, 1986).

38 Zhang Guogang, *Tangdai zhengzhi zhidu yanjiu lunji* (Taipei: Wenjin chubanshe, 1994), pp. 23–4.

39 Hamaguchi, "Fuhei seido yori shin heisei e," p. 1462.

40 Gu Jiguang, *Fubing zhidu kaoshi*, pp. 167–8, 188–9, 217–18.

41 Gu Jiguang, *Fubing zhidu kaoshi*, pp. 215–16.

42 Lai, "The Military and Defense System under the T'ang Dynasty," pp. 1, 54–5.

43 *Xin Tang shu*, ch. 50, pp. 1325–6; *Jiu Tang shu*, ch. 43, p. 1834.

44 Gu Jiguang, *Fubing zhidu kaoshi*, p. 175.

45 Gu Jiguang, *Fubing zhidu kaoshi*, pp. 148–50.

46 Gu Jiguang, *Fubing zhidu kaoshi*, pp. 155–7; also see Hamaguchi, "Fuhei seido yori shin heisei e," pp. 1265, 1440–1, and *Xin Tang shu*, ch. 37, p. 961.

47 Kikuchi Hideo, "Tō setsushōfu no bunpu mondai ni kansuru ichi kaishaku," *Tōyōshi kenkyū*, 27 (1968), p. 128.

48 Zhang Guogang, *Tangdai zhengzhi zhidu yanjiu lunji*, p. 23–4.

49 Cen Zhongmian, *Fubing zhidu yanjiu* (Shanghai: Shanghai renmin chubanshe, 1957), p. 59.

50 Edwin G. Pulleyblank, *The Background of the Rebellion of An Lu-shan* (London: Oxford University Press, 1955), pp. 75–80.

51 Kikuchi, "Tō setsushōfu no bunpu mondai," pp. 135–6.

52 *Tang lü shu yi* (Shanghai: Commercial Press, 1933), Section 3, ch. 16, p. 25. Mobilization procedures and safeguards are discussed in Gu Jiguang, *Fubing zhidu kaoshi*, pp. 163–4, and Hamaguchi, "Fuhei seido yori shin heisei e," pp. 1282–3.

53 *Xin Tang shu*, ch. 50, p. 1328.

54 Sun Jimin discusses the difference between the two types of expeditionary army commander in his *Tangdai xingjun zhidu yanjiu*, pp. 141–7.

55 For more information on the *bingmu*, see Kikuchi Hideo, "Tōdai heibo no seikaku to meishō to ni tsuite," *Shien*, 68 (May 1956), pp. 75–98; Tang Geng'ou, "Tangdai qianqi de bingmu," *Lishi yanjiu*, 1981, No. 4, pp. 159–72; and Zhang Guogang, *Tangdai zhengzhi zhidu yanjiu*, pp. 29–53.

56 Sun Jimin, *Tangdai xingjun zhidu yanjiu*, pp. 114, 115; Zhang Guogang, *Tangdai zhengzhi zhidu yanjiu lunji*, pp. 97–8, 100–1; Zhang Qun, *Tangdai fanjiang yanjiu* (Taipei: Lianjing, 1986), p. 96.

57 Sima Guang, *Zizhi tongjian*, ch. 199, pp. 6274–5.

58 The fragments of Li Jing's work have been conveniently gathered in a modern annotated edition; see Deng Zezong, *Li Jing bingfa jiben zhuyi* (Beijing: Jiefangjun chubanshe, 1990).

59 Du You, *Tong dian*, ch. 148, pp. 3792–3; ch. 149, p. 3813.

60 *Tong dian*, ch. 148, p. 3794.

61 Gu Jiguang, *Fubing zhidu kaoshi*, p. 166; Lai, "The Military and Defense System under the T'ang Dynasty," p. 32.

62 *Tong dian*, ch. 148, p. 3794; ch. 149, p. 3812; ch. 157, pp. 4026 and 4035.

63 *Tong dian*, ch. 149, pp. 3813–14; ch. 157, p. 4033.

64 *Tong dian*, ch. 149, p. 3812; ch. 157, p. 4026. Gu Jiguang has suggested that the *tong*, not the *dui*, was the most important level of combat organization in early Tang armies; see his *Fubing zhidu kaoshi*, p. 166.

65 *Tong dian*, ch. 157, p. 4033.

66 *Tong dian*, ch. 148, p. 3789.

67 *Tong dian*, ch. 149, p. 3813.

68 *Tong dian*, ch. 149, pp. 3812, 3814.

69 *Tong dian*, ch. 149, p. 3824.
70 *Tong dian*, ch. 149, p. 3813; also see Deng Zezong, *Li Jing bingfa jiben zhuyi*, pp. 64, 74.
71 *Tong dian*, ch. 157, p. 4029.
72 George T. Dennis (trans.), *Maurice's Strategikon: Handbook of Byzantine Military Strategy* (Philadelphia: University of Pennsylvania Press, 1984), pp. xvi–xvii.
73 *Maurice's Strategikon*, pp. 19–20.
74 *Maurice's Strategikon*, p. 65.
75 *Maurice's Strategikon*, pp. 23, 80, 83, 87–8. This difference in attitude may have been due to the more finite resources of the Eastern Roman empire and its unenviable strategic position; see Walter Emil Kaegi, Jr., *Some Thoughts on Byzantine Military Strategy* (Brookline, Mass.: Hellenic College Press, 1983), p. 5 and passim.
76 Sima Guang, *Zizhi tongjian*, ch. 194, pp. 6110–13; *Jiu Tang shu*, ch. 67, p. 2481.
77 Sima Guang, *Zizhi tongjian*, ch. 196, pp. 6170–2.
78 Sima Guang, *Zizhi tongjian*, ch. 199, pp. 6262–4.
79 Sima Guang, *Zizhi tongjian*, ch. 200, pp. 6306–7.
80 Sima Guang, *Zizhi tongjian*, ch. 196, pp. 6169–70; Howard J. Wechsler, "T'ai-tsung (reign 626–49) the Consolidator," in Denis Twitchett (ed.), *The Cambridge History of China*, vol. 3: *Sui and T'ang China, 589–906, Pt. 1* (Cambridge: Cambridge University Press, 1979), pp. 233–4.
81 For these preparations, see Sima Guang, *Zizhi tongjian*, ch. 197, p. 6214, and *Jiu Tang shu*, ch. 199A, pp. 5322–3.
82 *Jiu Tang shu*, ch. 199A, p. 5321.
83 These events are described in Sima Guang, *Zizhi tongjian*, ch. 197, pp. 6218–21, and ch. 198, pp. 6222–3; and in *Jiu Tang shu*, ch. 199A, pp. 5323–4.
84 Sima Guang, *Zizhi tongjian*, ch. 198, pp. 6224–6; *Jiu Tang shu*, ch. 199A, p. 5324.
85 Sima Guang, *Zizhi tongjian*, ch. 198, pp. 6228–9; *Jiu Tang shu*, ch. 199A, pp. 5325–6.
86 Sima Guang, *Zizhi tongjian*, ch. 197, p. 6220; *Jiu Tang shu*, ch. 199A, p. 5325.
87 Sima Guang, *Zizhi tongjian*, ch. 198, p. 6230; *Jiu Tang shu*, ch. 199A, pp. 5325–6.
88 Sima Guang, *Zizhi tongjian*, ch. 198, pp. 6245–8.
89 *Jiu Tang shu*, ch. 199A, p. 5326.
90 Sima Guang, *Zizhi tongjian*, ch. 200, p. 6320; *Xin Tang shu*, ch. 220, p. 6195.
91 Sima Guang, *Zizhi tongjian*, ch. 200, p. 6321.
92 *Xin Tang shu*, ch. 220, pp. 6195–6; Sima Guang, *Zizhi tongjian*, ch. 200, pp. 6323–6.
93 For these events, see *Xin Tang shu*, ch. 220, pp. 6200–1; *Jiu Tang shu*, ch. 199A, pp. 5331–3; and Sima Guang, *Zizhi tongjian*, ch. 200, pp. 6323–4, 6329–30, and ch. 201, pp. 6336–8.
94 *Xin Tang shu*, ch. 220, pp. 6196–7; Sima Guang, *Zizhi tongjian*, ch. 201, pp. 6352–7.
95 John Charles Jamieson, "The Samguk Sagi and the Unification Wars" (Ph.D. dissertation, University of California, Berkeley, 1969), pp. 95–6, 115–16.
96 Sima Guang, *Zizhi tongjian*, ch. 201, p. 6359; *Xin Tang shu*, ch. 220, p. 6197.
97 *Xin Tang shu*, ch. 220, p. 6198; Sima Guang, *Zizhi tongjian*, ch. 201, p. 6364, and ch. 202, pp. 6367, 6370, and 6372.
98 Sima Guang, *Zizhi tongjian*, ch. 202, pp. 6372, 6375; Jamieson, "The Samguk Sagi and the Unification Wars," pp. 68–70, 74, 158, and 162.
99 Sima Guang, *Zizhi tongjian*, ch. 202, p. 6378.

CHAPTER TEN

The price of professionalism

In 664 Liu Rengui, commander of the Tang garrison in recently subjugated Paekche, sent a memorial to the emperor reporting that the morale of his conscript-recruits was extremely low. The most immediate problem was that the troops, now in their second year in Korea, had brought only enough clothing to last them a single year. (Evidently, a much shorter sojourn overseas had been expected.) But the soldiers' discontent extended far beyond the matter of insufficient clothing. The rewards they received for their service were much less generous than had been customary in the past, and men who had earned honorific ranks (*xun guan*) in earlier campaigns had been sent back into the field and "exposed to hardship with no distinction between themselves and ordinary commoners." Where men had once been quick to volunteer for military expeditions, the repeated dispatch of conscript-recruits to the Korean peninsula – and the fact that their merit was not properly rewarded – had created an aversion to military service. Strong young men from prosperous families used their influence to avoid conscription, while those who had no money and did not frequent local government offices, even if old and weak, were still hauled in for service. Some of them deserted or inflicted disabling injuries upon themselves in order to avoid taking ship for Korea.[1]

Liu's memorial was an early harbinger of the collapse of the system of ad hoc expeditionary armies that had worked so well in the days of Tang Taizong. Temporary armies composed of short-term conscripts and the farmer-soldiers of the *fubing* regiments were well suited for swift, aggressive campaigns of limited duration concluding with a convincing victory over the enemy. Li Jing's conquest of the Eastern Turks in 629–30 was the model of such a campaign. After the middle of the seventh century, however, the Tang empire became increasingly involved in conflicts with distant, well-organized, and militarily powerful states that were simply not susceptible to a single knockout blow. Koguryŏ was one such opponent, and Silla another. In the west, Tang China was confronted with the rapidly rising power of the Tibetan empire founded by Srong-btsan-sgam-po. In the early 660s, while Tang armies were occupied in the Korean peninsula, the Tibetans conquered the Tuyuhun territories in what is now Qinghai province. In 665 they began to challenge

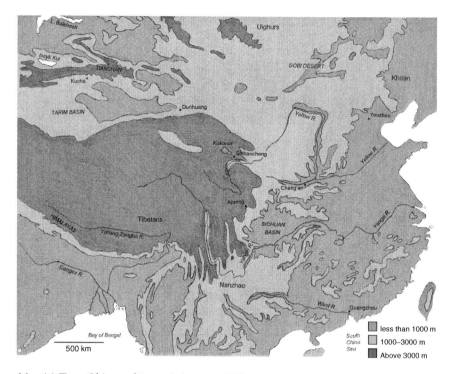

Map 16 Tang China and Inner Asia, *ca.* AD 750

Tang control of the oasis kingdoms of the Tarim Basin, and in the spring and summer of 670 they captured the key administrative center of Kucha and evicted Tang forces from almost all of the vast desert region between the Tianshan Mountains and the northern edge of the Tibetan plateau. In the eighth lunar month of 670, a large Tang army under Xue Rengui struck southward into the Tuyuhun country. Xue separated his best and most mobile troops from the baggage train and slower-moving elements and advanced toward the great lake of Kokonor, giving the Tibetans the opportunity to overrun the baggage train and then crush Xue's own light column at the battle of the Dafei River.[2] In 678 another Tang army campaigning in the Qinghai region was similarly exposed to defeat in detail at the hands of the Tibetans, and in 680 Tibetan forces captured the important fortress of Anrong in the mountainous borderland of northwestern Sichuan.[3] In all of these campaigns, Tang troops found themselves fighting in remote, sparsely populated, and inhospitable terrain that was the natural element of their Tibetan opponents. The heartland of the Tibetan state in the valley of the Yarlung Zangbo (Brahmaputra) River, meanwhile, was sheltered by so many geographical barriers as to be entirely immune to Chinese attack.

The military situation in the northwest deteriorated even further in 679 when the Eastern Turks, Tang vassals since 630, rebelled on the northern border of Hedong (modern Shanxi). Their initial rising was suppressed by Tang forces in 681, but at the end of the following year the revolt was renewed with greater success by Qutlugh Qaghan, a descendant of Xieli. The revived Eastern Turk qaghanate would dominate the Mongolian steppes for more than fifty years. The appearance of this hostile power to the north required the diversion of Tang forces that might otherwise have been directed against the Tibetans in the west, and the defection of the Eastern Turks also blunted the offensive power of Tang expeditionary armies that had formerly benefited from the speed, mobility, and martial prowess of their nomad auxiliaries.

The shift in the military balance between Tang China and its northern and western neighbors spelled the end of the expeditionary army system. The expeditionary armies were no longer able to inflict decisive defeats on their enemies and return home again within a reasonable period of time. Incapable of delivering a knockout blow, yet at the same time unable to withdraw when undefeated enemy forces were still in a position to threaten exposed border prefectures, more and more expeditionary armies found it necessary to settle down in static encampments which gradually evolved into permanent garrisons. In the year 677, for example, several static "army garrisons" (*jun zhen*) were established on the Tibetan frontier. The armies' change of posture was signalled by the title of "garrison defense commander-in-chief for the expeditionary army of the Taohe route" that Liu Rengui received when he was sent to take command of the northwestern frontier forces facing the Tibetans.[4] Initially set in motion by the Tibetan challenge, the establishment of a system of permanent frontier armies was nevertheless a gradual, start-and-stop process that was not completed until well into the eighth century. An army might garrison one location for a few years, then be reactivated as an expeditionary army, move to another location, and settle down there.[5] The last record of a specially constituted expeditionary army being sent into the field comes from 732, long after the older expeditionary forces had been converted into permanent garrisons.[6]

At first, no provision was made for the replacement or relief of the *fubing* and conscript-recruits who made up these campaign armies turned into garrisons. Men originally enlisted for the duration of what was expected to be a short campaign were kept away from home for years on end.[7] This must have had much the same depressing effect on morale that Liu Rengui observed in Korea in the early 660s, dampening the enthusiasm of both elite and commoners for military service. Within a few years of the military setbacks of the 670s, rotational systems were set up to cycle replacements − both *fubing* and conscript-recruits − in and out of the army garrisons on a regular basis.[8] The typical period of frontier duty was two or three years.[9] It is probably not coincidental that the period between 685 and 688 saw a major increase in the numerical strength of the *fubing*, with regimental quotas raised from 600 to 800 men for the smallest regiments and from 1000 to 1200 for the largest. The need to maintain strong, permanent forces on the frontier could not be met by the existing *fubing* establishment without disrupting the schedule of rotation for guard duty in the capital or keeping soldiers away from their homes for very extended periods. In addition to beefing up the existing *fubing* units, the Tang government also created a considerable number of new regiments in areas close to the northern border.[10] This had the advantage of minimizing the logistical costs associated with the movement of tens of thousands of troops to and from the border each year, and the new regiments appear to have been excused from rotational guard duty in the capital in return for their contribution to frontier defense.

In spite of all the measures to increase overall manpower and activate new regiments in frontier regions, there is ample evidence that the *fubing* system was in distress by the last years of the seventh century. In 695, for example, it was reported that many *fubing* in the Guanzhong region around Chang'an were absconding from their homes in order to escape the military service obligation, and in the following year the government found it necessary to raise an entirely new militia force to help resist an invasion of the Hebei region by the nomadic Khitan people of the northeast.[11] In addition to the new burden placed upon the *fubing* by the demands of frontier defense, the deterioration of the "equal-field" system of land redistribution also had a negative impact on the old regimental system. The entire structure was predicated on the assumption that the soldiers were small farmers who would not only be able to support themselves when they were not on active duty, but would even be able to provide some of their own equipment and supplies. The equal-field system was, *in theory*, supposed to provide each adult male with 100 *mu* of land, more than enough to support an average family.[12] Real land allotments, however, did not always conform to the standards stipulated in the land regulations. This was especially true in crowded regions such as Guanzhong, where so many of the regiments were concentrated. The problem only intensified as time passed. With wealthy and powerful families augmenting their landholdings by a variety of devices both legal and illegal, less and less land was available for distribution to ordinary farmers. The problem was already acute by the last years of the seventh century, and helps to explain why many of the *fubing* of the Guanzhong region were abandoning both their home districts and their military obligations.[13] The decline of the *fubing* was a gradual process that extended over several decades, but it is generally agreed that the system was completely moribund by 749 – the year in which the dispatch of fish-shaped copper tallies (or mobilization tokens) to the various regiments was halted on the grounds that there were no longer any troops available for service.[14]

In the early years of the eighth century, conscript-recruits serving limited tours of duty on the frontier were the single most important source of manpower for the army garrisons. However, the conscript-recruit system was not ideally suited to sustaining the frontier defenses. There were substantial costs associated with the constant movement of large bodies of men between the interior and the borders, and the limited tour of duty also meant that the most experienced troops were constantly being replaced by raw recruits.[15] Longer tours and more conscription from districts closer to the frontier did not solve the basic problem. In 717 the government sought to persuade conscript-recruits to remain with the armies past the expiration of their term of service by offering them material inducements.[16] With the breakdown of the equal-field system, the concentration of landownership in the hands of wealthy families, and the rise of vagrancy – all trends that were very much in evidence during the first half of the eighth century – there was no shortage of hard-pressed peasants who might be expected to respond to such offers.[17] Men who chose to remain on the frontier became known as "sturdy lads" (*jian'er*), a label that had original-ly been applied to elite elements among the conscript-recruits.[18] The year 737 saw a decisive shift toward voluntary recruitment of an *armée de métier* dedicated to long-term service on the frontiers. An imperial edict issued on June 12 of that year called upon frontier commanders to calculate their manpower needs and establish quotas to be filled by the recruitment of currently serving conscript-recruits and members of migrant familes to serve as long-term *jian'er*. As inducements, the government offered material compensation "above the usual standard," permanent exemption from taxes and corvée, and provision of farmland and dwellings for dependants who accompanied soldiers to the frontier.[19] The offer was apparently a great success. In the first month of 738, with the quotas already close to being filled, it was decreed that the remaining conscripts still serving on the frontier would be allowed to return home, and that henceforth no more men were to be conscripted for service in the army garrisons.[20]

By the middle of the eighth century, the *jian'er* were the most common and characteristic element of the frontier armies. But they were not the only element present. Peasant conscripts continued to appear even after 738, since the armies were not always able to fill their quotas entirely with volunteers. Moreover, the new *armée de métier* proved inadequate whenever it became necessary to raise large forces in a short period of time in order to field an unusually large campaign army or cope with a sudden emergency. The disastrous campaign against the southwestern kingdom of Nanzhao in 754 cost the lives of tens of thousands of hapless peasant conscripts, and when the great rebellion of An Lushan erupted at the end of 755 conscript-recruits were rushed to the defense of the capital.[21] Non-Chinese contingents continued to play a prominent role in the new frontier armies, and especially in their all-important cavalry forces. The losses caused by the defection of the Eastern Turks in 679 were made good in the early years of the eighth century as political instability and armed conflict on the steppe drove many tribal leaders to submit to Tang authority. As in the days of the expeditionary army system in the seventh century, non-Chinese units were a discrete element within the Tang military structure, but they tended to enjoy less autonomy than in the past and were bound more closely into the larger organizational framework.

Their status was less that of the ally and more that of the subordinate.[22] By the middle of the eighth century, the frontier armies and garrisons were polyglot communities composed of Chinese and steppe elements.

A list of the Tang frontier forces believed to date from 742 shows an arc of more than sixty army garrisons stretching from the Liao River valley in the northeast to Sichuan in the southwest.[23] In addition, there were several other garrisons located in what is now northern Vietnam, on the southeast coast, and on the Shandong peninsula. These units varied in size from a few hundred men to upwards of 30,000, with the great majority falling within the range of one thousand to ten thousand. The total number of soldiers was almost half a million, of whom no more than 80,000 appear to have been cavalry. Most of the units listed are designated as "armies" (*jun*); some are identified as "defense detachments" (*shouzhuo*) or "fortresses" (*cheng*). The defense detachments are usually – but not invariably – smaller than the armies. The status of these units was rather fluid; *shouzhuo* could be converted to armies, and armies reduced to *shouzhuo*.[24]

As of 742, all but a handful of the army garrisons had been organized into ten regional military commands, each responsible for the security of a large sector of the frontier. In most cases, these sectors corresponded to the frontier prefectures of one of the province-sized "circuits of inspection" (*dao*) that had been delineated in 733. The five largest commands each disposed of between 55,000 and 91,000 men, and covered the northern frontier from the area of modern Beijing to the Gansu corridor. Smaller regional commands projected bastion-like from the main line to hold the Liao River valley in the northeast and the Tarim basin and the Tianshan range in the northwest, and there were also separate and relatively small regional commands for the Sichuan frontier and the far south. A large northern command typically controlled about a dozen armies and defense detachments, with the bulk of these units positioned to guard prefectural seats and other key points along the frontier. In most regional commands, one army considerably larger than the others was based at the headquarters of the region's military commander and subject to his direct control. This army might account for as much as 45 percent of the region's total troop strength, including the lion's share of the cavalry. In some cases cavalry accounted for more than half of the headquarters army. Most army garrisons, in contrast, consisted of no more than 10 percent cavalry – if mounted troops were present at all. Most of the smaller frontier armies appear to have been best suited for the static defense of fortified positions. The large headquarters armies, meanwhile, provided each region with a relatively mobile strike force and strategic reserve. It could be moved rapidly to the support of threatened sectors and was large enough to undertake major campaigns and punitive expeditions beyond the frontier. The strategic functions that had once been performed by ad hoc expeditionary armies sent from the interior of the empire were now the responsibility of strong armies permanently stationed along the periphery.

Of the ten regional commands that existed in 742, nine were headed by "military governors" (*jiedushi*). These were extraordinary imperial commissionerships rather than regular bureaucratic offices. The title probably derives from the expression *jiedu*, meaning "to regulate with the insignia of command," that was used in early Tang to indicate the authority the commander-in-chief of an expeditionary army wielded over his subordinate commanders.[25] This etymology dovetails with the origin of the frontier forces in expeditionary armies compelled by circumstances to settle down as permanent garrisons. The post of military governor – and the regional commands themselves – would seem to have emerged gradually as an improvised response to the need for some sort of superior command authority to coordinate the operations of a number of army garrisons stationed in a particular geographical area and confronting the same opponent. After several decades of terminological chaos, the title of *jiedushi* had become the standard and almost universal appellation for the regional military commanders by the early 730s.

The substance of the position continued to evolve over time, however, with ever greater powers accruing to the incumbents. By 750, almost all of the military governors held commissionerships for public revenues and state lands concurrently with their *jiedushi* appointments. These posts were directly involved with the supply and support of the frontier armies, but at the same time they gave the military governor fiscal and economic authority that was province-wide rather than confined to a handful of frontier prefectures. Some military governors also held the office of investigating commissioner (*caifangshi*), which gave them extensive authority over the civil affairs of every prefecture in the circuit.[26] The office of the *jiedushi* was beginning to take on the character of a true provincial governorship. This was a development that the Tang state had taken pains to avoid in earlier times for fear that strong regional regimes might emerge to challenge the authority of the court. During the reign of Xuanzong (712–56), however, considerations of military efficiency and effectiveness tended to trump other arguments.

From the time of their inception, the military governorships had normally been entrusted to high-ranking Han Chinese officials who had already held some of the empire's top civil positions. These early *jiedushi* included members of powerful and prominent families with long traditions of officeholding, as well as relative parvenus who had entered government service by the increasingly prestigious route of the literary examinations. Among the latter sort was the noted statesman and poet Zhang Yue, who held several northern frontier commands in the years around 720.[27] Such men might return to court with enhanced prestige to serve the emperor as chief ministers. This pattern was altered in 747 when the then-dominant chief minister, Li Linfu, initiated a new policy of appointing non-Chinese officers to the key frontier commands on the grounds that they were more courageous and effective in combat. It has long been claimed that Li's real motive was to prevent members of the Chinese political elite from using military success on the frontier as a means of accumulating the political capital to challenge his own hold on the government.[28] This may well be true, but the rationale that he offered should not be dismissed out of hand. It must have sounded quite sensible to many of Li's contemporaries – including the emperor himself, who was notoriously hungry for military glory and always welcomed reports of victories over foreign enemies.[29]

The principal beneficiaries of the new personnel policy were Geshu Han and An Lushan. Both men were of foreign origin and mixed blood. Geshu's father was a Turk descended from the ruling subtribe of the Turgesh people, while his mother was a princess from the small Central Asian principality of Khotan. The father had served Tang as a frontier official, and Geshu followed a similar path. He became an officer of the Hexi and Longyou armies, sometimes fighting in the front ranks against the Tibetans. In 747 he was appointed military governor of Longyou, and from 753 he served concurrently as the military governor of neighboring Hexi. Geshu was not a simple "barbarian" soldier; his family had both money and a tradition of officeholding, and Geshu himself had enough education to be able to read classic texts such as the *Tradition of Zuo* (*Zuo zhuan*) and Ban Gu's *History of the Han Dynasty* (*Han shu*).[30] An Lushan came from a similar background, but was a more uncouth character. The son of a Turkish mother, he belonged to a Sogdian (Central Asian) family associated with the rulers of the second Eastern Turk qaghanate. In 716 a bloody coup at the Turkish court drove the An family to seek refuge in the Tang empire. An Lushan was only one of several relatives who eventually rose to high rank after entering the Tang frontier armies. In contrast to Geshu Han, An was not literate in Chinese, but this does not seem to have impeded his promotion. By 733 An was an important deputy of the Youzhou military governor Zhang Shougui. In 742 he was made military governor of Pinglu in southwestern Manchuria. Two years later he was transferred to the much more powerful Youzhou command (now called Fanyang) while retaining overall control of Pinglu. And in 751 yet another regional command, that of Hedong in what is now Shanxi, was added to An's purview.[31] Other foreigners, most notably the Korean Gao Xianzhi and An's kinsman An Sishun, also held military governorships during this period, but An Lushan and Geshu Han were the only ones permitted to control multiple frontier commands concurrently.

The power of these men was further enhanced by changes that were taking place at lower command levels. The shift from rotational duty to the stationing of a permanent, long-service soldiery along the northern frontier saw the emergence of a new sort of officer corps. Where the leadership of the *fubing* had been drawn largely from locally powerful and prominent families rooted in their home communities, the trend in the new frontier armies was to promote men from the ranks of the generally plebeian *jian'er* to serve as subalterns and middle-grade officers. It is possible that the allure of the civil bureaucracy, especially after the system of literary examinations became an important means of fast-track recruitment during the ascendancy of Empress Wu Zetian in the latter part of the seventh century, also brought a reduction in the number of young men of good family who chose to pursue military careers. In 702 Empress Wu introduced a new system of regular annual military qualification examinations (*wuju*) in order to attract a better class of military officer. Examinees were scored on their skill with bow and arrow and the cavalry lance, and were also tested for physical strength and command "presence." Those who passed with relatively high scores might be appointed to posts in the imperial guards.[32] In fact, the military examinations had no discernable influence on the composition of the Tang officer corps.[33] By the middle of the eighth century, it seems that the great majority of frontier officers at all levels were either Han Chinese from very humble backgrounds or non-Han, usually of steppe origin. Such men were often promoted from the ranks on the basis of local military examinations administered at their garrison by the army commander or military governor.[34] The military governors gained considerable power over the selection and promotion of their own subordinates, and their personnel decisions were routinely approved by the central authorities in Chang'an. At the beginning of 755, for example, An Lushan was allowed to replace thirty-two of his Han commanders with men of barbarian origin.[35] In the frontier garrisons, the loyalty of the officers came to be directed more toward their military governors than the distant Tang court.

Though not invariably victorious, the new professional frontier armies that emerged during Xuanzong's reign were generally successful in covering the borders, establishing strong positions well to the north and west of the major areas of Chinese settlement and projecting power outward to keep inveterate foes such as the Tibetans and the nomadic Khitan people of the northeast off balance. There were no incursions into Chinese territory at all comparable to the devastating Khitan invasion of Hebei that occurred in 696 during the reign of Empress Wu. In the far northwest, imperial forces were eventually able to reestablish firm control over the Tarim basin and Dzungaria and extend Tang suzerainty to many of the small states of the Pamirs and Transoxiana. The Anrong fortress on the mountainous Sichuan frontier, held by the Tibetans for sixty years, was recaptured in 740. In 747 Gao Xianzhi, a general of Korean (Koguryŏ) descent attached to the Anxi military command in the Tarim basin, led an army of 10,000 men on an epic march southward across the Pamirs to conquer the strategically located Tibetan client kingdom of Little Balur (Gilgit), cutting Tibet's communications with the Arabs and the Western Turks.[36] The Longyou military governor Geshu Han took the stronghold of Shibaocheng east of Kokonor – albeit at enormous cost – in 749. Geshu went on to eject the Tibetans from the "Nine Bends" region on the upper course of the Yellow River in 753. In what is now Mongolia, the Eastern Turk qaghanate disintegrated in 741 as a result of internal strife and was soon replaced by the Uighurs, whose basic policy was not antagonistic to Tang, as the hegemon of the northern steppe. On the northeastern frontier, the military governors of Youzhou (Fanyang) and Pinglu experienced both victory and

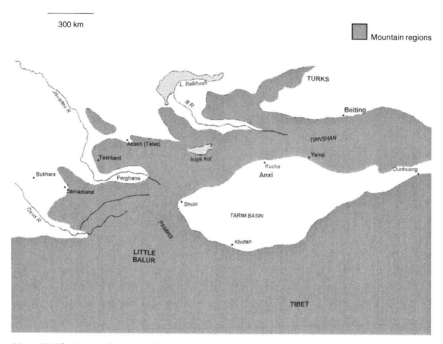

300 km

Mountain regions

Map 17 The Tarim basin and Transoxiana, *ca.* AD 750

defeat in their frequent encounters with the Khitan, but usually managed to retain the strategic initiative.[37]

When the Tang frontier armies suffered serious defeats, it was usually in the context of rash, ill-considered offensive operations. Later commentators attributed the sometimes foolhardy aggressiveness of the military governors to their desire to gain Xuanzong's favor by winning victories in the field.[38] The year 751 was especially ill-starred. In the late spring the Jiannan (Sichuan) military governor Xianyu Zhongtong led an army of 80,000 against the recently established kingdom of Nanzhao in what is now Yunnan province – and was utterly defeated with the loss of some three-quarters of his original force. The influential minister Yang Guozhong, Xianyu's patron at court and cousin of the emperor's favorite consort, somehow managed to conceal the defeat and was not deterred from making a second, equally disastrous attempt on Nanzhao in 754. During this second campaign the Nanzhao ruler avoided battle until the Tang army had eaten up its grain supplies and large numbers of men had been stricken with a "miasmal pestilence," then pursued and wiped out the intruders.[39] These defeats in the far southwest were not, strictly speaking, the fault of the new professional armies, since the huge forces fielded by the Sichuan commanders consisted largely of conscript-recruits – many of whom were drawn from North China and had no experience of or immunity to the microbes of the subtropical south.

Two other setbacks in the late summer and early autumn of 751 did involve the professional armies of the northern frontier, however. Striking deep into Khitan territory along the Tuluzhen (Laoha) River, the Fanyang military governor An Lushan was routed with heavy losses when a tribal contingent accompanying his army went over to the Khitan side after the battle had been joined. An was not helped by the fact that the torrential rains through which he had forced his advance had weakened the glue and sinew of his soldiers' composite bows.[40] More than two thousand miles to the west and perhaps two months earlier, a Tang army of 30,000 under Gao Xianzhi, now military governor of Anxi, had confronted an Arab army near the town of Atlakh on the Talas River. Gao had intervened on the side of one of the local principalities, Ferghana, in its conflict with neighboring Tashkent. This move prompted Ziyad bin Salih, governor of Samarkand for the Ummayyad caliphate, to lead his Arab army north to the assistance of Tashkent. The outcome of the battle was decided in much the same way as An Lushan's encounter with the Khitan: Gao's army was routed and nearly destroyed when an allied contingent of Qarluq Turks defected to the Arabs.[41] This contest, the only major battle ever fought between Chinese and Arab armies, was entirely without sequel. The Tang empire was soon distracted by its own internal difficulties, and the Arabs made no attempt to press forward into the Tarim Basin and Dzungaria.

Even without the additional expenses resulting from ill-advised expeditions and the occasional military catastrophe, the cost of maintaining large, permanent armies on the frontier was still substantial. The empire's military establishment in the middle of the eighth century was no smaller than it had been in the heyday of the *fubing*, but a very high proportion of the men in the ranks were now costly long-service veterans rather than part-time farmer-soldiers who made few demands on the state's resources. The new professional fighters not only contributed no tax revenue to the state's coffers, but required payments of cloth and grain that must have been well in excess of the subsistence rations provided for short-term conscripts. The shift toward an *armée de métier* meant a considerable increase in military expenditure. It was reported that before 712 frontier defense had cost no more than two million strings of copper cash each year, as opposed to twelve million strings in 742 and fourteen or fifteen million by 755.[42] There is reason to question whether the Tang empire's defense budget really grew sevenfold between 712 and 755, since the increase may in part represent an accounting change as conscript-recruits supported from prefectural resources were replaced by *jian'er* maintained with funds dispatched from the center.[43] Given the growing importance of material reward in attracting and retaining men for military service, however, there seems little reason to doubt that the trend of military expenditure was sharply upward. During the reign of Xuanzong, as both before and after, the cost of supporting the military was the single largest item of state expenditure.[44] In some regions, especially along the north-western frontier, the government attempted to save at least part of the cost of transporting grain over long distances by establishing large numbers of military agricultural colonies (*tuntian*) near the army garrisons.[45]

On the frontiers of the empire, the changes set in motion in the 670s had, by the middle of the eighth century, resulted in the formation of large standing armies composed of battle-hardened veterans. The new defense system was extremely powerful but also increasingly expensive, and it posed a potential threat to the supremacy of the Tang court. The government was not unaware of this danger, and several institutional mechanisms had long been in place to check the centrifugal tendencies of frontier commanders. The senior officers of army garrisons, like most other Tang officials, were supposed to be assigned to a single post for only a few years, after which time they were subject to reassignment.[46] Up until the 740s, the military governors themselves were normally replaced at frequent intervals. A second control mechanism was the assignment of censors – civil officials with an investigative function – to serve as "army supervisors" (*jianjun*). In the 730s, during Xuanzong's reign, the censors were replaced in this function by trusted eunuchs sent from the imperial palace. The supervisor, whether censor or eunuch, did not have the authority to issue orders to the general or military governor. His basic duties were to "oversee reward and punishment," uncover falsehoods, and report any illegal or treasonable activities to the emperor.[47] The efficacy of this system was somewhat reduced by the fact that army supervisors were appointed on a case-by-case basis. Gao Xianzhi was saddled with the eunuch supervisor Bian Lingcheng during his expedition to Little Balur in 747, but there is no evidence that the Fanyang military governor An Lushan, commander of much more powerful forces, ever had to put up with such an intrusive presence in *his* headquarters.[48] Old rules do not seem to have been enforced in the cases of favored commanders such as Geshu Han and An Lushan; by the autumn of 755, An was in his twelfth year as military governor of Fanyang.

By that time, there were no armed forces at the capital or elsewhere in the interior of the empire that were at all capable of counterbalancing the frontier armies. The old *fubing* system was completely moribund, and the palace armies in Chang'an were no more than a hollow shell. These forces were originally drawn from members of Li Yuan's original army who had settled near the capital at the time the Tang dynasty was founded, but had undergone repeated reorganizations since that time and had seen very little combat. By the middle of the eighth century the total manpower quota for all four of the palace armies was perhaps 60,000 men. Only a fraction of this number were actually on duty at any given time, however, and the quality of the troops was open to question. Many were registered inhabitants of districts near the capital who were selected for service in much the same manner as the *fubing*, while others were relatives of officials, sons of wealthy families, and even merchants. Persons of these sorts found membership in the palace armies attractive because it offered immunity from taxes and government labor exactions – as well as from military service on

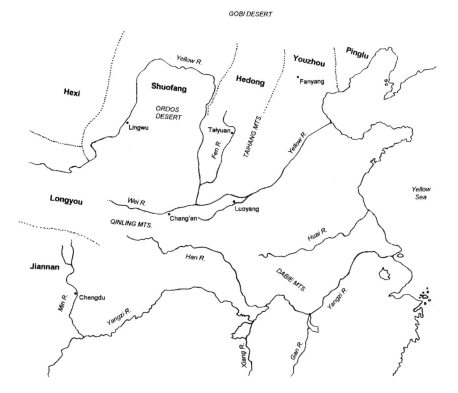

Map 18 Tang frontier commands in AD 755

the frontier. It does not seem that very much was demanded of them in return, nor that they constituted a disciplined, well-trained, and battle-ready force.[49]

The crisis came near the end of 755. An Lushan had enjoyed a good working relationship with Li Linfu, the dominant chief minister from 736 until his death in 752. Li did not consider the illiterate frontier general a threat to his position at court and allowed him to remain in office year after year, while An for his part seems to have stood in awe of Li. Matters were very different under Li's successor Yang Guozhong, a much less imposing figure who owed his power at court to the fact that he was a second cousin of Xuanzong's favorite consort. An still held the emperor's trust, but he quickly became involved in a power struggle with Yang Guozhong. After Yang began to arrest and eliminate his supporters in the capital, An finally rose in rebellion.[50] Claiming to have received a secret edict from Xuanzong instructing him to suppress Yang Guozhong, An marched south from his base at Fanyang on December 16, 755. After the deduction of contingents left to hold Fanyang and other frontier areas, An's main army consisted of perhaps 150,000 men. In addition to the experienced regular troops of the Fanyang command, this force also included large groups of Tongra, Xi, Khitan, and Malgal tribesmen recruited from the

217

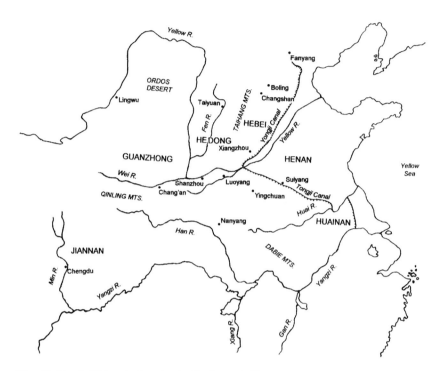

Map 19 North China during the An Lushan rebellion, AD 755–63

other side of the border.[51] Some 8000 of these barbarian warriors were attached to An Lushan by fictive kinship ties, forming detachments of "stepsons" (*jiazi*) that could be deployed to control less reliable units.[52] The rebel army was well supplied with horses, in part because An's concurrent appointment as Commissioner of Stables had enabled him to transfer the best animals from the pastures of the northwest to his own command.[53] It encountered no effective resistance as it swept down through Hebei toward the Yellow River, covering an average of about twenty miles a day.[54]

The news of An Lushan's rebellion travelled even faster; it reached Chang'an in only six days, carried by express riders who must have covered more than eighty miles a day.[55] Xuanzong's response was to send officers to raise conscript-recruits in Hedong (Shanxi) and Luoyang, and Feng Changqing, an experienced frontier general and former subordinate of Gao Xianzhi, was soon to take command of the forces being gathered at Luoyang. An Lushan's eldest son, who happened to be in Chang'an at this time, was seized and put to death, and An's cousin An Sishun was quickly removed from his position as military governor of Shuofang controlling the Yellow River frontier and the Ordos region directly to the north of the capital. An Lushan, meanwhile, effected a crossing of the Yellow River northeast of Luoyang on January 8, 756, and marched toward the eastern capital. With a hastily raised army of 60,000 conscripts and volunteers, Feng Changqing attempted to block the rebels' advance at the Hulao Pass, the same strategic chokepoint where Li Shimin had halted Dou Jiande in 621. On this occasion, however, the terrain advantage was not enough to compensate for the qualitative imbalance between the two sides, and Feng's untrained rabble was trampled beneath the hoofs of An Lushan's veteran cavalry. After two more clashes on the road to Luoyang, the rebels entered the city on January 19 as Feng and the remnants of his army fled westward to Shanzhou. There they joined forces with another government army under Gao Xianzhi, some 50,000 guardsmen, frontier troops, and volunteers recruited in Chang'an with gold and silk from the palace treasury. Gao and Feng soon decided to abandon their exposed position at Shanzhou and withdraw to the strategic Tong Pass, but the retreat quickly degenerated into a disorderly, panic-stricken flight. Although order was restored at Tong Pass, both generals were denounced by Gao's eunuch supervisor Bian Lingcheng and put to death on Xuanzong's orders.[56]

The remnants of the forces led by Gao and Feng were soon joined by more reliable troops. More than half of the regular soldiers garrisoning Hexi and Longyou under Geshu Han, some 80,000 men, were recalled from the northwestern frontier to strengthen the defenses of the Tong Pass. The total number of men guarding the pass was now reported to be 200,000, making the narrow defile between the Yellow River and the mountains all but impregnable. Xuanzong placed Geshu Han in overall command of this army, despite that fact that the general was in very poor health.[57] In the spring and early summer of 756, An Lushan made no attempt to force the strong position at Tong Pass. On February 5, the first day of the new lunar year, An had abandoned all pretense of loyalty to Xuanzong and proclaimed himself the first emperor of the new "Yan" dynasty.[58] For some time thereafter, he seems to have been preoccupied with the establishment of his new regime at Luoyang, and he also faced a serious threat to his communications with Fanyang. In February 756, Tang local officials who had not dared to challenge An's southward advance launched a popular uprising against his garrisons in central Hebei. An was compelled to dispatch strong forces under Shi Siming, a subordinate general of Turkish origin, to regain control of the region. No sooner had Shi's men made their presence felt in Hebei, however, than the local Tang loyalists were reinforced by a portion of the Shuofang army arriving from Hedong by way of the Jingxing Pass through the Taihang Mountains. When Shi Siming raced ahead with his mounted troops to attack the Shuofang column near the town of Changshan, the rebels' superiority in cavalry – usually the decisive element in Tang warfare and certainly the decisive factor in the campaign thus far – was negated by the skillful tactics of the Shuofang general Li Guangbi. Already in possession of Changshan, Li deployed his foot soldiers with their backs to the town wall and kept the enemy horsemen at bay with a dense spear formation and 1000 crossbowmen divided into four sections so as to keep up continuous volleys. Shi suffered heavy losses and was forced to retreat.[59] In May, Li was joined by the main body of the Shuofang army under its new military governor, Guo Ziyi, and Shi's rebel army was pushed back and besieged at Boling.

In midsummer, however, the fortunes of war shifted once more in the rebels' favor. Fearing that Geshu Han might use the immense force gathered at Tong Pass to carry out a coup in Chang'an, and encouraged by reports that the rebel forces outside the pass were weak and unprepared, Yang Guozhong persuaded Xuanzong to order the general to march east and attack the enemy. Geshu suspected a trap and other Tang commanders also had deep misgivings, but the order was obeyed. On July 5, the Tang army began to advance toward Shanzhou. Two days later, when they encountered rebel forces west of Lingbao, Geshu's suspicions were swiftly borne out. The Tang vanguard was drawn into an ambush in a narrow defile where the troops were packed too tightly to put their weapons to good use. Driven to flight by a Tongra cavalry attack against their rear, the vanguard troops communicated their panic to the main body which also dissolved into a mass of fugitives. The government army suffered terrible losses, with many men drowning in the Yellow River as they attempted to swim to safety, while the rebels followed up their success by storming Tong Pass. Geshu Han was captured and brought as a prisoner to Luoyang.[60]

With the capital now uncovered, Xuanzong, his favorite concubine Yang Guifei, her cousin Yang Guozhong, and an escort of imperial guards set out on the road to Sichuan. At the Mawei post station, about thirty-five miles west of Chang'an, the guardsmen mutinied and forced the emperor to have both of the Yangs – whom they blamed for the disaster – put to death. Xuanzong eventually arrived safely in Chengdu, but power was already slipping from his hands. The crown prince had fled northwest to Lingwu on the Yellow River – headquarters of the Shuofang army – to rally support, and on August 12 he proclaimed himself emperor. He received the allegiance of the Tang forces in North China and later the acquiescence of Xuanzong as well. A rebel army occupied Chang'an, while the Shuofang forces abandoned their campaign in Hebei and marched west to protect their new ruler (who would be known posthumously as Suzong).[61]

An Lushan's power reached its apogee with the capture of Chang'an and the recovery of Hebei, but at this point his armies stalled. The rebels inflicted several more defeats on Tang forces in Guanzhong, but were unable to extend their control beyond the immediate environs of the capital. Other rebel armies pushing southward toward the lower Yangzi region – the breadbasket of the empire, an important source of tax revenues and surplus grain whose loss would have crippled the Tang war effort – also made little headway. The stubborn defense of walled towns such as Yingchuan in central Henan, Suiyang on the Grand Canal, and Nanyang on the approach to the Han River completely frustrated the rebel efforts to reach the Yangzi. At Suiyang the defense was led by Zhang Xun, a local civil official and literary examination graduate who managed to hold the town for nearly a year. The rebels, presumably unwilling to leave a strong enemy position interdicting their canal supply line, did not attempt to bypass Zhang's stronghold.[62] The rebels' lack of offensive successes between the summer of 756 and the autumn of 757 was probably also influenced by weakness at the center. Early in 757, An Lushan – ailing and violently irascible – was murdered by a cabal of his closest associates, who installed his son An Qingxu as the new emperor of Yan. The result was much weaker central control over the various rebel field commanders. The son simply did not command the same respect in the rebel camp that his father had, and the assassination alienated many rebel officers of An Lushan's generation (among them Shi Siming).[63]

The Tang counterattack came in the autumn of 757. By this time, the loyalist cause had been bolstered by an alliance with the Uighurs, the most powerful of the Turkic Tiele peoples, who had replaced the Eastern Turks as rulers of the Mongolian steppe during the 740s. The alliance was negotiated by Pugu Huai'en, a Shuofang general of noble Tiele origin, and the Uighurs sent more than 4000 horsemen to join the Tang army in Guanzhong.[64] That army, now under the command of the Shuofang general Guo Ziyi, began its advance on Chang'an on October 29. On November 13, Guo met the rebels in a set-piece battle near the Xiangji Temple, about ten miles south of the capital. Guo deployed facing north, with the monastery behind him and his left flank resting on the Feng River, a north-flowing tributary of the Wei. The Tang line was driven back and thrown into confusion by the initial onslaught of the rebel army. Beyond the right flank, however, Tang reconnaissance discovered enemy cavalry who had been placed in ambush to fall upon the government army's rear at an opportune moment. Pugu Huai'en led the as-yet uncommitted Uighur cavalry in a devastating attack on this rebel detachment, then continued his advance to strike the rear of the enemy's main body. This blow brought about the complete collapse of the Yan army, and Chang'an was recovered by the Tang forces the next day.[65] The rebels retreated toward Luoyang with Guo's army in pursuit. They tried to make a stand in the narrow defiles between the Tong Pass and Shanzhou where Geshu Han's army had come to grief the year before, but were routed again by the Uighur cavalry on November 30.[66] The Tang army entered Luoyang on December 3, and An Qingxu escaped across the Yellow River to southern Hebei.

In the space of just a few weeks, both capitals had been recovered and a series of apparently decisive blows inflicted on the rebel forces. At this point, however, the government offensive ground to a halt. Organizational, jurisdictional, and logistical problems needed to be sorted out, and the mood in the Tang camp seems (not unnaturally) to have been one of relaxation rather than urgency.[67] Besides, the Uighurs, spearhead of the government's counterattack, had gone home after the recovery of Luoyang. The result was that An Qingxu was allowed a breathing space to rally and rebuild his forces in southern Hebei, and it was not until another year had passed that operations against him were resumed in earnest.

When the Tang offensive finally began in November of 758, it involved the forces of no fewer than nine different military governors. Only three of these men represented frontier commands that had existed before 755; all the others controlled new military provinces that had been carved out of the interior of North China in response to the exigencies of the rebellion. Their total force was reported to number more than 200,000 men, but shaky command arrangements meant that the whole was rather less than the sum of its parts. None of the generals was assigned to supreme command; instead, Yu Chao'en, a powerful eunuch who enjoyed Suzong's trust, was present in a coordinating role as army supervisor. This arrangement was said to have come about because neither of the two most powerful military governors, Guo Ziyi and Li Guangbi, could be made to serve under the other. It is also suggestive of the court's distrust of its own generals, and the extent to which those generals – though not yet independent warlords – had been able to free themselves from central control.[68] Despite the less than optimal command arrangements, the government's armies were able to defeat An Qingxu in the field and lay siege to his headquarters at Xiangzhou (today's Anyang) in southern Hebei. With his situation now desperate, An appealed to Shi Siming, whose forces were in control of Fanyang and northern Hebei. Shi was by this time no longer a subordinate of the Yan emperor, but an autonomous actor who had at one point even made a nominal submission to the Tang court. Shi sent a relatively small force to observe the situation at Xiangzhou, but it was not until the spring of 759 that he was willing to challenge the huge government army with his full strength. On April 7 he faced the Tang army north of the Anyang River. Just after the two sides had joined battle, however, a sudden dust storm cut visibility to just a few feet, provoking the flight of both armies. With the advantage of a unified command structure, Shi was able to get his men back under control relatively quickly. On the government side matters were far worse, with each of the nine military governors choosing to retreat in a different direction toward his own territorial base. None of them showed much confidence in his colleagues, and none was willing to risk facing the rebels alone.[69]

This "battle" saved Xiangzhou, but not An Qingxu. He was soon eliminated by Shi Siming, who made himself the new leader of the rebel movement. After consolidating his position in Hebei, Shi pushed south across the Yellow River in the autumn of 759. Instead of fighting to defend the eastern capital, his opponent Li Guangbi chose to retreat to the north side of the Yellow River at Heyang (about twenty-five miles northeast of Luoyang) and occupy a strong fortified position that could easily receive supplies and reinforcements from loyalist territory in today's Shanxi. Shi Siming occupied Luoyang, but Li's presence at Heyang – potentially a very serious threat to his flank and rear – prevented him from pressing westward toward Shanzhou, the Tong Pass, and Chang'an.[70]

The front line remained in the vicinity of Luoyang for three years. During this period the rebels experienced another violent change of leadership – the third since 757 – when Shi Siming was murdered by his son Shi Chaoyi (who had been set aside as heir apparent in favor of a younger brother) in the spring of 761. The military deadlock finally came to an end in the autumn of 762, when the Tang court was once again able to secure the assistance of the Uighurs. One Tang column, including Pugu Huai'en and the Uighur contingent, marched east from Shanzhou, while Li Guangbi advanced from central Henan and other Tang forces descended from the high country of southeastern Shanxi. The decisive encounter occurred outside of Luoyang in November. The rebel army was smashed, and Shi Chaoyi made his escape eastward with an escort of several hundred light cavalry. As had earlier been promised by the Tang authorities, the Uighurs were permitted to sack the city of Luoyang; it was reported that the civilian dead numbered in the tens of thousands, and that the fires continued to burn for weeks. Other Tang units plundered the surrounding prefectures mercilessly for several months on the grounds that they were "rebel territory."[71]

This time the rebels were not able to bounce back as they had in 759. The defeat at Luoyang convinced Shi Chaoyi's key subordinates, the generals holding key territories in Hebei and northeastern Henan, that both Shi and the rebellion were finished. One by one, these generals turned against their chief and refused to give him refuge. In a display of the "bandwagoning" behavior so often seen in China's civil wars, they now sought to make the best deal they could with the victors. The Tang court, for its part, was more than willing to accommodate the rebel generals in order to bring the long and bloody rebellion to a quick and inexpensive conclusion. Pugu Huai'en, the general commanding the pursuit into Hebei, allowed those rebel commanders who submitted to retain control of both their territories and their armies. This strategy evidently had the full blessing of the court, since the ex-rebels were soon formally installed as Tang military governors. And it was entirely successful in isolating Shi Chaoyi, who was hounded to his death on the northern frontier of Hebei at the beginning of 763. Shi's suicide marked the end of the rebellion that had been launched by An Lushan in 755.[72]

Notes

1 Liu's memorial can be found in *Jiu Tang shu*, ch. 84, pp. 2792–4.
2 Sima Guang, *Zizhi tongjian*, ch. 201, p. 6364; also see Christopher I. Beckwith, *The Tibetan Empire in Central Asia* (Princeton, N.J.: Princeton University Press, 1987), pp. 35–6.
3 Sima Guang, *Zizhi tongjian*, ch. 202, p. 6385.
4 *Jiu Tang shu*, ch. 84, p. 2795; *Xin Tang shu*, ch. 108, p. 4084; and Lei Jiaji, "Cong zhanlue fazhan kan Tang chao jiedu tizhi de chuangjian," *Jiandu xuebao*, 8 (November 1979), pp. 234–5, 240, and 249–50. Also see Edwin G. Pulleyblank, *The Background of the Rebellion of An Lu-shan* (London: Oxford University Press, 1955), p. 68, and Kang Le, *Tangdai qianqi de bianfang*, pp. 158, 175–7, 191–2.

5　Kikuchi Hideo, "Setsudoshisei kakuritsu izen ni okeru 'gun' seido no tenkai," *Tōyō gakuho*, 44 (1961), pp. 62–8.

6　Sima Guang, *Zizhi tongjian*, ch. 213, p. 6797; *Jiu Tang shu*, ch. 199B, p. 5353.

7　Kikuchi Hideo, "Fuhei seido no tenkai," p. 426; Tang Geng'ou, "Tangdai qianqi de bingmu," p. 167; Zhang Guogang, *Tangdai zhengzhi zhidu yanjiu lunji*, p. 36.

8　Kikuchi, "Fuhei seido no tenkai," p. 426; Tang Geng'ou, "Tangdai qianqi de bingmu," p. 167; Sun Jimin, *Tangdai xingjun zhidu yanjiu*, p. 103.

9　Zhang Guogang, *Tangdai zhengzhi zhidu yanjiu lunji*, pp. 37–8.

10　Kikuchi, "Fuhei seido no tenkai," p. 435.

11　Wang Pu (comp.), *Tang huiyao* (Beijing: Zhonghua shuju, 1990), ch. 85, pp. 1560–1; Sima Guang, *Zizhi tongjian*, ch. 205, p. 6507, and Hino Kaisaburō, "Dai Tō fuheisei jidai no danketsu hei ni tsuite," *Hōseishi kenkyū*, 5 (1954), pp. 79–133.

12　Kurihara Masuo, "Fuheisei no hōkai to shin heishu," *Shigaku zasshi*, 73 (1964), p. 128.

13　D. C. Twitchett, *Financial Administration under the T'ang Dynasty*, second edition (Cambridge: Cambridge University Press, 1971), pp. 9–17; Kurihara, "Fuheisei no hōkai to shin heishu," pp. 125–32.

14　*Xin Tang shu*, ch. 50, p. 1327; *Tang huiyao*, ch. 72, p. 1299; Gu Jiguang, *Fubing zhidu kaoshi*, pp. 230–3.

15　Tang Geng'ou, "Tangdai qianqi de bingmu," pp. 169–70; *Cefu yuangui*, ch. 124, p. 19a; *Tang da zhaoling ji*, ch. 2, p. 7.

16　*Tang da zhaoling ji*, ch. 107, p. 553. The edict does not indicate the nature or amount of the award. Another source tells us that *fubing* who elected to remain on the border for a second three-year tour received twenty lengths of hemp cloth; see Wang Yinglin, *Yu hai*, ch. 138, p. 21b.

17　For an overview of the economic conditions during this period, see Pulleyblank, *Background of the Rebellion of An Lu-shan*, ch. 3.

18　Zhang Guogang, "Tangdai de jian'er zhi," pp. 100–1.

19　*Cefu yuangui*, ch. 124, p. 21b, supplemented with information from Li Linfu et al., *Tang liudian* (Tokyo: Hiroike gakuen jigyōbu, 1973), ch. 5, p. 18b.

20　Sima Guang, *Zizhi tongjian*, ch. 214, p. 6832.

21　Zhang Guogang, "Tangdai de jian'er zhi," p. 102; *Jiu Tang shu*, ch. 107, p. 3262; Sima Guang, *Zizhi tongjian*, ch. 216, pp. 6906–7, and ch. 217, pp. 6926–7.

22　See, for example, Zhang Guogang, *Tangdai zhengzhi zhidu yanjiu lunji*, pp. 93–112; Kang Le, *Tangdai qianqi de bianfang*, pp. 162–4; and Zhang Qun, *Tangdai fanjiang yanjiu*, pp. 229, 235–8, and 243–6.

23　Variants of the list can be found in *Jiu Tang shu*, ch. 38, pp. 1385–9; Sima Guang, *Zizhi tongjian*, ch. 215, pp. 6847–51; *Tong dian*, ch. 172, pp. 4479–83; and Li Jifu, *Yuanhe junxian tuzhi* (Beijing: Zhonghua shuju, 1983), ch. 4, p. 92, ch. 13, pp. 361–2, ch. 34, p. 886, ch. 39, pp. 991–2, and ch. 40, p. 1018. The numerous minor discrepancies are discussed in Tang Changru, *Tang shu bingzhi jianzheng* (Beijing: Kexue chubanshe, 1957), pp. 34–7, and Cen Zhongmian, *Tongjian Sui Tang ji bi shi zhiyi* (Beijing: Zhonghua shuju, 1964), pp. 210–19.

24　Tang Changru, *Tang shu bingzhi jianzheng*, pp. 33, 42.

25　Pulleyblank, *The Background of the Rebellion of An Lu-shan*, pp. 149–52, n. 2.

26　Robert des Rotours, "Les Grandes fonctionnaires des provinces en Chine sous la dynastie des T'ang," *T'oung Pao*, 25 (1927), pp. 283–5, 297–301.

27　*Jiu Tang shu*, ch. 97, pp. 3052–4; *Xin Tang shu*, ch. 125, pp. 4407–9.

28　*Jiu Tang shu*, ch. 106, pp. 3239–40; Pulleyblank, *Background of the Rebellion of An Lu-shan*, pp. 94–5.

29　For Xuanzong's military predilections, see Du You, *Tong dian*, ch. 148, p. 3780.

30　*Jiu Tang shu*, ch. 104, pp. 3211–13; also see Pulleyblank, *Background of the Rebellion of An Lu-shan*, p. 11.

31 Pulleyblank, *Background of the Rebellion of An Lu-shan*, pp. 9–13, 18–19, 20–2, 83–4, and 165, n. 62.

32 For more detailed treatment of the military qualification examinations, see *Xin Tang shu*, ch. 44, p. 1170; this is translated by Robert des Rotours in *Traité des examens* (Paris: Librairie Ernest Leroux, 1932), pp. 209–12; Kao Ming-shih, "Tangdai de wuju yu wumiao," in *Di yi jie guoji Tangdai xueshu huiyi lunwenji* (Taipei: Zhonghua minguo Tangdai xuezhe lianyihui, 1989), pp. 1017, 1020–4; and O'Byrne, "Civil–Military Relations During the Middle T'ang: The Career of Kuo Tzu-i," pp. 20–7, 288. The edict establishing the examinations is mentioned in Sima Guang, *Zizhi tongjian*, ch. 207, p. 6558, and *Tang huiyao*, ch. 59, p. 1030.

33 The only graduate whose name is known to us is the great general Guo Ziyi, a prefect's son who rose to command the Shuofang army during the An Lushan rebellion. See *Jiu Tang shu*, ch. 120, p. 3449, and Kao Ming-shih, "Tangdai de wuju yu wumiao," pp. 1034, 1037.

34 Kao Ming-shih, "Tangdai de wuju yu wumiao," p. 1032. O'Byrne ("Civil–Military Relations," pp. 292–4) calculates that 21 percent of the men who served as military governors between 755 and 779 had risen from the ranks. Most would have begun their military careers before 755.

35 Sima Guang, *Zizhi tongjian*, ch. 217, p. 6929; also see *Jiu Tang shu*, ch. 200A, p. 5369.

36 Sima Guang, *Zizhi tongjian*, ch. 215, pp. 6884–6. Also see Gao's biography in *Jiu Tang shu*, ch. 104, pp. 3203–5, and Twitchett, "Hsüan-tsung (reign 712–56)," pp. 430–3.

37 See Pulleyblank, *Background of the Rebellion of An Lu-shan*, pp. 19–23 and ch. 7.

38 Du You, *Tong dian*, ch. 148, p. 3780.

39 Sima Guang, *Zizhi tongjian*, ch. 216, pp. 6906–7; ch. 217, p. 6927.

40 Sima Guang, *Zizhi tongjian*, ch. 216, pp. 6908–9; Pulleyblank, *Background of the Rebellion of An Lu-shan*, p. 98.

41 The Chinese account of the battle can be found in Sima Guang, *Zizhi tongjian*, ch. 216, pp. 6907–8. The Arab accounts are translated in D. M. Dunlop, "A New Source of Information on the Battle of Talas or Atlakh," *Ural-Altaische Jahrbücher*, 36 (1964), pp. 326–30. The exact site of the battle is not known, but is surely very close to what is now the border of Kyrgystan and Kazakhstan south of the town of Dzambul.

42 Du You, *Tong dian*, ch. 148, p. 3780. The exact level of remuneration for *jian'er* in this period is not recorded. One source indicates that after 755 the standard rate for regular troops may have been twelve lengths of cloth and 7.2 *shi* of grain per annum. See Li Quan, *Taibai yinjing*, ch. 5, pp. 558, 561.

43 Kikuchi Hideo, "Tōdai heibo no seikaku to meishō to ni tsuite," *Shien*, 68 (May 1956), pp. 88, 98.

44 Twitchett, *Financial Administration*, p. 86.

45 See Denis Twitchett, "Lands under State Cultivation under the T'ang," *Journal of the Economic and Social History of the Orient*, 2 (1959), pp. 152–203.

46 See Jonathan K. Skaff, "Barbarians at the Gates? The Tang Frontier Military and the An Lushan Rebellion," *War and Society*, 18.2 (October 2000), pp. 33–4.

47 Zhang Guogang, "Tangdai jianjun zhidu kaolun," *Zhongguo shi yanjiu*, 1981, No. 2, pp. 122–4.

48 *Jiu Tang shu*, ch. 104, pp. 3204, 3206; Pulleyblank, *Background of the Rebellion of An Lu-shan*, p. 74.

49 For the palace armies, see *Tang huiyao*, ch. 72, pp. 1293, 1300; *Jiu Tang shu*, ch. 50, pp. 1326–7; Hamaguchi, "Fuhei seido yori shin heisei e," pp. 1498–500; and Pulleyblank, *Background of the Rebellion of An Lu-shan*, p. 67.

50 For An's relationships with Li and Yang, and associated political maneuverings, see Twitchett, "Hsüan-tsung," pp. 427–52.
51 Sima Guang, *Zizhi tongjian*, ch. 217, pp. 6934–5.
52 *Xin Tang shu*, ch. 225A, p. 6414; Kurihara Masuo, "Tō Godai no karifushi teki ketsugo no seikaku," *Shigaku zasshi*, 62 (1953), pp. 520–3.
53 Twitchett, "Hsüan-tsung," p. 448; Sima Guang, *Zizhi tongjian*, ch. 217, pp. 6923–4.
54 O'Byrne, "Civil–Military Relations during the Middle T'ang," p. 69.
55 Li Shu-t'ung, "Tangdai de ma yu jiaotong," in idem, *Tang shi yanjiu* (Taipei: Taiwan Commercial Press, 1979), p. 326.
56 For these events, see Sima Guang, *Zizhi tongjian*, ch. 217, pp. 6935–40, 6942; *Jiu Tang shu*, ch. 104, pp. 3206, 3209–11.
57 Sima Guang, *Zizhi tongjian*, ch. 217, pp. 6943–4; Twitchett, "Hsüan-tsung," p. 448.
58 Edwin G. Pulleyblank, "The An Lu-shan Rebellion and the Origins of Chronic Militarism in Late T'ang China," in John Curtis Perry and Bardwell L. Smith (eds.), *Essays on T'ang Society* (Leiden: E. J. Brill, 1976), p. 41.
59 Sima Guang, *Zizhi tongjian*, ch. 217, pp. 6954–5.
60 Sima Guang, *Zizhi tongjian*, ch. 218, pp. 6966–9.
61 For more information on these events, see Twitchett, "Hsüan-tsung," pp. 460–1.
62 David A. Graff, "Meritorious Cannibal: Chang Hsün's Defense of Sui-yang and the Exaltation of Loyalty in an Age of Rebellion," *Asia Major* (3rd series), 8.1 (1995), pp. 1–15. For Yingchuan and Nanyang, see *Jiu Tang shu*, ch. 114, p. 3365.
63 Pulleyblank, "The An Lu-shan Rebellion and the Origins of Chronic Militarism," p. 43, and Charles A. Peterson, "Court and Province in Mid- and Late T'ang," in Denis Twitchett (ed.) *The Cambridge History of China*, vol. 3, p. 479; the assassination is described in Sima Guang, *Zizhi tongjian*, ch. 219, pp. 7011–12.
64 Sima Guang, *Zizhi tongjian*, ch. 220, p. 7032.
65 Sima Guang, *Zizhi tongjian*, ch. 220, pp. 7033–4.
66 Sima Guang, *Zizhi tongjian*, ch. 220, p. 7040.
67 For explanations of this hiatus in military operations, see Peterson, "Court and Province," p. 480, and Pulleyblank, "The An Lu-shan Rebellion and the Origins of Chronic Militarism," pp. 54–5.
68 Sima Guang, *Zizhi tongjian*, ch. 220, pp. 7061–2; Pulleyblank, "The An Lu-shan Rebellion and the Origins of Chronic Militarism," p. 45.
69 Sima Guang, *Zishi tongjian*, ch. 221, pp. 7069–70; Pulleyblank, "The An Lu-shan Rebellion and the Origins of Chronic Militarism," pp. 45, 55.
70 Sima Guang, *Zizhi tongjian*, ch. 221, pp. 7081–3; Pulleyblank, "The An Lu-shan Rebellion and the Origins of Chronic Militarism," p. 45.
71 Sima Guang, *Zizhi tongjian*, ch. 222, pp. 7133–5.
72 Sima Guang, *Zizhi tongjian*, ch. 222, pp. 7135–40; Peterson, "Court and Province," pp. 483–4; Pulleyblank, "The An Lu-shan Rebellion and the Origins of Chronic Militarism," pp. 46–7.

CHAPTER ELEVEN

Consequences of the
An Lushan rebellion

In November of 763, scarcely a year after the termination of the great rebellion, a large Tibetan army suddenly advanced against the Tang capital of Chang'an. Descending rapidly into the Wei River valley from the northwest, the Tibetans defeated an inferior Tang force at Zhouzhi, about thirty miles west of the capital, on November 12. The very next day the emperor (now Daizong, who had succeeded his father Suzong in the middle of 762) decamped for the relatively safe haven of Shanzhou, on the road to Luoyang. On November 18 the Tibetans entered the city and installed an elderly cousin of Daizong on the imperial throne. They proceeded to plunder the palace and the city, setting fires as they went. Dispersed Tang troops took the opportunity to join in the looting, while much of the populace sought refuge in the hills to the south of the city. The Tibetans were not, however, in a position that was tenable for the long term. Recalled from retirement to deal with the crisis, the great loyalist general Guo Ziyi rallied Tang troops at Shangzhou and moved on Chang'an from the southeast by way of the Wu Pass, while other Tang commanders brought their troops down from the prefectures immediately to the north of the Wei River valley. With Tang forces gathering around them, the Tibetans evacuated the city on November 30, dragging a large number of women, scholars, and craftsmen into captivity, but abandoning their puppet emperor of twelve days to his fate. The capital was secured by Tang troops in December, and Daizong returned to his palace early in 764.[1]

The temporary loss of Chang'an was a dramatic indicator of the extent to which Tang power had been diminished by the An Lushan rebellion. The immediate opening for the Tibetan advance was created by the defection of a key fortress guarding the valley of the Jing River, but the groundwork had been prepared over the course of several years. As veteran Tang troops were recalled from the western frontier to be thrown into the struggle against the rebels, the ambitious Tibetan ruler Khri-srong-lde-brtsan threw his forces against the greatly weakened Chinese defenses. Each year, more towns fell to the Tibetans. Most of the Longyou region was eventually overrun, and the frontier shifted more than 150 miles to the east. Even after the Tibetans retreated from the Tang capital in 763, they remained entrenched on the headwaters of the Wei and Jing rivers, still within striking distance of Chang'an.[2] The areas north and west of the capital were disturbed by Tibetan incursions throughout the the 760s and 770s, and the threat would not be removed until the collapse of the Tibetan state in the middle of the ninth century.

The Tibetan advance was significant not only because of the prolonged threat to the capital region, but also because it engulfed the pasture lands where most of the Tang government's horses had been bred in the years before the An Lushan rebellion. The imperial herds had counted 325,700 horses in 754.[3] After the rebellion, however, government armies were often short of horses, and frontier commanders complained that their meager cavalry forces were hopelessly outnumbered by those of the Tibetans.[4] This was an important and lasting cause of Tang military weakness, not only vis-à-vis the Tibetans and other Inner Asian peoples, but also against the various military governors who had been able to carve out autonomous and semi-autonomous domains in the interior of the empire during the course of the great rebellion.[5]

It was fortunate for the Tang empire that the Uighurs, the dominant power on the northern steppe from the 740s until their overthrow by Kirghiz invaders in 840, had no interest in acquiring Chinese territory. On occasion, as in 757 and 762, Uighur rulers even took action to support the Tang court. Their stance, however, seems to have been shaped by ruthless self-interest rather than real friendship. For them, the Chinese agrarian economy was a resource to be exploited. This exploitation took the form of a frontier trade in which Uighur horses were exchanged for Chinese silk. The animals surrendered by the Uighurs were often small, weak, or unhealthy, and the prices demanded were exorbitant – as much as forty lengths of silk for a single horse. In view of their relative weakness, the Chinese had little choice but to accept these terms, and to overlook the many acts of violence committed by Uighur visitors to Chang'an. In the 840s, after the collapse of the qaghanate, Tang military power would be turned against the Uighur remnants on the steppe frontier; within China, Uighur residents and the Sogdian merchants who had traded under Uighur protection were subjected to savage persecution.[6]

From the An Lushan rebellion to the end of the Tang dynasty in the early years of the tenth century, despite the Tibetan pressure and occasional friction with the Uighurs, China's military power was for the most part absorbed in internal conflicts. The rebellion had been made possible by the establishment of powerful, potentially autonomous military commands on the frontiers, and its suppression had in turn brought about the transplantation of the frontier model into the interior of the empire. Not only were the surrendered rebel generals in Hebei permitted to retain control of their armies and territories, but many new regional military commands had been hastily set up to arrest the progress of the rebels in the earlier stages of the conflict. Their commanders were granted the authority to requisition manpower and provisions from these territorial bases in order to maintain their armies in the field.[7] When the rebellion was over, the new military provinces remained as more or less permanent features of the political landscape. The ex-rebels and their successors ran largely autonomous warlord regimes that appointed their own officials, paid no taxes to the center, and had to be held in check by strong loyalist forces stationed nearby. For this reason alone the new military commands in the interior became indispensable. But many of the loyalist provinces also displayed autonomous tendencies, and some – most notably Pinglu in what is now Shandong province and Huaixi in south-central Henan – came to differ very little from the former rebels in Hebei.

The turbulent years from 755 to 763 saw the number of military provinces increase from the original ten frontier commands to approximately forty, most of which were located in the interior of the empire. These territories ranged in size from two or three prefectures to as many as fifteen.[8] Some were headed by military governors (*jiedushi*) who usually held concurrent authority as civil governors (*guanchashi*), others by civil governors who also held local military authority as "chief commissioner for military training" or "chief defense commissioner."[9] In almost all of the provinces, both civil and military authority resided in the same individual.

There were significant differences among the provinces both in their level of militarization and their basic orientation toward the Tang court. Representing one extreme were the ex-rebel provinces of Hebei: Wei-Bo in the south along the Yellow River; Chengde at the mouth of the Jingxing Pass in central Hebei; and Youzhou with its headquarters at Fanyang on the northern frontier, the old base of An Lushan. (A fourth rebel province, Zhaoyi in the southwestern corner of Hebei, had switched to the loyalist camp in 775 after losing much of its territory to aggression by Wei-Bo.) They were armed to the teeth, paid little more than lip service to imperial authority, and insisted on the right of hereditary succession to the office of military governor. Although it had been founded by forces that fought on the side of the court during the An Lushan rebellion (and drew its name from the old frontier command in southern Manchuria where its men had originally been based), the Pinglu command in today's Shandong was also a member of this group until its dismemberment in 819. Inheriting the ethnically mixed character of the old frontier armies, some of these military provinces were led by men of non-Chinese origin. The pattern was most pronounced in Chengde, which was established by a rebel general of Xi origin named Li Baochen. In 782 Li's son was overthrown by his principal cavalry commander, a Khitan named Wang Wujun whose descendants continued to rule the province until 820. In 821 power was seized by an officer of Uighur origin whose heirs were still ruling the province at the beginning of the tenth century.[10] Pinglu was in the hands of a Korean dynasty from 765 to 819, and Youzhou was ruled by Uighur generals for ten years in the second half of the ninth century.[11] It should be noted, however, that the ordinary people of these territories were overwhelmingly of Han Chinese stock, and the behavior of the "barbarian" rulers of Chengde and Pinglu differed little from that of the members of the Chinese Tian family who governed Wei-Bo.

Facing these recalcitrant provinces along a confrontation line in Shanxi and Henan was a string of loyalist provinces which maintained very powerful military forces: Hedong, Ze-Lu (the remnants of Zhaoyi), Bian-Song, and Xuzhou. The military provinces in Henan were especially sensitive for the Tang court because they guarded the Bian Canal, the principal route for tax and tribute revenues from the rich lower Yangzi region and therefore the financial and logistical lifeline of the government. These provinces normally accepted court appointees – including civil officials as well as military men – but some were especially prone to coups and mutinies, and there were occasionally open rebellions against imperial authority, as in Bian-Song in 777 and Ze-Lu in the early 840s. Another group of heavily militarized provinces was located to the north and west of the capital. Their primary responsibility was to protect Chang'an from the Tibetans, who were in the habit of launching attacks in the autumn when their horses were in top condition after spring and summer grazing. Since these provinces were located in close proximity to the seat of imperial authority and were, moreover, dependant on supplies brought up from the south and channeled through the capital, they were relatively easy to control – until the last years of the dynasty, when central armies no longer existed to hold them in check. In contrast to North China, the rich provinces of the south that provided the economic basis for imperial power were only lightly garrisoned. Their governors tended to be civil officials, and rebellions in this region were rare occurrences.[12]

Provincial armies varied greatly in size. The largest military establishments were found in the most independent of the northern regional commands, which possessed rich, populous territories and had to be on constant guard against the forcible reassertion of central authority. Pinglu, the largest of all, maintained an army of 100,000 men, and Wei-Bo followed closely with perhaps 70,000. Chengde had about 50,000.[13] Some of the loyalist armies in the north were also extremely large; the army of Bian-Song, positioned to confront Pinglu, itself approached 100,000 men in the late eighth century.[14] In the south, however, it was a very different situation. In 859, for example, the provincial governor of Zhedong (eastern Zhejiang) had only a few hundred troops at his disposal.[15] Most provincial military establishments were some-where between these extremes, perhaps 15,000 men in the late 770s. The center imposed upper limits on these forces, but such limits were easily circumvented and sometimes ignored altogether.[16]

The armies of the military governors, and especially those of the large northern provinces, had complex command structures and were split into several distinct components. The main army in each province was concen-trated at the prefectural city that served as the headquarters of the military governor. Divided into several large units under troop commanders (*bing ma shi*), it was by far the largest force in the province and formed the nucleus of its field army in the event of war.[17] In addition to the main army, a provincial governor's forces also included a number of outlying garrisons. These were deliberately kept small, seldom exceeding 2000 men, so as not to pose a threat to the authority of the governor. Garrisons were positioned to defend prefectural cities and other strategic points in the province, including mountain passes, river crossings, and locations of economic importance such as salt pans and rural markets. Garrisons normally occupied fortified positions, ranging from walled towns to earthworks and palisades, and dense networks of small forts were the key to the defense of some of the autonomous military provinces.[18] Local forces commanded by the prefects were the third component of the late Tang provincial armies. Prefects were primarily civil administrators, but had military leadership thrust on them during the An Lushan rebellion; from 756 it became usual for prefects to serve concurrently as militia training commissioners.[19] While the men of the main army and the outlying armies were full-time professional soldiers of the *jian'er* type, prefectural forces tended to be made up of militiamen who supported themselves by farming, received periodic training during the winter slack season, and rendered part-time military service in exchange for exemption from taxes and corvée. When called to duty, they were employed primarily in defensive roles in their home areas. They provided military governors with a valuable supplement to their regular troops, but the regulars were the largest and most important component of all of the strong northern armies.[20]

The tripartite force structure of main army, outlying garrisons, and prefectural forces was intended to guarantee the authority of the military governor within his own province without compromising its defense against external threats. Outlying garrisons dominated the prefectures, while the main army was in most cases more than sufficient for dealing with a rebellious garrison.[21] The ultimate guarantee of a governor's power was his main army, but this was also the weak point in the system. Its soldiers enjoyed better pay and more privileges than the men of other units, but this by no means assured their loyalty. In many provinces these forces became known for their arrogance and unruliness; they developed praetorian tendencies, were easily manipulated by ambitious officers, and often drove out unpopular governors and replaced them with men more to their liking. All this was especially true of the elite headquarters units that formed the innermost core of the provincial army and provided the immediate guard for the governor's headquarters. The classic example is the Wei-Bo "headquarters guard" (*yajun*), an elite corps that had been formed by that province's first military governor, Tian Chengsi. The men of this force, originally 5000 strong, were chosen for their size and strength; they were much better rewarded than the rest of the army, and membership eventually became a hereditary privilege that was passed from father to son. Extremely jealous of their privileges, they came to dominate the politics of Wei-Bo in the ninth century and intervened to install military governors of their own choosing in 812, 822, 829, 870, 883, and 888. After narrowly

Map 20 Tang provinces in AD 785

surviving an unsuccessful coup attempt in 905, the then military governor, Luo Shaowei, arranged the massacre of the entire headquarters guard with the assistance of a strong force sent by his ally, the Bianzhou warlord Zhu Quanzhong.[22]

Massacres of this sort were, however, a last resort. The usual, and, by the middle of the ninth century, almost universal response of military governors to the threat posed by their headquarters garrisons was to hold them in check by creating new bodyguard units composed of personal retainers. Known variously as "private troops," "intimate troops," or "household troops," these forces were often formed from the household servants and slaves of the military governor, reinforced by fugitives from justice and other desperadoes who had sought his protection. Such forces varied in size. In 784 the rebellious Youzhou military governor Zhu Tao was reported to have no less than 10,000 private retainers, amounting to one-sixth of his army, but private forces of a few hundred or perhaps one or two thousand men were much more common.[23]

Though seldom a match for the headquarters garrison in numbers, they insulated the military governor from pressures that might be brought to bear by his unruly soldiery and provided him with a reliable corps of military police. The loyalty of private retainers was sometimes reinforced through the establishment of fictive kinship ties, with military governors recognizing key subordinates or even entire units as their adopted sons.[24]

Fictive kinship and the private retainer corps were only two of the many tools employed by military governors to maintain control of their armies and provinces. They also exploited real kinship ties by appointing close relatives to key command positions and forming marriage alliances with the families of important subordinates. Prudent military governors made sure that the officers and regular troops of the provincial army were generously rewarded, and the elite headquarters guard units and private retainer groups were rewarded most generously of all. Coercion also had a role to play. Family members of outlying garrison commanders were sometimes held hostage at the governor's head-quarters, and spies and informers found ample employment.[25] One of the most important officers on a military governor's staff was the provost marshal (*duyuhou*), responsible for maintaining military discipline and ferreting out disloyalty.[26] Such measures were essential to the security of the more independent of the military governors, who were in an especially vulnerable position insofar as they could not assume that they would always enjoy the prestige of court-bestowed appointment to help them keep their armies under control.[27]

Just as the military governors were faced with the problem of maintaining control over their forces, the principal political–military challenge confronting the Tang court for more than a century after the suppression of the An Lushan rebellion was to strengthen central control over the military provinces. A variety of institutions and policies were adopted to this end. The employment of court eunuchs as army supervisors (*jianjunshi*), only haphazardly applied during the pre-rebellion period, was expanded and systematized. Eunuch supervisors were now assigned to almost all of the provincial military commands on a regular basis. These supervisors served for three-year terms. They had their own administrative and clerical staff, and some of them brought armed retinues that could be as large as several thousand men. The army supervisor was supposed to be equal to the governor in status. While the governor exercised command authority, the supervisor's job was to keep the court informed of developments in the garrison and to act as necessary to put down mutinies and prevent rebellion.[28] Another tool of control was a rebuilt and greatly enlarged Imperial Palace Army based in and around Chang'an. The nucleus of this force was the Shence ("inspired strategy") Army, a veteran frontier unit that had been redeployed to fight the An Lushan rebels. The Imperial Palace Army quickly came under the administrative and operational control of senior court eunuchs, and eventually grew to number more than 150,000 men.[29] It helped to defend the northwestern frontier against Tibetan incursions, served as a deterrent to potential rebels, and reduced the court's dangerous dependence on the "loyal" provincial armies. From the 760s until its destruction in 880 during the Huang Chao rebellion, the Imperial Palace Army was the mainstay of central military power and an important factor contributing to the survival of the dynasty. At the same time, however, it also enabled the eunuchs to dominate court politics – even to the point of manipulating the imperial succession in the first half of the ninth century.[30]

The increased power and prominence of eunuchs as provincial army supervisors and Imperial Palace Army controllers were in part a reflection of the court's distrust of military men in the wake of the An Lushan rebellion. The reassertion of civilian control over the military became one of the central goals of the Tang government, and military leaders who had made their careers entirely within the military establishment came to be regarded with deep suspicion. During the half-century after 755, the court's relations with its generals were often badly strained. Guo Ziyi, a figure of exemplary loyalty and one of the government's most successful generals, was not entrusted with a field command during the last three years of the rebellion. Guo's Shuofang colleague Li Guangbi fell under suspicion shortly before his death in 764. Lai Tian, who had won the sobriquet "Bite-Iron" during his stubborn defense of Yingchuan against An Lushan's men, was denounced by eunuchs and forced to commit suicide at the beginning of 763. During this same period in 763–4, Pugu Huai'en – architect of the Uighur alliance and pacifier of the Hebei rebels – was badgered into rebellion by a cabal of military rivals and hostile eunuchs. The pattern was repeated during the civil war of the early 780s, when suspicion and misunderstanding pushed yet another Shuofang general, Li Huaiguang, to the brink of revolt.[31]

With political reliability now the paramount consideration in selecting military leaders, important commands were often entrusted to civil officials or eunuchs rather than experienced generals. Pei Du, who directed the successful military operations against the rebellious province of Huaixi in 814–15, was a literary examination graduate who had served as investigating censor, court diarist, president of the Censorate, and vice-president of the Chancellery before he was given overall command of the field armies in Henan.[32] Wherever local circumstances permitted, the court preferred to appoint civil bureaucrats to serve as military governors. In response to the enhanced power and autonomy of the empire's military elites in the post-rebellion period, there were new assertions of the fitness of scholars and civil officials for military command. The historical writing of the late Tang and the succeeding Five Dynasties period (907–60) offers many examples of civil officials who were able to beat the military men at their own game. One such man was Wang Jin, who held several military governorships during the 770s and brought the unruly Hedong garrison to heel by executing several insubordinate troop commanders who had scorned him as a mere scholar.[33] Another was Xin Mi, a prefect who put down a local rebellion in the southeast at the beginning of the ninth century.[34] Where the early Tang idea of military command had emphasized personal leadership on the battlefield, the post-rebellion period gave more attention to strategic acumen, administrative talent, and understanding of human relations as attributes of the successful general: "In antiquity, those who were considered famous generals had no need of the ability to fight in the front rank, or the strength to wrestle with tigers and bears. What is important is that one begins and ends with righteousness, and succeeds through one's skill at making plans."[35]

Eunuch supervisors, imperial appointment of military governors, and – as a last resort – the power of the Imperial Palace Army served to keep most of the "loyal" provinces obedient to the center most of the time. These devices, however, were largely inapplicable to the autonomous, heavily militarized provinces in Hebei and Shandong, which claimed the right of hereditary succession to the office of military governor. In its dealings with these hard-case provinces the court was normally content to pursue a policy of "indulgence," routinely bestowing the title of *jiedushi* on local dynasts who were willing to uphold the façade of imperial unity by paying lip service to the authority of the emperor. Concerned primarily with maintaining control over their own provinces and armies, these military governors were seldom interested in challenging the status quo. It was only when the court attempted to deprive them of their accustomed autonomy that they rose in open rebellion. The first large-scale revolt came in the early 780s. A vigorous young emperor, Dezong, came to the throne in 779 determined to reassert central authority over the autonomous provinces. When the military governor of Chengde died in 781, Dezong refused to recognize his heir as the new *jiedushi*. This precipitated a revolt in which Chengde was supported by Wei-Bo and Pinglu. Youzhou, however, sided with the court, and for a brief period at the beginning of 782 it appeared that Dezong's intransigence would be crowned with success. After repeated defeats by the armies of Youzhou, the leader of Chengde was overthrown by one of his generals, the Khitan Wang Wujun, who made his submission to the imperial court. At this point, however, both Wang and the Youzhou military governor Zhu Tao were disappointed with the rewards they had received from the court and rebelled in unison in the spring of 782. Dezong now faced a united front of all the northeastern provinces, and the situation deteriorated even further at the end of the year when Li Xilie, the military governor of Huaixi in south-central Henan who had previously been in the government's camp, decided to launch his own rebellion. Li cut the Bian Canal, and the court was soon hard-pressed both financially and militarily.[36]

On November 2, 783, troops from the northwestern frontier province of Jing-Yuan, passing through Chang'an on their way to the battlefront in Henan, rioted when they found that the government was giving them only a fraction of the bounty normally paid to soldiers setting out on a campaign. Joined by an urban mob embittered by the special exactions that had been imposed to support the war effort, the Jing-Yuan troops stormed and plundered the palace and took control of the capital. Their former commander Zhu Ci (the elder brother of the Youzhou military governor Zhu Tao) emerged from retirement to lead them. Dezong fled to the town of Fengtian, some fifty miles northwest of Chang'an, where he was besieged by the mutineers for more than a month before he was rescued by government forces hastily recalled from the campaign in Hebei.[37] The emperor's fortunes improved in 784. An offer of amnesty, recognition, and restoration of the status quo ante persuaded Wang Wujun to turn against Zhu Tao, who was preparing to lead a large army westward to support his brother in Guanzhong. Wang joined forces with a loyalist army from Shanxi to inflict a decisive defeat on Zhu Tao near Beizhou in central Hebei on May 29, 784.[38] Chang'an was recovered three weeks later, though the last of the rebel leaders, Li Xilie, was not eliminated until 786 – poisoned by one of his subordinates who brought Huaixi back to nominal allegiance to the Tang court. All but one of the provinces that had been in rebellion at one time or another between 781 and 786 managed to retain their independence; their leaders were once again recognized as *jiedushi* in return for their nominal obeisance to imperial authority. More than ten years passed before Dezong was again willing to risk offensive action against a recalcitrant province, waging a relatively restrained (and unsuccessful) war against Huaixi in 799–800.

The status quo ante was restored so easily because the ambitions of most of the autonomous provincial military leaders did not extend beyond holding on to their own territories, armies, and customary privileges, and at most increasing their domains by small increments at the expense of their immediate neighbors. Leaders with empire-wide ambitions, such as Zhu Tao of Youzhou, were relatively rare, and Zhu died of natural causes soon after his defeat at Beizhou. There was a general tendency to form coalitions against whoever happened to represent the greatest threat to the existing order. When the young emperor Dezong, determined to crush the autonomy of the provincial leaders, was the principal threat to the status quo, he was opposed by an alliance of several provinces. When a string of successes by government forces made the restoration of centralized imperial rule appear probable, Zhu Tao, hitherto a supporter of the court, switched sides and threw in his lot with the rebels. By 784, in the wake of the Jing-Yuan mutiny, it was no longer Dezong but Zhu Tao who seemed to be the rising menace. At this juncture Zhu was abandoned by his allies, who joined forces with the loyalists to deal him a crushing defeat. The long-lasting equilibrium that existed between the autonomous provinces and the Tang court has long been remarked by Chinese scholars. The great seventeenth-century thinker Gu Yanwu observed that the Hebei leaders did not dare to threaten the court because of their distrust of one another, while the survival of the court as a powerful external pressure served to maintain the balance among the various provinces and prevent any one of them from subduing the others and emerging as preeminent.[39]

The next great challenge to the equilibrium came from another ambitious, centralizing emperor. This was Dezong's grandson Xianzong, who ruled from 806 to 820. He enjoyed several advantages that Dezong had not had in the

780s, including a full treasury and a much stronger Imperial Palace Army, and with benefit of hindsight he proceeded in a much more circumspect manner, usually concentrating on the subjugation of one recalcitrant province at a time. His reign opened with easy victories over provincial leaders who were reaching for greater autonomy in Sichuan and the lower Yangzi region, and in 809 he was emboldened to attack the much more heavily militarized province of Chengde in central Hebei. This campaign ended in failure, with peace restored in 810, but two years later the military governor of neighboring Wei-Bo chose to surrender his autonomy and place his province at the disposal of the court. Between 815 and 817, Xianzong waged an arduous but ultimately successful campaign against the province of Huaixi in south-central Henan. Government armies totalling 90,000 men – some three times the size of the regular army of Huaixi – surrounded the province but made very little headway for more than two years. They were hindered by a divided command structure, with some twenty small contingents from as many provinces distributed among five separate armies, and by a tenacious defense based on both walled towns and networks of small forts. The campaign was finally brought to a successful conclusion near the end of 817 when Li Su, the commander of one of the five government armies, made a daring and unconventional thrust through the enemy's outer defenses to penetrate the heart of the province. Advancing under cover of darkness and a fortuitous snowstorm, Li was able to achieve complete surprise and capture the all-but-undefended provincial capital and Huaxi's military ruler along with it. The province was soon partitioned among three neighboring loyalist provinces.[40]

A similar fate befell Xianzong's next target, the very large and powerful province of Pinglu in today's Shandong. As government forces massed along its borders in 819, the military governor was killed by his own subordinates. They surrendered to the court, and Pinglu was divided to form three new (and relatively weak) provinces. By the time of Xianzong's death in 820, all of the autonomous provinces – even Chengde – had either been conquered or had submitted voluntarily. This was the zenith of the Tang court's power in the post-755 period, and it lasted only a brief moment. The arrogance of the civil bureaucrats sent to govern Youzhou in 821 quickly antagonized the military men of the province, who were told, "Now that the empire is at peace, fellows like you who can pull a strong bow are not worth as much as someone who can recognize the simplest written character!"[41] In that same year an ill-advised scheme to have the Hebei provinces swap military governors also led to unrest in Wei-Po and Chengde. By the middle of 822 mutinies had occurred in all three provinces and autonomy-minded local military men were back in power. The new emperor lacked his father's ability and drive, and the three provinces were allowed to go their own way after the failure of yet another military campaign aimed at bringing them to heel.[42] They retained their autonomy for the rest of the Tang and on into the Five Dynasties period (907–60) that followed. The other military provinces also remained an important part of the late Tang political landscape, and their loyalty could not always be taken for granted by the center.[43] When the great bandit armies led by Huang Chao swept across China between 875 and 884, it was ultimately the power of the Tang court in Chang'an that suffered the most serious damage. The leaders of the military provinces, on the other hand, gained much greater freedom of action, with the province becoming the key unit of political organization. This situation continued for some time after the fall of the Tang dynasty in 907. As we shall see, the institutions of the Tang military province had a significant and lasting influence on the structure of power in both the Five Dynasties and Northern Song (960–1127).

One of the most obvious consequences of provincial autonomy in the latter half of the Tang period was the pervasive militarization of the empire. There had been perhaps 600,000 soldiers, almost all located on the frontiers, on the eve of the An Lushan rebellion. There were approximately 800,000 in 805, at the beginning of Xianzong's reign, and by the time of his successor the number had grown to nearly a million.[44] The majority of these men were not on the frontiers, but in provincial armies that eyed one another warily in the interior of China. According to one modern estimate, their upkeep cost twenty million strings of cash per annum, amounting to more than two-thirds of the state's total annual revenue.[45] The care and feeding of the provincial army was undoubtedly the single largest item of expenditure for most of the military governors, especially those in North China.[46] As in the years before the outbreak of the rebellion, regular troops were obtained primarily through the enlistment of willing recruits. The greatest reservoir of potential recruits was provided by the landless, desperate, and destitute, and particularly by peasants who were no longer able to wrest a living from the land after the breakdown of the government's land redistribution system and the formation of private estates.[47] Once they entered an army, they became full-time mercenary soldiers who were almost entirely dependant on the pay they received from their commanders in order to sustain both themselves and their families. This pay included a grain ration for the soldier and enough silk or hemp cloth to provide him with outfits of winter and spring clothing, and there might also be allowances of salt, wine, soy sauce, and vinegar. Soldiers also expected to receive grain rations for their dependants.[48] In addition to their regular provisions, soldiers might also receive special rewards of various sorts. There were bonuses of silk cloth for men setting out on campaign, and further rewards followed successes in the field. In some provinces, the soldiers received bonuses at major holidays and on the occasion of the installation of a new military governor.[49] The men of elite headquarters units were especially well rewarded. Those who guarded the governor's yamen at Xuzhou, for example, were treated to daily banquets.[50]

In the professional armies of late Tang, remuneration was the key to loyalty. When an ambitious officer attempted to supplant his military governor, the typical course of action was to bribe the soldiers of the garrison in order to secure their support.[51] Conversely, any reduction of customary rewards and bonuses could easily lead to violent mutiny. The Xuanwu Army, based at Bianzhou on the Grand Canal, was especially known for its turbulence. When an officer named Lu Changyuan took over as acting military governor in 799, he made the mistake of refusing to distribute the customary gift of silk and hemp cloth to the troops. Already unpopular for his strict discipline, Lu was killed, sliced up, and eaten by the enraged soldiery.[52] A modern Chinese historian has counted ninety-nine instances of mutiny in the late Tang provincial armies, with issues of remuneration and reward the most common source of the soldiers' discontent.[53]

The unruly behavior of the late Tang soldiery, with "soldiers bullying the subalterns and subalterns bullying the generals," was a new development in Chinese social and political history. As the eighteenth-century historical commentator Zhao Yi observed, "From the time of Qin and Han and the Six Dynasties there had been rebellious generals but no such thing as rebellious soldiers. After the middle years of the Tang, however, mutinies in the provincial garrisons happened all the time."[54] This development had many causes. Removed from agriculture and gathered in garrison towns, entirely reliant on military service for their livelihood, the soldiers were in a good position to develop a keen sense of corporate identity and collective self-interest – and to strike out violently when they perceived their interests to be threatened. Unlike so many of the fighting men of Wei-Jin and the northern and southern dynasties, they were not members of a semi-servile hereditary status group bound to their commanders by traditional ties of dependence. They must have been keenly aware of the extent to which their generals were reliant on *them* for their survival. And they belonged to a society in which commerce and market transactions were playing an ever-increasing role. Determined to exact the best possible deal for themselves, the professional soldiers of late Tang came to resemble a privileged and parasitic caste. Some units took on a hereditary character as sons followed fathers in the ranks; when a man was killed in battle a son or brother might claim the privilege of inheriting his military status and emoluments.[55] Soldiers were unwilling to give up their rice bowl when they became too old for combat, with the result that in some provincial armies many of the troops were not fit for duty.[56] Attempts at force reduction often led to mutiny, and on those occasions when men were discharged from service they showed a distressing tendency to turn to banditry as their new source of livelihood.[57] The predatory mercenary soldier, essentially a product of the new conditions of late Tang, was part of the Tang legacy to Song and would be a recurring problem in China's later history – including the first half of the twentieth century.

The rise of provincial authority and provincial autonomy in the wake of the An Lushan rebellion had other social and economic consequences that extended far beyond the military. The Tang government, like many of its predecessors, had sought to maintain a very high degree of control over economic activity. The Tang founders had retained the "equal-field" system of land distribution, originally introduced in North China by the Northern Wei dynasty in the last years of the fifth century. Under its terms all farmland was supposed to belong to the state, and was periodically reallocated to rural households on an equitable basis (with a standard allocation for each adult male and supplemental allotments for other family members and dependants). The farm families were in turn responsible for providing the state with corvée labor (or paying a corvée exemption tax), and for paying a standard, fixed amount of annual tax for each taxable adult in the household. Taxes were usually collected in kind, that is, in grain and silk or hemp cloth. There were many additional complexities and actual conditions did not always follow the statutes, but there is ample evidence that the "equal-field" system did not exist only on paper but was actually put into practice during the first half of the Tang dynasty.[58] Commercial activity was also tightly constrained by governmental regulation. In all urban centers from the capital down to the county seats, the authorities established one or several official markets in fixed locations and required that all buying and selling take place within their confines. These markets were closely supervised by government officials, who enforced the use of standard weights and measures, made sure that trading occurred only during specified hours of the day, and determined (and publicly announced) the fair market price for goods and commodities at ten-day intervals.[59] Not all economic activity was subject to official supervision; there were, for example, many small, informal rural markets that were beyond the government's purview. Government control over the possession and use of farmland was also less than complete. Wealthy and powerful families were able to build up large estates by means both legal and illegal, and peasant taxpayers – especially those with inadequate allotments – absconded to become their tenants. This trend was already well underway in the years before the An Lushan rebellion, but the central government's control of the economy was far weaker in the new political landscape that existed after 755.

The new provincial administrations emerged as important economic actors in the post-rebellion period. Many sought to encourage the growth of new centers of trade within their boundaries as new sources of tax revenue that would be firmly under provincial control. Many of the informal, extra-legal rural markets eventually developed into important market towns as decentralization of administrative control promoted "a general increase in economic activity." Another reason that the new political order had a stimulating effect on the economy was because a greater proportion of the tax revenue collected locally was now spent within the provinces in order to support the administrations and armed forces of the military governors.[60] After the An Lushan rebellion, the Tang court lost the ability to enroll, enumerate, and impose taxes directly upon the majority of China's peasant households. This development is dramatically illustrated by the decline of the registered population from approximately nine million households in 755 to less than two million in 760.[61]

Trends already visible before the rebellion were now accelerated as the government lost the ability to control and reallocate land in accordance with the "equal-field" system and a private market in land developed. The obstacles that had once made it difficult (but not impossible) for wealthy families to become estate owners and landlords were now largely removed. At the same time, the post-rebellion political economy created new opportunities for men to acquire wealth that could be invested in landownership. Among the winners were merchants, military officers, men serving on the administrative staffs of the military governors, and officials working for new, specialized bureaucratic agencies such as the Salt and Iron Commission which administered the government's salt monopoly.[62]

The creation of the salt monopoly was as much a consequence of the An Lushan rebellion (and a reflection of the needs of the time) as was the division of the empire into military provinces. With the equal-field system largely moribund and direct taxation no longer an option, the court turned to indirect taxation. The initial moves toward control of salt production and distribution were made between 756 and 758, at the height of the rebellion when the government's need for revenue was acute. The salt monopoly soon became the center's single most important source of revenue, accounting for more than 50 percent of income by 780 (though it became somewhat less important thereafter). Salt was produced by government workers both at suitable sites on the seashore and at inland salt pools, then sold to merchants at an inflated price that was many times the cost of production. The Salt and Iron Commission, which was largely staffed by men from the mercantile world rather than conventional scholarly backgrounds, ran the operation, and its officials enjoyed many opportunities for personal enrichment.[63] The various military provinces similarly held out opportunities for new men to rise in government service and enrich themselves in the process. Military governors generally had the authority to appoint their own staff and subordinates, appointments which were approved automatically by the center. In many cases, their choice fell on soldiers and other men who lacked the education, credentials, social standing, and connections that would have qualified them for government office in the pre-rebellion period. These men often plowed their emoluments (and the proceeds of their peculations) into landownership, and contributed to the formation of the more broadly based, educated, landowning elite stratum from which the officials of the Song dynasty would be recruited by means of the civil service examinations.[64] An "enlarged class of educated landowners" would remain the source of both local power and official recruitment until the last days of the empire, and a more vigorous commercial economy and a free market in land would also be key features of "late imperial China" from Song to Qing.

Not all members of society benefited equally from the developments of late Tang, however. Peasants were heavily taxed to support both the imperial court and the provincial military regimes, and the most hard-pressed were driven to banditry. By the 830s and 840s small bandit gangs were active on the plains of

Henan and pirates were operating on the Yangzi River. In 859 a larger but still localized bandit revolt broke out in coastal Zhejiang and was not suppressed by government forces until the following year. A much more serious uprising broke out in the far southwest in the summer of 868, among troops from one of the Henan garrisons who had been sent there by the court to guard the frontier against the powerful kingdom of Nanzhao (in today's Yunnan). After six years on the frontier – or twice the three-year tour of duty to which they had originally been committed – the men mutinied under the influence of officers who were former bandits. They chose a supply officer named Pang Xun as their leader, marched northward toward their home province on the Bian Canal, and actually succeeded in capturing the provincial capital near the end of 868. Though they were finally crushed in the autumn of 869, the episode did not bode well for the established order. The mutineers had travelled a vast distance through the interior of the empire without being checked by government forces, and cavalry contributed by the Shatuo Turks (who had emerged as an important power on the Mongolian steppe after the fall of the Uighur empire) played a major role in their eventual suppression.[65]

In the early 870s, drought and famine led to an intensification of bandit activity in Henan as desperate peasants swelled the ranks of the roaming gangs. Small groups coalesced into larger forces hundreds strong and began to attack walled cities and fight pitched battles with government troops sent to hunt them down. While the great majority of the bandits surely came from the lowest strata of rural society, many of their leaders were "local strongmen" from families with some wealth and influence in the village community, and some had actually acquired a certain amount of education.[66] Huang Chao, the man who emerged as the dominant bandit leader in 878, was an unsuccessful examination candidate from Caozhou in today's Shandong whose family had become wealthy by selling salt. "Expert at striking with a sword and at mounted archery, he was but superficially instructed in letters, yet possessed verbal eloquence."[67] By the time that Huang took over the leadership, his following was many thousands strong. Between 875 and 878 the bandits had operated between the Yellow River and the Yangzi. Then, under pressure from government forces in the north, Huang led his followers across the Yangzi and marched south to sack the wealthy south seas entrepot of Guangzhou (Canton) in the summer of 879. From there he moved north again, and a local military governor allowed him to get across the Yangzi unopposed in the late summer of 880. This was not the first sign that government commanders and provincial leaders were beginning to put their own interests ahead of those of the imperial court. Many had avoided confrontations with Huang's army, and at least one passed up an opportunity to destroy the enemy on the grounds that he had more to fear from a victorious court than from the rebels.[68]

Aided by the unwillingness of the provincial armies to face him in battle, Huang Chao swept north through Henan at the end of 880, gathering recruits as he went. He captured Luoyang on December 22, then turned westward immediately to threaten Chang'an. As Huang approached the capital, the Shence Army, the core of the Imperial Palace Army, was sent out to block his advance at the Tong Pass. By this time, however, the palace army was no longer the formidable force that it had been in the days of Dezong and Xianzong. A great many merchants and wealthy young men of the capital had bribed the eunuchs to have their names inscribed on the roster of the Shence Army in order to gain privileges such as exemption from corvée labor obligations, but now that actual fighting loomed they hired substitutes to take their places in the ranks. Many of these replacements were old, infirm, and entirely uninstructed in the use of weapons, and they were easily routed by the rebels during the first week of January.[69] The emperor (Xizong) followed the precedent set by his ancestor Xuanzong and decamped for the safe haven of Sichuan. Huang Chao entered Chang'an on January 8 and soon proclaimed himself emperor, but the empire did not fall into line behind him. The savage behavior of his bandit followers, including a great deal of violence directed at the educated elite, denied him the aura of legitimacy that literati support might have conferred, and his military position in Guanzhong was far from secure. He held the capital itself, but the place was ringed by hostile military provinces whose troops prevented him from dominating the countryside. In spite of the great difficulty of securing adequate food supplies, Huang's men held on until 883 when the court called in a steppe army led by the twenty-eight-year-old Shatuo leader Li Keyong. Badly defeated by Li and other government commanders at the battle of Liangtian Hill, Huang evacuated Chang'an in May and retreated eastward into Henan. He found scant welcome there, however, for the followers whom he had earlier installed as military governors, sensing the direction the wind was blowing, had by now gone over to the side of the Tang court. He fought on for another year, but his forces became bogged down in a long, unsuccessful siege of Chenzhou and suffered repeated defeats at the hands of loyalist forces. Huang finally retreated into the familiar territory of his native Shandong, where he was hunted down and killed in the summer of 884.[70]

In 885, Xizong returned to Chang'an, but the new 54,000–man mercenary army recruited in Sichuan by his chief eunuch Tian Lingzi was soon destroyed in battle when Tian attempted to subdue two of the powerful northern military governors. Without a strong, effective military force at their disposal, Xizong and his successors Zhaozong (r. 888–904) and Ai Di (r. 904–7) became pawns in the hands of the military governors, who were now for all practical intents and purposes independant warlords. Real power was in the hands of some fifty different provincial regimes.[71] The situation was relatively stable in the less militarized south, where several durable and defensive-minded states were formed in territories corresponding to modern provinces – including Wu-Yue in Zhejiang, Min in Fujian, and Han in Guangdong. One of these "Ten Kingdoms," Wu-Yue, was established by the leader of a militia force that had been formed by local elites to protect their communities in these troubled times, and defensively oriented local militarization was also quite pronounced in Sichuan.[72] In the north, on the other hand, military governors struggled with one another for dominance. By the end of the ninth century, two of them had emerged as preeminent. One was the Shatuo leader Li Keyong, who had compelled the Tang court to recognize him as military governor of Hedong in modern Shanxi; the other was Huang Chao's former subordinate Zhu Quanzhong, who was based at the strategic center of Bianzhou (modern Kaifeng), on the Bian Canal in Henan. The two men were bitter foes after Zhu had made a treacherous but unsuccessful attempt to murder Li in 884. Zhu had the upper hand initially. He extended his power over most of the North China Plain, made the last two Tang emperors his captives, and finally proclaimed himself first emperor of the new Liang dynasty in 907. However, Zhu's realm did not long survive his own death in 912. Only eleven years later, Liang was conquered by Li Keyong's heir Li Cunxu, founder of the Later Tang dynasty. The rest of the north's "Five Dynasties," the Jin (937–46), Han (947–50), and Zhou (951–60), were short-lived military regimes that emerged from the carcass of the Later Tang through a string of coups d'état. The Song dynasty emerged from the Zhou in the same manner, but its founders were able to fashion a more lasting imperial order and succeeded in restoring unity to almost all of China's territory, north and south, by 979.[73]

The institutions of the late Tang military province had a major influence not only on the unstable regimes of the Five Dynasties, but also on the structure and policies of the Song state. The office of military governor was the springboard to imperial power for the founders of both Liang and Later Tang, and their imperial states became a sort of military province writ large. Zhu Quanzhong maintained his grip on his army with the help of a strong personal retainer corps, and he used his main army to dominate subordinate provinces in much the same way that provincial armies had once dominated the prefectures. The key contribution of the Later Tang was the creation of the "Emperor's Army" in 926; patterned after the elite headquarters force of a Tang military governor but on a much larger scale, it provided the ruler with a powerful force to keep his military governors in line.[74] This was of great benefit to the cause of centralization, but just as in the Tang military provinces it could also be a source of instability. The Han dynasty was replaced by the Zhou as the result of a coup d'état led by Guo Wei, the commander of the Emperor's Army. Guo formed a more intimate force, the Palace Corps, to protect himself against a similar maneuver by the Emperor's Army, but to no avail; in 960 his heir was overthrown in a coup led by the commander of the Palace Corps.[75]

This was Zhao Kuangyin, the founder of the Song dynasty. Zhao and his successor were the ones who finally succeeded in bringing the military firmly under control through a range of new institutional measures. They divided the central army into three separate elements (the Emperor's Army, the Palace Corps, and an elite imperial bodyguard unit), which they placed under the command of different officers and used to balance one another. They rotated units between the capital and the frontier to disrupt the ties between generals

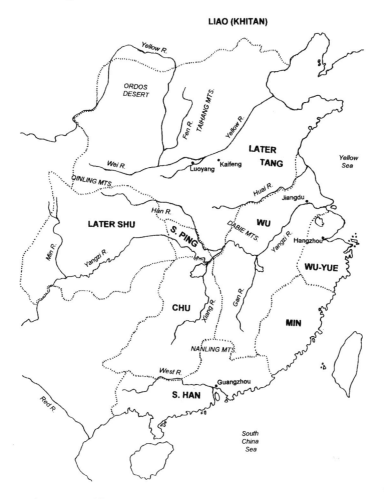

Map 21 China in AD 930

and their subordinates, and formed their campaign armies from diverse elements that included units from both the central army and the prefectural defense forces. They made sure that command authority was divided between the Bureau of Military Affairs (*shu mi yuan*), which was responsible for setting armies in motion, and the generals who were responsible for leading those armies in the field. Army supervisors, including both trusted officers and eunuchs, were assigned as a matter of course.[76] From the time of the second Song emperor (Taizong, r. 976–97) the principle of civilian supremacy over the military was firmly established, and during the course of the eleventh century it became quite common for civil officials to be entrusted with important military commands. The Song rulers and statesmen were generally successful in their efforts to keep the military on a tight leash, though it has often been asserted that this success came only at the price of reduced military effectiveness. The dynasty was never able to recover the "sixteen prefectures" in the area of today's Beijing that had been taken by the Khitan in the first half of the tenth century; all of North China was lost to the Jurchen invaders from Manchuria in 1126, and the whole of the country fell under Mongol rule in 1279.

The controls imposed by the early Song rulers were clearly a reaction to the rampant warlordism of late Tang and the menacing mercenary soldiery that was part of the Tang legacy to the Five Dynasties and Song.[77] Beyond this, however, it has also been suggested that the negative experience of late Tang gave rise to "antimilitarist sentiment" and contributed to the dominance of a "civilian ethic," a sort of allergy to soldiers, armies, and all things military, that is supposed to have colored Chinese attitudes from Song times down to the twentieth century.[78] It was, after all, the Song period that is supposed to have given us the famous adage, "Good iron is not made into nails, nor are good men made into soldiers."[79] Yet, even if we leave aside the complicated question of whether an antimilitary bias was really prevalent in late imperial China, the notion that the Tang–Song divide was a turning point in this regard seems somewhat overdrawn. The early Tang statesman Wei Zheng, who refused to watch a performance by dancers with armor and halberds in commemoration of Taizong's military victories, was by no means the only scholar of his time (or earlier) to express a disdain for military affairs.[80] Both before and after the An Lushan rebellion, there were educated men and civil officials who led armies – and others who shunned them.

Nor was the Tang–Song transition an obvious turning point in other respects. The most important development in military technology, the introduction of gunpowder weapons, appears to have had very little impact on strategy and the basic patterns of warfare.[81] Many of the military institutions of early imperial China – such as hereditary military households and various forms of militia organization – can also be found on the other side of the Tang–Song divide.[82] The number of soldiers did increase, rising to 1,250,000 by the middle of the eleventh century and to as many as four million in the later years of the Ming dynasty (1368–1644), but this surely owed something to China's population growth and cannot be represented as a "military revolution."[83] Almost all of the various institutional devices used to restrain the Song military, taken individually, had respectable precedents in Han, Tang, or the age of the northern and southern dynasties. The division of command authority between "inner" and "outer" armies was old hat, as was the employment of army supervisors. The rotational system of the *fubing* had worked to prevent soldiers and generals from becoming too well acquainted with one another, and Tang expeditionary armies had been put together from diverse elements that served under a single commander only for the duration of a single campaign. The assignment of scholars and civil officials to military command under the Song dynasty was not an entirely new development, either. Certain patterns of behavior, such as the militarization of rural society in response to the breakdown of central authority, can be seen from antiquity straight through to the early twentieth century.[84] Perhaps most important of all, the basic problem confronted by the rulers of late imperial China was not fundamentally different from that faced by Han and Tang: how to maintain the military force to defend the frontiers and deter internal revolt, without allowing that force to become a threat to the throne itself.

Yet the complexion of the military *was* somehow different in Song times and after, and different choices were made. The middle Tang (that is, the years before, during, and immediately after the An Lushan rebellion) was the beginning of this transition, and the consolidation of the Song dynasty marked its completion. Under Xuanzong, earlier institutional controls were relaxed in order to maximize the military effectiveness of the frontier armies, but after 755 a high price was paid for the temporary successes that had been gained by these means. The rise of autonomous and semi-autonomous provincial military regimes was accompanied by an upsurge of the commercial economy, and the full-time mercenary soldiery quickly developed into a self-aware, self-interested political pressure group. The policies of the Song rulers and the attitudes of the Song elite emerged in reaction to the new military conditions of late Tang. Few elements of the policy mix were entirely new. What was different was the entire *combination*: a range of controls was now employed rigorously and systematically to rein in a new type of professional soldiery, and old attitudes of disdain for the military were given a new edge and spread more widely than before among a much larger civilian elite. The Song response to the Tang crisis was by and large a success. It became fashionable for Song literati to mourn the passing of the *fubing* system, and to condemn the mercenaries of their own time as both less effective and more expensive than the farmer–soldiers of early Tang.[85] Yet the Song dynasty and its successors never faced a military revolt comparable to that of An Lushan, nor were they prey to the sort of praetorian politics characteristic of late Tang and the Five Dynasties. Song and Ming never came close to duplicating the military glories of Tang Taizong's reign, but they were able to hold their own against formidable steppe opponents for long periods of time. There would be intervals of warlordism and disunity as one dynasty gave way to another, but never again would imperial China experience a prolonged period of fragmentation comparable to the two centuries between the An Lushan rebellion and the Song consolidation.

Notes

1 For these events, see Sima Guang, *Zizhi tongjian*, ch. 223, pp. 7151–7.

2 Sima Guang, *Zizhi tongjian*, ch. 223, p. 7157. Also see Michael T. Dalby, "Court Politics in Late T'ang Times," in Denis Twitchett (ed.), *The Cambridge History of China*, vol. 3: *Sui and T'ang China, 589–906, Pt. 1* (Cambridge: Cambridge University Press, 1979), pp. 568–9.

3 *Xin Tang shu*, ch. 50, p. 1338; also see Song Changlian, "Tangdai de mazheng," *Dalu zazhi* 29.1–2 (July 15 and 31, 1964), pp. 29–30, 61.

4 Dalby, "Court Politics in Late T'ang Times," p. 569.
5 There is already a large literature dealing with the influence of horses on the military fortunes of the Tang dynasty. See Chen Yinke, "Lun Tangdai zhi fanjiang yu fubing," in *Chen Yinke xiansheng wen shi lunji* (Hong Kong: Wen wen chubanshe, 1972), vol. 2, p. 32; Li Shu-t'ung, "Tangdai zhi junshi yu ma," p. 241ff; and Fu Lecheng, "Huihe ma yu Shuofang bing," in idem, *Han Tang shi lunji* (Taipei: Lianjing, 1977), pp. 313–14.
6 For the Tang–Uighur relationship, see Colin Mackerras, "The Uighurs," in Denis Sinor (ed.), *The Cambridge History of Early Inner Asia* (Cambridge: Cambridge University Press, 1990), pp. 317–42; Colin Mackerras, *The Uighur Empire According to the Tang Dynastic Histories* (Columbia, S.C.: University of South Carolina Press, 1973); and Fu Lecheng, "Huihe ma yu Shuofang bing."
7 Edwin G. Pulleyblank, "The An Lu-shan Rebellion and the Origins of Chronic Militarism in Late T'ang China," in John Curtis Perry and Bardwell L. Smith (eds.), *Essays on T'ang Society* (Leiden: E. J. Brill, 1976), pp. 53–5; Sima Guang, *Zizhi tongjian*, ch. 218, pp. 6983–4.
8 Hino Kaisaburō, *Shina chūsei no gunbatsu* (Tokyo: Sanseido, 1942), p. 38; Kurihara Masuo, "An-Shi no ran to hanchin taisei no tenkai," in *Iwanami kōza: sekai rekishi*, vol. 6 (Tokyo: Iwanami shoten, 1970), p. 164. Pinglu, the largest of the northern commands, had fifteen prefectures. Several larger provinces could be found in the south, but these were much less heavily militarized.
9 Wang Shou-nan, *Tangdai fanzhen yu zhongyang guanxi zhi yanjiu* (Taiwan: Jiaxin shuini gongsi wenhua jijinhui, 1968), pp. 115–16; Hino, *Shina chūsei no gunbatsu*, p. 37.
10 For the history of Chengde, see *Jiu Tang shu*, ch. 142, pp. 3865–92.
11 *Xin Tang shu*, ch. 212, p. 5983; ch. 213, pp. 5989–95; Wu Tingxie, *Tang fangzhen nianbiao* (Beijing: Zhonghua shuju, 1980), ch. 4, p. 570.
12 These regional differences are discussed in Denis C. Twitchett, "Varied Patterns of Provincial Autonomy in the T'ang Dynasty," in Perry and Smith, *Essays on T'ang Society*, pp. 98–102; and in Zhang Guogang, *Tangdai fanzhen yanjiu* (Changsha: Hunan jiaoyu chubanshe, 1987), pp. 23–5.
13 Sima Guang, *Zizhi tongjian*, ch. 222, p. 7144; ch. 225, p. 7250; ch. 226, p. 7277; and *Jiu Tang shu*, ch. 141, p. 3838.
14 Hori Toshikazu, "Hanchin shineigun no kenryoku kōzō," *Tōyō bunka kenkyūjō kiyō*, No. 20 (March 1960), p. 90.
15 Sima Guang, *Zizhi tongjian*, ch. 249, p. 8077; ch. 250, p. 8079.
16 Hino, *Shina chūsei no gunbatsu*, pp. 67–8.
17 Yen Keng-wang, "Tangdai fangzhen shifu liaozuo kao," in idem, *Tang shi yanjiu conggao* (Hong Kong: Xin Ya yanjiusuo, 1969), p. 219; Zhang Guogang, *Tangdai zhengzhi zhidu yanjiu lunji*, pp. 162, 164–5.
18 Hino, *Shina chūsei no gunbatsu*, pp. 48–55; Charles A. Peterson, "Regional Defense against the Central Power: The Huai-hsi Campaign, 815–817," in Frank A. Kierman, Jr. and John K. Fairbank (eds.), *Chinese Ways in Warfare* (Cambridge, Mass.: Harvard University Press, 1974), pp. 146–8.
19 Hino, *Shina chūsei no gunbatsu*, pp. 36, 50, 55–6; *Jiu Tang shu*, ch. 44, p. 1923; Du You, *Tong dian*, ch. 33, p. 909. In the more recalcitrant of the Hebei provinces, it was not unusual for a military man trusted by the governor to act as both garrison commander and prefect.
20 Hori, "Hanchin shineigun no kenryoku kōzō," pp. 82–3.
21 Hino, *Shina chūsei no gunbatsu*, pp. 140–1.
22 Sima Guang, *Zizhi tongjian*, ch. 238, p. 7694; ch. 265, pp. 8644, 8656–7; *Jiu Tang shu*, ch. 141, p. 3838; ch. 181, pp. 4686–7, 4688, 4690, 4692.
23 See Hori, "Hanchin shineigun no kenryoku kōzō," pp. 103–20.

24 For more on this subject, see Kurihara Masuo, "Tō Godai no karifushi teki ketsugo no seikaku," pp. 514–43; and Yano Chikara, "Tōdai ni okeru kashisei ni tsuite," in *Shigaku kenkyū kinen ronsō* (Kyoto: Ryūgen shoten, 1950), pp. 231–57.

25 Charles A. Peterson, "The Autonomy of the Northeastern Provinces in the Period Following the An Lu-shan Rebellion" (Ph.D. dissertation, University of Washington, 1966), pp. 141–2.

26 Yen Keng-wang, "Tangdai fangzhen shifu liaozuo kao," pp. 220–5; Zhang Guogang, *Tangdai fanzhen yanjiu*, pp. 169–70.

27 Zhang Guogang, *Tangdai fanzhen yanjiu*, p. 110.

28 Zhang Guogang, "Tangdai jianjun zhidu kaolun," pp. 123–7.

29 Sima Guang, *Zizhi tongjian*, ch. 235, p. 7580; *Xin Tang shu*, ch. 50, p. 1334; Song Minqiu (comp.), *Tang da zhaoling ji*, ch. 2, p. 12.

30 The most comprehensive modern study of the Imperial Palace army is He Yongcheng, *Tangdai Shence jun yanjiu* (Taipei: Taiwan Commercial Press, 1990).

31 Tensions between the Tang court and its generals are examined in Pulleyblank, "The An Lu-shan Rebellion and the Origins of Chronic Militarism in Late T'ang China," pp. 54–8; Charles A. Peterson, "P'u-ku Huai-en and the T'ang Court: The Limits of Loyalty," *Monumenta Serica*, 29 (1970–1), pp. 423–55; Wang Jilin, "Tangdai de Shuofang jun yu Shence jun," in *Di yi jie guoji Tangdai xueshu huiyi lunwenji* (Taipei: Zhonghua minguo Tangdai xuezhe lianyihui, 1989), pp. 914–21; and Zhang Qun, "Pugu Huai'en yu Li Huaiguang de fanpan," in Cho-yun Hsu et al., *Zhongguo lishi lunwenji* (Taipei: Taiwan Commercial Press, 1986, pp. 87–119).

32 *Jiu Tang shu*, ch. 170, p. 4413 ff; *Xin Tang shu*, ch. 173, p. 5209 ff.

33 *Jiu Tang shu*, ch. 118, p. 3417.

34 *Jiu Tang shu*, ch. 157, pp. 4150–1.

35 *Jiu Tang shu*, ch. 161, p. 4237. Changes in military elites and the conceptualization of military leadership from early to late Tang are examined in greater detail in David A. Graff, "The Sword and the Brush: Military Specialisation and Career Patterns in Tang China, 618–907," *War and Society*, 18.2 (October 2000), pp. 9–21.

36 Dalby, "Court Politics in Late T'ang Times," pp. 582–3; *Jiu Tang shu*, ch. 142, pp. 3872–3.

37 For these events, see Sima Guang, *Zizhi tongjian*, ch. 228, pp. 7351–68; and ch. 229, pp. 7369–75.

38 Sima Guang, *Zizhi tongjian*, ch. 231, p. 7432; *Jiu Tang shu*, ch. 143, p. 3898.

39 Gu Yanwu, *Rizhilu jishi* (Taipei: Shijie shuju, 1968), vol. 1, pp. 220–1.

40 For these events, see Charles A. Peterson, "Regional Defense against the Central Power: The Huai-hsi Campaign, 815–817," pp. 123–50. Li Su's exploit is described in Sima Guang, *Zizhi tongjian*, ch. 240, pp. 7740–3.

41 *Jiu Tang shu*, ch. 129, p. 3611.

42 Dalby, "Court Politics in Late T'ang Times," pp. 637–8.

43 The "loyalist" province of Ze-Lu in southeastern Shanxi rebelled against the court in the early 840s, for example.

44 Hino, *Shina chūsei no gunbatsu*, pp. 209–10.

45 Fang Jiliu, "Guanyu Tangdai mubing zhidu de tantao," *Zhongguo shi yanjiu*, 1988, No. 3, pp. 110–20.

46 Zhang Guogang, *Tangdai fanzhen yanjiu*, pp. 71–3.

47 Kurihara, "An Shi no ran to hanchin taisei no tenkai," pp. 165–6; Hino, *Shina chūsei no gunbatsu*, pp. 59, 209.

48 Zhang Guogang, "Tangdai de jian'er zhi," pp. 106–7; Sima Guang, *Zizhi tongjian*, ch. 225, p. 7245. There is some evidence that the standard was 7.2 *shi* (432 liters) of hulled grain, six lengths of silk cloth, and six lengths of hemp cloth per man during the An Lushan rebellion. See Li Quan, *Taibai yinjing*, ch. 5, pp. 558–9, 561.

49 Fang Jiliu, "Guanyu Tangdai mubing zhidu de tantao," pp. 114–15.
50 *Jiu Tang shu*, ch. 19A, p. 653; Hori, "Hanchin shineigun no kenryoku kōzō," pp. 91–3.
51 See, for example, Sima Guang, *Zizhi tongjian*, ch. 230, p. 7413.
52 *Jiu Tang shu*, ch. 145, pp. 3937–8.
53 Zhang Guogang, *Tangdai fanzhen yanjiu*, p. 106; also see Wang Shou-nan, *Tangdai fanzhen yu zhongyang guanxi zhi yanjiu*, p. 228.
54 Zhao Yi, *Nian'er shi zhaji* (Taipei: Dingwen shuju, 1975), ch. 20, p. 267. Also see Sima Guang's comments in *Zizhi tongjian*, ch. 220, pp. 7065–6.
55 Fang Jiliu, "Guanyu Tangdai mubing zhidu de tantao," p. 116; Zhang Guogang, "Tangdai de jian'er zhi," p. 108.
56 Fang Jiliu, "Guanyu Tangdai mubing zhidu de tantao," pp. 115–16.
57 Zhang Guogang, *Tangdai fanzhen yanjiu*, p. 74; Hino, *Shina chūsei no gunbatsu*, p. 214.
58 Twitchett, *Financial Administration under the T'ang Dynasty*, pp. 1–9, 24–34.
59 Denis Twitchett, "The T'ang Market System," *Asia Major* (new series), 12.2 (1966), pp. 221, 243–8.
60 Twitchett, "The T'ang Market System," pp. 240–1.
61 Twitchett, *Financial Administration under the T'ang Dynasty*, p. 17.
62 Denis Twitchett, *The Birth of the Chinese Meritocracy: Bureaucrats and Examinations in T'ang China*. The China Society Occasional Papers, No. 18 (London: The China Society, 1976), pp. 31–2.
63 Twitchett, *Financial Administration under the T'ang Dynasty*, pp. 50–8.
64 Twitchett, *The Birth of the Chinese Meritocracy*, pp. 31–2. For an overview of changes in the character of the elite from late Tang to Song, see Peter K. Bol, *"This Culture of Ours": Intellectual Transitions in T'ang and Sung China* (Stanford, Ca.: Stanford University Press, 1992), pp. 36–75.
65 See Robert des Rotours, "La Révolte de P'ang Hiun (868–69)," *T'oung Pao*, 56 (1970), pp. 229–40.
66 Robert M. Somers, "The End of the T'ang," in Denis Twitchett (ed.), *The Cambridge History of China*, vol. 3, pp. 720–26.
67 *Biography of Huang Ch'ao*, trans by Howard S. Levy (Berkeley and Los Angeles: University of California Press, 1961), p. 8, and p. 46, n. 3.
68 Somers, "The End of the T'ang," p. 741.
69 Sima Guang, *Zizhi tongjian*, ch. 254, pp. 8237–9; Liu Yat-wing, "The Shen-ts'e Armies and the Palace Commissions in China, 755–875 A.D." (Ph.D. dissertation, University of London, 1970), pp. 394–5.
70 These events are covered in much greater detail in Somers, "The End of the T'ang," pp. 745–62.
71 Somers, "The End of the T'ang," pp. 762–81.
72 Tanigawa Michio, "Tōdai no hanchin ni tsuite: Sessai no ba'ai," *Shirin*, 35.3 (October 1952), pp. 87–8; Kurihara Masuo, "Tōmatsu no dogōteki zaichi seiryoku ni tsuite: Shisen no I Kunsei no ba'ai," *Rekishigaku kenkyū*, No. 243 (1960), pp. 1–14.
73 Wang Gungwu, *The Structure of Power in North China during the Five Dynasties* (Stanford, Ca.: Stanford University Press, 1967) remains the best survey of Five Dynasties political history.
74 Wang, *The Structure of Power*, pp. 3–6, 149, 158, 160–1.
75 John Richard Labadie, "Rulers and Soldiers: Perception and Management of the Military in Northern Sung China (960–ca. 1060)" (Ph.D. dissertation, University of Washington, 1981), pp. 33–4; Edmund H. Worthy, Jr., "The Founding of Sung China, 950–1000: Integrative Changes in Military and Political Institutions" (Ph.D. dissertation, Princeton University, 1975), pp. 106–7.

76 Worthy, "The Founding of Sung China," pp. 138–9, 173, 187–9, 195–7, 243–4; Wang Zengyu, *Songchao bingzhi chutan* (Beijing: Zhonghua shuju, 1983), pp. 1, 3–4, 32–3, 61.

77 See, for example, the comments of the investigating censor Li Jing quoted in Labadie, "Rulers and Soldiers," pp. 111–12.

78 Pulleyblank, "The An Lu-shan Rebellion and the Origins of Chronic Militarism in Late T'ang China," pp. 35, 59–60.

79 Labadie, "Rulers and Soldiers," p. 5.

80 Li Fang (comp.), *Taiping guangji*, ch. 203, p. 1534. For literati attitudes, also see McMullen, "The Cult of Ch'i T'ai-kung and T'ang Attitudes to the Military," pp. 59–103.

81 Edward L. Dreyer, "Military Continuities: The PLA and Imperial China," in William W. Whitson (ed.), *The Military and Political Power in China in the 1970's* (New York: Praeger, 1972), pp. 3–24.

82 The Ming dynasty, for example, had a system of hereditary military households. See Romeyn Taylor, "Yüan Origins of the Ming Wei-so System," in Charles O. Hucker (ed.), *Chinese Government in Ming Times: Seven Studies* (New York: Columbia University Press, 1969), pp. 23–40.

83 For the eleventh-century figure, see Labadie, "Rulers and Soldiers," p. 47; for the Ming figure, see Hucker, *A Dictionary of Official Titles in Imperial China*, p. 79.

84 See Philip A. Kuhn, *Rebellion and its Enemies in Late Imperial China: Militarization and Social Structure, 1796–1864* (Cambridge, Mass.: Harvard University Press, 1970), and Perry, *Rebels and Revolutionaries in North China*.

85 See, for example, Ouyang Xiu's comments in *Xin Tang shu*, ch. 50, especially pp. 1323–4 and 1328; Zhang Ruyu, *Qunshu kaosuo xuji*, Siku quanshu edition (Taipei: Taiwan Commercial Press, 1983), ch. 43, p. 7b; Ma Duanlin, *Wenxian tongkao*, Siku quanshu edition (Taipei: Taiwan Commercial Press, 1983), ch. 154, p. 28b and passim.

Conclusion

During the six centuries covered by this volume China went from the unified imperial order of the Western Jin dynasty to the chaos of the barbarian conquest of the north and the ensuing north–south division, and from there to the restoration of the unified empire by the Sui and Tang dynasties. After the An Lushan rebellion of 755, the empire again began to slide into division and civil war, with unity not being restored until after the establishment of the Song dynasty in 960. During most of this period of 600 years China was not at peace, nor was the outlook of rulers and key elites at all pacific. Almost without exception, the many changes of dynasty and regime during this period came about through military action, whether armed rebellion, war of invasion, or coup d'état. When the empire was united, strong dynasties projected their power outward in efforts to subjugate neighboring states and peoples; when the Chinese world was divided, conflicts among the various regional regimes were the order of the day. War and its preparations had an enormous and multifaceted influence on the fortunes of states and dynasties, on institutional structures and the social order, and on the lives of ordinary people.

Military events determined whether the people of China would live in a unified, prosperous, and (relatively) peaceful empire or in a congeries of squabbling regional statelets subject to banditry and invasion. The collapse of the Western Jin empire that initiated the medieval period was made possible by military institutions – the command authority given to the imperial princes, a hereditary and dependant soldiery, and a heavy reliance on the cavalry forces of steppe peoples both inside and outside the empire – and triggered by civil wars of the princes. The consequences were profound and long-lasting. The empire was divided, the north fell under barbarian rule, and large numbers of people migrated from the northern plains to the Yangzi valley in order to escape the prevailing violence and disorder. The reunification of the empire, a process begun by the Western Wei/Northern Zhou regime and completed by its Sui and Tang successors, was also the result of military operations and the development of new military institutions. Of particular importance was the creation of the *fubing* territorial soldiery by the Western Wei and Northern Zhou. Originally a matter of necessity for the outnumbered western state led by

Yuwen Tai, the *fubing* system enabled his successors to build a powerful but cost-effective army by incorporating Chinese local elites and farmers. Again, the consequences were profound and farreaching. The new armies made possible the Zhou conquest of the North China Plain in 577 and the Sui conquest of the south in 589, and contributed to the emergence of the vigorous, mixed-blood Sino-Xianbei aristocracy that governed all of China under the Sui and early Tang. That the Tang dynasty and not the Sui was the ultimate beneficiary of the process of reunification was also the result of military action, in this case Emperor Yang's massive, costly, and unsuccessful campaigns against Koguryŏ in 612–14 that destroyed both his own prestige and the power of the Sui empire.

The mid-Tang crisis and its consequences affords yet another example of the impact of war and the preparations for war on the political and social structure of medieval China, and on the lives of the people. The great rebellion of the frontier general An Lushan in 755 was made possible by new military institutions, namely the powerful, permanent armies of long-service veterans created to meet the needs of frontier defense in the first half of the eighth century. Here, too, the consequences were profound and farreaching. The An Lushan rebellion weakened the authority of the Tang court and left the empire deeply divided, a condition that facilitated the rise of a more vigorous market economy, private ownership of land, and a new landowning bureaucratic elite sprung from diverse origins. These would remain important features of Chinese society under the Song, Ming, and Qing dynasties – down to the twentieth century, in fact.

During the centuries treated here, much was happening elsewhere in the world. To focus only on the western fringes of the Eurasian land mass, the opening of this study around the year 300 coincides with the revival of the fortunes of the late Roman empire under Diocletian and Constantine. The centuries that followed saw the fall of the Roman empire in the west, the establishment of a number of regional successor states under Germanic princes, and the efforts of the Eastern Roman Emperor Justinian to recover Italy and Africa from the barbarians. The seventh century witnessed the stunning emergence of the Arabs from their desert homeland to put an end to the Sasanid Persian empire and strip the Eastern Roman empire of Egypt, Syria, and North Africa, making their Muslim caliphate a major world power. The eighth century saw the rise of the Carolingian Franks, culminating in Charlemagne's extensive conquests and his efforts to revive the Roman empire in the west, and with the ninth century came the depredations of the Northmen and then the Magyars. The endpoint of this volume coincides roughly with the Vikings' siege of Paris and the deposition of Charles the Fat, leading to the permanent division of Charlemagne's empire. In the eastern Mediterranean, the Eastern Roman (or Byzantine) empire was experiencing a modest revival of its military fortunes, while the caliphate was beginning its long decline.

How unique was the Chinese experience of warfare during this period?

What, if anything, did the Chinese have in common with the peoples at the other end of Eurasia, and what was different? The first step in answering this question is to narrow the comparison. Is China to be compared with the Roman empire of Diocletian and Constantine, the Frankish state of the Merovingians, the empire of Charlemagne, Saxon England, Lombard Italy, Visigothic or Muslim Spain, the Muslim caliphate, or the Eastern Roman empire of Justinian and his successors? The closest comparison would seem to be with the Eastern Roman or Byzantine empire, though it had only a fraction of China's population and was limited to a much smaller territory. Like most of the Chinese states of the medieval period, the Byzantine empire was both autocratic and bureaucratic, with a sophisticated system of civil administration staffed by highly literate officials. Just as medieval Chinese states were the successors of earlier imperial dynasties and heirs to China's ancient civilization, the Byzantines (who never ceased to call themselves "Romans") were the direct inheritors of Greco-Roman cultural traditions and the political legacy of the Roman empire. In sharp contrast to both Byzantium and China, "no western European monarch" of the early medieval period "had at his command an organized, literate civil service which could deal with fiscal matters on a state-wide basis."[1]

For the most part, the military tools and techniques of medieval China would have been familiar to a Byzantine visitor (and vice versa). The level of military technology was essentially the same. Both Chinese and Byzantine armies relied upon a cavalry composed of both mounted archers and armored lancers as their main strike force, but supported this with infantry armed with spears, swords, and bows. Many of the specific military practices of the Sui–Tang empire in China and the Byzantine empire, such as the arrangement made to protect the baggage train while an army was on the march, were remarkably similar.[2] Both civilizations were heirs to a substantial literature dealing with the art of war. The medieval Chinese had the classic treatises of the Warring States period, most notably Sunzi's *Art of War*, while the Byzantines inherited a tradition of Greek strategic writing dating back to the fourth century BC that included the works of Aeneas the Tactician, Asclepiodotus, Onasander, and Polyaenus among others.[3] To these they added a great many military treatises of their own, including the works traditionally attributed to the emperors Maurice (r. 582–602) and Leo VI (r. 886–912). These treatises borrow so freely from one another and from the earlier Greek tradition of Hellenistic and Roman times that one modern authority has pronounced that all the Greek and Byzantine military writings belong to a single, integral tradition.[4] In Byzantium, as in China, there was no sharp break with antiquity, and the accumulated wisdom of the ancients was always available for consultation.

The Chinese and the Byzantines also shared some common attitudes toward war. For the soldiers of both empires, war was not just a trial of strength and courage, but rather an actvitiy requiring the application of intellect, cunning, and trickery to gain every possible advantage. It was not an end in itself, an opportunity to demonstrate one's manhood or justify one's privileged position in society. It was seen as a serious and dangerous business, not to be undertaken lightly. The famous passage in the ancient Daoist classic, the *Laozi*, that "arms are instruments of ill omen" is echoed by the anonymous author of a mid-sixth-century Byzantine military text: "war is a great evil and the worst of all evils."[5] In both cultures, generals sought to postpone engagements until the time was ripe, to increase the likelihood of success through artful maneuver or clever stratagems. Battle was to occur under the most favorable conditions that could be obtained. As the same anonymous Byzantine author put it, "If conditions are equal on both sides and the victory could go either way, we should not advance into battle before the enemy have become inferior to us in some respect." Both he and his near contemporary, the Tang general Li Jing, provided lists of the situations in which the enemy could be attacked with the greatest likelihood of success.[6]

Both China and Byzantium found defense against the incursions of nomadic peoples from the neighboring steppes to be among the most serious and intractable of their military problems, and both were profoundly influenced by this contact, whether it meant borrowing from the military techniques of the nomads or developing new methods by which to resist them.[7] A favorite steppe tactic employed by both Chinese and Byzantine soldiers was the feigned flight to draw the enemy into an ambush or set him up for a counterattack.[8]

There were also significant differences between Byzantium and medieval China. These were found not in the pragmatics of warfare, but in the relationship between the military and the civil authority of the state. Medieval China certainly had its share of military insubordination. Most of the southern dynasties of the period of division were overturned by revolts or coups led by military commanders, and in the aftermath of the An Lushan rebellion the professional armies of the military provinces frequently deposed their own commanders and sometimes even rebelled against the imperial court to protect their own customary privileges. It was not until the very end of the Tang dynasty that provincial military leaders became strong enough to depose emperors, but the praetorian politics of the provincial garrisons migrated to the center of power during the ensuing Five Dynasties period (907–960), when one ephemeral dynasty after another in North China was brought down by military coup d'état. Compared to the situation in the Byzantine empire, however, the Chinese military and its leaders were relatively tame. As Warren Treadgold has pointed out, "acclamation by the army, not coronation or inheritance, was what made a man emperor. The army overthrew twenty-odd rulers, and tried to oust many more."[9] In contrast, almost all of China's Tang emperors came to throne by peaceful inheritance, and few if any were challenged by their *armies* (as opposed to eunuchs, provincial governors, and imperial princes who happened to have a modicum of armed force at their disposal).

Approximately two-thirds of the Byzantine emperors were men who had led troops before their accession to the throne, and it was commonplace for reigning emperors to command armies on campaign.[10] This was not the norm in medieval China. The emperor as warrior and war leader was a common pattern in the age of division, especially in the barbarian-influenced north, but it is noteworthy that during the Han period the only rulers who actually led armies were Liu Bang and Liu Xiu, the respective founders of the Western and Eastern Han dynasties. Their successors were not generals; they ruled from the capital through ritual, symbol, and the mechanism of the imperial bureaucracy. Even during the period of division, the rulers of the southern dynasties normally followed this model. After the empire was reunited at the end of the sixth century, Emperor Yang of Sui and Tang Taizong (Li Shimin) with their great Korean campaigns were significant exceptions to the Han pattern, representing the lingering influence of North Asian ideas of rulership among mixed-blood elites in North China. The steppe influence did not continue past the time of Tang Taizong. Later Tang emperors would sometimes speak of leading their armies in person, but none actually chose to do so. Rulership again came to be exercised from the palace, through ritual and symbol and the imperial bureaucracy. This outcome is suggestive of the tremendous staying power of the tradition of sacred kingship inherited from very early times, and of the Confucian ideal of government through virtuous example and proper ritual forms. Even Tang Taizong, one of the greatest warriors in all of Chinese history, saw fit to call for a proper balance of civil and military virtues in the government of the empire.[11]

The influence of what we may loosely term "Confucian values" extended well beyond the confines of the imperial palace. Together with the survival of an effective and literate state administration which obviated the need for feudal-type grants of land and authority to local elites, they helped to ensure that medieval China would not develop a true military aristocracy. Elite families would use armed force when they felt the need to do so, but it never became the central element of their class identity and claims to superior status. Even the powerful mixed-blood aristocracy that emerged in the northwest under Western Wei and Northern Zhou, with its archery and horsemanship, its love of the chase and its talent for military leadership, lasted for only a few generations; under the changed conditions of the Tang consolidation its member families soon began to produce civil bureaucrats and men of culture rather than warriors. In spite of all of the violence and warfare of China's medieval period, the cultural legacy of antiquity made the significance of things military very different from what it was in Byzantium or the Latin West.

Notes

1 Beeler, *Warfare in Feudal Europe*, p. 11.
2 *Three Byzantine Military Treatises* trans. by George T. Dennis (Washington, D.C.: Dumbarton Oaks, 1985), p. 279; Sima Guang, *Zizhi tongjian*, ch. 181, p. 5660.

3 For a comprehensive listing of the texts which make up the Greco-Byzantine military tradition, see Alphonse Dain, "Les Stratégistes byzantins," *Travaux et Mémoires*, 2 (1967), pp. 317–92.

4 Dain, "Les Stratégistes byzantins," p. 319; also see his "La Tradition des stratégistes byzantins," *Byzantion*, 20 (1950), p. 315.

5 *Tao Te Ching*, trans. by D. C. Lau (Harmondsworth: Penguin, 1985), p. 89; *Three Byzantine Military Treatises*, p. 21.

6 *Three Byzantine Military Treatises*, pp. 103–5; *Tong dian*, ch. 150, pp. 3839, 3842.

7 For the steppe influence on the Byzantine military, see Eugène Darkó, "Influences touraniennes sur l'évolution de l'art militaire des Grecs, des Romains, et des Byzantins," *Byzantion*, 10 (1935), pp. 443–69.

8 *Maurice's Strategikon*, pp. 52–3. Examples in the Chinese histories are legion.

9 Treadgold, *Byzantium and its Army*, p. 1.

10 Treadgold, *Byzantium and its Army*, p. 1.

11 *Tang Taizong ji* (Xi'an: Shaanxi renmin chubanshe, 1986), p. 122.

Bibliography

Primary sources and traditional Chinese works

Ban Gu. *Han shu* (History of the Han dynasty). Beijing: Zhonghua shuju, 1962.

Biography of Huang Ch'ao. Translated by Howard S. Levy. Berkeley and Los Angeles: University of California Press, 1961.

Chan-Kuo Ts'e. Translated by J. I. Crump, Jr. Oxford: Clarendon Press, 1970.

Deng Zezong. *Li Jing bingfa jiben zhuyi* (Reconstituted text of Li Jing's military methods with translation and annotation). Beijing: Jiefangjun chubanshe, 1990.

Du You. *Tong dian* (Encyclopedic history of institutions). Beijing: Zhonghua shuju, 1988.

Fan Ye. *Hou Han shu* (History of the Later Han dynasty). Beijing: Zhonghua shuju, 1965.

Fang Xuanling et al. *Jin shu* (History of the Jin dynasty). Beijing: Zhonghua shuju, 1974.

Gu Yanwu. *Rizhilu jishi* (Collected notes on the *Record of knowledge gained day by day*). Taipei: Shijie shuju, 1968.

Gu Zuyu. *Dushi fangyu jiyao* (Essentials of geography for reading history). 1879 Sichuan Tonghua shuwu edition. Reprint, Taipei: Xinxing shuju, 1967.

Li Baiyao. *Bei Qi shu* (History of the Northern Qi dynasty). Beijing: Zhonghua shuju, 1972.

Li Fang. *Taiping guangji* (Wide gleanings made in the Taiping era). Beijing: Renmin wenxue chubanshe, 1959.

Li Fang et al. *Taiping yulan* (Imperially reviewed encyclopedia of the Taiping era). In *Guoxue jiben congshu*. Taipei: Xinxing shuju, 1959.

—— *Wenyuan yinghua* (Beautiful flowers from the garden of literature). Taipei: Huawen shuju, 1965.

Li Jifu. *Yuanhe junxian tuzhi* (Maps and gazetteer of the commanderies and counties in the Yuanhe period). Beijing: Zhonghua shuju, 1983.

Li Linfu et al. *Tang liudian* (Compendium of administrative law of the six Tang ministries). Tokyo: Hiroike gakuen jigyōbu, 1973.

Li Quan. *Taibai yinjing* (Secret classic of the white planet). In *Zhongguo bingshu jicheng* (Collectanea of Chinese military writings), vol. 2. Beijing and Shenyang: Jiefangjun chubanshe and Liao-Shen shushe, 1988.

Li Yanshou. *Bei shi* (History of the Northern dynasties). Beijing: Zhonghua shuju, 1974.

—— *Nan shi* (History of the Southern dynasties). Beijing: Zhonghua shuju, 1975.

Linghu Defen. *Zhou shu* (History of the Northern Zhou dynasty). Beijing: Zhonghua shuju, 1971.

Liu Chung-p'ing [Liu Zhongping]. *Weiliaozi jin zhu jin yi* (Modern annotation and translation of the *Weiliaozi*). Taipei: Taiwan Commercial Press, 1975.

Liu I-ch'ing. *Shih-shuo hsin-yü: A New Account of the Tales of the World.* Translated by Richard B. Mather. Minneapolis: University of Minnesota Press, 1976.

Liu Xu et al. *Jiu Tang shu* (Old Tang history). Beijing: Zhonghua shuju, 1975.

Loewe, Michael. *Records of Han Administration.* Cambridge: Cambridge University Press, 1967.

Ma Duanlin. *Wenxian tongkao* (General history of institutions and critical examination of documents and studies). Siku quanshu edition. Taipei: Taiwan Commerical Press, 1983.

Maurice's Strategikon: Handbook of Byzantine Military Strategy. Translated by George T. Dennis. Philadelphia: University of Pennsylvania Press, 1984.

Ouyang Xiu. *Xin Tang shu* (New Tang history). Beijing: Zhonghua shuju, 1975.

Quan Tang wen (Complete prose literature of the Tang). Compiled by Dong Hao. Taipei: Jingwei shuju, 1965.

Shen Yue. *Song shu* (History of the Liu Song dynasty). Beijing: Zhonghua shuju, 1974.

Sima Guang. *Zizhi tongjian* (Comprehensive mirror for aid in government). Beijing: Guji chubanshe, 1956.

Sima Qian. *Shi ji* (Records of the Grand Historian). Beijing: Zhonghua shuju, 1959.

—— *Records of the Grand Historian.* Translated by Burton Watson. Hong Kong: Columbia University Press, 1993.

Sun Tzu. *The Art of War.* Translated by Samuel B. Griffith. New York: Oxford University Press, 1971.

Sunzi jiaoshi (Collation and explanation of Sunzi). Edited by Wu Jiulong. Beijing: Junshi kexue chubanshe, 1990.

Tang da zhaoling ji (Collected edicts of the Tang). Compiled by Song Minqiu. Beijing: Commercial Press, 1959.

Tang huiyao (Important documents of the Tang). Compiled by Wang Pu. Beijing: Zhonghua shuju, 1990.

Tang lü shuyi (Tang code with commentary). Shanghai: Commercial Press, 1933.

Tang Taizong ji (Collected writings of Tang Taizong). Xi'an: Shaanxi renmin chubanshe, 1986.

Tangdai muzhiming huibian fukao (Collection of Tang tomb inscriptions with analysis). Edited by Mao Han-kuang. Taipei: Institute of History and Philology of Academia Sinica, 1984–94.

Tao Te Ching. Translated by D. C. Lau. Harmondsworth: Penguin, 1985.

The Seven Military Classics of Ancient China. Translated by Ralph D. Sawyer. Boulder, Colo.: Westview Press, 1993.

Three Byzantine Military Treatises. Translated by George T. Dennis. Washington, D.C.: Dumbarton Oaks, 1985.

Traité des examens. Translated by Robert des Rotours. Paris: Librairie Ernest Leroux, 1932.

Traité des fonctionnaires et Traité de l'armée. Translated by Robert des Rotours. Leiden: E. J. Brill, 1947.

Wang Qinruo et al. *Cefu yuangui* (Outstanding models from the storehouse of literature). Taipei: Taiwan Zhonghua shuju, 1967.

Wang Yinglin. *Yu hai* (Ocean of jade). Reprint of 1337 edition. Taipei: Huawen shuju, 1964.

Wei Shou. *Wei shu* (History of the Wei dynasty). Beijing: Zhonghua shuju, 1974.

Wei Zheng et al. *Sui shu* (History of the Sui dynasty). Beijing: Zhonghua shuju, 1973.

Wen Daya. *Da Tang chuangye qiju zhu* (Court diary of the founding of great Tang). Shanghai: Shanghai Guji chubanshe, 1983.

Wu Jing. *Zhenguan zhengyao* (Essentials of the good government of the Zhenguan period). Shanghai: Shanghai Guji chubanshe, 1978.

Xiao Zixian. *Nan Qi shu* (History of the Southern Qi dynasty). Beijing: Zhonghua shuju, 1972.

Xu Song. *Tang liang jing chengfang kao* (A study of the walls and wards of the two Tang capitals). In *Tōdai no Chōan to Rakuyō* (Tang dynasty Chang'an and Luoyang), edited by Hiraoka Takeo. Kyoto: Jimbunkagaku kenkyūsho, Kyoto University, 1956.

Yao Silian. *Chen shu* (History of the Chen dynasty). Beijing: Zhonghua shuju, 1972.

—— *Liang shu* (History of the Liang dynasty). Beijing: Zhonghua shuju, 1973.

Yen Chih-t'ui. *Family Instructions for the Yen Clan (Yen-shih chia-hsün).* Translated by Teng Ssu-yü. T'oung Pao Monographs, vol. 4. Leiden: E. J. Brill, 1968.

Zeng Gongliang. *Wujing zongyao* (Essentials of the military classics). In *Zhongguo bingshu jicheng* (Collectanea of Chinese military writings), vol. 3. Beijing and Shenyang: Jiefangjun chubanshe and Liao-Shen shushe, 1988.

Zhang Ruyu. *Qunshu kaosuo xuji* (Sequel to inquiries into literature). Siku quanshu edition. Taipei: Taiwan Commercial Press, 1983.

Zhao Yi. *Nian'er shi zhaji* (Critical notes on the twenty-two histories). Taipei: Dingwen shuju, 1975.

Selected literature

Andreski, Stanislav. *Military Organization and Society.* Berkeley and Los Angeles: University of California Press, 1971.

Asami Naoichirō. "Yōdai no dai ichi ji Kōkuri enseigun: sono kibo to heishu" (Yangdi's first Koguryŏ expedition: its scale and troop types). *Tōyōshi kenkyū*, 44.1 (June 1985), pp. 23–44.

Bachrach, Bernard S. "Charlemagne's Cavalry: Myth and Reality." *Military Affairs*, 47.4 (December 1983), pp. 181–7.

Barfield, Thomas J. *The Perilous Frontier: Nomadic Empires and China, 221 BC to AD 1757.* Oxford: Basil Blackwell, 1989.

Barnes, Gina L. *The Rise of Civilization in East Asia: The Archaeology of China, Korea and Japan.* London: Thames and Hudson, 1999.

Beckwith, Christopher I. *The Tibetan Empire in Central Asia.* Princeton, N.J.: Princeton University Press, 1987.

Beeler, John. *Warfare in Feudal Europe, 730–1200.* Ithaca and London: Cornell University Press, 1971.

Bielenstein, Hans. "The Census of China during the Period 2–742 A.D." *Bulletin of the Museum of Far Eastern Antiquities* (Stockholm), 19 (1947), pp. 125–63.

—— *The Restoration of the Han Dynasty*, vol. 2: *The Civil War.* In *Bulletin of the Museum of Far Eastern Antiquities* (Stockholm), 31 (1959), pp. 1–287.

—— *The Bureaucracy of Han Times.* Cambridge: Cambridge University Press, 1980.

Bingham, Woodbridge. *The Founding of the T'ang Dynasty: The Fall of Sui and Rise of T'ang*. Baltimore: The Waverly Press, 1941. Reprint, New York: Octagon Books, 1970.

Black, Jeremy. "Global Military History: The Chinese Dimension." In *Warfare in Chinese History*, edited by Hans van de Ven, pp. 428–42. Leiden: E. J. Brill, 2000.

Bol, Peter K. *"This Culture of Ours": Intellectual Transitions in T'ang and Sung China*. Stanford, Ca.: Stanford University Press, 1992.

Boodberg, Peter A. "The Art of War in Ancient China." Ph.D. dissertation, University of California, 1930.

—— "Marginalia to the Histories of the Northern Dynasties." In *Selected Works of Peter A. Boodberg*, compiled by Alvin P. Cohen, pp. 265–349. Berkeley and Los Angeles: University of California Press, 1979.

Cen Zhongmian. *Fubing zhidu yanjiu* (Researches on the *fubing* system). Shanghai: Shanghai renmin chubanshe, 1957.

—— *Tongjian Sui Tang ji bi shi zhiyi* (Comparison and questioning of the Sui and Tang annals in the *Comprehensive mirror*). Beijing: Zhonghua shuju, 1964.

Chang, Chun-shu. "Military Aspects of Han Wu-ti's Northern and Northwestern Campaigns." *Harvard Journal of Asiatic Studies*, 26 (1966), pp. 148–73.

Chen Baoqiu. *Zhongguo lidai bingyi zhidu* (Systems of military service in China under successive dynasties). Taipei: Hua shi chubanshe, 1981.

Chen Yinke. *Tangdai zhengzhi shi shulun gao* (Draft explanatory essays on Tang political history). Beijing: Sanlian, 1956.

—— "Lun Tangdai zhi fanjiang yu fubing" (On the barbarian generals and *fubing* of the Tang dynasty). In *Chen Yinke xiansheng wen shi lunji* (Collected literary and historical essays of Mr. Chen Yinke), vol. 2, pp. 27–40. Hong Kong: Wenwen chubanshe, 1972.

—— *Wei Jin Nanbeichao shi jiangyanlu* (A record of lectures on Wei, Jin, and the Northern and Southern dynasties). Edited by Wan Shengnan. Hefei: Huangshan shushe, 1987.

Clark, Colin, and Margaret Haswell. *The Economics of Subsistence Agriculture*. 4th edn. London: St Martin's Press, 1970.

Contamine, Philippe. *War in the Middle Ages*. Translated by Michael Jones. Oxford: Basil Blackwell, 1984.

Crowell, William G. "Northern Émigrés and the Problems of Census Registration under the Eastern Jin and Southern Dynasties." In *State and Society in Early Medieval China*, edited by Albert E. Dien, pp. 171–209. Stanford, Ca.: Stanford University Press, 1990.

Dain, Alphonse. "La Tradition des stratégistes byzantins." *Byzantion*, 20 (1950), pp. 315–16.

—— "Les Stratégistes byzantins." *Travaux et Mémoires*, 2 (1967), pp. 317–92.

Dalby, Michael T. "Court Politics in Late T'ang Times." In *The Cambridge History of China*, vol. 3: *Sui and T'ang China, 589–906, Pt. 1*, edited by Denis Twitchett, pp. 561–681. Cambridge: Cambridge University Press, 1979.

Darkó, Eugène. "Influences touraniennes sur l'évolution de l'art militaire des Grecs, des Romains, et des Byzantins." *Byzantion*, 10 (1935), pp. 443–69.

de Crespigny, Rafe. *Northern Frontier: The Policies and Strategy of the Later Han Empire*. Canberra: Faculty of Asian Studies, Australian National University, 1984.

—— *Generals of the South: The Foundation and Early History of the Three Kingdoms*

State of Wu. Canberra: Faculty of Asian Studies, Australian National University, 1990.

DeFrancis, John. "Biography of the Marquis of Huai-yin." *Harvard Journal of Asiatic Studies*, 10.2 (September 1947), pp. 179–215.

Delbrück, Hans. *Numbers in History.* London: University of London Press, 1913.

Demiéville, Paul. "Le Bouddhisme et la guerre." In *Choix d'études bouddhiques (1929–1970)*, pp. 261–99. Leiden: E. J. Brill, 1973.

des Rotours, Robert. "Les Grandes fonctionnaires des provinces en Chine sous la dynastie des T'ang." *T'oung Pao*, 25 (1927), pp. 219–332.

—— "La Révolte de P'ang Hiun (868–69)." *T'oung Pao*, 56 (1970), pp. 229–40.

Di Cosmo, Nicola. "The Northern Frontier in Pre-Imperial China." In *The Cambridge History of Ancient China*, edited by Michael Loewe and Edward Shaughnessy, pp. 885–966. Cambridge: Cambridge University Press, 1999.

Dien, Albert E. "The Use of the *Yeh-hou chia-chuan* as a Historical Source." *Harvard Journal of Asiatic Studies*, 34 (1974), pp. 221–47.

—— "The Bestowal of Surnames under the Western Wei–Northern Chou: A Case of Counter-Acculturation." *T'oung Pao*, 63 (1977), pp. 137–77.

—— "A Study of Early Chinese Armor." *Artibus Asiae*, 43 (1982), pp. 5–66.

—— "The Stirrup and its Effect on Chinese Military History." *Ars Orientalis*, 16 (1986), pp. 33–56.

—— "The Role of the Military in the Western Wei/Northern Chou State." In *State and Society in Early Medieval China*, edited by Albert E. Dien, pp. 331–67. Stanford, Ca.: Stanford University Press, 1990.

Dreyer, Edward L. "Military Continuities: The PLA and Imperial China." In *The Military and Political Power in China in the 1970's*, edited by William W. Whitson, pp. 3–24. New York: Praeger, 1972.

Drompp, Michael R. "Supernumerary Sovereigns: Superfluity and Mutability in the Elite Power Structure of the Early Türks." In *Rulers from the Steppe: State Formation on the Eurasian Periphery*, edited by Gary Seaman and Daniel Marks, pp. 92–115. Los Angeles: Ethnographics Press, 1991.

Dunlop, D. M. "A New Source of Information on the Battle of Talas or Atlakh." *Ural-Altaische Jahrbücher*, 36 (1964), pp. 326–30.

Eberhard, Wolfram. *Conquerors and Rulers: Social Forces in Medieval China.* 2nd edn, rev. Leiden: E. J. Brill, 1965.

Eisenberg, Andrew. "Warfare and Political Stability in Medieval North Asian Regimes." *T'oung Pao*, 83 (1997), pp. 300–28.

Engels, Donald W. *Alexander the Great and the Logistics of the Macedonian Army.* Berkeley and Los Angeles: University of California Press, 1978.

Fang Jiliu. "Guanyu Tangdai mubing zhidu de tantao" (A study of the voluntary recruitment system of the Tang dynasty). *Zhongguo shi yanjiu*, 1988, No. 3, pp. 110–20.

Fitzgerald, C. P. *Son of Heaven: A Biography of Li Shih-min, Founder of the T'ang Dynasty.* Cambridge: Cambridge University Press, 1933.

Franke, Herbert. *Studien und Texte zur Kriegsgeschichte der südlichen Sungzeit.* Wiesbaden: Otto Harrassowitz, 1987.

—— "Warfare in Medieval China: Some Research Problems." In *Zhongyang yanjiuyuan di er jie guoji hanxue huiyi lunwenji* (Proceedings of the second international sinological conference at Academia Sinica), vol. 5, p. 806. Taipei: Academia Sinica, 1989.

Fu Lecheng. "Huihe ma yu Shuofang bing" (Uighur horses and Shuofang soldiers). In *Han Tang shi lunji* (Collected essays on Han and Tang history), pp. 305–17. Taipei: Lianjing, 1977.

—— "Wei Jin Nanbeichao zhanshi" (History of warfare in Wei, Jin, and the Northern and Southern dynasties). In *Zhongguo zhanshi lunji* (Essays on the history of warfare in China), 3rd edn. Taipei: Zhongguo wenhua xueyuan chubanbu, 1980.

Fuller, J. F. C. *A Military History of the Western World*. New York: Funk and Wagnalls, 1954–6.

Gao Min. "Cao Wei shijia zhidu de xingcheng yu yanbian" (Formation and evolution of the system of military households under the Cao Wei dynasty). *Lishi yanjiu*, 1989, No. 5, pp. 61–75.

Goodrich, Chauncey S. "Riding Astride and the Saddle in Ancient China." *Harvard Journal of Asiatic Studies*, 44.2 (December 1984), pp. 279–306.

Graff, David A. "The Battle of Huo-i." *Asia Major*, 3rd ser., 5.1 (1992), pp. 33–55.

—— "Early T'ang Generalship and the Textual Tradition." Ph.D. dissertation, Princeton University, 1995.

—— "Meritorious Cannibal: Chang Hsün's Defense of Sui-yang and the Exaltation of Loyalty in an Age of Rebellion." *Asia Major*, 3rd ser., 8.1 (1995), pp. 1–15.

—— "The Sword and the Brush: Military Specialisation and Career Patterns in Tang China, 618–907." *War and Society*, 18.2 (October 2000), pp. 9–21.

—— "Strategy and Contingency in the Tang Defeat of the Eastern Turks, 629–630." Forthcoming.

Grafflin, Dennis. "The Great Family in Medieval South China." *Harvard Journal of Asiatic Studies*, 41.1 (June 1981), pp. 65–74.

Gu Jiguang. *Fubing zhidu kaoshi* (Examination and explanation of the *fubing* system). Shanghai: Shanghai renmin chubanshe, 1962. Reprint, Taipei: Hongwenguan chubanshe, 1985.

Haldon, John. *Warfare, State and Society in the Byzantine World, 565–1204*. London: UCL Press, 1999.

Hamaguchi Shigekuni. "Fuhei seido yori shin heisei e" (From the *fubing* system toward a new military system). *Shigaku zasshi*, 41 (1930), pp. 1255–95, 1439–1507.

—— *Shin Kan Zui Tō shi no kenkyū* (Researches on Qin-Han and Sui-Tang history). Tokyo: Tokyo University Press, 1966.

He Yongcheng. *Tangdai Shence jun yanjiu* (Researches on the Shence army of the Tang dynasty). Taipei: Taiwan Commercial Press, 1990.

He Ziquan. "Wei Jin Nanchao de bingzhi" (Military institutions of Wei, Jin, and the Southern dynasties). *Bulletin of the Institute of History and Philology of Academia Sinica*, 16 (1948), pp. 229–71.

—— *Wei Jin Nanbeichao shilue* (A brief history of Wei, Jin, and the Northern and Southern Dynasties). Shanghai: Shanghai renmin chubanshe, 1958.

Hino Kaisaburō. *Shina chūsei no gunbatsu* (Medieval Chinese warlords). Tokyo: Sanseido, 1942.

—— "Dai Tō fuheisei jidai no danketsu hei ni tsuite" (Concerning the *tuanjie* troops in the time of the Tang *fubing* system). *Hōseishi kenkyū*, 5 (1954), pp. 79–133.

Holcombe, Charles. *In the Shadow of the Han: Literati Thought and Society at the Beginning of the Southern Dynasties*. Honolulu: University of Hawaii Press, 1994.

Holmgren, Jennifer. *Annals of Tai: Early T'o-pa History According to the First Chapter of the Wei-shu*. Canberra: Australian National University Press, 1982.

——"The Making of an Élite: Local Politics and Social Relations in Northeastern China during the Fifth Century A.D." *Papers on Far Eastern History*, 30 (September 1984), pp. 1–79.

Honey, David B. *The Rise of the Medieval Hsiung-nu: The Biography of Liu Yüan*. Papers on Inner Asia, No. 15. Bloomington, Ind.: Research Institute for Inner Asian Studies, 1990.

——"Lineage as Legitimation in the Rise of Liu Yüan and Shih Le." *Journal of the American Oriental Society*, 110.4 (October–December 1990), pp. 616–21.

Hoplites: The Classical Greek Battle Experience. Edited by Victor Davis Hanson. London and New York: Routledge, 1991.

Hori Toshikazu. "Hanchin shineigun no kenryoku kōzō" (The power structure of the military governor's bodyguard corps). *Tōyō bunka kenkyūjō kiyō*, No. 20 (March 1960), pp. 75–147.

Hsu, Cho-yun. *Ancient China in Transition: An Analysis of Social Mobility, 722–222 B.C.* Stanford, Ca.: Stanford University Press, 1965.

——"The Roles of the Literati and of Regionalism in the Fall of the Han Dynasty." In *The Collapse of Ancient States and Civilizations*, edited by Norman Yoffee and George L. Cowgill, pp. 176–95. Tucson: University of Arizona Press, 1988.

Hu Rulei. "Lue lun Li Mi" (Brief discussion of Li Mi). In *Zhongguo nongmin zhanzheng shi yanjiu* (Researches on the history of peasant wars in China), vol. 2, pp. 55–62. Shanghai: Shanghai renmin chubanshe, 1982.

Huang Huixian. "Sui mo nongmin qiyi wuzhuang qianxi" (A superficial analysis of the armed forces of the peasant uprising at the end of Sui). In *Tang shi yanjiuhui lunwenji* (Proceedings of the Tang history research conference), pp. 170–97. Xi'an: Shaanxi renmin chubanshe, 1983.

——"Lun Sui mo Tang chu de 'Shandong haojie'" (On the "heroes east of the mountains" at the end of Sui and beginning of Tang). In *Zhongguo nongmin zhanzheng shi luncong* (Essays on the history of China's peasant wars), vol. 5, pp. 61–116. N.p.: Zhongguo shehui kexue chubanshe, 1987.

Huang Lie. "Tuoba Xianbei zaoqi guojia de xingcheng" (The formation of the early Tuoba Xianbei state). In *Wei Jin Sui Tang shi lunji* (Collected essays on Wei-Jin and Sui-Tang history), vol. 2, pp. 60–94. Beijing: Zhongguo shehui kexue chubanshe, 1983.

Huang, Ray. *1587, A Year of No Significance: The Ming Dynasty in Decline*. New Haven: Yale University Press, 1981.

Huang Yongnian. *Tang Taizong Li Shimin* (Biography of Li Shimin). Shanghai: Shanghai renmin chubanshe, 1987.

Hucker, Charles O. *A Dictionary of Official Titles in Imperial China*. Stanford, Ca.: Stanford University Press, 1985.

Jamieson, John Charles. "The Samguk Sagi and the Unification Wars." Ph.D. dissertation, University of California at Berkeley, 1969.

Jenner, W. J. F. *Memories of Loyang: Yang Hsüan-chih and the Lost Capital (493–534)*. Oxford: Clarendon Press, 1981.

Jiang Fuya. *Qian Qin shi* (History of the Former Qin dynasty). Beijing: Beijing shifan xueyuan chubanshe, 1993.

Jin Fagen. *Yongjia luan hou beifang de haozu* (Powerful families in North China after the chaos of the Yongjia period). Taipei: Taiwan Commercial Press, 1964.

Jones, Archer. *The Art of War in the Western World.* London and New York: Oxford University Press, 1989.

Kaegi, Walter Emil, Jr. *Some Thoughts on Byzantine Military Strategy.* Brookline, Mass.: Hellenic College Press, 1983.

Kang Le. *Tangdai qianqi de bianfang* (Frontier defense in the early period of the Tang dynasty). Taipei: National Taiwan University, 1979.

Kao Ming-shih. "Tangdai de wuju yu wumiao" (Military examinations and military temples under the Tang dynasty). In *Di yi jie guoji Tangdai xueshu huiyi lunwenji* (Proceedings of the first International Tang Studies Conference), pp. 1016–69. Taipei: Zhonghua minguo Tangdai xuezhe lianyihui, 1989.

Kawakatsu Yoshio. "Tō Shin shizokusei no kakuritsu katei – gunjiryoku to no kanren no moto ni" (The process of establishing the aristocratic system of Eastern Jin: on the basis of the connection to military power). *Tōhō gakuhō,* 52 (1980), pp. 317–40.

Keegan, John. *The Mask of Command.* New York: Viking, 1987.

—— *A History of Warfare.* New York: Alfred A. Knopf, 1993.

Kegasawa Yasunori. "Gyōkasei kō" (A study of the *xiaoguo* system). *Ōryō shigaku,* 11 (1986), pp. 59–84.

—— "Zui Yōdai ki no fuheisei o meguru ichi kōsatsu" (A study revolving around the *fubing* system of Sui Yangdi's time). In *Ritsuryōsei: Chūgoku, Chōsen no hō to kokka* (The *ritsuryō* system: law and the state in China and Korea), pp. 445–81. Tokyo: Kyūko shoin, 1986.

—— "Zenki fuheisei kenkyū josetsu – sono seika to ronten o megutte" (Introductory remarks on researches dealing with the *fubing* system of the early period: revolving around their conclusions and disputed points). *Hōseishi kenkyū,* 42 (1992), pp. 123–51.

Kierman, Frank A., Jr. "Phases and Modes of Combat in Early China." In *Chinese Ways in Warfare,* edited by Frank A. Kierman, Jr., and John K. Fairbank, pp. 27–66. Cambridge, Mass.: Harvard University Press, 1974.

Kikuchi Hideo. "Tōdai heibo no seikaku to meishō to ni tsuite" (Concerning the character and appellation of the conscript-recruits of the Tang dynasty). *Shien,* 68 (May 1956), pp. 75–98.

—— "Hokuchō gunsei ni okeru iwayuru kyōhei ni tsuite" (Concerning the so-called local troops in the military system of the Northern Dynasties). In *Shigematsu sensei koki kinen Kyūshū Daigaku tōyōshi ronsō* (Collected essays in oriental history published by Kyushu University on the occasion of the seventieth birthday of Professor Shigematsu), pp. 95–139. Fukuoka: Kyushu University, 1957.

—— "Setsudoshisei kakuritsu izen ni okeru 'gun' seido no tenkai" (The development of the "army" system before the establishment of the system of military governors). *Tōyō gakuho,* 44 (1961), pp. 54–88.

—— "Tō setsushōfu no bunpu mondai ni kansuru ichi kaishaku" (An explanation concerning the problem of the distribution of the Tang regiments). *Tōyōshi kenkyū,* 27 (1968), pp. 121–57.

—— "Fuhei seido no tenkai" (The development of the *fubing* system). In *Iwanami kōza: sekai rekishi* (Iwanami lectures: world history), vol. 5, pp. 407–39. Tokyo: Iwanami shoten, 1970.

Klein, Kenneth Douglas. "The Contributions of the Fourth Century Xianbei States to the Reunification of the Chinese Empire." Ph.D. dissertation, University of California Los Angeles, 1980.

Kuhn, Philip A. *Rebellion and its Enemies in Late Imperial China: Militarization and Social Structure, 1796–1864.* Cambridge, Mass.: Harvard University Press, 1970.

Kurihara Masuo. "Tō Godai no karifushi teki ketsugo no seikaku" (The character of the fictive kinship bond in Tang and the Five Dynasties). *Shigaku zasshi*, 62 (1953), pp. 514–43.

——"Tōmatsu dogōteki zaichi seiryoku ni tsuite: Shisen no I Kunsei no ba'ai" (Concerning the local power-holders at the end of the Tang: the case of Wei Junjing in Sichuan). *Rekishigaku kenkyū*, No. 243 (1960), pp. 1–14.

——"Fuheisei no hōkai to shin heishu" (The collapse of the *fubing* system and the new troop types). *Shigaku zasshi*, 73 (1964), pp. 121–46, 269–91.

——"An-Shi no ran to hanchin taikei no tenkai" (The An Lushan rebellion and the development of the military garrison system). In *Iwanami kōza: sekai rekishi* (Iwanami lectures: world history), vol. 6, pp. 161–96. Tokyo: Iwanami shoten, 1970.

Labadie, John Richard. "Rulers and Soldiers: Perception and Management of the Military in Northern Sung China (960–ca. 1060)." Ph.D. dissertation, University of Washington, 1981.

Lai, Swee Fo. "The Military and Defense System under the T'ang Dynasty." Ph.D. dissertation, Princeton University, 1986.

Lao Gan. "Handai bingzhi ji Hanjian zhong de bingzhi" (The military system of the Han dynasty and the military system in the Han strips). *Bulletin of the Institute of History and Philology of Academia Sinica* 10 (1943), pp. 23–55.

——"Zhanguo shidai de zhanzheng fangfa" (Methods of warfare in the Warring States period). In *Lao Gan xueshu lunwenji* (Collected academic essays of Lao Gan), pt. 1, vol. 2, pp. 1167–83. Banqiao, Taiwan: Yiwen yinshuguan, 1976.

Ledyard, Gari. "Galloping Along with the Horseriders: Looking for the Founders of Japan." *Journal of Japanese Studies*, 1.2 (Spring 1975), pp. 217–54.

Lei Haizong. *Zhongguo wenhua yu Zhongguo de bing* (Chinese culture and the Chinese soldier). Changsha: Commercial Press, 1940.

Lei Jiaji. "Cong zhanlue fazhan kan Tangchao jiedu tizhi de chuangjian" (Viewing the creation of the Tang system of military governors from the standpoint of the development of military strategy). *Jiandu xuebao*, 8 (November 1979), pp. 215–59.

Lewis, Mark Edward. *Sanctioned Violence in Early China.* Albany: State University of New York Press, 1990.

——"The Han Abolition of Universal Military Service." In *Warfare in Chinese History*, edited by Hans van de Ven, pp. 33–76. Leiden: E. J. Brill, 2000.

Li Jiping. *Fei shui zhi zhan* (Battle of the Fei River). Shanghai: Shanghai renmin chubanshe, 1955.

Li Shu-t'ung [Li Shutong]. "Tangdai de ma yu jiaotong" (Horses and transportation in the Tang period). In *Tang shi yanjiu* (Researches in Tang history), pp. 277–334. Taipei: Taiwan Commercial Press, 1979.

——"Tangdai zhi junshi yu ma" (Horses and military affairs in the Tang period). In *Tang shi yanjiu*, pp. 231–76. Taipei: Taiwan Commercial Press, 1979.

Li Tse-fen [Li Zefen]. *Liang Jin Nanbeichao lishi lunwenji* (Collected essays on the history of the Two Jin and the Northern and Southern dynasties). Taipei: Taiwan Commercial Press, 1987.

——*Sui Tang Wudai lishi lunwenji* (Essays on the history of Sui, Tang, and the Five Dynasties). Taipei: Taiwan Commercial Press, 1989.

Littauer, Mary Aiken. "Early Stirrups." *Antiquity*, 55 (1981), pp. 99–105.

Liu, Yat-wing. "The Shen-ts'e Armies and the Palace Commissions in China, 755–875 A.D." Ph.D. dissertation, University of London, 1970.

Loewe, Michael. *Military Operations in the Han Period*. London: The China Society, 1961.

—— "The Campaigns of Han Wu-ti." In *Chinese Ways in Warfare*, edited by Frank A. Kierman, Jr., and John K. Fairbank, pp. 67–122. Cambridge, Mass.: Harvard University Press, 1974.

—— "The Heritage Left to the Empires." In *The Cambridge History of Ancient China*, edited by Michael Loewe and Edward Shaughnessy, pp. 967–1032. Cambridge: Cambridge University Press, 1999.

Lü Simian. *Liang Jin Nanbeichao shi* (History of the Two Jin and the Northern and Southern dynasties). Shanghai: Shanghai Guji chubanshe, 1983.

Lynn, John A. (ed.). *Feeding Mars: Logistics in Western Warfare from the Middle Ages to the Present*. Boulder, Colo.: Westview Press, 1993.

Mackerras, Colin. *The Uighur Empire According to the T'ang Dynastic Histories*. Columbia, S.C.: University of South Carolina Press, 1973.

—— "The Uighurs." In *The Cambridge History of Early Inner Asia*, edited by Denis Sinor, pp. 317–42. Cambridge: Cambridge University Press, 1990.

Mao Han-kuang. "Bei Wei Dong Wei Bei Qi zhi hexin jituan yu hexin qu" (The core group and core area of Northern Wei, Eastern Wei, and Northern Qi). In *Zhongguo zhonggu zhengzhi shi lun* (Essays on the political history of medieval China), pp. 29–98. Taipei: Lianjing, 1990.

—— "Bei chao Dong Xi zhengquan zhi Hedong zhengduo zhan" (The wars between the eastern and western political authorities for control of Hedong during the northern dynasties). In *Zhongguo zhonggu zhengzhi shi lun*, pp. 131–66. Taipei: Lianjing, 1990.

—— "Xi Wei fubing shi lun" (On the history of the *fubing* of Western Wei). In *Zhongguo zhonggu zhengzhi shi lun*, pp. 169–94. Taipei: Lianjing, 1990.

Mather, Richard B. *Biography of Lü Kuang*. Berkeley and Los Angeles: University of California Press, 1959.

McMullen, D. L. *State and Scholars in T'ang China*. Cambridge: Cambridge University Press, 1988.

—— "The Cult of Ch'i T'ai-kung and T'ang Attitudes to the Military." *T'ang Studies*, 7 (1989), pp. 59–103.

Miyakawa, Hisayuki. "An Outline of the Naito Hypothesis and its Effects on Japanese Studies of China." *Far Eastern Quarterly*, 14.4 (August 1955), pp. 533–52.

Miyazaki Ichisada. "Tokushi satsuki" (Critical notes from the reading of history). *Shirin*, 21.1 (1936), pp. 124–58.

Morohashi Tetsuji. *Dai Kan Wa jiten* (Great Chinese–Japanese dictionary). Tokyo: Taishūkan, 1966.

Needham, Joseph. *Science and Civilisation in China*, vol. 3: *Mathematics and the Sciences of the Heavens and the Earth*. Cambridge: Cambridge University Press, 1959.

—— *Science and Civilisation in China*, vol. 4: *Physics and Physical Technology*, pt. 2: *Mechanical Engineering*. Cambridge: Cambridge University Press, 1965.

—— *Science and Civilisation in China*, vol. 4: *Physics and Physical Technology*, pt. 3: *Civil Engineering and Nautics*. Cambridge: Cambridge University Press, 1971.

Needham, Joseph, and Robin D. S. Yates. *Science and Civilisation in China*, vol. 5: *Chemistry and Chemical Technology*, pt. 6: *Military Technology: Missiles and Sieges*. Cambridge: Cambridge University Press, 1994.

Ni Jinsheng. "Wu Hu luan Hua qianye de Zhongguo jingji" (China's economy on the eve of the disordering of China by the five barbarian peoples). *Shi huo banyuekan*, 1.7 (March 1, 1935), pp. 38–49.

——— "Wu Hu luan Hua mingri de Zhongguo jingji" (China's economy on the morrow of the disordering of China by the five barbarian peoples). *Shi huo banyuekan*, 1, No. 8 (March 16, 1935), pp. 18–24.

Nunome Chōfū. "Ri En no kigi" (The uprising of Li Yuan). In *Zui Tō shi kenkyū* (Researches on Sui and Tang history), pp. 101–49. Kyoto: Tōyōshi kenkyūkai, Kyoto University, 1968.

O'Byrne, Terrence Douglas. "Civil–Military Relations During the Middle T'ang: The Career of Kuo Tzu-i." Ph.D. dissertation, University of Illinois at Urbana-Champaign, 1982.

Ochi Shigeaki. "Tō-Shin chō chūgen kaifuku no ichi kōsatsu" (An examination of the recovery of the central plain by the Eastern Jin court). *Tōyō gakuhō*, 38.1 (June 1955), pp. 73–88.

Otagi Hajime. "Tōdai shū ken jōkaku no kibo to kōzō" (The scale and construction of the walls of prefectural and county seats during the Tang dynasty). In *Di yi jie guoji Tangdai xueshu huiyi lunwenji* (Proceedings of the first International Tang Studies Conference), pp. 647–95. Taipei: Zhonghua minguo Tangdai xuezhe lianyihui, 1989.

Pan, Yihong. *Son of Heaven and Heavenly Qaghan*. Bellingham, Wash.: Western Washington University, 1997.

Pearce, Scott A. "The Yü-wen Regime in Sixth-Century China." Ph.D. dissertation, Princeton University, 1987.

People's Republic of China Atlas. N.p.: U.S. Central Intelligence Agency, 1971.

Perry, Elizabeth. *Rebels and Revolutionaries in North China, 1845–1945*. Stanford, Ca.: Stanford University Press, 1980.

Peterson, Charles A. "The Autonomy of the Northeastern Provinces in the Period Following the An Lu-shan Rebellion." Ph.D. dissertation, University of Washington, 1966.

——— "P'u-ku Huai-en and the T'ang Court: The Limits of Loyalty." *Monumenta Serica*, 29 (1970–1), pp. 423–55.

——— "Regional Defense against the Central Power: The Huai-hsi Campaign, 815–817." In *Chinese Ways in Warfare*, edited by Frank A. Kierman, Jr., and John K. Fairbank, pp. 123–50. Cambridge, Mass.: Harvard University Press, 1974.

——— "Court and Province in Mid- and Late T'ang." In *The Cambridge History of China*, vol. 3: *Sui and T'ang China, 589–906, Pt. 1*, edited by Denis Twitchett, pp. 464–560. Cambridge: Cambridge University Press, 1979.

Pulleyblank, Edwin G. *The Background of the Rebellion of An Lu-shan*. London: Oxford University Press, 1955.

——— "Registration of Population in China in the Sui and T'ang Periods." *Journal of the Economic and Social History of the Orient*, 4 (1961), pp. 289–301.

——— "The An Lu-shan Rebellion and the Origins of Chronic Militarism in Late T'ang China." In *Essays on T'ang Society*, edited by John Curtis Perry and Bardwell L. Smith, pp. 33–60. Leiden: E. J. Brill, 1976.

Qi Xia. "You guan Sui mo nongmin qiyi de jige wenti" (Several question concerning the peasant uprising at the end of Sui). In *Zhongguo nongmin qiyi lunji* (Collected essays on China's peasant uprisings), edited by Li Guangbi et al., pp. 97–118. Beijing: Sanlian, 1958.

Qi Zebang. "Lun Dong Wei-Bei Qi de daotui" (On the fall of Eastern Wei/Northern Qi). In *Wei Jin Nanbeichao shi yanjiu* (Researches on the history of Wei, Jin, and the Northern and Southern dynasties), pp. 383–403. Chengdu: Sichuan sheng shehui kexue yuan chubanshe, 1986.

Qian Jianfu. "Shi lun Qin Han de 'zheng zu' yaoyi" (On the corvée service of full conscripts in Qin and Han). *Zhongguo shi yanjiu*, 1982, No. 3, pp. 3–11.

Ramsay, J. H. "The Strength of English Armies in the Middle Ages." *English Historical Review*, 29 (1914), pp. 221–7.

Rogers, Michael C. *The Chronicle of Fu Chien: A Case of Exemplar History*. Berkeley and Los Angeles: University of California Press, 1968.

—— "The Myth of the Battle of the Fei River." *T'oung Pao*, 54 (1968), pp. 50–72.

Schafer, Edward H. *The Golden Peaches of Samarkand: A Study of T'ang Exotics*. Berkeley and Los Angeles: University of California Press, 1963.

Schreiber, Gerhard. "The History of the Former Yen Dynasty." *Monumenta Serica*, 15 (1956), pp. 1–141.

Senger, Harro von. *The Book of Stratagems*. New York: Viking Penguin, 1991.

Shi Suyuan. "Cong san da zhanyi kan jiechu junjia Li Shimin" (Looking at the outstanding military commander Li Shimin through three great battles). *Renwen zazhi*, 1982, No. 3, pp. 95–9.

Sinor, Denis. "The Establishment and Dissolution of the Türk Empire." In *The Cambridge History of Early Inner Asia*, edited by Denis Sinor, pp. 285–316. Cambridge: Cambridge University Press, 1990.

Skaff, Jonathan Karam. "Barbarians at the Gates? The Tang Frontier Military and the An Lushan Rebellion." *War and Society*, 18.2 (October 2000), pp. 23–35.

Smith, John Masson, Jr. "Ayn Jālūt: Mamlūk Success or Mongol Failure?" *Harvard Journal of Asiatic Studies*, 44.2 (December 1984), pp. 307–45.

Somers, Robert M. "The End of the T'ang." In *The Cambridge History of China*, vol. 3: *Sui and T'ang China, 589–906, Pt. 1*, edited by Denis Twitchett, pp. 682–789. Cambridge: Cambridge University Press, 1979.

—— "Time, Space, and Structure in the Consolidation of the T'ang Dynasty (A.D. 617–700)." *Journal of Asian Studies*, 45.5 (1986), pp. 971–94.

Song Changlian. "Tangdai de mazheng" (Horse administration under the Tang dynasty). *Dalu zazhi*, 29.1–2 (July 15 and 31, 1964), pp. 29–33, 61–6.

Southern, Pat, and Karen Ramsey Dixon. *The Late Roman Army*. New Haven and London: Yale University Press, 1996.

Sun Ji. "Tangdai de maju yu mashi" (Horse trappings and decorations of the Tang period). *Wen wu*, 1981, No. 10, pp. 82–8.

Sun Jimin. *Tangdai xingjun zhidu yanjiu* (Researches on the expeditionary army system of the Tang dynasty). Taipei: Wenjin chubanshe, 1995.

Sun Yancheng. "Qin Han de yaoyi he bingyi" (Corvée and military service in Qin and Han). *Zhongguo shi yanjiu*, 1987, No. 3, pp. 77–85.

Sun Yutang. "Xi Han de bingzhi" (The military institutions of Western Han). *Zhongguo shehui jingji shi jikan*, 5.1 (March 1937), pp. 1–74.

—— "Dong Han bingzhi de yanbian" (Evolution of the military institutions of Eastern Han). *Zhongguo shehui jingji shi jikan*, 6.1 (June 1939), pp. 1–34.

Tamura Jitsuzo. *Chūgoku shijō no minzoku idō ki* (The age of ethnic migration in Chinese history). Tokyo: Sōbunsha, 1985.

Tan Qixiang. *Zhongguo lishi dituji* (Historical atlas of China). Shanghai: Cartographic Publishing House, 1982.

Tang Changru. "Jindai beijing ge zu 'bianluan' de xingzhi ji Wu Hu zhengquan zai Zhongguo de tongzhi" (The nature of the "rebellions" of the peoples of northern frontier during the Jin period and the rule of political authorities of the five barbarian peoples within China). In *Wei Jin Nanbeichao shi luncong* (Essays on the history of Wei, Jin, and the Northern and Southern dynasties), pp. 127–92. Beijing: Sanlian, 1955.

—— "Wei Zhou fubing zhidu bianyi" (Changes in the *fubing* system of Wei and Zhou). In *Wei Jin Nanbeichao shi luncong*, pp. 250–88. Beijing: Sanlian, 1955.

—— *Tang shu bingzhi jianzheng* (Notes and corrections to the military treatise in the *New History of the Tang Dynasty*). Beijing: Kexue chubanshe, 1957.

—— "Xi Jin fenfeng yu zongwang chu zhen" (Western Jin enfeoffment and the appointment of imperial princes to regional commands). In *Wei Jin Sui Tang shi lunji* (Essays on the history of Wei, Jin, Sui, and Tang), vol. 1, pp. 1–12. Beijing: Zhongguo shehui kexue chubanshe, 1981.

—— "Wei Jin Nanbeichao shiqi de ke he buqu" (Guests and retainers in the Wei, Jin, and Northern and Southern dynasties period). In *Wei Jin Nanbeichao shilun shiyi* (Addenda to essays on the history of Wei, Jin, and the Northern and Southern dynasties), pp. 1–24. Beijing: Zhonghua shuju, 1983.

—— "Wei Jin zhou jun bing de shezhi he feiba" (The establishment and abolition of the provincial and commandery troops under Wei and Jin). In *Wei Jin Nanbeichao shilun shiyi*, pp. 141–50. Beijing: Zhonghua shuju, 1983.

—— *Wei Jin Nanbeichao Sui Tang shi san lun* (Three discourses on the history of Wei, Jin, the Northern and Southern dynasties, Sui, and Tang). Wuhan: Wuhan daxue chubanshe, 1993.

Tang Geng'ou. "Tangdai qianqi de bingmu" (Conscript-recruits of the early Tang). *Lishi yanjiu*, 1981, No. 4, pp. 159–72.

Tanigawa Michio. "Tōdai no hanchin ni tsuite: Sessai no ba'ai" (Concerning the Tang military provinces: the case of Zhexi). *Shirin*, 35.3 (October 1952), pp. 70–89.

—— "Fuheisei kokka ron" (On the *fubing*-system state). *Ryūkoku daigaku ronshū*, No. 443 (December 1993), pp. 1–26.

—— "Zui matsu no nairan to minshū: hyōraku to jiei" (Internal disorder and the populace at the end of Sui: robbery and self-defense). *Tōyōshi kenkyū*, 53.4 (1995), pp. 173–92.

Taylor, Romeyn. "Yüan Origins of the Ming Wei-so System." In *Chinese Government in Ming Times: Seven Studies*, edited by Charles O. Hucker, pp. 23–40. New York: Columbia University Press, 1969.

Treadgold, Warren. *Byzantium and its Army, 284–1081*. Stanford, Ca.: Stanford University Press, 1995.

Tu Cheng-sheng, "'Bian hu qi min' de chuxian ji qi lishi yiyi" (The emergence of "registering households and ordering the people" and its historical significance). *Bulletin of the Institute of History and Philology of Academia Sinica*, 54.3 (September 1982), pp. 77–111.

Twitchett, Denis. "Lands under State Cultivation under the T'ang." *Journal of the Economic and Social History of the Orient*, 2 (1959), pp. 152–203.

—— "The T'ang Market System." *Asia Major*, n.s., 12.2 (1966), pp. 202–48.

—— *Financial Administration under the T'ang Dynasty*. 2nd edn. Cambridge: Cambridge University Press, 1971.

—— *The Birth of the Chinese Meritocracy: Bureaucrats and Examinations in T'ang China*. The China Society Occasional Papers, No. 18. London: The China Society, 1976.

—— "Varied Patterns of Provincial Autonomy in the T'ang Dynasty." In *Essays on T'ang Society*, edited by John Curtis Perry and Bardwell L. Smith, pp. 90–109. Leiden: E. J. Brill, 1976.

—— "Hsüan-tsung (reign 712–56)." In *The Cambridge History of China*, vol. 3: *Sui and T'ang China, 589–906, Pt. 1*, edited by Denis Twitchett, pp. 333–463. Cambridge: Cambridge University Press, 1979.

—— *The Writing of Official History Under the T'ang*. Cambridge: Cambridge University Press, 1992.

van Creveld, Martin. *Command in War*. Cambridge, Mass.: Harvard University Press, 1985.

Verbruggen, J. F. *The Art of Warfare in Western Europe during the Middle Ages*. Translated by Sumner Willard and S. C. M. Southern. Amsterdam and New York: North-Holland Publishing Company, 1977.

Waldron, Arthur. *The Great Wall of China: From History to Myth*. Cambridge: Cambridge University Press, 1990.

Waley, Arthur. "The Fall of Lo-yang." *History Today*, 1 (1951), pp. 7–10.

Wallacker, Benjamin E. "Studies in Medieval Chinese Siegecraft: The Siege of Yü-pi, A.D. 546." *Journal of Asian Studies*, 28.4 (August 1969), pp. 789–802.

—— "Studies in Medieval Chinese Siegecraft: The Siege of Chien-k'ang, A.D. 548–549." *Journal of Asian History*, 5.1 (1971), pp. 35–54.

Wang, C. H. "Towards Defining a Chinese Heroism." *Journal of the American Oriental Society*, 95.1 (1975), pp. 25–35.

Wang, Gungwu. *The Structure of Power in North China during the Five Dynasties*. Stanford, Ca.: Stanford University Press, 1967.

Wang Jilin. "Tangdai de Shuofang jun yu Shence jun" (The Tang Shuofang army and Shence army). In *Di yi jie guoji Tangdai xueshu huiyi lunwenji* (Proceedings of the first International Tang Studies Conference), pp. 914–21. Taipei: Zhonghua minguo Tangdai xuezhe lianyihui, 1989.

Wang Jun. *Tang Taizong*. Shanghai: Xuexi shenghuo chubanshe, 1955.

Wang Qian. *Wang Qian Sui Tang shi lungao* (Wang Qian's draft essays on Sui and Tang history). Edited by Tang Changru. Beijing: Zhongguo shehui kexue chubanshe, 1983.

Wang Shou-nan. *Tangdai fanzhen yu zhongyang guanxi zhi yanjiu* (Researches on relations between the center and the military provinces of the Tang dynasty). [Taiwan]: Jiaxin shuini gongsi wenhua jijinhui, 1968.

Wang Zengyu. *Songchao bingzhi chutan* (Preliminary investigation of the military institutions of the Song dynasty). Beijing: Zhonghua shuju, 1983.

Wang Zhongluo. *Wei Jin Nanbeichao shi* (History of Wei, Jin, and the Northern and Southern dynasties). Shanghai: Shanghai renmin chubanshe, 1979.

Warfare in Chinese History. Edited by Hans van de Ven. Leiden: E. J. Brill, 2000.

Wechsler, Howard J. *Mirror to the Son of Heaven: Wei Cheng at the Court of T'ang T'ai-tsung*. New Haven: Yale University Press, 1974.

—— "T'ai-tsung (reign 626–49) the Consolidator." In *The Cambridge History of China*, vol. 3: *Sui and T'ang China, 589–906, Pt. 1,* edited by Denis Twitchett, pp. 188–241. Cambridge: Cambridge University Press, 1979.

—— *Offerings of Jade and Silk: Ritual and Symbol in the Legitimation of the T'ang Dynasty.* New Haven: Yale University Press, 1985.

Weinstein, Stanley. *Buddhism under the T'ang.* Cambridge: Cambridge University Press, 1987.

Worthy, Edmund H., Jr. "The Founding of Sung China, 950–1000: Integrative Changes in Military and Political Institutions." Ph.D. dissertation, Princeton University, 1975.

Wright, Arthur F. "The Formation of Sui Ideology, 581–604." In *Chinese Thought and Institutions,* edited by John K. Fairbank, pp. 71–104. Chicago: University of Chicago Press, 1957.

—— "Sui Yang-Ti: Personality and Stereotype." In *The Confucian Persuasion,* edited by Arthur F. Wright, pp. 47–76. Stanford, Ca.: Stanford University Press, 1960.

—— *The Sui Dynasty.* New York: Alfred A. Knopf, 1978.

—— "The Sui Dynasty." In *The Cambridge History of China,* vol. 3: *Sui and T'ang China, 589–906, Pt. 1,* edited by Denis Twitchett, pp. 48–149. Cambridge: Cambridge University Press, 1979.

Wu Feng. *Sui Tang Wudai shi* (History of Sui, Tang, and the Five Dynasties). Beijing: Renmin chubanshe, 1958.

Wu Tingxie. *Tang fangzhen nianbiao* (Chronological tables for the Tang military provinces). Beijing: Zhonghua shuju, 1980.

Xu Hui. "Nanbeichao zhanzheng tedian tanxi" (Investigation and analysis of the characteristics of the wars between the Northern and Southern dynasties). *Jiang hai xuekan,* 1991, No. 3, pp. 118–23.

Yang, Chung-i. "Evolution of the Status of 'Dependents.'" In *Chinese Social History,* edited by E-tu Zen Sun and John DeFrancis, pp. 142–56. Washington, D.C.: American Council of Learned Societies, 1956.

Yang Hong. *Zhongguo gu bingqi luncong* (Essays on ancient Chinese weapons). Beijing: Wenwu chubanshe, 1980. Reprint, Taipei: Mingwen shuju, 1983.

—— *Gudai bingqi shihua* (Popular history of ancient weapons). Shanghai: Shanghai kexue jishu chubanshe, 1988.

Yang, Lien-sheng. "Notes on the Economic History of the Chin Dynasty." In *Studies in Chinese Institutional History,* pp. 119–97. Cambridge, Mass.: Harvard University Press, 1961.

—— "Numbers and Units in Chinese Economic History." In *Studies in Chinese Institutional History,* pp. 75–84. Cambridge, Mass.: Harvard University Press, 1961.

Yano Chikara. "Tōdai ni okeru kashisei ni tsuite" (Concerning the institution of adopted sons in the Tang dynasty). In *Shigaku kenkyū kinen ronsō,* pp. 231–57. Kyoto: Ryūgen shoten, 1950.

Yasuda Jirō. "Shinan Ō Shi Kun no hanran ni tsuite – Nanchō monbatsu kizoku taisei to gōzoku dogō" (Concerning the rebellion of Zixun, prince of Jin'an: the aristocratic system of the Southern dynasties and the local powerholders). *Tōyōshi kenkyū,* 25.4 (1967), pp. 414–38.

—— "Shin-Sō kakumei to Yōshū (Jōyō) no kyōmin – gunsei shihai kara minsei shihai e" (The Jin-Song revolution and the émigrés of Yongzhou: from military government to civil government). *Tōyōshi kenkyū,* 42.1 (June 1983), pp. 110–35.

Yates, Robin D. S. "New Light on Ancient Chinese Military Texts: Notes on their

Nature and Evolution, and the Development of Military Specialization in Warring States China." *T'oung Pao*, 74 (1988), pp. 211–48.

Yen Keng-wang [Yan Gengwang]. "Tangdai fangzhen shifu liaozuo kao" (A study of headquarters staff of the Tang military provinces). *Tang shi yanjiu conggao* (Draft researches on Tang history), pp. 177–236. Hong Kong: Xin Ya yanjiusuo, 1969.

Yoshimori Kensuke. "Shin-Sō kakumei to Kōnan shakai" (The Jin-Song revolution and Jiangnan society). *Shirin*, 63.2 (1980), pp. 208–34.

Zang Rong. "Lun Dou Jiande de chenggong yu shibai" (On the success and defeat of Dou Jiande). In *Zhongguo nongmin zhanzheng shi yanjiu jikan* (Collected research on the history of China's peasant wars), No. 3, pp. 69–76. Shanghai: Shanghai renmin chubanshe, 1983.

Zang Zhifei. "Qin Han 'zheng zu' bianxi" (An analysis of the full conscripts of Qin and Han). *Zhongguo shi yanjiu*, 1988, No. 1, pp. 95–8.

Zhang Guogang. "Tangdai jianjun zhidu kaolun" (A study of the Tang system of army supervisors). *Zhongguo shi yanjiu*, 1981, No. 2, pp. 120–32.

—— *Tangdai fanzhen yanjiu* (Researches on the military provinces of the Tang dynasty). Changsha: Hunan jiaoyu chubanshe, 1987.

—— "Tangdai fubing yuanyuan yu fanyi" (The origins of the Tang *fubing* and the system of rotational service). *Lishi yanjiu*, 1989, No. 6, pp. 145–58.

—— "Tangdai de jian'er zhi" (The Tang system of long-service troops). *Zhongguo shi yanjiu*, 1990, No. 4, pp. 100–9.

—— *Tangdai zhengzhi zhidu yanjiu lunji* (Collected essays on the political institutions of the Tang dynasty). Taipei: Wenjin chubanshe, 1994.

Zhang Qun. "Pugu Huai'en yu Li Huaiguang de fanpan" (The rebellions of Pugu Huai'en and Li Huaiguang). In *Zhongguo lishi lunwenji* (Collected essays on Chinese history), pp. 87–119. Taipei: Taiwan Commercial Press, 1986.

—— *Tangdai fanjiang yanjiu* (Researches on barbarian generals of the Tang dynasty). Taipei: Lianjing, 1986.

Zhang Tieniu and Gao Xiaoxing. *Zhongguo gudai haijun shi* (History of the Chinese navy in ancient times). Beijing: Bayi chubanshe, 1993.

Zhao Dongjie et al. *Sishui xian zhi* (Gazetteer of Sishui county). Shanghai: Shijie shuju, 1929. Reprint, Taipei: Chongwen chubanshe, 1968.

Zhao Keyao and Xu Daoxun. *Tang Taizong zhuan* (Biography of Tang Taizong). Beijing: Renmin chubanshe, 1984.

Zhao Wenrun. "Lun Xi Wei yu Dong Wei zhijian de ji ci zhanyi" (On several battles between Western Wei and Eastern Wei). *Beichao yanjiu*, 1996, No. 2, pp. 11–12.

Zhongguo junshi shi (Chinese military history), vol. 3: *Bingzhi* (Military Institutions). Beijing: Jiefangjun chubanshe, 1987.

Zhongguo junshi shi, vol. 6: *Bing lei* (Fortifications). Beijing: Jiefangjun chubanshe, 1991.

Zhou Nianchang. "Dong Jin bei fu bing de jianli ji qi tedian" (The establishment of the Eastern Jin northern headquarters troops and their special characteristics). *Wei Jin Sui Tang shi lunji* (Essays on Wei, Jin, Sui, and Tang history), vol. 2, pp. 149–67. Beijing: Zhongguo shehui kexue chubanshe, 1983.

Zhou Weizhou. *Han Zhao guo shi* (History of the states of Han and Zhao). Taiyuan: Shanxi renmin chubanshe, 1986.

Zhou Yiliang. "Wei Jin bingzhi shang de yige wenti" (A problem in the Wei-Jin military system). In *Wei Jin Nanbeichao shi lunji* (Essays on the history of Wei, Jin, and the Northern and Southern dynasties), pp. 1–11. Beijing: Zhonghua shuju, 1963.

——"Beichao de minzu wenti yu minzu zhengce" (Ethnic problems and ethnic policies of the Northern dynasties). In *Wei Jin Nanbeichao shi lunji*, pp. 117–76. Beijing: Zhonghua shuju, 1963.

——"Bei Wei zhen shu zhidu kao ji xu kao" (A study of the system of garrisons and outposts in Northern Wei). In *Wei Jin Nanbeichao shi lunji*, pp. 199–219. Beijing: Zhonghua shuju. 1963.

Zhu Dawei. "Wei Jin Nanbeichao nongmin zhanzheng de jige wenti" (Several problems regarding peasant wars of Wei, Jin, and the Northern and Southern dynasties). In *Wei Jin Sui Tang shi lunji* (Collected essays on the history of Wei-Jin and Sui-Tang), vol. 2, pp. 10–59. Beijing: Zhongguo shehui kexue chubanshe, 1983.

——"Wei Jin Nanbeichao shi nongmin zhanzheng de shehui houguo" (Social consequences of peasant wars in Wei, Jin, and the Northern and Southern dynasties). In *Zhongguo nongmin zhanzheng shi luncong* (Essays on the history of Chinese peasant wars), vol. 5, pp. 1–60. N.p.: Zhongguo shehui kexue chubanshe, 1987.

Zou Bentao. "Xi Han nan bei jun kaobian" (Investigation and analysis of the northern and southern armies of Western Han). *Zhongguo shi yanjiu*, 1988, No. 1, pp. 85–94.

Zou Yuntao. "Shi lun San Guo shiqi nan bei junshi de xingcheng ji qi pohuai" (Preliminary discussion of the formation of the north–south balance during the Three Kingdoms period and its destruction). In *Wei Jin Nanbeichao shi yanjiu* (Research in the history of Wei, Jin, and the Northern and Southern dynasties), pp. 128–45. Chengdu: Sichuan sheng shehui kexue yuan chubanshe, 1986.

Zuixin shiyong Zhongguo dituce (Newest practical atlas of China). Xi'an: Zhongguo ditu chubanshe, 1992.

Index